The Greater New York Sports Chronology

Jeffrey A. Kroessler

The Greater New York Sports Chronology

To Harry —
A true New Yorker —
Jeffy Kroessler

Columbia University Press

New York

Columbia University Press
Publishers Since 1893
New York   Chichester, West Sussex
Copyright © 2010 Jeffrey A. Kroessler

Library of Congress Cataloging-in-Publication
    Data
Kroessler, Jeffrey A.
    The greater New York sports chronology /
        Jeffrey A. Kroessler.
            p. cm.
    Includes index.
    ISBN 978-0-231-14648-7 (cloth : alk. paper)
    ISBN 978-0-231-14649-4 (pbk. : alk. paper)
    ISBN 978-0-231-51827-7 (e-book)
 1. Sports—New York (State)—History—
    Chronology.   I. Title.
    GV584.5.N4K76 2010
    796.09747—dc22   2009019465

Columbia University Press books are printed
    on permanent and durable acid-free paper.
This book is printed on paper with recycled
    content.

Printed in the United States of America

Designed by Lisa Hamm

c 10 9 8 7 6 5 4 3 2 1
p 10 9 8 7 6 5 4 3 2 1

To the memory
of Richard C. Wade
Historian, friend,
and the soul
of urban liberalism

■ ■ ■ ■ ■

Contents

Foreword

This book is not one that should be resting on a shelf. Instead, it's one that should be constantly within reach of readers because they'll go to it more often than any other book they've ever read. There is so much in it, so very much, for sports enthusiasts and lovers of history alike. Jeffrey Kroessler has put hours of research, a love of sports, and great patience into this enormous work, which chronicles the happenings—small or major—of sports in New York City.

I have spent a good deal of my life in arenas, rinks, ballparks, football stadiums, and basketball courts and at ringside, and I think that the world of sports has all the aspects of life. Sports expresses everything we do from the time we are able to reason. Just think about how all our lives we have experienced joy and defeat. It's the same in sports. There is always failure and triumph. Always the struggle to win and yet the courage to endure a loss.

The baseball field was a place I loved to be when I was growing up. There was no Little League then, but our season was just as organized. We ran our own clubs, playing other neighborhood teams on the ample sandlot ball fields of Astoria. Being a boy is having sports heroes like Joe DiMaggio and

Don Mattingly and never once being disappointed by them.

I grew up around boxing, which may explain why I like the sport, particularly the combat of it. It's such a basic thing, one man against another. You can't possibly argue that boxing isn't brutal. Brutal it is. One man is trying to knock out another man with his fist, which is essentially a club. But sometimes it gets into the category of art, and that's when you marvel at it. You marvel at the moves of Willie Pep, great boxer that he was, and Sugar Ray Robinson and Muhammad Ali. You marvel at how the great ones escape punches. For some reason, people want to see one man pitted against another. It's the element of danger we grew up with, especially as a kid in New York.

When Joe Louis was champion, all the white guys I knew rooted for him, and he fought mainly white fighters. This was a tribute to the man, for he *was* boxing in those days.

You will find people in sports, be they stars or just good, striving for a perfection they can't possibly achieve. Some will come close, but they are the extraordinary ones—like Babe Ruth, Joe DiMaggio, Muhammad Ali, Jim Brown, Michael Jordan, Tiger Woods, and Joe Montana. But even these great gifts to sports had their share of failure, and they knew how to deal with it.

Drama is another part of life we see in sports, and it was never displayed more than on October 3, 1951, when Bobby Thomson of the New York Giants connected with a Ralph Branca fastball, sending it into the seats of the Polo Grounds. The Giants won the pennant with that one blast off that unlucky Dodger pitcher. At the time, it was deemed a miracle. "The Shot Heard 'Round the World" is carved in stone in the annals of sports. In one autumn day, we saw great joy in triumph and great despair in losing. There we saw Thomson, full of elation while being carried off like the hero he was by his teammates, while on the dingy steps going into the Dodger locker room was Branca, lying face down, sobbing, and repeatedly saying, "Why me? Why me?"

This was life in the raw, an unbelievable drama. You could not make it up.

For another example of "sports and life are kin," I take you to Madison Square Garden, May 8, 1970: the NBA finals, pitting the New York Knicks against the Los Angeles Lakers. Willis Reed is out with a leg injury. He is sorely needed but is seemingly lost for the game. Suddenly, from the Knicks locker room, out comes a limping Reed to join his team on the floor. He takes only two shots, and both go in the basket. The Knicks win, and Reed is hailed as he limps off the court.

There, folks, was an important element in life, undaunted courage and a never-say-die will.

Another type of courage was displayed by Jackie Robinson in 1947 when he was chosen to single-handedly break the shameful color line our country had imposed on black ballplayers. "Blacks are not allowed to play this game reserved for WHITES ONLY" were the words that were invisibly written at all major league ballparks. When most clear-thinking Americans finally absorbed these words, they saw the hateful bigotry in them.

When I was a kid in Astoria, I was teased about my Spanish heritage. At first I fought it, but then I learned to laugh at it. It became a joke when I realized that it was coming from people like me. Everybody has to overcome something. When you grow up in that neighborhood, you are not prejudiced, because everyone's in the same boat. Once you understand that, it melts all that stuff down.

Robinson, who was forever to be known in baseball as "THE FIRST," led the way to putting a stop to this despicable display of bigotry in baseball. The man stood alone in fighting ignorant and profane acts against him as he was coming to the plate or running out to his position at second base. Robby not only did it with a fierce type of courage, but was able to restrain a justifiably vengeful heart and refrain from poking the insulters on the nose.

The saga of Jackie Robinson was life, all of it, and displayed by just one man. It's terrific that the Mets named the rotunda in their new ballpark in his honor. I wish they could have honored Casey Stengel and Gil Hodges, too. And why isn't Hodges in the Hall of Fame?

But let me go back to this marvelous history book by Jeffrey Kroessler, which you are about to read. You couldn't write this book about Philadelphia, and I'm sure W. C. Fields would agree. When it comes to sports, amateur or professional, New York City has unquestionably the greatest audience in the world. Where can you find such die-hard honest-to-goodness rooters as in this town? The Yankees, the Mets, the football Giants, the Rangers, and the Islanders and Knicks have the best fans anywhere.

New York gave us the greatest football game ever played when the Baltimore Colts beat the Giants in Yankee Stadium in 1958, and New York gave us the greatest boxing event of the twentieth century when on March 8, 1971, Muhammad Ali met Joe Frazier for the heavyweight championship of the world.

New York, when you think of its vastness, is more like a country than a city. What other town could claim Joe Louis and Jack Dempsey, Joe Lapchick and Lou Carnesecca, Yogi and the Scooter? How can any city or burg match the excitement of the 1969 Miracle Mets when they won the World Series? In the same year—the year of the moon landing—the Jets, with the popular Joe Namath directing the club, pulled a surprise by upsetting the 18$^1/_2$-point favorite Colts. And that's just one year.

This book deals with life, and you will see it in its pages. It's all there. It's quite an effort on Jeffrey Kroessler's part and something I would never attempt. Enjoy it, you fans of sports and history. It's a fine and ambitious tome, and I enjoyed it immensely. And remember, keep it close. You'll be reaching for it again and again.

Bill Gallo, *Daily News*

Preface

As I neared completion of *New York, Year by Year*, in 2001, the editor said (1) it's too big (how can any chronology of the great city be too big?), and (2) it includes too many entries about sports. The solution was obvious: cut many of the items about baseball, football, and the like and start a volume on sports. *The Greater New York Sports Chronology* is the result. Researching this book was more involved than I ever imagined, more surprising, and more rewarding. My intention was to produce a compendium of value to both true fans and historians, a work at the same time informative and entertaining. Many of the facts on these pages need no elaboration, but I hope that this book raises questions as well, pointing researchers in unexpected directions.

This chronology could never be complete, and I have certainly omitted many great players, many outstanding performances, many inspiring or tragic moments. Should I have included every singles champion at Forest Hills? Every trade that sent a fan favorite out of town? Every New York–born athlete who went on to greatness elsewhere? Here a historian's judgment comes into play. Always, a historian must distinguish between events and individuals of lasting significance and those of only momentary interest or celebrity. This is perhaps easier the farther we recede from the events. I confess that the chapter on the 2000s includes too much, but it all seemed vital at the time.

For the purposes of this work, I defined Greater New York as the area within a radius of roughly 75 miles from Manhattan and all of Long Island. Accordingly, many events that took place in New Jersey are included, although I focused more consistently on teams, players, and universities based in the five boroughs.

Chief Librarian Larry Sullivan and my colleagues at Lloyd Sealy Library at John Jay College were supportive, encouraging, and generous in granting me time to complete this work. This book was supported, in part, by a grant from The City University of New York PSC-CUNY Research Award Program.

I owe a debt of gratitude to the readers of this manuscript for Columbia University Press: Clifton Hood of Hobart and William Smith Colleges and Joseph Dorinson of Long Island University, both of whom completed a close reading and offered many, many useful comments. My editor at the press, Philip Leventhal, asked the right questions and pointed out the glaring omissions; as a sports fan, he wanted it to be right. Thanks to friends and colleagues who contributed ideas, suggestions, and the kind of details only long-suffering sports fans would know: Timothy Coogan, Richard Flanagan, Jay Hogge, Peter Salwen, and Roger Whitney. Arieh Sclar provided research assistance for the colonial era. Joy Kestenbaum connected me with a sports photographer. Jim Brennan, a true Yankees fan, was encouraging from the start. My agent, Rita Rosenkranz, was a dedicated champion for this manuscript. And Richard C. Wade, always my example, my adviser, and my friend.

Many librarians and archivists also gave generously of their time, tracking down images from their collections and making them available: Janet Munch, Lehman College; Steve Barto, Queens College; James Kaser, College of Staten Island; Wally Broege, Suffolk County Historical Society; Melanie Bower, Museum of the City of New York; Peter Derrick, Bronx County Historical Society; Christina Benson, New York City Department of Parks and Recreation; Bob Congialese, Belmont Park; and John Hyslop, Long Island Division of the Queens Borough Public Library.

Of course, I especially thank my wife, Laura, for her never flagging love and confidence. And, finally, my father, Andy Kroessler, goalie on the 1935 Brooklyn Tech city champion hockey team, a lifelong golfer, who sadly passed away while this book was nearing completion. My joy is diminished by his absence.

A Note on the Illustrations

The images in this volume came from many libraries, archives, and private collections. Every effort has been made to trace the copyright holders; to the best of my knowledge, I acquired the appropriate publication rights for every illustration, and each has been properly credited. Any failures in that regard were certainly inadvertent, and I will include the appropriate acknowledgements in future editions. The sources are Andra Douglas; Bill Gallo; Bob and Adam Coglianese Photographs; The Bronx County Historical Society; College of Staten Island, Archives and Special Collections; Dan Goldfarb; Jeffrey A. Kroessler; June Harrison; Lehman College, Bronx Chamber of Commerce Collection; Library of Congress, George Grantham Bain Collection, Prints and Photographs Division; Museum of the City of New York; Nassau County Museum Collection, Long Island Studies Institute, Hofstra University; New York City Parks Photo Archive; New York Public Library; Queens Borough Public Library, Long Island Division; Queens College; Suffolk County Historical Society; and Zurita Architects.

The Greater New York Sports Chronology

Introduction

In 2008, the Yankees drew 4,298,543 fans to the Bronx, more than 50,000 a game. It was the third straight year in which attendance topped the 4 million mark, and in every season since 1999 the team has drawn over 3 million. With that recent history, it is certainly difficult to imagine the circumstances that led to the firing of Red Barber in 1966.

On September 22, a cool, unpleasant afternoon, only 413 faithful passed through the turnstiles to see the Bronx Bombers play a meaningless game as they tumbled toward last place. Barber was calling the game on television that day (when all Yankee games were broadcast over WPIX, and when day games were not an oddity). A native of Florida, Walter Lanier Barber had been a familiar voice in New York since he first announced Dodger games in 1939. His soft, southern intonation seemed perfectly suited to fans in Brooklyn and the Bronx. Looking out over more than 60,000 empty seats, Barber asked the cameraman to scan the cavernous stadium. Wisely, perhaps, the director refused. Even without the visual support, Barber told his audience, "I don't know what the paid attendance is today, but whatever it is, it is the smallest crowd in the history of the stadium . . . and this smallest crowd is the story, not the ball game." Barber always saw himself as a journalist, and his primary loyalty was to his profession; he never thought that broadcasters should shill for the team. A few days later, Barber met team president Michael Burke for breakfast at the Plaza Hotel; before the Old Redhead finished his first cup of coffee, he had been fired. For most of Burke's seven-year tenure, the Yankees remained in the second division.

Once, this tale was known to all who followed the Yankees, baseball, and broadcasting. Today, few even remember the gracious Red Barber. How many more once prominent sports figures, men and women who dominated the arena and the press, have been consigned to oblivion? Heavyweight champion James J. Braddock would have remained forgotten, just another name on a list of titleholders, had not *Cinderella Man* been brought to the screen in 2004. Emile Griffith, too, is on that list. At Madison Square Garden in 1962, he met Benny "Kid" Paret in a welterweight title fight and literally beat him to death. At the weigh-in, Paret, who had taken the title from Griffith six months before, called him a *maricón*.

And what of Jack Dempsey? No, not the Manassa Mauler, the heavyweight champion of the Roaring

Twenties who later opened what would today be called a sports bar in Times Square. The original Jack Dempsey, the "Nonpareil." Born John Kelly in County Kildare in 1862, he fought out of Brooklyn under the name Jack Dempsey. He reigned as lightweight and middleweight champion in the 1880s and 1890s, when boxing was illegal in the New York State and the underground bouts lasted for 50 rounds and longer, not stopping until one of the fighters was battered to the ground. Nonpareil Jack died of tuberculosis, no doubt hastened by drink, alone and impoverished in 1895, but he was memorialized in a poem: "The Nonpareil's Grave." So legendary was the Nonpareil's career, in fact, that William Harrison Dempsey boxed under the name Jack in his honor.

These are all great sports figures and great sports stories, and they are all New York stories. Without question, the history of sport in Greater New York is the history of sport in the United States. As Toots Shor once boasted, "I have the best saloon in America, because to me, New York is America." Yogi Berra, of course, famously remarked, "Toots Shor's is so crowded nobody goes there anymore."

In any top-ten list, how many memorable, inspiring, embarrassing, or infamous moments in the history of American sports would be New York stories? The list would surely include Bobby Thomson's ninth-inning home run off Ralph Branca at the Polo Grounds and radio announcer Russ Hodges's unforgettable call, "The Giants win the pennant! The Giants win the pennant! The Giants win the pennant!" It was the first baseball game broadcast live coast-to-coast, which certainly factored into its legend. The overtime victory of the Colts over the Giants at Yankee Stadium in the National Football League title game in 1958—"the greatest game ever played"—has to be included. So would the bouts between Joe Louis and Max Schmeling at Yankee Stadium. In 1936, Schmeling knocked out the Brown Bomber

in the twelfth round; in the rematch two years later, Louis recorded the quickest knockout of his career. These fights were certainly among the most significant in history, with a black American who embodied the contradictions of race in the United States facing a German who represented the Nazi ideology of racial supremacy. (In fact, Louis and Schmeling became lifelong friends.)

The Kentucky Derby may be the most famous horse race in the country, but the Belmont Stakes—the "Test of the Champion"—has the real drama, as the best thoroughbreds vie for greatness by winning the Triple Crown. Secretariat won the Triple Crown in 1973, but it was how he won at Belmont that secured his place among the greatest, shattering the track record and finishing 31 lengths ahead of the field. That race deserves to be on any top-ten list, of course, but perhaps we should also include the match race between Eclipse, the champion thoroughbred of the North, and Sir Henry, the champion of the South, at Union Course in Woodhaven, Queens, in 1823. A throng numbering 60,000 saw the New York horse triumph. Never before in the United States had so many men and women of all classes and races come together to view a sporting event.

Sport, whether amateur or professional, casual or organized, is integral to the story of New York. What other city has been the scene of so many great moments and historic firsts? The first organized horse races in America were staged on the plains of Long Island soon after the English took New Amsterdam from the Dutch in 1664. The first recorded baseball game, the first intercollegiate lacrosse match, the first million-dollar gate for a prizefight, the first radio broadcast of the World Series, the first televised sporting events—all occurred in New York. The schooner *America*, built in an East River shipyard for the New York Yacht Club, was the first winner of the trophy known since as the America's Cup.

Manhattan, not Cooperstown, is the birthplace of baseball, and Brooklyn is where our national pastime grew up. The first leagues were organized in the 1840s in New York, and New York is where the rules were codified. The National League was organized in the city, and where else would baseball have taken the overdue step toward integration but in Brooklyn? Contrary to popular belief, however, the Dodgers' move in 1947 did not herald a flood of black ballplayers into the majors. Not surprisingly, the Giants were the second National League club to break the color line, but that came two years later, and the Yankees did not field a black player until 1955. Still, a sports chronology has its limits. A decade after Jackie Robinson made Brooklyn proud, John Hope Franklin became chair of the Department of History at Brooklyn College, an appointment sufficiently momentous to warrant a front-page story in the *New York Times*. Despite the accolades, Professor Franklin found it almost impossible to buy a house in the Borough of Churches. One player on a professional ball club does not a racial utopia make.

The integration of major league baseball, however, is only part of the story. While black players were barred from the majors and minors, barnstorming black clubs regularly took on white semi-pro teams from the 1880s into the 1950s. So great a draw were those matchups that for years Dexter Park in Woodhaven was reserved for Negro League doubleheaders on Memorial Day, July Fourth, and Labor Day. Did those games attract only black crowds? Of course not. Baseball fans flocked to see good baseball. At least in New York, the fans accepted integration on the field long before the big leagues dared embark on "baseball's great experiment."

Today, college football has bypassed New York, but the city once was the obvious site for the annual contests to determine the national champion. In the first half of the twentieth century, Yankee Stadium and the Polo Grounds hosted many historic intercollegiate football games, most memorably the annual clash between Army and Notre Dame at the Stadium. Fordham, with the legendary "Seven Blocks of Granite" (including Vincent Lombardi, class of 1937), and even New York University were once proud football powers. In the early 1940s, NYU generated considerable controversy by adhering to the "gentlemen's agreement" whereby northern schools would keep their black players off the field if they visited a school in the segregated South. In 1933, Manhattan College played in the first Festival of Palms in Miami, precursor of the Orange Bowl. Columbia, however, set a National Collegiate Athletic Association record for consecutive losses on the gridiron in the 1980s.

Most fans know that the Giants are one of the oldest franchises in the National Football League and that the Jets won Super Bowl III for the upstart American Football League. They are New York teams still, even though their home field is in East Rutherford, New Jersey. But what of the Bulldogs and the Tigers, not to mention the Staten Island Stapletons? Who remembers the New Jersey Generals of the United States Football League, let alone the Yankees of the All-America Football Conference? The Giants and Jets are sold out for every game, and there is a generations-long waiting list for season tickets. Most fans can follow their teams only on radio and television, in the newspapers, or online. Has this made it possible for more of them to identify with their teams, or has this created a gulf, rendering fandom less immediate? And by selling "personal seat licenses" costing many thousands of dollars to finance their new stadium, the Giants and Jets priced not a few longtime season-ticket holders out of their seats.

What city has more famous sports venues than New York? In baseball, there is Yankee Stadium, of course, and Shea Stadium, but also the Polo

Grounds, Ebbets Field, and Washington Park, so-named because it was located on part of the site of the Battle of Long Island in 1776. No ballpark today would honor such a heroic moment in American history. And, really, how many sports fans even know about the Battle of Long Island? The new home for the Mets is Citi Field, and Citigroup is paying plenty for the privilege.

Whereas New York once dominated horse racing, today only Aqueduct Racetrack remains within the five boroughs, with Belmont Park, Yonkers Raceway, the Meadowlands, and Monmouth Park just beyond. In the antebellum years, Centerville Race Course, Union Course, and Fashion Race Course in Queens attracted tens of thousands of spectators for historic match races pitting North against South. While a few intersectional match races were held in Baltimore and Washington, Southerners usually traveled north to Long Island. Other tracks have come and gone: Jamaica Race Track in Queens; Jerome Park (where the Belmont Stakes originated in 1867) and Morris Park in the Bronx; Sheepshead Bay Race Track, Brighton Beach Race Course, and Gravesend Racetrack in Brooklyn; and Roosevelt Raceway on Long Island. Protestations about "improving the breed" to the contrary, what has always driven horse racing is gambling. (Indeed, gambling stimulates interest in all sports; almost every year just before the Super Bowl, one district attorney or another announces the arrest of individuals involved in an organized-crime gambling ring.) New York banned the sport from 1802 to 1821 and for the next hundred years sought to regulate the action at the tracks and in gambling dens. At the turn of the twentieth century, New York was the horse-racing capital of the country. The industry generated millions of dollars and employed thousands in the state. Regardless, New York almost killed the sport in 1910 by outlawing gambling at the tracks and making track owners liable for any such activity on their premises. All tracks in the Big Apple—a term that came out of the racing world in the early 1920s—shut down until 1913. Campaigns against gambling and sports arose from the same roots as Prohibition, with the same results. Since the 1960s, public interest in the Sport of Kings has steadily eroded, and in the future, racetracks will be kept afloat not by the diminishing sums wagered on horses but by the revenue generated by slot machines and video poker.

Soccer arrived in the late nineteenth century, but for generations never migrated far beyond the bounds of immigrant neighborhoods. As a city of immigrants, New York supported the game long before it became a suburban cliché. Metropolitan Oval in Maspeth, Queens, is the oldest soccer field in continuous use in the United States, and teams representing the city's ethnic communities— Greeks and Germans and Hungarians—regularly won the national amateur championships. In 1975, Pelé arrived from Brazil to join the Cosmos and rescue the fledgling North American Soccer League. When he took the field for his first game at Downing Stadium on Randall's Island (site of the 1936 and 1964 Olympic track and field trials), the field was in such poor condition that the groundskeepers had to spray-paint the dirt green. For Pelé's retirement two years later, Giants Stadium was completely sold out. Does his arrival merit inclusion on the list of the top ten American sporting events? Would he have had the same impact had he signed with, say, the Tampa Bay Rowdies or even the Chicago Sting?

If sport in America had an epicenter, it was surely Madison Square Garden. From basketball to boxing to bicycle racing, from track and field to hockey, from the Westminster Dog Show to the National Horse Show, the Garden has seen it all. The Millrose Games, first staged in 1908 by employees of John Wanamaker & Company, a department store, is the oldest and most prestigious indoor track and field event in the nation, but it is the last of its kind. In the past, the Garden's winter schedule was peppered with meets, keeping public interest in the sport high.

Birthplace of the National Invitational Tournament, the Garden was practically synonymous with the rise of college basketball. The game grew with local talent—Irish, black, and Jewish kids—and City College, Long Island University, New York University, Manhattan College, and St. John's University dominated the sport under legendary coaches like Clair Bee, Joe Lapchick, and Nat Holman. But the Garden was also linked to the sport's corruption. The point-shaving scandals of the 1950s and 1960s ended the golden age of big-time basketball in the city. The University of Kentucky, Bradley University, and other schools beyond the Hudson were brought down by the scandal, but the shame was most deeply felt at City College, involving as it did members of the 1950 national championship team.

Surprisingly, and with not a little embarrassment, only two championship banners hang from the Garden's rafters for the Knicks, one of the original franchises in the National Basketball Association. The first basket in NBA history was scored by Ossie Schectman of LIU, one of six Jewish players on the Knicks. The great teams of the early 1950s never won a title, and until the glory years of the early 1970s under coach Red Holzman, the Knicks remained one of the consistently worst teams in the league. The Patrick Ewing–led teams of the 1990s always fell just short of the gold ring, but still had a New York toughness.

The peripatetic Nets began as the New Jersey Americans in the American Basketball Association, hosting their home games in the Teaneck Armory. Renamed the New York Nets, they played at the Long Island Arena in Commack (gone), the Island Garden in West Hempstead (gone), and the Nassau Veterans Memorial Coliseum, before re-

turning to New Jersey and settling into the Brendan Byrne Arena, renamed the Continental Airlines Arena, now the Izod Center. As the future Brooklyn Nets, they await a final (!) move to a new home in downtown Brooklyn—the Barclays Center. For all the cynical nostalgia about bringing a professional team back to Brooklyn, naming rights for their home court went to a London-based bank, with no branches in the city, to the tune of $400 million over 20 years. And the arena itself is merely the wedge for a massive real-estate development that will require hundreds of millions of dollars in public subsidies. The economic collapse in 2008 put that project on hold, and when—or if—the Nets move to Brooklyn is in doubt.

Ironically, that site is where Walter O'Malley tried to pressure the city into subsidizing a new stadium for the Dodgers half a century before. Robert Moses vehemently opposed the idea: "Acquiring land for sale to Walter O'Malley is not a public purpose and would be a scandalous procedure anyway." Moses offered a location in Flushing Meadows, but O'Malley refused and moved the team to Los Angeles. How the relationship between sports teams and municipal government has changed.

From the 1920s into the 1970s, Madison Square Garden, the "Temple of Fistiana," was the international capital of boxing, hosting more title fights than any other venue. The reason for that virtual monopoly was rather more complicated than sheer glamour or innate greatness. Tex Rickard, the greatest sports promoter of the early twentieth century, wrote into the contract of every boxer who fought in the Garden that his first title defense would be held there. Backed by sportswriter Damon Runyon and others, Mike Jacobs formed the Twentieth Century Sporting Club in 1933, ultimately partnering with Madison Square Garden to dominate boxing. He retired in 1949, and control of the sport passed to Frankie

Carbo, a mobster who served his apprenticeship with Murder, Inc., and Billy Brown, the Garden's matchmaker. Throughout the 1950s, their International Boxing Club monopolized bouts at Yankee Stadium, the Polo Grounds, St. Nicholas Arena in Manhattan, Chicago Stadium, the Detroit Olympia, and the Arena in St. Louis, as well as the popular Friday night fights on television. Boxers who objected to the IBC's dominance did not get a shot. In 1959, Carbo, the "boxing commissioner of the underworld," went to jail for his role in the boxing game. How many bouts were clean, and how many boxers had to throw a fight to get a shot at the title? Middleweight Jake LaMotta admitted that he had done just that. He took a dive against Billy Fox at the Garden in 1947 and won the title a year later. (Martin Scorcese's film *Raging Bull* tells LaMotta's story.) Even so, no fighter would argue with Buddy McGirt, veteran of 25 bouts at the Garden, who recalled, "The first time you're coming through that tunnel, knowing you're here in this arena with its history, you can't describe it."

My grandfather was a boxer. Born in Germany, Oswald Alp grew up in Liverpool and worked as a stevedore. He also boxed. When he came to Brooklyn with his family in 1924, he took any jobs he could, and he boxed. But he never went far. My uncle says it was because he would not go along with the crooked-fight game. He never took a dive, but he was never knocked out, either. For a man who had worked on the Liverpool docks and frequented gyms, Ozzie had the best manners of any man I've known.

New York was once the undisputed capital of sport in America. Whether horse racing or horsemanship; football or soccer; boxing, baseball, or basketball; chess or bridge, New York's preeminence was undisputed. That is no longer true. Greater New York has no shortage of professional and amateur events, but there is no reason that any particular event has to be there. It is startling to realize how ordinary, even insignificant, recent sporting contests seem, at least in comparison with those of decades past.

There are multiple explanations. With national media, there is no need for a concentration of sport in any one city. Everyone can view everything. Once, New York alone had the concentration of population and wealth required to consistently support the sporting world. Today, the gate is secondary to the viewing audience. It was altogether different in 1949 when Ted Collins, owner of the NFL's New York Bulldogs, turned down an offer from a local television station to broadcast all his games because he feared that it would diminish the paid attendance. His team folded anyway.

The city's once vibrant sporting culture has been waning for decades, due in no small part to the migration to the suburbs in the postwar years and the dilution of the immigrant communities that sustained sport. The gyms that fostered local boxing talent and the smaller arenas where young men built their reputations are no longer found in every neighborhood. Ridgewood Grove, Sunnyside Garden, the Bronx Coliseum, Eastern Parkway Arena, St. Nicholas Arena—all gone. New York was once a great baseball town, not only because of the Yankees, Dodgers, and Giants, but also because of the semi-pro teams that generated players and fan interest, not to mention the high school players. Today, it is a challenge to maintain baseball fields in public parks and school yards. In Astoria Park, the Department of Parks and Recreation actually removed the backstop and infield and planted trees to prevent team play (more soccer than baseball in recent years); in 2006, it evicted the Sunset Park Boxing Club from the Sunset Park Recreation Center, the last such club operating out of a Parks Department facility in Brooklyn. The ring took up too much space, it said.

Where will boys learn to box? And what is a recreation center for, computer classes?

While New York is no longer at the center, no other city has supplanted it. Rather, the diffusion of wealth and population has fostered a national sports scene. In 1957, Frank McGuire, who learned basketball with his brothers on the playgrounds of Queens, recruited seven players from the city to the University of North Carolina and won the NCAA championship. While it is certainly possible to import an imposing starting five from New York today, there is no guarantee that they would overwhelm the opposition. Every region of the country generates talented players and coaches; indeed, beyond the metropolitan area, the players may be better coached. And while many players still dream of competing in Madison Square Garden, it is no longer necessary for teams to win there to cement their reputation. The Garden may indeed be the "World's Most Famous Arena," but fame and dominance are not synonymous; events that would have been a natural for the Garden in decades past now take place in Atlantic City, Las Vegas, or other gambling towns.

Sport, and wagering, have been present almost from the founding of New Amsterdam, but not until the arrival of the Famine Irish in the mid-nineteenth century did New York's sporting culture take shape. Indeed, it is startling to realize the degree to which the Irish created and sustained that culture. Visit present-day Dublin, and you find a constant stream of billiards, horse racing, soccer, and Irish football on television; fans still turn out in impressive numbers to support local teams; and every neighborhood has its storefront betting parlors. How familiar must it have been for Irishmen at the Polo Grounds in the 1880s when manager Jim Mutrie led fans in his "We are the people" cheer after a Giants victory.

The history of sport in New York is more than wins and losses, teams winning championships or falling short. It is the story of race relations and ethnicity; real estate, urban development, and suburbanization; politics and economics; gambling, crime, and corruption; loyalties honored and loyalties betrayed; even religion and public morality. Running through this chronology is a current of antagonism between those who love sport and all that entails—violence, blood, gambling, a frivolous investment of time and resources—and those who would prohibit such enjoyment in the name of moral uplift. In the early nineteenth century, blood sports were the target, and ultimately bullbaiting, rat baiting, and cockfighting were indeed banned.

Peter Stuyvesant tried in vain to prevent New Amsterdamers from indulging in games and other pastimes on the Sabbath. The English were less concerned with strict Calvinist practice; they did, after all, introduce horse racing into the colony. As quaint as those blue laws now seem, it was not until 1919 that the city legalized Sunday baseball, and into the 1920s Protestants sought to prevent the holding of sports contests on Sundays. Noting that out of 70,000 football fans who filled the Polo Grounds in November 1925 to see Red Grange and the Bears take on the Giants, only one person filed a complaint, magistrate James M. Burns remarked in dismissing the case, "That is just about the ratio between those who want Sunday sports and those who do not—70,000 to 1."

Boxing was a particular target of reformers. Until the last quarter of the nineteenth century, the sport was not regulated, but New York eventually sought to eliminate or at least closely circumscribe it. The police raided matches, often just breaking up the proceedings, but sometimes arresting those involved, even at Madison Square Garden. The spectacle of two men battering each other was deemed barbaric, appealing to the baser motives of the lower classes. When the state finally lifted the ban on the sweet science in 1920,

New York at once became the boxing capital of the world. Today, the sport seems to be fading, in part because of its own corruption and the multiplicity of titles, in part because of the decline of local clubs. Yet a new, more brutal sport is growing—ultimate fighting, or mixed martial arts. New York outlawed such "human cockfights" in 1997, but will that prohibition stand? Should it?

In athletic competition, we encounter individuals who demonstrate great heroism and others who display tragic flaws. At times, following sports can be disheartening. On July 25, 2007, the sports section of the *New York Times* published a story about an NBA referee providing information to gamblers; another about an NFL quarterback arrested for running a dogfighting operation; a third about the leader of the Tour de France dropping out of the race amid suspicions of doping; yet another linking baseball's home run king with steroid use (and, no, Babe Ruth's legendary capacity for beer is not analogous); and, finally, a fifth about a pending lawsuit over the rules for the next America's Cup. In December 2007, former senator George Mitchell issued his report about illicit steroid use in baseball, naming dozens of current and former major leaguers, including Cy Young Award winner Roger Clemens and other Yankees and Mets. Does this tarnish the Yankee championships of the late 1990s and early 2000s? Sadly, and emphatically, yes.

If sport is truly a mirror of society, should we not shrink from what we see reflected? Were we better off when the press hid such failings from the public?

Another change in the culture of sports—locally, nationally, and internationally—is the growing corporate captivity of teams and events. Corporate logos are prominently displayed along the route of the New York City Marathon, and employees of those companies are heard cheering on cue. The America's Cup is perhaps the most com-

pelling example. Always an endeavor of only the wealthiest, the race has morphed into another beast entirely. What historically had been a contest between yachtsmen of different nations has become a competition between corporations. The 2007 series saw the Swiss defender, *Alinghi*, vanquish *Emirates Team New Zealand*. *Alinghi*'s skipper and helmsman were New Zealanders, and the crew included not a single Swiss national. The ostensibly Kiwi challenger was sponsored by a Middle Eastern airline, a Japanese automobile manufacturer, and a Spanish beer company. Contrast this with the English manufacturer Thomas Octave Murdoch Sopwith's challenges with *Rainbow* in 1934 and *Ranger* in 1937. A self-made man who had delivered the famed Sopwith Camel fighter to the Royal Air Force in World War I, he not only personally bankrolled his effort, but also was at the helm for every race. Is it any wonder that Sopwith and his English crew could engage the public imagination, while today's America's Cup races are irrelevant?

Regardless, we cannot dismiss sports. Fans retain an emotional attachment to their teams no matter how many times they might curse George Steinbrenner or rage at higher ticket prices or turn in disgust from a player's behavior. For despite everything, there remains a nobility in competition: spectators in a packed Madison Square Garden cheering Russian high jumper Valeri Brumel at the height of the Cold War; Don Larsen hurling a perfect game in the World Series at Yankee Stadium; Joe Frazier sending Muhammad Ali to the canvas in the fifteenth round at the Garden; Willis Reed limping onto the floor and inspiring the Knicks to the NBA championship; Affirmed and Alydar battling to the wire at Belmont; Sir Thomas Lipton challenging for the America's Cup five times, demonstrating a well-earned reputation for sportsmanship; chess grand master Garry Kasparov playing a supercomputer to a draw at the

New York Athletic Club; Glenn Cunningham winning the Wanamaker Mile six times in the 1930s and Eamonn Coughlin winning seven times in the 1970s and 1980s. We are drawn to sports for such moments.

Finally, the New York sporting scene has generated some of our most colorful and memorable quotations. After Max Schmeling lost a close decision at the Madison Square Garden Bowl in Long Island City—the so-called Jinx Bowl—his manager, Joe Jacobs, grabbed the radio microphone and blurted out the immortal words, "We wuz robbed!" Asked for the secret of his success at the plate, Wee Willie Keeler replied, "Hit 'em where they ain't." (A lifetime .343 hitter, Keeler was the first man to wear the uniform of all three New York major league teams.) Yankee owner Jacob Ruppert said, "There is no charity in baseball. I want to win the pennant every year." In 1962, Casey Stengel offered his legendary lament about the Mets: "Can't anybody here play this game?" We could scarcely omit Lou Gehrig's poignant speech at Yankee Stadium on July 4, 1939, after he had been diagnosed with amyotrophic lateral sclerosis: "Today, I consider myself the luckiest man on the face of the earth." Contrast that with the words of Micheal Ray Richardson of the Knicks, who famously said of his team, "The ship be sinking." Perhaps the most civil remark ever uttered about competition came at the finish line of the New York City Marathon in 2005. After winning by less than half a second, Paul Tergat of Kenya comforted second-place finisher Hendrick Ramaala of South Africa, saying softly, "Take it easy. This is sport."

1600—1799

The Dutch clearly relished their leisure hours, even though the activities they enjoyed often conflicted with the demands of strict religious observance. Much of what we know of the recreational pursuits of New Amsterdamers comes from official efforts to suppress such enjoyments. Director General Peter Stuyvesant repeatedly tried, and failed, to enforce respect for the Sabbath, evidence that the pursuit of fun and sport has been deeply ingrained in the city's culture from the beginning. The arrival of the English in 1664 brought horse racing to the colony, as well as blood sports like bullbaiting. Like the Dutch, the English sought to prohibit sports and other recreation on the Sabbath, but their half-hearted efforts proved futile. By the time of the Revolution, games of cricket, the first team sport in New York, were common.

1652

As "many guns" were "daily discharged and fired at partridges and other game" within the city limits of New Amsterdam, Peter Stuyvesant and his council banned the activity, with violators subject to the payment of fines and the loss of their firearms.

1654

On February 25, Peter Stuyvesant issued an edict on forbidding "certain farmers' servants to ride the goose on the feast of Bacchus at Shrovetide." Despite the ban, the event went off. The sport of plucking, pulling, or riding the goose involved smearing the neck and head of a goose with oil or soap and tying the bird between two poles. Contestants on horseback rode at full gallop and attempted to seize the prize. Alternatively,

Pulling the goose. (Author's collection)

a goose was dangled above the water, with the contestant balancing on a board on a small boat. Whoever carried off the goose was declared to be king of the festival. Harmen Smeeman and others were briefly jailed for participating in the competition and for laughing at the court proceedings.

1655

On February 8, farmers petitioned the New Amsterdam Council to permit riding the goose, but it was again prohibited.

▪ ▪ ▪

Peter Stuyvesant set aside August 25 as a day of general fasting, thanksgiving, and prayer for invoking the divine blessing on the impending expedition against the Swedes on the Delaware River. All common business—including "ploughing, sowing, fishing, hunting, etc., as well as all games of tennis, ballplaying, tapping, and drinking"—was forbidden "on pain of arbitrary correction."

1661

On June 27, tavern keeper Hendrick Assueros was fined for having sold liquor and permitted patrons to play ninepins during church services.

1663

Distressed that New Amsterdamers still did not properly observe the Sabbath, Peter Stuyvesant proposed that harsher restrictions be in effect from sunrise to sunset, not merely when church services were being conducted. In addition to doing "ordinary labor" and sitting in "drinking clubs," the edict banned "all extraordinary exercises, such as Gaming, Boating, Riding in cars or wagons, Fishing, Fowling, Running and roving in search of Nuts and Strawberries, Trading with Indians, or any such like, and, among the rest, the too unrestrained and excessive Playing, Shouting and screaming in the Streets and Highways." On March 18, 1664, with the act still not approved, the city fathers explained that while it might be necessary, the measure was "too severe and too much opposed to Dutch liberties."

1664

On March 17, several individuals were fined for having shot pigeons in the woods on Manhattan on Sunday, contrary to an ordinance.

1665

On May 1, six months after the English took New Netherland from the Dutch, Governor Richard Nicolls established a racecourse on the Hempstead Plains, on Long Island, calling it Newmarket after the English course. His avowed purpose was not "the divertissement of youth" but "to encourage the bettering of the breed of horses, which through great neglect was impaired."

1669

Following the practice of his predecessor, Governor Francis Lovelace announced that a horse race

Spectators and jockeys at Newmarket racecourse on the Hempstead Plains, the first track in the colonies. (Author's collection)

would be held on Long Island in May; subscriptions cost 1 crown in silver or the equivalent in good wheat.

1676

On November 13, the city fathers decreed "that no Inhabitant Merchant or Trades Man Or other Person or Persons . . . shall . . . prophane the Sabbath daye By Buyinge or Sellinge of any wares of Merchantdizes . . . or by Unlawfull Playinge att Cards Dice Tables or other Unlawfull Games whatsoever Either In Sermon Time or without. . . . As alsoe the disorderly Assemblys of Children in ye streets or other Places To the disturbances of Others with Noyse Upon the Sabbath Day which is to be Understood from Sun Riseinge Till Sunn Settinge."

1695

On October 22, the New York provincial legislature passed "An Act against the Profanation of the Lord's Day, called Sunday," decreeing that "there shall be no travelling, servile labouring and Working, shooting, fishing, sporting, playing, Horseracing, hunting, or frequenting of Tippling-Houses, or the using of any other Exercises or pastimes."

1699

On August 9, the Common Council ordered "that if Any Children Youth or Other persons doe fire Any Gun or Pistoll att Any Mark or Att Random Against any fence poles or within Any Orchard Garden or Other Inclosure or in Any place where persons frequent to walke on the South Side of the fresh water [the Collect, now Foley Square] of this Citty [they] Shall for Every Such offense forfeit the sum of twenty Shillings."

1700

By at least this year, there was a racecourse around Beaver Pond in Jamaica, Queens (now 155th Street and Liberty Avenue). This was the second track in New York.

1709

On May 6, the Common Council banned "play acting and prize fighting."

1721

On February 24 "was a famous Horse Race, run for the Sum of Sixty Pounds, between the Inhabitants of Queens County on the Island of Nassau and Samuel Byard of the City of New-York, Merchant, where the latter gained but little."

1733

On March 12, the Common Council authorized the "enclosure of Bowling Green for the ornament of the said street as well as for the Recreation and Delight of the Inhabitants of the City." The annual rent for this first public park was one peppercorn.

▪ ▪ ▪

An advertisement dated November 5 announced: "To be Run for, on the Course at New York, the 8th of this Month, a Purse upwards of 4 pounds value, by any Horse, Mare, or Gelding carrying 12 Stone and paying 5 shilling entrance, which entrance Money is to be given to the second Horse, unless distanced."

1735

A shooting contest was held from April 7 to 10 at the sign of the Marlborough's Head in Bowery Lane. The fee was 5 shillings for every shot; the contestant making the best hit at 100 yards won a lot of 37 feet, 6 inches, in breadth on Sackett Street.

1741

A law passed in November prohibited "playing Billiard Trucks or Cards in any publick House."

1749

In November, John Bonnin advertised a contest in the *New York Post-Boy*: "To be Shot for at Capt. Benj. Kiersted's. . . . A Large Rose Diamond Ring, value Six Pounds. Each Person who inclines to try his Skill . . . is to pay Twenty Shillings."

1750

In the issue of May 31, the *New York Post-Boy* reported on a "great Horse Race" held on Hempstead Plains. It "engaged the attention of so many in this City, that upwards of 70 Chairs and Chaises were carried over the Ferry from hence the day before, besides a far greater Number of horses; and it was thought that the Number of Horses on the Plains at the Race, far exceeded a Thousand."

1751

On April 29, a company of Londoners faced a company of New Yorkers in "a great Cricket Match" for a "considerable Wage" on the Commons (now City Hall Park). They played 11 a side, "according to the London Method." The New Yorkers prevailed, 167–80.

1757

The first running of the New York Purse was held in Jamaica.

1762

The *New York Mercury* of February 22 announced that a new racecourse in Harlem would be the scene for the running of the "New-York Race," with a purse of £100.

1763

On April 4, Martin Pendergrast advertised for sale his "Good new commodious Dwelling House and Lot of Ground. . . . It has all the Conveniences fit for a Tavern, is now kept as much [and] has a very fine Tennis-Court or Fire Alley."

▪ ▪ ▪

A "Bull-beating," or bullbaiting, was held in Bowery Lane near the DeLancey Arms Tavern on October 1.

▪ ▪ ▪

"An Act to prevent the Practice of Cock-fighting" was presented in the assembly on December 15. There is no record of its passage.

1777

Captain Pennington of the Guards killed J. Tollemache, captain of the man-of-war *Zebra*, in a duel in an upstairs room of Hull's Tavern, also known as the City Arms Tavern, at 115 Broadway. Wounded many times, Pennington finally pierced Tollemache through the heart.

1778

On May 16, the general orders of the day for the occupying British Army directed that "Officers or Non-Commissioned Officers Commanding Guards are to send Patrols to apprehend any Persons Gaming in the Streets or Ruins near their Posts; They are to send such persons to the Main

Guard and a Report is to be made immediately to the Commandant of the City."

An advertisement in the *Royal Gazette* on June 13 announced a "Game of Cricket, to be played on Monday next, the 14th instant, at Cannon's Tavern, at Corlear's Hook. Those Gentlemen that choose to become members of the Club are desired to attend. The Wickets to be picht at two o'Clock." On August 9, "a Set of Gentlemen" played a match "on the Cricket ground near Brooklyn ferry," inviting "any Gentleman to join the set in the exercise." The ground had "a large Booth for the accommodation of spectators." They played every Monday through the summer.

1779

On September 19, a cricket match for 50 guineas was played between the Brooklyn Club and the Greenwich Club at the House of Loosely and Elma's.

A notice in the November 8 issue of the *New York Mercury* warned the public against gamblers: "The Market-People and others are cautioned against being enticed into Public Houses or other Places by Strangers pretending Business with them, as there is a most infamous set of Gamblers in this City, who had lately defrauded sundry Persons from the Country, of large Sums of Money, after inviting them into Taverns, under pretense of wanting to buy Country Produce."

1780

A cricket match was held on June 19 and every Monday throughout the summer "on the Ground ... near the Jews' Burying Ground" (off Chatham Square). Newspapers regularly carried challenges

for cricket matches between Americans and Englishmen

1781

On June 6, horse racing commenced "on Ascot Heath, five miles from Brooklyn Ferry."

The *Royal Gazette* announced that "a Bull Baiting, after the true English manner," would take place at the Brooklyn ferry on June 20: "Taurus will be brought to the Ring at 3 o'Clock; some good dogs are already provided, but every assistance of that sort will be esteemed a favour. A Dinner exactly British will be upon Loosely's table, after which there is not the least doubt that the song called 'O! the Roast Beef of old England' will be sung with harmony and glee." On August 30, Thomas McMullen hosted a bullbaiting at his tavern; his notice promised that "the Bull is active and very vicious, therefore hopes the spectators will have satisfactory diversion."

The Brooklyn Hunt took place on November 14, commencing at 9:00 A.M., with dinner at Brooklyn Hall at 3:00 P.M.: "A Guinea or more will be given for a good strong Bag Fox by Charles Loosely."

1783

On April 16, a notice in the *Royal Gazette* advertised "Cock Gaffs, For the Royal Pastime of Cock Fighting."

1785

According to a petition to the mayor: "It is a very general complaint that there is not in this great city, nor its environs, any one proper spot where its numerous inhabitants can enjoy, with convenience, the exercise that is necessary for health and amusement."

1789 ....

On August 13, a yacht race took place "without the Hook" (Sandy Hook, New Jersey). The pilot boat *York* beat the Virginia-built schooner *Union*, covering 14 leagues in 5 hours. According to the *New York Journal*, the owners of the yacht reportedly wagered nearly £2,000 on the outcome.

1797 ....

On April 17, a bearbaiting was held "near Bunker's Hill, which terminated unfortunately to the sporters; for the bear got loose and hugged, most fraternally, some of the spectators."

1800—1849

In the first half of the nineteenth century, the population of New York (defined as the area of the five boroughs) grew from fewer than 80,000 to nearly 700,000, making it the largest city in the nation. Rapid urbanization still left much open space for organized sports or casual recreation, although such activities increasingly migrated to the outskirts of the city. In an early skirmish between the lovers of sport and the opponents of gambling, New York State outlawed horse racing in 1802. The ban was lifted in 1821, and the city quickly established itself as the racing capital of America, hosting many famous match races between northern and southern horses. Most significantly, baseball was born in New York during these decades, with the first organized teams and the first codified rules: the Knickerbocker Rules. Accompanying and fostering this sporting culture was the first weekly publication devoted to sports.

1801

In April, a bear- and bullbaiting was held at the New Circus in the Bowery. All "true lovers of Sport" were invited, with "dogs of the first blood" promised: "The Urus and Bull will be fought alternatively with the same dogs, not only to gratify the spectators, but to convince the public that the Urus, though far inferior to the Bull in size and diminutive in appearance, is greatly superior in strength, activity, mettle, and management." Writing in the *American Citizen* on April 15, "Philanthropist" decried the exhibition: "Amongst the various amusements that have lately been offered to the public, there is none so inconsistent with the manners of the age as that of Bull or Urus baiting. . . . The owner or owners of the Urus has built a large circus in the Seventh ward of this city for the purpose of continuing those scenes of cruelty. . . . It might be proper for the authority to interfere." The spectacle apparently continued into the summer.

1802

The New York legislature passed the "Act to Prevent Horseracing," abolishing the sport in the state for nearly 20 years.

1803

The New York Cricket Club adopted the Bunch of Grapes, a tavern at 11 Nassau Street, as its official meeting place.

1808 ....

On July 4, the Corlear's Hook Circus exhibited a tiger attacking first a bull and then a wild bear.

1811 ....

On April 8, the Common Council passed a measure "to prevent gambling in the Streets and public grounds in the City of New York."

1818 ....

In an illegal race at Newmarket on Long Island in May, Nathaniel Coles's four-year-old Eclipse ran for the first time and easily won the $300 purse. Early the next year, Coles sold the horse to noted horseman Cornelius Van Ranst for $3,000.

1819 ....

On August 9, the Common Council passed a law "to prevent the use of Velocipedes in the public places and on the side walks in the City of New York."

1820 ....

In the spring, John Cox Stevens, Cornelius Van Ranst, and other prominent horsemen founded the New York Association for the Improvement of the Breed of Horses and immediately lobbied the state legislature to lift the ban on horse racing.

1821 ....

Almost 20 years after prohibiting horse racing, the state reversed its decision and permitted "trials of speed" twice yearly in Queens. The New York Association for the Improvement of the Breed of Horses soon opened the Union Course racetrack in Woodhaven (now Seventy-eighth to Eighty-second Streets, and Atlantic to Jamaica Avenues; the road to the track was known as Trotting Course Lane). In the first legal horse races, held

Union Course in Woodhaven. (Queens Borough Public Library, Long Island Division, Eugene Armbruster Photographs)

on October 15, Cornelius Van Ranst's Eclipse easily bested Lady Lightfoot, a renowned Virginia mare.

1822

At Union Course in the spring and again in October, eight-year-old Eclipse easily defeated Sir Walter, a Pennsylvania horse bred from Virginia's best. In November, Cornelius Van Ranst took his horse to National Course in Washington, where Eclipse beat the southern champion Sir Charles without difficulty.

1823

I was last Saturday much pleased in witnessing a company of active young men playing the manly and athletic game of "base-ball." . . . [I]t is innocent amusement, and healthy exercise, attended with but little expense, and has no demoralizing tendency.

"A SPECTATOR"

A letter from "A Spectator" in the daily *National Advocate* on April 25 provides the first known mention of baseball in any newspaper:

I was last Saturday much pleased in witnessing a company of active young men playing the manly and athletic game of "base-ball" at the Retreat in Broadway (William Jones's tavern, between 8th Street and Washington Place). I am informed they are an organized association. . . . Any person fond of witnessing this game may avail himself of seeing it played with consummate skill and wonderful dexterity. It is surprising, and to be regretted that the young men of our city do not engage more in this manual sport; it is innocent amusement, and healthy exercise, attended with but little expense, and has no demoralizing tendency.

On May 27, before 60,000 spectators at Union Course, nine-year-old Eclipse, champion of the North, bested four-year-old Sir Henry, the standard-bearer of the South trained by William Ransom Johnson of Virginia, in a best-of-three series for a $20,000 purse. Carrying 108 pounds, Sir Henry took the initial 4-mile heat—the first horse ever to beat Eclipse—in the record time of 7 minutes, 37 seconds. With Samuel Purdy in the saddle, Eclipse, carrying 126 pounds, won the next two heats. Aaron Burr, Vice President Daniel Tompkins, and Andrew Jackson attended the race. The *New York Evening Post* ran a special edition to announce the result, the first ever sports extra. Eclipse never raced again; he was sold for stud and lived until 1833.

1824

Rowing the Brooklyn-built gig *American Star*, Whitehall boatmen easily bested an English crew in *Dart* (formerly *Sudden Death*), champion boat of the Thames, for the $1,000 prize. A gig is a long, light ship's boat, usually for the captain's use.

1825

Local horsemen organized the New York Trotting Association. The next year, they opened the Centerville Racecourse in Queens (now Woodhaven to Rockaway Boulevards).

In an intersectional match race at Union Course, Ariel, a daughter of Eclipse, lost to Flirtilla, a half-sister of Sir Henry, in three heats.

1829

Again at Union Course, Eclipse's daughter Black Maria vanquished the Virginia-bred colt Brilliant in another match race.

1831

In December, William T. Porter introduced the city's first sports weekly: *Spirit of the Times, a Chronicle of the Turf, Field, Sports, Literature and the Stage*. It was published until June 22, 1861.

1835

John Cox Stevens offered $1,000 to any man who could cover 10 miles in under an hour. Before 20,000 spectators at Union Course, Henry Stannard, a Connecticut farmer, made the distance in 59 minutes, 48 seconds.

1837

The Gotham Base Ball Club was founded. The members introduced the rule that to make an out, the throw went to the base, not at the runner.

■ ■ ■

The Beacon Course for horse racing opened in November in Hoboken, New Jersey.

1840

The Eagle Base Ball Club was founded.

■ ■ ■

Irish immigrant Kit Burns (Christopher Keybourn) opened Sportsman's Hall at 273 Water Street, a saloon infamous for rat baiting. Dozens of rats were loosed in the pit, a wooden oval 8.5 feet across and 17 feet long, and then a terrier was set down among them. The best ratters could dispatch a hundred rats within minutes. Years later, when hauled into court by the Society for the Prevention of Cruelty to Animals, Burns contended that rats were not animals like horses: "I know rats. I know they're vermin and they ought to be killed. And if we can get a little sport out of their killing, so much the better."

1842

At Union Course in May, Fashion, champion of the North, met Boston, a Virginia horse, for a $20,000 purse. The crowd was over 50,000, but the amount wagered was disappointing. Furthermore, the $10 admission fee dampened the enthusiasm of the spectators (even though it bought a season pass). Fashion won both 4-mile heats, taking the first by one length in the world-record time of 7 minutes, $32\frac{1}{2}$ seconds, and the second by 60 yards.

■ ■ ■

In an illegal bout on Hart Island, off the Bronx, James "Yankee" Sullivan (born James Ambrose in Ireland) defeated Englishman Billy Bell after 24 rounds.

■ ■ ■

In Hastings on September 13, Christopher Lilly knocked out Tom McCoy in the 119th round. McCoy died from the blow. Lilly fled to England, while 18 others involved with the bout, Yankee Sullivan among them, were arrested and convicted of fourth-degree manslaughter.

1843

The first chess tournament in the country was held in Manhattan.

1844

The New York Cricket Club was founded, with William T. Porter, publisher of the *Spirit of the Times*, as president.

■ ■ ■

John Cox Stevens founded the New York Yacht Club aboard his yacht *Gimcrack* on July 30.

1845

In May, a throng estimated at between 70,000 and 100,000 flocked to Union Course to witness

Peytona and Fashion racing at Union Course, May 1845, as illustrated in a lithograph by Nathaniel Currier. (Queens Borough Public Library, Long Island Division)

Fashion, the champion horse of New York, take on Peytona, a challenger from the South. The underdog, Peytona, won both very close heats.

▪ ▪ ▪

The New York Yacht Club held its first Annual Regatta in the harbor on July 17.

▪ ▪ ▪

On September 11, the *New York Morning News* published the first account of a baseball game.

▪ ▪ ▪

Alexander Cartwright, a twenty-five-year-old clerk, organized the Knickerbocker Base Ball Club of New York on September 23. (The name honored the volunteer fire company to which Cartwright belonged). The officers were Duncan Curry, president; William Wheaton, vice president; and William Tucker, secretary-treasurer. Cartwright penned the "20 Original Rules of Baseball," better known as the Knickerbocker Rules, establishing three strikes, three outs, tags and force-outs (rather than throwing the ball at the runner), and

fair and foul territory. Soon after the codification of the rules, Archibald Gourlie of the Knickerbockers was fined 6 pence for having protested the umpire's call, the first fine imposed on a ballplayer. Cartwright left New York for the West in 1849.

1846

Daniel "Doc" Adams succeeded Duncan Curry as president of the Knickerbockers. At Elysian Fields in Hoboken, New Jersey, on June 19, they faced the New York Base Ball Club, also called the New York Nine, in the first recorded game played according to the Knickerbocker Rules. The Knickerbockers lost, 23–1.

1847

Irish-born Michael Phelan opened his first establishment in Manhattan, the Arcadia Billiard Parlor.

The city's undefeated champion, he manufactured billiard tables and wrote *Billiards Without a Master* (1850), *The Game of Billiards* (1857), *The Illustrated Hand-Book of Billiards* (1862), and *The American Billiard Record: A Compendium of Important Matches Since 1854* (1870).

1849

On March 25, Captain Robert Waterman brought the *Sea Witch* into New York Harbor 74 days, 14 hours after leaving Hong Kong, a record for a sailing vessel that stood until 2003.

□ □ □

Daniel "Doc" Adams, president of the Knickerbockers, was credited with creating the shortfielder, or shortstop, position.

1850—1879

The mid-nineteenth century brought the professionalization of baseball and the first true leagues, and New York had its first baseball dynasty—the Atlantics of Brooklyn. Other sports attracted growing interest or curiosity, including wrestling, pedestrian contests (walking marathons), rat baiting (which brought the intervention of the Society for the Prevention of Cruelty to Animals), and, of course, horse racing. The *Police Gazette*, the premier men's publication of the era, glamorized and sensationalized sport, especially boxing, and fed a growing public fascination with celebrity athletes. Members of society's upper crust, including James Gordon Bennett, publisher of the *New York Herald*, were visible participants in sports, from yachting to shooting to foxhunting. The Jockey Club was founded to regulate horse racing and stave off state interference, and the New York Yacht Club staged the first defense of the America's Cup in the harbor.

1851

Your Majesty, there is no second.

REPLY TO QUEEN VICTORIA

Designed and built by James R. Steers and George Steers in their East River shipyard for John C. Stevens, founder of the New York Yacht Club, the schooner *America* won the Royal Yacht Squadron's regatta around the Isle of Wight on August 22. Observing the finish, Queen Victoria asked which yacht was second. "Your Majesty," came the reply, "there is no second." The 100 Guinea Cup was given to the New York Yacht Club under a deed of gift, making the trophy "a perpetual challenge cup for friendly competition between nations." Thus originated the America's Cup (named for the yacht). Stevens then offered to sail *America* against any English competitor for any wager. Robert Stephenson accepted for £100, but *America* easily distanced his *Titania* over a 40-mile course on August 28.

1853

On May 14, Frank Queen and Harrison Trent began to publish the *New York Clipper*, a

The America's Cup. (Author's collection)

sports weekly. Henry Chadwick covered baseball for the paper from 1858 to 1886.

1854 ....

Representatives of the Knickerbockers, the Gothams, and the Eagles met on April 1 to revise Alexander Cartwright's "20 Original Rules of Baseball," or Knickerbocker Rules. One change mandated that the batter following the player who makes the last out of an inning leads off the next inning.

On June 24, Fashion Race Course in Corona, Queens, opened; it was later renamed the National Race Course.

The Empire Base Ball Club was organized on October 23.

1855 ....

On January 29, the *New York Tribune* published the city's first account of rat baiting, or, more accurately, rat killing.

The Excelsior Base Ball Club of Brooklyn, 1860: (*left to right*) Raynolds, J. Whiting, James Creighton, Polhemus, Pearsall, Russell, Leggett, Brainard, and Flanly. (Photography Collection, Miriam and Ira D. Wallach Division of Art, Prints and Photographs, The New York Public Library, Astor, Lenox and Tilden Foundations)

Mechanics and shipwrights in Brooklyn founded the Eckford Base Ball Club, taking its name from one of the richest shipbuilders in the city.

1856 ....

The Excelsior Base Ball Club was founded in Brooklyn.

In Palisades, New Jersey, on September 18, bantamweight Charles Lynch knocked out Andy Kelly in the eighty-sixth round of their bout. Kelly died as a result.

Baseball was referred to as the "national pastime" in print for the first time in the *New York Mercury* on December 5.

The Brooklyn Hunt was organized. Its foxhunts ceased when the Civil War began.

1857 ....

On January 22, representatives from 14 New York and Brooklyn baseball clubs attended a convention to standardize the rules for players and clubs. Daniel "Doc" Adams presided. They agreed that games would last for nine innings, rather than continue until a team scored 21 runs, and set the bases 90 feet apart and the pitcher's mark 45 feet from home plate.

Billiard table manufacturer and champion player Michael Phelan patented a cushion made of strips of rubber to give a uniform carom. Competitors quickly appropriated his design.

Paul Morphy of New Orleans won the first American Chess Congress tournament, held at 764 Broadway, in November.

Chess champion Paul Morphy, as portrayed in *Harper's New Monthly Magazine*, 1888. (Author's collection)

1858

On March 10, representatives from 26 New York and Brooklyn baseball clubs attended the second baseball convention and formed the National Association of Base Ball Players. In all, there were 96 baseball teams in the area, up from 12 three years earlier.

▪ ▪ ▪

The commissioners of Central Park accepted the Greensward Plan of Frederick Law Olmsted and Calvert Vaux.

▪ ▪ ▪

All-star teams—"Picked Nines"—from Manhattan and Brooklyn met in a best-of-three series at Fashion Race Course in Corona on July 13. Thousands of fans paid admission: 10 cents a person, with an additional 20 cents for a one-horse vehicle and 40 cents for a two-horse vehicle. This was the first time fans paid to see a baseball game, ostensibly to support the widows and orphans of firemen. New York won the first game, 22–18; on August 17, Brooklyn took the second, 29–8; and on September 10, New York won the third, 29–18. The *New York Times* published an account of the third game on page 1, a first.

1859

In January, the Lake in Central Park (between Seventy-second and Seventy-eighth Streets on the west side of the park) opened for ice-skating. Although ladies were permitted to skate everywhere, only they were allowed on the upper Lake, a rule enforced by the Central Park Police. The next season, that rule was abandoned.

▪ ▪ ▪

In Detroit on April 12, Michael Phelan, New York's undefeated billiard champion and unceasing promoter of the sport, bested Jim Secreiter in a match for the American championship and $15,000.

▪ ▪ ▪

On September 10, George Wilkes published the first issue of *Wilkes' Spirit of the Times: A Chronicle of the Turf, Field, Sports, Literature and the Stage,*

Ice-skating on the Lake in Central Park, 1894. (Museum of the City of New York)

covering baseball, boxing, and horse racing. It became *Spirit of the Times* on July 4, 1868, and ceased publication on December 13, 1902.

* * *

Atlantic of Brooklyn won the National Association of Base Ball Players championship.

1860

The Excelsiors and the Atlantics met in a best-of-three series for the championship of Brooklyn. Before 10,000 spectators on their home field on July 19, the Excelsiors, with James Creighton Jr. on the mound, won the first game, 24–8. On August 2, the Atlantics solved Creighton's pitching and prevailed, 15–14, on their field in Bedford. With 20,000 on hand for the third game at the Putnam Grounds on August 23, the Excelsiors were leading, 8–6, when the crowd became unruly and play was suspended.

* * *

The Atlantics again won the National Association of Base Ball Players championship. The *Brooklyn Eagle* opined, "If we are ahead of the big city in nothing else, we can beat her in baseball."

1861

For the third straight year, the Atlantics won the National Association of Base Ball Players championship.

1862

At Chris O'Connor's billiard rooms on Fourteenth Street on July 17, John Deery of New York defeated William Goldthwaite of Boston in the second of two matches. (Goldwaithe had won in Boston in June.)

* * *

The Union Grounds in Williamsburg, Brooklyn (between Rutledge and Lynch Streets, and Harrison and Marcy Avenues) hosted its first baseball game on August 15. William H. Cammeyer had opened the grounds the previous year.

* * *

On October 14, James Creighton Jr., the twenty-one-year-old star of the Excelsiors, injured himself while batting and died of internal bleeding four days later. He is buried in Green-Wood Cemetery, Brooklyn, beneath a 7-foot stone obelisk adorned with crossed bats.

* * *

The Eckfords won the National Association of Base Ball Players championship.

1863

In a tournament at Irving Hall on June 11, New York's Dudley Kavanaugh won the American billiard championship. On August 19, at Kavanaugh's billiard rooms, Kavanaugh defeated Isidore in a match for $200, plus side bets. They

The Excelsiors and the Atlantics playing the first game for the baseball championship of Brooklyn, July 19, 1860. (Queens Borough Public Library, Long Island Division, Eugene Armbruster Photographs)

Union Grounds in Williamsburg, Brooklyn. (Queens Borough Public Library, Long Island Division, Eugene Armbruster Photographs)

played the three-ball carom game on a four-pocket table.

■ ■ ■

The Eckfords repeated as champions of the National Association of Base Ball Players.

1864

The Atlantics won the National Association of Base Ball Players championship.

■ ■ ■

The Hoboken Race Course opened. It closed in 1868.

1865

After the Eckfords defeated the New York Mutuals, 23–11, it became known that catcher William Wansley had taken $100 (which he split with two other players) from gamblers to throw the game—the first known game-fixing scandal in baseball history.

■ ■ ■

For the fifth time in seven years, the Atlantics won the National Association of Base Ball Players championship.

■ ■ ■

Soon after arriving in the city, Captain George Henry Mackenzie of Scotland, a Civil War veteran, won the championship of the New York Chess Club. He won it the next three years also.

1866

Ladies unaccompanied by gentlemen are not allowed to enter the grand stand.

SIGN AT JEROME PARK

A sizable crowd of genuine sportsmen attended a grand fox chase at Union Course on January 11. Six foxes were released in turn, each torn to pieces by a pack of hounds. An editorial in the *New York Times* exclaimed, "If that is deemed 'manly sport,' we must plead to a dullness of vision quite unable to see it."

■ ■ ■

Many thousands of ice-skaters went to Central Park each day, and new gas lamps permitted skating at night.

■ ■ ■

Henry Bergh founded the Society for the Prevention of Cruelty to Animals to suppress such "sports" as dogfighting and rat baiting.

■ ■ ■

Spectators at Jerome Park. (The Bronx County Historical Society)

In the office of Leonard W. Jerome on April 17, 27 gentlemen organized the American Jockey Club; in September, August Belmont was named presiding steward. On September 25, they opened Jerome Park in West Farms in the Bronx (now the site of the reservoir and Lehman College). The two-tiered grandstand could hold 8,000 spectators; entry was $1; and signs announced, "Ladies unaccompanied by gentlemen are not allowed to enter the grand stand." The racetrack closed in 1889.

Manhattan sportsmen purchased an inn on the Connetquot River in Suffolk County and formed the South Side Sportsmen's Club, a private hunting and fishing preserve with its own trout hatchery. The state took it over in 1963 and has maintained it as a nature preserve, restocking the stream annually from the Cold Spring Harbor fish hatchery.

The Atlantics won their third straight National Association of Base Ball Players championship.

1867

The Eckfords and the Fultons played a baseball game on ice skates at the Satellite Skating Park in Williamsburg on January 12.

The Knickerbocker Base Ball Club declared the last Thursday of each month to be Ladies' Day, when players were encouraged to bring their wives and sweethearts to the game.

At Jerome Park on June 19, Ruthless won the first running of the Belmont Stakes for three-year-olds. The race was named for financier August Belmont, presiding steward of the American Jockey Club.

On July 1, the first International Caledonian Games were staged at Jones Wood on the East Side of Manhattan, attracting contestants from Canada and Scotland. The New-York Caledonian Club had hosted local games since 1857.

In a trotting match for $2,000 at Fashion Race Course, an estimated 20,000 spectators saw Ethan Allen defeat the renowned Dexter in three straight heats.

Union of Morrisania won the National Association of Base Ball Players championship, the first time the winners did not hail from Brooklyn.

1868

Henry Buermeyer, John Babcock, William Curtis, and 11 others met in the Knickerbocker Cottage to organize the New York Athletic Club. At the Empire City Skating Rink (Third Avenue, between Sixty-third and Sixty-fourth Streets) on November 11, the NYAC hosted the first indoor amateur athletic games, featuring track and field events and the first bicycle—or velocipede—race in the United States.

The New York Mutuals won the National Association of Base Ball Players championship.

In December, the Pearsall brothers opened the city's first velocipede riding school, at 932 Broadway.

1869

In a hall on Chatham Street, Peter Goulding and Jim Miles faced off in a 1,000-mile pedestrian contest. Miles quit after 877 miles and, an hour later, shot his trainer, James Ross, severely wounding him in the neck.

□ □ □

At Leider's Café Europa, at 12–14 Division Street, the Fourth Grand National Chess Tournament began on June 21. Captain George Henry Mackenzie won the six-week tournament and took the $38 first prize.

□ □ □

The Atlantics again won the National Association of Base Ball Players championship.

1870

On April 2, Captain George Henry Mackenzie won the Brooklyn Chess Club tournament that had begun in February.

□ □ □

At the Capitoline Skating Lake and Base-Ball Ground in Brooklyn on June 14, the Atlantics defeated the Cincinnati Red Stockings, the first pro-

Capitoline Skating Lake and Base-Ball Ground, Brooklyn. (Queens Borough Public Library, Long Island Division, Eugene Armbruster Photographs)

fessional baseball team, before 20,000 spectators. With the score tied at 5–5 after nine innings, both teams agreed to play "extra innings" for the first time. The Atlantics won, 8–7, in the eleventh inning, ending the Red Stockings' two-year undefeated streak. Baseball pioneer Harry Wright called it "the finest game ever played." The Atlantics went on to win the championship that year.

□ □ □

Englishman James Ashbury issued the first challenge for the America's Cup, known then as the Queen's Cup. He sailed into New York Bay aboard his yacht, *Cambria*, on July 27: 23 days, 5 hours after leaving the English Channel and 1 hour, 10 minutes ahead of James Gordon Bennett's *Dauntless*. During the transatlantic crossing, *Dauntless* lost two men overboard in a storm. Over a course

The Red Stockings and the Atlantics playing in Brooklyn, as illustrated in *Harper's Weekly*, July 2, 1870. (Photography Collection, Miriam and Ira D. Wallach Division of Art, Prints and Photographs, The New York Public Library, Astor, Lenox and Tilden Foundations)

in Lower New York Bay on August 8, *Cambria* took on 17 yachts of the New York Yacht Club and finished eighth; *Magic* won. Admiral David Porter, commander of the Brooklyn Navy Yard, had the schooner *America* (which had seen service in the Civil War) recommissioned and refitted for the regatta; it finished fourth. In a match race off Newport, Rhode Island, on August 16, *Magic* again bested *Cambria*.

On July 30, John F. Chamberlin opened the original Monmouth Park in Long Branch, New Jersey. He had purchased 128 acres of the Corlies Estate the year before.

On November 21, Henry Bergh of the SPCA and the police raided Kit Burns's saloon, the Band Box, and broke up a rat baiting, arresting Burns and 38 others. They put the surviving rats into a cage and tossed them into the river, and destroyed the fighting dogs; Burns was sued by the dogs' owners for their value. Burns died before the trial, and the other men were acquitted.

1871 ....

No one who has closely observed the conduct of the people who visit the Park can doubt that it exercises a distinctly harmonizing and refining influence upon the most unfortunate and lawless classes of the city,—an influence favorable to courtesy, self-control, and temperance.

FREDERICK LAW OLMSTED

For $40,000, the New York and Hempstead Railroad bought the Centerville Race Course for a right of way; the track had opened in 1826.

The first professional baseball league, the National Association of Professional Base-Ball Players, commenced its inaugural season on March 17. The New York Mutual was one of the clubs that joined the new league and abandoned the original amateur association. The league folded in 1875.

The first pigeon shoot on Staten Island was staged on the grounds of the Richmond Club on July 13. The participants were well known in the city's financial circles.

The tenth annual regatta of the Empire City Rowing Club, held in the Harlem River off 114th Street on September 25, featured two races for women. Amelia Shean won the singles race in a 17-foot workboat, and Elizabeth Custace and Anne Harris won the doubles.

On October 7, billiard table manufacturer and champion player Michael Phelan died in a yachting accident.

Englishman James Ashbury again challenged for the America's Cup, a best-of-seven series pitting his *Livonia* against three boats representing the New York Yacht Club: *Columbia*, *Dauntless*, and *Sappho*. *Columbia* took the first two races, but lost to *Livonia* in the third; *Sappho* won the next two, taking the fifth and deciding race on October 23. Ashbury filed a protest after the second race, however, claiming that *Columbia* had rounded a mark to port instead of to starboard. The New York Yacht Club dismissed his protest. In a match race held on October 24, James Gordon Bennett's *Dauntless* bested *Livonia*. In gale-force winds and rough seas the next day, *Dauntless* and *Livonia* were again set to race, but *Dauntless* lost a crewmember overboard and withdrew; *Livonia* sailed to the start alone and claimed victory. The New York Yacht Club disagreed and, despite Ashbury's legal challenges, kept the America's Cup.

Central Park attracted about 10 million visitors during the year. Frederick Law Olmsted earlier had remarked, "No one who has closely observed the conduct of the people who visit the Park can doubt that it exercises a distinctly harmonizing and refining influence upon the most unfortunate and lawless classes of the city,—an influence favorable to courtesy, self-control, and temperance."

1872

The Atlantics and the Eckfords joined the National Association of Professional Base-Ball Players. The Eckfords played for one season; the Atlantics, until the league collapsed in 1875.

1873

About 1,000 spectators attended the first annual prize meeting of the National Rifle Association at the Creedmoor Shooting Range, in Queens, on October 8. W. M. Robertson of the Seventy-ninth Regiment took first prize, a $50 silver cup; O. Schricel Ocks won the sportsman's match, open to all comers.

▪ ▪ ▪

New York University fielded its first football team. The university abandoned football after

Members of the New York National Guard taking target practice at Creedmoor, 1890. John Jacob Astor is in the light shirt. (Queens Borough Public Library, Long Island Division, Illustrations Collection)

the 1952 season, with a record of 199–226–31 over 79 seasons.

1874

The Young Men's Hebrew Association was founded in the home of Dr. Simeon N. Leo on March 22. Lewis May was the first president.

▪ ▪ ▪

On April 14, a grand jury in Hempstead declined to indict J. Schwallenburg, proprietor of Schwallenburg's Hotel in Dutch Kills, for having held a cockfight in January. Those called to testify for allegedly having attended the event included Alderman George Hunter of Long Island City, Constable W. J. Rooney, Fire Commissioner J. Stephens, and Commissioner of Public Works A. Moran.

▪ ▪ ▪

On June 6 and 13, the National Rifle Association held its spring meeting at Creedmoor. Colonel John Bodine won the long-range rifle match for the Remington diamond badge, presented by the Remington Arms Company. According to the rules, the prize had to be won three times before passing permanently into the winner's possession.

▪ ▪ ▪

A foxhunt was staged on Staten Island on November 11. Since there were no foxes on the island, the

Creedmoor Shooting Range. (Queens Borough Public Library, Long Island Division, Illustrations Collection)

Members of Company F, Eighth Regiment, New York National Guard, in front of the Creedmoor Hotel. (Queens Borough Public Library, Long Island Division, Illustrations Collection)

unfortunate creature was brought over from New Jersey.

1875

On May 31, Lieutenant F. W. Hofele of the Eighth Regiment of the New York National Guard won the spring meeting of the National Rifle Association at Creedmoor. The third annual meeting was held there on September 28.

Travis C. Van Buren of the Long Island Shooting Association bested James Gordon Bennett, publisher of the *New York Herald*, in a pigeon-shooting match on the William Douglas Estate on Flushing Bay before about 50 invited guests on December 7. Bennett had imported about 250 birds identified as "English Blue Lock" at a cost of $1,250.

1876

On January 6, a foxhunt was staged at Bull's Head on Staten Island.

At 7:00 P.M. on January 15 at Giehl's Mammoth Garden in Williamsburg, Peter Goulding and John De Witt stepped off in a contest to walk 1,000 miles in 1,000 hours for a $1,000 prize, plus side bets. They finished together on February 26, but as there was no winner, they continued to walk.

Meeting at the Grand Central Hotel on February 2, club owners formed the eight-team National League of Professional Base Ball Clubs; William Hulbert was named president. The New York Mutual abandoned the National Association of Professional Base-Ball Players to join the new league. To save expenses at the end of a losing season, Mutuals owner William H. Cammeyer declined to send his team on a final road trip, angering the other owners. In December, they expelled the Mutuals from the league.

Captain George Henry Mackenzie won an international chess tournament held in New York.

The Westchester Polo Club was founded. The members played their matches at Jerome Park.

On March 29, before a rather small audience at Beethoven Hall on Fifth Street, William J. Austin defeated Tishler Fernando in three straight falls

Chess champion George Henry Mackenzie, as portrayed in *Harper's New Monthly Magazine*, 1888. (Author's collection)

in a Greco-Roman wrestling match. At Central Park Garden (Seventh Avenue, between Fifty-eighth and Fifty-ninth Streets) on April 22, Henry Howard bested Austin in a wrestling match for the light-heavyweight championship of America and $250 a side. On August 9, also at Central Park Garden, about 500 spectators witnessed a Greco-Roman wrestling match between two boxers: Joseph Coburn and John Dywer. Dywer prevailed in the two-of-three-falls match, $250 a side.

■ ■ ■

Off Sandy Hook on August 12, the New York Yacht Club's *Madeleine* defeated Canada's *Countess of Dufferin* by 27 minutes, 14 seconds to take the best-of-three series in two straight and successfully defend the America's Cup.

■ ■ ■

The New York Athletic Club held its seventh annual fall games and the first national track and field championships at its grounds in Mott Haven (150th Street and Mott Avenue) on September 30.

■ ■ ■

Colonel James H. McLaughlin and Jacob H. Martin, both of Michigan, met in a championship "collar and elbow" wrestling match before 800 spectators at Central Park Garden on October 16. McLaughlin prevailed, the stakes being $500 a side.

■ ■ ■

In a pedestrian contest at Central Park Garden that began on November 5, Bertha Von Hillern completed 323.5 miles to defeat Mary Marshall on November 12. At the same venue four days later, Marshall beat Peter Van Ness of Philadelphia in a 20-mile walking match. She covered the distance in 5 hours, 11 minutes, finishing 1 mile—eight laps—ahead of Van Ness.

■ ■ ■

At an athletic exhibition at Central Park Garden on Christmas, Emil Regnier and a bear engaged in a Greco-Roman wrestling match. Regnier prevailed in the tedious affair.

1877

In the wake of the heavy wagering on the outcome of the presidential election between Samuel J. Tilden and Rutherford B. Hayes, the New York State legislature banned auction-pool betting. In that system, bettors bid for exclusive betting rights to horses; the total bets were pooled and divided among those winners; and the auctioneer claimed a commission. As a result, bookmaking developed, with bettors putting money on any horse at posted odds.

■ ■ ■

The Westminster Kennel Club (originally the Westminster Breeding Club) held the first annual New York Bench Show of Dogs in the Hippodrome at Gilmore's Garden from May 8 to 11; about 1,200 dogs were entered. The club was named for the founders' favorite gathering place, the bar at the Westminster Hotel.

■ ■ ■

The Manhattan Chess Club was founded.

■ ■ ■

Irish immigrant Richard K. Fox acquired the *Police Gazette* and transformed it into the nation's premier sports publication (featuring also crime, vice, sexual transgressions, and other topics prone to prurient sensationalism). To promote his paper, he sponsored many sporting events and donated $1 million in prize money over the years, including the heavyweight-title belt, studded with diamonds, emeralds, sapphires, and rubies. To a great extent, he was responsible for the growth of a sporting culture in the city. But by the time of his death, on November 14, 1922, the world of sport had long left his publication behind.

■ ■ ■

In what was billed as a world championship Greco-Roman wrestling match at Terrace Garden before 1,000 spectators, William Miller of Baltimore defeated André Christol of France in two straight falls on June 15.

Led by F. Gray Griswold, Master of the Hounds and Huntsman, the Queens County Hunt set off on its inaugural meeting from the Garden City Hotel on October 3. The hunts typically covered about 7 miles over farms and fields, and the club regularly paid for damages to property.

On November 22, Manhattanville College and New York University met in Central Park in the first intercollegiate lacrosse game. New York University won, 2–0.

1878

On April 27, at Central Park Garden, John Hughes completed a six-day pedestrian challenge—walking 378 miles, 3,485 feet over 144 hours—but falling considerably short of the record he had set out to better: Daniel O'Leary's mark of 520 miles, 1,320 feet. The men met at Gilmore's Garden in the fall, completing a six-day pedestrian contest at 1:00 A.M. on October 5, O'Leary covering 403 miles to Hughes's 310.

At the St. George's Cricket Grounds in Hoboken, New Jersey, on November 28, a crowd of 2,000 saw Princeton defeat Yale by a "touchdown and a goal" for the Intercollegiate Football Association championship.

1879

Hotelier William A. Engeman formed the Brighton Beach Racing Association, and on June 28, a crowd of about 2,000 attended the opening day of racing at his Brighton Beach Race-Course. The track was built on sand and could not properly support the thoroughbreds. That first season, two horses perished each week, and the course became known as the Coney Island Slaughter-house.

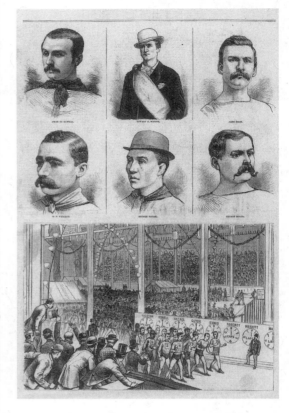

Start of the six-day pedestrian contest at Madison Square Garden, as illustrated in *Frank Leslie's Illustrated Newspaper*, October 4, 1879. (Author's collection)

It shut down in 1910 when New York State outlawed wagering.

At 1:00 A.M. on Monday, September 22, at Madison Square Garden, 13 contestants stepped off for the six-day pedestrian contest for the Astley Belt. (The odd time was to avoid the Sunday blue laws.) Englishman Charles Rowell walked 530 miles and took the $26,000 top prize; eight men completed 450 miles to qualify for a share of the gate.

1880—1889

Baseball and horse racing matured into modern form, while boxing remained disreputable and illegal. Even so, heavyweight champion John L. Sullivan often boxed in the city, and Jack Dempsey, the "Nonpareil," became the undefeated lightweight champion while dodging authorities intent on preventing the bouts. In baseball, the Gothams became the Giants and moved to the Polo Grounds; Brooklyn joined the American Association; and the first Mets came and went. New racetracks opened, even as the state attempted to combat gambling. The New York Yacht Club successfully defended the America's Cup in races off Sandy Hook; fox-hunting expanded in rural areas; the first horse show was staged at Madison Square Garden; tennis gained a foothold among the well-to-do; and the nation's first golf club was founded in Yonkers. The popular press covered those upper-class pursuits, generating interest in activities beyond the reach of most readers. Excluded from white sports, black athletes and fans developed parallel teams and champions. College football became a regular feature of the autumn calendar, and cycling evolved from a curiosity into a sport.

1880

Captain George Henry Mackenzie won the fifth American Chess Congress tournament.

◼ ◼ ◼

On May 11, the three-day Westminster Kennel Club Bench Show opened at Madison Square

Entrants in the Westminster Kennel Club Bench Show, as shown in the *Illustrated American*, February 22, 1890. (Author's collection)

Garden, the event's home ever since (except for five years). It is one of four events held in each incarnation of the Garden (the others being the horse show, the circus, and boxing).

▫ ▫ ▫

At Jerome Park on June 8, the fourteenth running of the Belmont Stakes introduced the post parade. Whereas the horses used to proceed directly from the paddock to the start, they were now walked in front of the grandstand.

▫ ▫ ▫

The Coney Island Jockey Club—established by Leonard W. Jerome, August Belmont, and William Travers—opened Sheepshead Bay Race Track on June 19. It shut down in 1910 when New York State banned gambling.

▫ ▫ ▫

John B. Day and James Mutrie formed the New York Metropolitans—the original Mets—as an independent baseball team. In the fall, they leased a polo field at 110th Street and Sixth Avenue from James Gordon Bennett Jr., and the Mets played a successful 24-game stand in their new home field, the Polo Grounds.

▫ ▫ ▫

Before they could begin a gloved bout to be fought according to Marquis of Queensbury rules for a $25

purse at Harry Hill's Variety Theatre on September 20, Jack Boylan and Jack Dempsey (born John Kelly in County Kildare in 1862) were arrested.

▫ ▫ ▫

At Tammany Hall on October 4, George F. Slosson defeated Jacob Schaefer for the American billiard championship and a $1,000 prize.

▫ ▫ ▫

After a ride by the Queens County Hunt over their fields, several New Rochelle farmers submitted bills for damages to their fences, fields, and crops.

1881

In March, the Kings County Wheelmen's Association was founded to encourage cycling and advocate for improved roads.

▫ ▫ ▫

On September 24, Judge Donohue of the New York State Supreme Court granted the American Jockey Club an injunction to bar police from interfering with bookmaking at Jerome Park. According to the club's vice president, Leonard W. Jerome, it had sold bookmaking privileges since 1878.

▫ ▫ ▫

The Meadow Brook Hunt was organized on Long Island: "[T]he object and nature of the business for which said corporation is to be formed is to support and hunt a pack of foxhounds in the proper seasons, and to promote other sports." A. Belmont Purdy was the first Master of Hounds. The club lasted into the 1960s.

▫ ▫ ▫

On November 10, the New York Yacht Club won its fourth defense of the America's Cup. *Mischief* defeated Canada's *Atalanta* by 39 minutes, 4 seconds over a course off Sandy Hook, taking the best-of-three series in two straight. *Mischief* was selected over the faster *Gracie* because its owner was William Krebs, chairman of the club's America's Cup committee.

Sheepshead Bay Race Track. (Queens Borough Public Library, Long Island Division, Post Card Collection)

Scenes from a ride of the Meadow Brook Hunt, as illustrated in *Frank Leslie's Illustrated Newspaper*, November 26, 1887. (Author's collection)

■ ■ ■

Members of the Seventh Regiment and their lady friends organized a tennis association and set up courts on the drill floor of the Seventh Regiment Armory. For years, they held championships on New Year's Day.

■ ■ ■

Meeting for the collegiate football championship for a sixth year, Yale and Princeton played to a scoreless draw in the annual Thanksgiving Day game at the Polo Grounds. An estimated 10,000 spectators braved the freezing conditions.

1882 ....

The race presented a striking spectacle at first from the imposing array of queer-looking vehicles and the skill with which they were handled, but after the first

Tennis players in the Seventh Regiment Armory, as illustrated in *Harper's Weekly*, December 10, 1881. (Author's collection)

impressions wore away it became rather monotonous.

REPORTER FOR THE *NEW YORK TIMES*

A six-day pedestrian match at Madison Square Garden ended on March 4. George Hazael had walked 600 miles to victory. According to the *Brooklyn Eagle*,

The attempt to push the powers of human endurance to the utmost limit must necessarily be attended with suffering. How intense the agony endured by the plucky little Englishman, Rowell, before he yielded to the inevitable and reluctantly retired from the race, a beaten but not dishonored competitor, none but he can tell. And even to the victors, if outward indications are to be accepted, the prizes won are after all but slight recompense for the physical pains and penalties undergone in their winning. The walkers who have stuck to their six days' work with a pertinacity and courage which would be counted heroic if displayed in a loftier cause are fitter objects for commiseration, as far as the end draws near, than admiring contemplation, so far as appearances go; and it is undoubtedly the fact that of the hundreds of spectators who shouted themselves hoarse over the finish of the race last night, there were few who did not turn from the final scene with feelings of sympathy rather than of exultation.

• • •

In a steady rain at Washington Park (Seventieth Street at the East River) on the Fourth of July, John L. Sullivan battered Jim Elliot senseless in three rounds; Sullivan had offered Elliot $500 if he lasted for four rounds. Five thousand fans paid between $1 and $5 to see Sullivan fight Englishman Tug Wilson at Madison Square Garden on July 17. Wilson survived four rounds with the champion by skipping away and intentionally falling to the floor. In addition to the usual sporting crowd of gamblers, many from the upper crust were in attendance.

• • •

Five contestants entered a 50-mile bicycle race at the Manhattan Athletic Club Grounds (Fifty-sixth Street and Eighth Avenue) on September 9. V. C. Place won in 3 hours, 27 minutes, 11 3/4 seconds—a new American record for open-air cycling. A reporter for the *New York Times* wrote: "The race presented a striking spectacle at first from the imposing array of queer-looking vehicles and the skill with which they were handled, but after the first impressions wore away it became rather monotonous. True, the monotony was relieved by occasional spurts on the part of one or other of the riders, at which the spectators lustily cheered; also by the incessant freebooting attacks from the licentious mosquito."

• • •

At Harry Hill's Variety Theatre on December 7, Charles Hadley of Bridgeport, Connecticut, met Morris Grant of New York for what was called the Colored Boxing Championship of America and for permanent possession of the Richard K. Fox

Harry Hill's Variety Theatre, 1878. (Picture Collection, The Branch Libraries, The New York Public Library, Astor, Lenox and Tilden Foundations)

Medal (each man had won the medal twice). Hadley prevailed in two rounds.

• • •

On December 28, a benefit was held at Madison Square Garden for pugilist Joe Coburn, recently released from prison after serving six years for assault, to raise funds for him to buy a saloon. John L. Sullivan engaged in friendly sparring with Coburn, to the crowd's delight.

1883 ....

At the Manhattan Chess Club on February 2, Wilhelm Steinitz, a recent Austrian immigrant, prevailed over Captain George Henry Mackenzie, the city's champion, in a six-game match.

• • •

The New York Metropolitans joined the American Association for the league's second season. In their first game, on May 12, the Mets lost to Philadelphia, 11–4. James Mutrie and John B. Day, owners of the Metropolitans, also had organized a new franchise in the National League, the New York Gothams. In their first game at the Polo Grounds, on May 1, the Gothams defeated Boston, 7–5, before 15,000 spectators, including former president Ulysses S. Grant. The Gothams played in the southeast corner of the grounds, and the Mets played in the southwest corner. At the urging of baseball pioneer A. G. Spalding, National League officials ordered the Gothams to shutter the liquor stand at the Polo Grounds.

▪ ▪ ▪

George Taylor, Charles Byrne, Joseph Doyle, and Frederick Abell obtained a franchise in the short-lived Interstate Association and built Washington Park in Brooklyn (Third to Fifth Streets, and Fourth and Fifth Avenues). The name honored George Washington because the park was built on the site of intense fighting during the Battle of Long Island in 1776. The owners' most important hire was twenty-four-year-old Charles Ebbets, who did everything. On opening day, May 12, a crowd of about 6,000 saw the Brooklyn Grays defeat Trenton, 13–6.

▪ ▪ ▪

At Madison Square Garden on May 14, John L. Sullivan battered Englishman Charlie Mitchell. Police captain Alexander "Clubber" Williams stopped the fight in the third round, although Mitchell seemed willing to continue. (It was Williams who dubbed the vice district the "Tenderloin.") On May 28, about 4,000 witnessed Sullivan pitch for a semi-pro team at the Polo Grounds, for which he received half the gate: $1,585.90.

▪ ▪ ▪

On May 28, the League of American Wheelmen held its third annual meet, with a parade of cyclists up Fifth Avenue to 116th Street, and then through Central Park, which was normally closed to cyclists. In June, the league succeeded in hav-

Members of the League of American Wheelmen cycling on Riverside Drive during their third annual meet, May 28, 1883, as illustrated in *Harper's Weekly*. (Museum of the City of New York)

ing Central Park and Riverside Drive open for cycling between sunrise and 9:00 A.M., although cyclists could enter and exit Central Park only at Fifty-ninth Street and Eighth Avenue or 110th Street and Seventh Avenue.

▪ ▪ ▪

Driven out of Maguire's Saloon in Blissville by the Long Island City police on the morning of September 3, Jack Dempsey and Harry Force searched for another site for their $250 lightweight bout. They finally began the proceedings in the open air at Coney Island, but police chief John Y. McKane broke up the match in the ninth round and hauled both fighters to the Gravesend jail.

▪ ▪ ▪

On September 22, two women's baseball teams, the Blondes and the Brunettes, met at the Manhattan Athletic Club Grounds (Fifty-sixth Street and Eighth Avenue). Before about 1,500 spectators, the Brunettes prevailed in five innings, 54–22. According to the promoters, the players were selected from 200 applicants, "variety actresses" and "ballet girls" being barred.

▪ ▪ ▪

The first National Horse Show, held at Madison Square Garden, as illustrated in *Frank Leslie's Illustrated Newspaper,* October 27, 1883. (Author's collection)

From October 22 to 26, the first National Horse Show was held at Madison Square Garden. Except for 1989 to 1995, when it took place at the Meadowlands, the event was staged at the Garden through 2001, when it moved to Florida.

1884

Brooklyn joined the American Association, playing its home games at Washington Park. Over the years, the team was variously known as the Bridegrooms, the Superbas, the Robins, and the Trolley Dodgers.

The American Kennel Club was founded, and the Westminster Kennel Club became the first member. Westminster remained the only all-breed club in the AKC until 1897.

On July 30, after several aborted efforts, middleweights Jack Dempsey and George Fulljames finally met in a ring at Great Kills Point on Staten Island. Dempsey prevailed, but on August 9 he was arrested while strolling on the Bowery and booked on Staten Island. On August 27, the charges were dismissed, as none of the witnesses could swear that Dempsey was the man they had seen box. After this bout, the Nonpareil won 41 straight fights before losing to heavyweight champion Bob Fitzsimmons in 1891.

In their second season in the league, the Metropolitans won the American Association pennant. They challenged the Providence Grays, champions of the National League, to a best-of-five series for the Championship of America, but lost in three straight.

German immigrants in Brooklyn founded the German-Americans, a sports club for track and field, boxing, wrestling, and later soccer.

1885

My giants!

JAMES MUTRIE

Inspector Thorne and Captain Alexander "Clubber" Williams stepped into the ring at Madison Square Garden on January 19 to stop a prizefight between John L. Sullivan and Paddy Ryan. At least 10,000 spectators had jammed the arena, including politicians, society types, and the usual sporting crowd.

Grand opening of the new clubhouse of the New York Athletic Club, as illustrated in *Harper's Weekly*, February 14, 1885. (Author's collection)

The new clubhouse of the New York Athletic Club, located at the southwest corner of Fifty-fifth Street and Sixth Avenue, opened with a formal affair on February 5.

The Guttenberg Racetrack, controlled by gamblers and local politicians, opened in Hudson County, even though gambling was illegal in New Jersey. The track closed in 1893.

William Wallace founded the Ridgewood Baseball Club and built Wallace's Ridgewood Grounds (Irving Avenue and Halsey Street). From 1886 to 1889, the Brooklyn club in the American Association played its Sunday games there, as the blue

laws were not enforced as strictly in Queens as in Brooklyn. The ballpark was expanded to hold 11,000 in 1902; in 1928, it was sold to real-estate developers.

After a thrilling extra-inning win over Philadelphia on June 3, Jim Mutrie, manager and co-owner of the New York Gothams, called his players "my giants!" giving his team a new nickname. (Fans and reporters had been referring to the team as the Giants for some time.) After battling for first place all season, the Giants dropped three of four to the Chicago White Stockings, who took the pennant.

William A. Engeman, owner of the Brighton Beach Race-Course, was arrested for permitting gambling at the track. He was arrested again the next year.

Over a course off Sandy Hook, the New York Yacht Club's *Puritan* defeated the English cutter *Genesta* by 1 minute, 38 seconds to take the best-of-three series for the America's Cup on September 16.

Frank P. Thompson, headwaiter at the Argyle Hotel in Babylon on Long Island, organized a black baseball team to entertain guests. Originally called the Athletics, the team barnstormed after the hotel closed for the season, winning most of its games but losing to the Metropolitans, 11–3, on

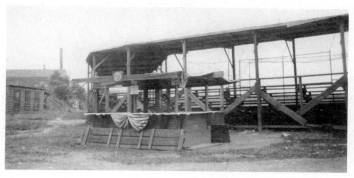

Wallace's Ridgewood Grounds, 1922. (Queens Borough Public Library, Long Island Division, Eugene Armbruster Photographs)

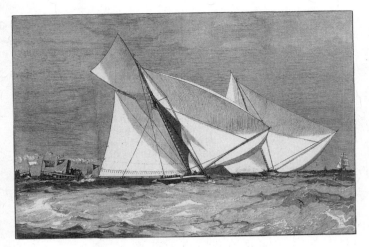

The America's Cup defender, *Puritan*, and the English challenger, *Genesta*, running downwind in the second race, as illustrated in *Harper's Weekly*, September 26, 1885. (Author's collection)

October 5. The team, renamed the Cuban Giants in 1886, became one of the most successful barnstorming clubs of the era.

▪ ▪ ▪

On October 1, the Metropolitans played their final game at the Polo Grounds, defeating the Cincinnati Red Stockings, 5–1. On December 5, Erastus Wiman acquired the team, intending to move it to a field on Staten Island (he had an interest in the ferry); three days later, the other club owners revoked New York's franchise and awarded it to Washington, D.C. Wiman sued and on December 19 won the right to stay in the American Association.

New grounds of the New York Metropolitans on Staten Island. (Picture Collection, The Branch Libraries, The New York Public Library, Astor, Lenox and Tilden Foundations)

▪ ▪ ▪

Unhappy at the club owners' attempt to limit salaries, players founded the Brotherhood of Professional Base Ball Players on October 22. Their goal was "to protect and benefit ourselves collectively and individually; to promote a high standard of professional conduct; to foster and encourage the interests of the game of baseball." John Montgomery Ward of the Giants was the first president of the union.

1886

On January 15, at a benefit held in his honor at the Germania Assembly Rooms in the Bowery following his American tour, during which he was undefeated, middleweight champion Jack Dempsey took on three boxers for four rounds each: Jimmy Murray, Tom Henry, and "Professor" Mike Donovan. On February 3, after 27 rounds fought in 1 hour, 47 minutes—the exact location was secret because the bout was illegal—Dempsey knocked out Jack Fogarty of Philadelphia, breaking his nose and jaw. In an improvised ring in Larchmont before a select crowd of gamblers on March 14, Dempsey knocked out George LaBlance of Boston in the thirteenth round.

▪ ▪ ▪

The Brooklyn Jockey Club opened the Gravesend Racetrack, joining the Brighton Beach Race-Course and Sheepshead Bay Race Track to make southern Brooklyn a national center of horse racing. The track shut down in 1910.

▪ ▪ ▪

William Travers, president of the New York Athletic Club, arranged the purchase of the club's summer home in Pelham, on Long Island Sound. The facility features playing fields, a saltwater pool, and a clubhouse.

▪ ▪ ▪

Track and field events at the New York Athletic Club grounds at Travers Island, as shown in the *Illustrated American*, June 28, 1890. (Author's collection)

The New York Yacht Club's *Mayflower* successfully defended the America's Cup, taking the second race of the best-of-three series from the English challenger, *Galatea*, over a course off Sandy Hook on September 11.

In a series of matches held in New York, St. Louis, and New Orleans, Austrian-born Wilhelm Steinitz defeated Johann Zukertort for the first world chess championship. Steinitz had settled in New York and became a citizen on November 23, 1888, after five years' residency in the United States.

1887

The Flushing Athletic Club (renamed Old Country Club) was founded (Bayside and Whitestone Avenues, Willets Point Boulevard, and 149th Street). The golf course, the second designed by Walter Travis, opened in 1902.

The New York State legislature passed the Ives Anti-Poolroom Law, forbidding off-track betting and allowing wagering only at racetracks. In 1888, the major bookmakers formed the Metropolitan Turf Alliance to monopolize wagering at local tracks. Democratic Party politician and bookmaker Timothy D. Sullivan was the secretary of the association.

Long Island City poolroom (betting parlor), as illustrated in *Harper's Weekly*, September 2, 1882. (Author's collection)

Captain George Henry Mackenzie, the foremost player in New York, won the International Chess Congress tournament in Frankfurt, Germany, to become "Chess Champion of the World."

Madison Square Garden received a full saloon license on August 15.

The League of Colored Baseball Clubs was organized with eight teams, including one in New York. Although recognized as an official minor league under baseball's national agreement, the association folded after only 13 games.

On September 30, the New York Yacht Club's *Volunteer* defeated Scotland's *Thistle* to win the America's Cup in two straight in the best-of-three series, held off Sandy Hook.

On October 3, Erastus Wiman sold the Metropolitans of the American Association to the owners of the Brooklyn club for $25,000. They kept the best players and sold the franchise to Kansas City.

Before a large and enthusiastic crowd estimated at 15,000 at the Polo Grounds on Thanksgiving Day, Yale defeated Harvard, 17–8, for the collegiate football championship.

In a bout on Long Island on December 13, Jack Dempsey knocked out Johnny Reagan in the forty-fifth round.

1888

The Country Club Association purchased land near Pelham Bay Park and built the Country Club of Westchester, with a golf course and a polo field. The club sold the property after the clubhouse burned in 1922.

At the Westminster Dog Show, Anna Whitney became the first woman judge in America; she judged the 177 Saint Bernards entered in the competition.

Just after midnight on Monday, May 7, 47 men stepped off for the six-day pedestrian contest at Madison Square Garden. The winner was George Littlewood of England, who covered 611 1/4 miles, but fell short of Peter Albert's record of 621 5/8 miles. He received $3,974.12. Seven contestants endured to the end.

At Sheepshead Bay Race Track on September 3, the gelding Proctor Knott won the first Futurity Stakes, taking home a $41,675 prize, the richest stakes race for two-year-olds to date. Winners have included Man o' War, Citation, Secretariat, and Affirmed. The event continues at Belmont Park.

At the Polo Grounds on October 4, the Giants defeated the Chicago Cubs, 1–0, for their first National League pennant, finishing the season with a 84–47 record. The lineup had six future Hall of Famers: Roger Connor, Mickey Welch, Buck Ewing, John Montgomery Ward, Jim O'Rourke, and Tim Keefe. The Giants then took on the St. Louis Brown Stockings of the American Association for the world championship. In St. Louis on October 25, the Giants prevailed by 11–3 to take the 10-game series. After the season, the city condemned the Polo Grounds to cut through 111th Street.

At the polo grounds of the Rockaway Hunt Club in Cedarhurst on November 3, the Hempstead Coursing Club held the first meeting of its second season. Rabbits were loosed in the enclosure, and trained terriers chased them down. Officers of the Society for the Prevention of Cruelty to Animals then arrested members of the club.

• • •

Scotsman John Ried, "the father of American golf"; Robert Lockart; H. O. Talmadge; Harry Holbrook; and John B. Upham organized the St. Andrews Golf Club in Yonkers on November 14. The club had begun in February, when Reid introduced his friends to the game on three improvised holes in a field; their "clubhouse" was an ancient apple tree. They moved to Hastings-on-Hudson in 1897, and the club is now the oldest in continuous operation in the nation.

1889

The leading players in almost any American chess club are still foreigners. The tournament has undoubtedly helped to arouse popular interest in one of the most interesting of all pastimes, but it is a pity for American chess that the championship could not have fallen to an American player.

EDITORIAL IN THE *NEW YORK TIMES*

The Knickerbocker Field Club was founded in Flatbush, on East Eighteenth Street near Church Avenue. The club built some of the first tennis courts in Brooklyn.

• • •

On April 8, a dinner at Delmonico's celebrated the baseball players who had just returned from A. G. Spalding's around-the-world tour. Luminaries in attendance included Theodore Roosevelt and Mark Twain.

• • •

Mikhail Tschigorin and Max Weiss shared top honors in an international chess championship held in the city. In an editorial published on May 19, the *New York Times* complained that the event produced no American champion:

Mr. Lipshutz, who entered as an American player, is not more American than Capt. Mackenzie, if as much. He decidedly leads all the players whose Americanism is better established, and he has but sixth place. It happens that the leading chess player now living, Mr. Steinitz, is a resident of the United States . . . but it would be absurd to describe Mr. Steinitz or Capt. Mackenzie as a representative of American chess. Their residence in this country may perhaps be held to show that it offers more opportunities than other countries for professional chess players, but the result of the tournament makes it plain that chess is not so well established or so well cultivated in this country as it deserves to be. The leading players in almost any American chess club are still foreigners. The tournament has undoubtedly helped to arouse popular interest in one of the most interesting of all pastimes, but it is a pity for American chess that the championship could not have fallen to an American player.

• • •

Eric won the final running of the Belmont Stakes at Jerome Park on June 13. The American Jockey Club, founded in 1866, dissolved at the end of the year and transferred the track to the Jerome Park Villa Site and Improvement Company. The 800 members were welcomed into the New York Jockey Club.

• • •

Leonard W. Jerome opened Morris Park, between Bronxdale Avenue and Williamsbridge Road in the Bronx. Named for Jerome's partner John A. Morris, the track closed in 1904.

• • •

After the city evicted the team from the original Polo Grounds, Giants owner John B. Day built a new Polo Grounds at Coogan's Hollow, at 155th Street and Eighth Avenue. The team played the early part of the season on the road, including two games at Oakland Park in New Jersey and 23 games before sparse crowds in St. George on

The grandstand at Morris Park. (The Bronx County Historical Society)

Staten Island. They played their first game in their new 15,000-seat ballpark on July 8, defeating Pittsburgh, 7–5. The Giants again won the pennant, finishing the season with an 83–43 record. On October 5, the Giants defeated Cleveland, 5–3, to repeat as National League champions. The Brooklyn Dodgers, or Bridegrooms, won the American Association pennant. On October 18, the teams met at the Polo Grounds in a best-of-11 championship series. The Dodgers took the first three games, but the Giants won the next six.

1890—1899

In the last decade of the nineteenth century, sports expanded in almost every arena. The second Madison Square Garden opened, bringing together entertainment and sport, high society and the sporting class. Golf courses were built from Shinnecock Hills in Southampton to Baltusrol in New Jersey to Van Cortlandt Park in the Bronx—the first public course in the United States—and the first amateur and professional championships were held. Aqueduct Racetrack opened, and although leading turfmen formed a new Jockey Club to oversee the sport, both New York and New Jersey enacted laws against gambling. New York attempted to limit boxing to private clubs, even as the nascent movie industry began filming bouts for mass distribution. More than ever, baseball became big business. To resist control by the owners, players formed their own short-lived Players League. The Giants moved into the third and last Polo Grounds, and Brooklyn joined the National League. The New York Athletic Club sent athletes to the first modern Olympic Games in Athens, a legacy that continues into the present.

1890 ....

Players have been bought, sold, or exchanged as

though they were sheep, not American citizens.

JOHN MONTGOMERY WARD

Racing against Jules Verne's fictional hero Phileas Fogg, reporter Nellie Bly arrived at the office of Joseph Pulitzer's *New York World* on January 25, completing her trip around the world in 72 days, 6 hours, 11 minutes—including a visit with the author in Paris. She had sailed from New York on November 14, 1889.

▪ ▪ ▪

Led by lawyer and ballplayer John Montgomery Ward, disgruntled professional baseball players formed the Players League to challenge the owners of the National League and the American Association. "Players have been bought, sold, or exchanged as though they were sheep, not American citizens," he said. The New York team built Brotherhood Park adjacent to the Polo Grounds in the upper section of Coogan's Hollow. On April 19, both New York teams held their season openers against Philadelphia clubs. About 12,000 saw the Players League game in Brotherhood Park, and 5,000 were in the Polo Grounds to see the Giants. Both home teams lost.

▪ ▪ ▪

Brooklyn abandoned the American Association and joined the National League. The new Brooklyn Gladiators joined the American Association for one season; in their first game at Ridgewood Park, their home field, they lost to Syracuse, 3–2. They finished with a 26–73 record, 45½ games out of first. John Montgomery Ward organized the Brooklyn Wonders in the Players League and built Eastern Park in East New York. In their first home game, on April 28, they defeated Philadelphia, 3–1. Sometimes all three Brooklyn teams had home games on the same day. With the new competition, the National League club's home attendance fell to only 37,000 from 350,000 in the previous season.

. . .

The second Madison Square Garden (Madison Avenue, between Twenty-sixth and Twenty-seventh Streets) opened on June 16, with prominent members of society and many elected officials in attendance for a concert of waltzes and polkas conducted by Edward Strauss (of the Vienna Strausses). Designed by Stanford White, it was the largest venue in the country. The 80-foot high auditorium could hold 8,000, with additional seating on the floor; there was also a 1,200-seat theater, a 1,500-seat concert hall, and a roof garden (where Harry Thaw would murder White in 1906). Augustus Saint-Gaudens's scandalous gilded statue of a nude Diana drawing her bow crowned the tower, consciously modeled after the Giralda in Seville.

. . .

In the Coney Island Jockey Club's Suburban Handicap at Sheepshead Bay Race Track on June 17, Salvator, with the great black jockey Isaac Murphy in the irons, bested rival Tenny, with white jockey Edward "Snapper" Garrison up, setting up a much-touted match race at the same track a week later. Running the mile and a quarter on June 25, Salvator beat Tenny by a head in 2 minutes, 5 seconds, cutting 1½ seconds off the previous record.

The second Madison Square Garden, designed by Stanford White. (Author's collection)

. . .

The new Monmouth Park racetrack opened in the rain on the Fourth of July.

. . .

Thomas Hitchcock, the Master of Hounds at the Meadow Brook Hunt, introduced foxhunting with English hounds.

. . .

In the World Series, Brooklyn met Louisville of the American Association. Each team won three games, and one ended in a tie.

1891

Reeling from the disastrous 1890 season, club owners from the National League, the American Association, and the Players League met in the

Thomas Hitchcock and the foxhounds of the Meadow Brook Hunt, ca. 1900. (Nassau County Museum Collection, Long Island Studies Institute, Hofstra University)

city on January 16 and agreed on a new alignment, with eight teams in both the National League and the American Association. The Players League disbanded, but all the member ballplayers received amnesty. The Brotherhood of Professional Base Ball Players collapsed.

▪ ▪ ▪

Leonard W. Jerome, one of the city's premier turfmen and a founder of the American Jockey Club, died on March 3 and was buried in Green-Wood Cemetery in Brooklyn. He had built Jerome Park and Morris Park in the Bronx and Sheepshead Bay Race Track in Brooklyn. (He was also the grandfather of Winston Churchill.)

▪ ▪ ▪

Captain George Henry Mackenzie, the city's longtime chess champion, was found dead in his room in the Cooper Union Hotel, at St. Mark's Place and Third Avenue, on April 14.

▪ ▪ ▪

The Giants acquired Brotherhood Park—home of the Players League team for its only season—and it became the third and last Polo Grounds. The Giants abandoned the ballpark they had built in 1889, directly adjacent. In their first game in their new home, on April 22, the Giants fell to Boston, 4–3, before 17,835. Brooklyn's National League franchise moved to Eastern Park—former home of the Brooklyn Wonders of the Players League—losing their first game there, 6–5, to the Giants on April 27. It was at this time that the team became generally known as the Dodgers—because of the tangle of trolley tracks that fans had to cross to reach the park.

The New York Giants at the Polo Grounds, 1892. (The Bronx County Historical Society)

▪ ▪ ▪

Amos Rusie pitched the first no-hitter in the history of the Giants, stopping Brooklyn 6–0, at the Polo Grounds on July 31. After the season, club co-founder James Mutrie was forced out as the Giants manager. Famous for leading Giants fans in his "We are the people!" cheer, Mutrie won three pennants and two world championships, with a winning percentage of .611. Patrick Thomas Powers took over for 1892.

▪ ▪ ▪

Because the New Jersey legislature did not pass laws to legalize gambling at racetracks, the Monmouth Park Racing Association leased Jerome Park in the Bronx for its summer meeting.

1892

Representatives of champion John L. Sullivan and challenger James J. "Gentleman Jim" Corbett met at the office of the *New York World* on March 15 to arrange a championship bout scheduled for September 7 in New Orleans, with a winner-take-all purse of $45,000. The "Sullivan Special" left New York on September 1. Corbett won the historic

bout. In 1902, he bought a house in Queens at the corner of 221st Street and Bayside Boulevard, which became Corbett Road.

▪ ▪ ▪

George Washington Plunkitt pushed a measure through the New York State legislature to create a 2-mile speedway for horsemen in Central Park, and Governor Roswell P. Flower signed the bill on March 17. Public outrage quickly forced its repeal. A year later, public funding was secured for the Harlem Speedway, a 3-mile course for trotters and pacers to be built north of 155th Street.

▪ ▪ ▪

The West Side Tennis Club was founded in Manhattan on April 22. In 1908, the club moved to 238th Street and Broadway and built a facility with 12 grass courts and 15 clay courts; six years later, the club relocated to Forest Hills.

▪ ▪ ▪

In May, John Y. McKane, Democratic boss in Gravesend, together with other Kings County politicians, organized the Coney Island Athletic Club to host boxing matches.

▪ ▪ ▪

The Shinnecock Hills Golf Club, founded in 1891 as the first incorporated golf club in the country, opened in Southampton. Stanford White designed the clubhouse. The club hosted the United States Men's Open in 1896, 1995, and 2004.

▪ ▪ ▪

After the baseball season, Eddie Talcott and John T. Brush, minority owners of the Giants, forced out John B. Day, who, with James Mutrie, had founded the team.

1893

Hermann Helms became the chess editor of the *Brooklyn Eagle*, a position he held until the paper folded in 1955.

▪ ▪ ▪

With the passage of the Parker Acts, New Jersey legalized gambling at racetracks. In 1894, Republicans repealed the measures.

◦ ◦ ◦

John Montgomery Ward left Brooklyn to manage the Giants. He brought back slugger Roger Connor (baseball's all-time home run leader before Babe Ruth), but traded Wee Willie Keeler to the Dodgers. Shortstop George Davis hit .355, had 119 RBIs, and set two franchise records still standing: a 33-game hitting streak and 27 triples.

◦ ◦ ◦

A benefit for former middleweight champion Jack Dempsey—Nonpareil Jack—was held on September 4 at Grand Palace Hall (Forty-third Street and Lexington Avenue). Bob Fitzsimmons, who had dethroned Dempsey, and Gentleman Jim Corbett attended, and each gave a sparring demonstration. Dempsey received $2,469.57 from the affair.

◦ ◦ ◦

A letter to the *New York Times* from Episcopalian minister James H. Darlington of Christ Church in Brooklyn, published on September 29, thanked the paper for its opposition to prizefighting, particularly a proposed match between Jim Corbett and English boxer Charles Mitchell at the Coney Island Athletic Club: "Not alone will the churches and a great majority of our citizens support your cause, but all true lovers of manly sports will unite in the severest condemnation of the half-dozen mercenary politicians who, under the fair-sounding name of an 'athletic club' try to introduce and popularize prizefighting. True strength despises brutality, as a brave man does a swaggering rowdy." Brooklyn district attorney James Ridgeway had thus far refused to interfere with the bouts, and one of his supporters replied: "What does 'Jim' care for the parsons, anyhow? He is under no obligation to them. He was elected in the face of their opposition and naturally he's not going to bother himself about what they say now he's in office. He don't owe them anything." The Corbett–Mitchell bout was shifted to Jacksonville, Florida.

◦ ◦ ◦

Vigilant, owned by J. Pierpont Morgan, commodore of the New York Yacht Club, defeated Lord Dunraven's cutter *Valkyrie II* by 40 seconds—the closest margin of any America's Cup race to date—to take the third and deciding race in the best-of-three series on October 13.

1894

After defeating Charles Mitchell in Jacksonville, Florida, heavyweight champion James J. Corbett received a hero's welcome at Madison Square Garden on January 27. He and other boxers engaged in exhibition bouts, and Corbett took home $5,000 for the evening. The *New York Times* described the crowd as "largely composed of broken-down sporting men, prize fighters, gamblers, and crooks, the class that prize fighters cater to and the class who encourage men to make brutes of themselves."

◦ ◦ ◦

On February 13, gentlemen representing the Monmouth Park Racing Association, the Brooklyn Jockey Club, and the New York Jockey Club formed the Jockey Club to revise the racing rules and regulate the sport; the Coney Island Jockey Club initially refused to participate, but joined a few months later. According to James R. Keene, "The Jockey Club will give a good, firm, and strong government to racing and correct abuses that have crept in and which furnish a continual theme for newspapers to attack. . . . If the club has fifty or seventy-five honest citizens, it will act as a barrier at Albany against hostile legislation." The Jockey Club counted among its members August Belmont II, William Whitney, and Jacob Ruppert.

◦ ◦ ◦

The New York Yacht Club, after much internal debate, admitted Lucy Carnegie as the first woman member.

• • •

English immigrant Harry M. Stevens took over the concessions at the Polo Grounds. (He started out in the 1880s by selling scorecards in ballparks in the Midwest.) He later acquired the concessions at Ebbets Field, Yankee Stadium, Madison Square Garden, and Belmont Park. Stevens is credited with selling the first frankfurters in a bun at the Polo Grounds.

• • •

Robert Chinnock, a former employee of Thomas Edison, filmed a boxing match between Robert T. Moore and James W. Lahey on the roof of a building at 1729 St. Marks Avenue in East New York, Brooklyn, the first film shot in the city.

• • •

The Morris County Golf Club in Morristown, New Jersey, was organized. The first club founded and operated by women, it joined the United States Golf Association in 1895.

• • •

After the New Jersey legislature forced racetracks in the state to shut down, the New-Jersey Jockey Club leased old Jerome Park for the summer. The final day of racing at the historic track, site of the first running of the Belmont Stakes, was on October 4. The city acquired the property for a reservoir.

• • •

Meeting in New York, the owners of six National League baseball clubs organized the American League of Professional Football, the nation's first avowedly professional soccer league. The Brooklyn Bridegrooms finished on top, with a 5–1 record, and the New York Giants finished with a record of 2–4. There was no second season.

• • •

On September 27, the Queens County Jockey Club opened Aqueduct Racetrack (named for the conduit that carried water from Long Island reservoirs to Brooklyn). It had purchased the site for $50,000.

• • •

The Giants finished with an 88–44 mark, two games behind the Baltimore Orioles. Before about 10,000 fans at the Polo Grounds on October 8, the Giants beat the Orioles, 16–3, to capture the Temple Cup in four straight (in 1884, William Temple, owner of the Pirates, had offered the cup to the winner of a series between the league's top two teams) and again capture the National League flag. The clubs split $21,000, 65 percent going to the winner.

• • •

On November 6, New York State voters approved a new constitution, including an amendment that prohibited pool-selling or auction pools, bookmaking, and gambling. Previously, pool-selling and bookmaking were allowed at racetracks on the day of the race. In 1895, the legislature created a racing commission to regulate the sport in cooperation with the Jockey Club.

1895

Tammany-connected businessman Andrew Freedman purchased a majority interest in the Giants for $48,000 on January 17 and promptly fired manager John Montgomery Ward, the first of many managerial changes during his regime. Freedman was a thoroughly difficult individual, unpopular with players, fans, and the other club owners. On August 18, angry at a critical story by Sam Crane, Freedman banned the sportswriter from the press box; when Crane bought a ticket, he was refused admission to the Polo Grounds. Other scribes fed Crane the details of the game, and he filed the story from a nearby saloon. With Ward as his attorney, Crane sued Freedman, whose relations with the press and fans further deteriorated.

On January 18, before 3,500 spectators at Coney Island's Sea Beach Pavilion, Tommy Ryan of Chicago battered Brooklyn's own Jack Dempsey, who reportedly had been drinking heavily before the match; he was also suffering from tuberculosis. The embarrassing performance was the Nonpareil's final fight. His record was 50 victories, 26 by knockout; three defeats; and eight draws. He died alone and in poverty in Oregon on November 2.

In February, A. G. Spalding & Brothers opened an athletic goods store exclusively for women at 126–130 Nassau Street.

On May 8, in the concert hall at Madison Square Garden, 200 felines were on display at the first National Cat Show.

Baltusrol Golf Club was founded in Springfield, New Jersey; it was named for a farmer who had been found murdered in his home in the Watchung Mountains in 1831. The club hosted the United States Open seven times; the Professional Golfers Association Championship once; and the United States Women's Open, twice. A. W. Tillinghast designed the Lower and Upper Courses between 1918 and 1922; Robert Trent Jones redesigned several holes in 1954.

The Manhattan Beach Bicycle Track opened.

The Van Cortlandt Park Golf Course opened, the oldest public golf course in the country. Anyone with a permit from the Park Board could play at any time, although the course was closed on Sundays. Tom Bendelow redesigned the course and expanded it to eighteen holes in 1898.

About a year and a half after George Hunter introduced the sport to Staten Island, a nine-hole

Quill Club racers at the Manhattan Beach Bicycle Track, 1897. (Suffolk County Historical Society, Hal B. Fullerton Collection)

golf course was laid out adjacent to the clubhouse of the Richmond County Country Club. In May, a group of Staten Island women organized their own golf club, with a nine-hole course on Castleton Avenue; Marion Heineken was the club president.

In the third and final race for the America's Cup, on September 12, Lord Dunraven's *Valkyrie III* crossed the starting line, but immediately turned around, apparently to protest the large fleet of spectator craft along the course in New York Harbor. The English boat had seemingly won the second race, but the victory was awarded to the New York Yacht Club's *Defender* on a foul.

On October 7, the Agricultural and Horticultural Society of Newtown scheduled a fair to run for 40 days at its grounds in Maspeth, with three running and three trotting horse races daily. The next day, Judge William J. Gaynor told the grand jury in Long Island City: "When you and I were boys we knew what county fairs were with a meeting of one to three days, but here is a fair that is to be continued forty days and nights. It is the duty of the Grand Jury to investigate this matter and determine upon the genuineness of this fair. The law is quick to recognize a sham."

* * *

At the Meadow Brook Hunt Club on Long Island on November 9, Mrs. Charles S. Brown of the Shinnecock Hills Golf Club won the first United States Women's Amateur Golf Championship over 12 other competitors.

1896

On April 18, Governor Levi P. Morton signed the Horton Law, which prohibited boxing matches except in clubs that held yearlong leases on their buildings.

* * *

The Cosmopolitan Race, the nation's second automobile race, was staged on Memorial Day, running from City Hall Park to the Ardsley Country Club and back. The brothers Frank and Charles Duryea finished first and second in identical Duryea Motor Wagons.

* * *

On June 27, the Good Roads Association of Brooklyn staged a procession of 10,000 bicyclists to celebrate the opening of a 5-mile cycle path

Parade of cyclists to celebrate the opening of the bicycle path between Prospect Park and Coney Island, June 27, 1896. (Museum of the City of New York)

from Prospect Park to Coney Island. An estimated 100,000 spectators lined the way.

* * *

At the Shinnecock Hills Golf Club on July 15, H. J. Whigham of Scotland won the United States Men's Amateur Golf Championship over American Joseph G. Thorp, 8 and 7. In the second United States Open championship, held the next day, James Foulis, a Chicago professional, won the 36-hole match by three strokes over Horace Rawlins. Two of the 28 competitors lived on the nearby Shinnecock Indian reservation.

* * *

Thomas Burke of the New York Athletic Club won gold medals in track in the 100 meters and 400 meters at the first modern Olympic Games in Athens. At the 2004 Games in Athens, the NYAC sponsored 39 athletes; over the years, NYAC-sponsored athletes have won 123 gold, 39 silver, and 52 bronze medals at the Olympics.

* * *

At the Morris County Golf Club on October 9, sixteen-year-old Beatrix Hoyt, granddaughter of Salmon P. Chase, secretary of the treasury in the Lincoln administration, won the second United States Women's Amateur Golf Championship and took home the Robert Cox Cup, named for the Scotsman who had donated the trophy. Twenty-five golfers entered the tournament.

* * *

At the Ardsley Country Club on November 7, Yale's six-man team easily defeated Columbia to win the first intercollegiate golf tournament.

1897

Soon after returning to New York to make his way as a chess player, Frank J. Marshall, born in Manhattan in 1877 and raised in Montreal, won the New York junior chess championship.

* * *

Ninth hole and clubhouse at the Shinnecock Hills Golf Club, Southampton. (Suffolk County Historical Society, Hal B. Fullerton Collection)

An amendment to the New Jersey constitution outlawed gambling at racetracks, shutting down the sport in the state until 1939.

• • •

The private Dyker Meadow Golf Club, designed by Tom Bendelow, opened. The city acquired the club in the 1920s and renamed it the Dyker Beach Golf Course. In 1935, it was redesigned by John Van Kleek.

• • •

In September, the League of American Wheelmen announced that Robert Buggelyn of Corona, Queens, was the organization's 100,000th member.

• • •

A municipal park opened at Mulberry Bend, site of the notorious slum described by Jacob Riis in *How the Other Half Lives*. Located in Little Italy in Lower Manhattan, it is now called Columbus Park.

1898 ....

In January, Charles Ebbets became president of the Brooklyn Dodgers. He moved the team from distant Eastern Park to a new Washington Park, situated between First and Third Streets, and Third and Fourth Avenues (part of the clubhouse wall survives at the Con Edison facility at 221 First Street). On April 30, the Dodgers lost to the Phillies, 6–4, in their first game there.

• • •

At the Polo Grounds on July 25, Oriole outfielder Ducky Holmes, a former Giant, responded to heckling fans, "Well, I'm damn glad that I don't work for a Sheeny any more." ("Sheeny" is a nineteenth-century derogatory term for a Jew.) Giants owner Andrew Freedman demanded that the umpire toss Holmes, but the umpire claimed not to have heard the remark and refused. Freedman then ordered his team off the field and forfeited the game, even refunding the fans' money.

• • •

Superintendent Charles H. Hankinson of the Brooklyn Society for the Prevention of Cruelty to Animals and two detectives raided a cockfight in

Harlem Speedway, with High Bridge and Washington Bridge in the background. (Author's collection)

Blissville in Long Island City on August 15 and arrested 28 participants and spectators.

Lillian Wald, Mary Simkhovitch, Nathan Straus, Nicholas Murray Butler, Samuel Gompers, Bishop Henry Potter, and other reformers founded the Outdoor Recreation League to advocate for small parks and playgrounds in immigrant neighborhoods in order to foster the assimilation of the children. In 1899, they opened a recreation ground in what became Seward Park; the city completed the job in 1903.

The $3 million Harlem Speedway opened, a 3-mile course built exclusively for trotters and pacers.

On September 17, Findlay S. Douglas of Scotland won the United States Men's Amateur Golf Championship at the Morris County Golf Club.

At the Ardsley Country Club on October 15, Beatrix Hoyt won her third consecutive United States Women's Amateur Golf Championship, defeating Maude K. Wetmore, 5 and 3.

1899

With the amalgamation of the Brooklyn and Baltimore clubs, Ned Hanlon became manager of the Dodgers. The team was sometimes called the Superbas after a vaudeville act, Hanlon's Superbas.

At the Sportsmen's Show at Madison Square Garden on March 8, champion diver Thomas Donaldson died after diving from the rafters into an 8-foot tank, 54 feet below, crushing his skull. He had performed the feat successfully twice a day for the first five days of the show.

On March 8, the Parks Department hired Tom Bendelow for $100 a month to manage the links in Van Cortlandt Park and enforce the rules among players new to the sport.

The Far Rockaway Country Club was founded, with a nine-hole golf course. It disbanded in 1923.

The Garden City Golf Club was incorporated. Its 6,170-yard, 18-hole course was among the longest and most challenging in the nation.

Woman teeing off at the Far Rockaway Country Club, 1903. (Queens Borough Public Library, Long Island Division, Illustrations Collection)

Garden City Golf Club, ca. 1910. (Nassau County Museum Collection, Long Island Studies Institute, Hofstra University)

* * *

At the New Coney Island Sporting Club on June 9, James J. Jeffries knocked out champion Robert Fitzsimmons in the eleventh round for the world heavyweight championship; each fighter received about $25,000. At the Coney Island Athletic Club on November 3, Jeffries won a 25-round decision over challenger Tom Sharkey. Both Vitagraph and Biograph filmed the bout.

* * *

On June 30, bicyclist Charles Minthorn Murphy set a new record for the mile, covering the distance in 59.8 seconds and reaching 70 miles an hour. He rode in the vacuum created behind a modified Long Island Rail Road train between Farmingdale and Maywood, pedaling on a wooden track set between the rails. He became known as Mile-a-Minute Murphy.

* * *

In an open-air ring at the Westchester Athletic Club in Tuckahoe on July 1, Brooklyn's Terry McGovern battered Johnny Richie in three rounds for the bantamweight championship of America. A brass band accompanied the action at ringside. On the afternoon of September 12, 10,000 spectators jammed the club for a title fight between McGovern and English boxer Pedlar Palmer. McGovern scored a knockout at 2 minutes, 32 seconds of the first round, winning the $10,000 purse. Vitascope filmed the bout and made all the

arrangements, making this boxing match, perhaps, the first instance of mass media dictating the circumstances of a sports event.

* * *

Brooklyn won the National League pennant with a record of 101–47.

* * *

Charles Minthorn "Mile-a-Minute" Murphy. (Suffolk County Historical Society, Hal B. Fullerton Collection)

Mile-a-Minute Murphy and his specially modified train at the start of his race against the clock, South Farmingdale, June 30, 1899. (Suffolk County Historical Society, Hal B. Fullerton Collection)

Sir Thomas Lipton's *Shamrock*, the challenger for the America's Cup in 1899. (Museum of the City of New York)

Over a 30-mile course off Sandy Hook on October 20, the New York Yacht Club's *Columbia* defeated Sir Thomas Lipton's *Shamrock* by over 6 minutes to retain the America's Cup in three straight. Lipton challenged for the cup five times, never succeeding but earning a well-deserved reputation for sportsmanship.

1900—1909

The new century welcomed a new sport: automobile racing. Stock car racing was born with events in Westchester and Riverhead (which continues a racing tradition). William K. Vanderbilt sponsored the Vanderbilt Cup Race on Long Island and built the Long Island Motor Parkway, the nation's first limited-access toll road. Several older racetracks converted to accommodate automobile races, with speed records repeatedly set and broken. Jamaica Race Track and Belmont Park opened, even as the state sought to prevent gambling. New York also banned prizefighting. John McGraw began his 30-year tenure as manager of the Giants, and Christy Mathewson emerged as one of the greatest pitchers in baseball history. The Highlanders began to play in the new American League. Concerned about the ill effects of slums on children, educators founded the Public Schools Athletic League to foster athletic contests for schoolboys, with a division for girls founded soon after; wealthy New Yorkers generously supported these efforts.

1900 . . . .

At the Broadway Athletic Club on January 9, bantamweight champion Terry McGovern, "the Brooklyn Terror," knocked out George Dixon to win the world featherweight title and the $10,000 prize. The African American challenger's manager threw in the sponge (literally) after the eighth round. On March 10, McGovern defended his featherweight crown by knocking out Oscar Gardner in the third round at the same club. Before 12,000 at Madison Square Garden on July 16, he knocked out Frank Erne at 2 minutes, 18 seconds of the third round. When New York banned prize fighting, McGovern had to fight in other states, losing the featherweight title in San Francisco in 1903.

▪ ▪ ▪

On March 29, the New York State legislature repealed the Horton Law, essentially prohibiting prizefighting in the state as of September 1. The law had permitted bouts only in certain clubs.

▪ ▪ ▪

Interstate Park, a venue for pigeon- and trapshooting, opened in Queens Village. Thousands of birds were shot during the day-long competitions. Annie Oakley won a contest there in April.

▪ ▪ ▪

Before the start of the Long Island Automobile Club's race at Decker's store in Springfield, April 14, 1900. (Queens Borough Public Library, Long Island Division, Hal B. Fullerton Photographs)

The Long Island Automobile Club's race in Springfield, April 14, 1900. (Queens Borough Public Library, Long Island Division, Hal B. Fullerton Photographs)

Nine cars entered the Long Island Automobile Club's first race, held on April 14, running for 50 miles from Merrick Road in Springfield, Queens, to Babylon, in Suffolk County, and back. Driving an electric vehicle, A. L. Riker of Brooklyn won in 2 hours, 3 seconds.

. . .

On May 11, before a crowd of 7,000 at the Seaside Athletic Club in Coney Island, James J. Jeffries knocked out former champion James J. "Gentleman Jim" Corbett in the twenty-third round to retain the heavyweight crown.

. . .

On June 10, National Leaguers formed the Protective Association of Professional Baseball Players to negotiate with club owners for the elimination of the reserve clause, according to which owners retained exclusive rights to a player, thus preventing him from negotiating with other teams as a free agent. The owners refused, but the new American League met many of the players' demands, speeding the defection of veteran players to the Junior Circuit.

. . .

Tom Smith organized the Brighton Baseball Team of East New York. Its diamond was south of Pitkin Avenue, between Elton and Ashford Streets. The Brightons won the Standard Union Cup as the best semi-pro team in Brooklyn.

. . .

On July 7, Walter Travis of the United States defeated Findlay S. Douglas of Scotland for the United States Men's Amateur Golf Championship at the Garden City Golf Club.

. . .

Members of the New York Athletic Club took home 20 medals in track and field from the Summer Olympic Games in Paris.

. . .

At the Shinnecock Hills Golf Club on September 1, Frances C. Griscom was the surprise winner of the United States Women's Amateur Golf Championship. Three-time champion Beatrix Hoyt had been expected to prevail on her home course.

. . .

For a second year, the Brooklyn Superbas won the National League pennant. After the season, they went to Pittsburgh for a best-of-five series against the second-place Pirates. To dwindling public interest, Brooklyn took the series in four games,

Frances C. Griscom at the Shinnecock Hills Golf Club, 1900. (Suffolk County Historical Society, Hal B. Fullerton Collection)

Frances Griscom and Beatrix Hoyt on the eighteenth green at the Shinnecock Hills Golf Club, 1900. (Suffolk County Historical Society, Hal B. Fullerton Collection)

winning the Chronicle-Telegraph Cup and half the gate receipts.

On October 22, the Empire City Race Track opened in Yonkers for thoroughbred racing, although the hard track had been built for harness racing. It closed in 1942, but reopened in 1950 as Yonkers Raceway.

Madison Square Garden hosted the nation's first automobile show on November 3.

1901

On January 20, the New York Yacht Club, founded in 1844, dedicated its new building, at 37 West Forty-fourth Street, its sixth and final home. The architect was Whitney P. Warren.

The Long Island Automobile Club staged a 100-mile endurance run on April 20. Fourteen vehicles began in cold and rainy conditions at Petitt's Hotel in Jamaica, Queens; nine finished. The route went through Flushing, Port Washington, Amityville, Freeport, Garden City, Lake Success, Valley Stream, Springfield, and back to the starting point. The drivers were to complete the course in no less than 8 hours, 22.5 minutes, and no longer than 12 hours, 32.5 minutes, in accordance with the new law limiting automobiles to 15 miles an hour on open roads and 8 miles an hour in towns.

Sports cartoonist Tad Dorgan coined the term "hot dog" when he could not spell the word

The model room of the New York Yacht Club, on West Forty-fourth Street. (Library of Congress, George Grantham Bain Collection, Prints and Photographs Division)

Entrants at Parsons Boulevard and Jamaica Avenue before the Long Island Automobile Club's endurance run, April 20, 1901. (Queens Borough Public Library, Long Island Division, Hal B. Fullerton Photographs)

"dachshund," as in the "red hot dachshund sausage" sold at the Polo Grounds.

⬛ ⬛ ⬛

The nine-hole Forest Park Golf Links, designed by Tom Bendelow opened; in 1905, it was expanded to 18 holes, and the clubhouse was built. Also, the nine-hole Pell Golf Course, designed by Lawrence Von Etten, opened in the Bronx; it expanded to 18 holes in 1914. In 1936, it was redesigned by John Van Kleek and renamed the Pelham Golf Course.

⬛ ⬛ ⬛

On June 9, the Giants whacked a record 31 hits in a 25–13 victory over the Cincinnati Reds, with

Forest Park Golf Links. (Queens Borough Public Library, Long Island Division, Post Card Collection)

Al Selbach going 6 for 7. On July 15, Christy Mathewson pitched his first no-hitter, beating the St. Louis Cardinals, 5–0.

⬛ ⬛ ⬛

In races off Sandy Hook for the America's Cup, the New York Yacht Club's *Columbia* bested Sir Thomas Lipton's *Shamrock II* in three straight, winning the third race by 2 seconds actual time (with time allowance, the margin was adjusted to 41 seconds) on October 4.

⬛ ⬛ ⬛

At Baltusrol Golf Club in Springfield, New Jersey, on October 12, Genevieve Hecker won the United States Women's Amateur Golf Championship.

1902 ....

I see no good reason why New York, the best baseball town in the country, should not have a team which will be in the first division this year and be head of the list next season. I have orders to spend any amount of money I feel disposed to in order to strengthen the team.

JOHN MCGRAW

The Newark Indians joined the new International League as a charter member.

⬛ ⬛ ⬛

The Long Island Automobile Club's second 100-mile endurance test, held on April 26, attracted 67 entrants, most of them automobile manufacturers. Drivers started and finished in Jamaica and had to adhere to the speed limit of 15 miles an hour; 14 drivers were disqualified for finishing too soon.

⬛ ⬛ ⬛

Yachtsmen formed the Bayside Yacht Club at Little Neck Bay on July 9.

⬛ ⬛ ⬛

On July 9, twenty-nine-year-old shortstop John McGraw signed as manager of the Giants, a post

Bayside Yacht Club. The club dissolved in 2007, and the clubhouse was demolished to make way for a church. (Library of Congress, George Grantham Bain Collection, Prints and Photographs Division)

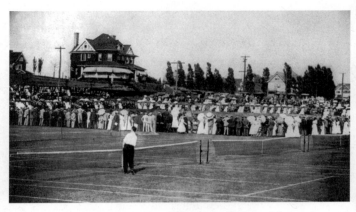

Tennis courts at the Crescent Athletic Club in Bay Ridge, 1909. (Library of Congress, George Grantham Bain Collection, Prints and Photographs Division)

he held for the next 30 years. Given control over personnel at the same time, he stated, "I see no good reason why New York, the best baseball town in the country, should not have a team which will be in the first division this year and be head of the list next season. I have orders to spend any amount of money I feel disposed to in order to strengthen the team, and I will set about that task at once."

□ □ □

Laurie Auchterionie of Scotland won the United States Open at the Garden City Golf Club.

□ □ □

On August 8, at the Crescent Athletic Club in Bay Ridge, Brooklyn (Eighty-fifth Street and Shore Road), the United States defeated Great Britain, 3–2, to retain the Davis Cup.

□ □ □

Andrew Freedman sold his majority interest in the Giants to former Cincinnati Reds owner John T. Brush for $125,000 on September 29. (He had bought the team in 1895 for $48,000.)

□ □ □

The Circumnavigators Club was founded in December. The principle qualification for membership is crossing each meridian in the same direction on the same trip.

□ □ □

On December 29, a crowd of 3,500 witnessed the first professional football game at Madison Square Garden. Syracuse beat New York, 5–0. In a preliminary game, the Monitor Athletic Club of New York beat the Colonial Football Club of New Jersey, 17–5. The Garden's wooden floor was removed and replaced with dirt for the game, creating a field 70 yards long and 35 yards wide.

1903 ....

It has always been my ambition to play in New York City. Brooklyn is all right, but if you're not with the Giants you might as well be in Albany.

BILL DAHLEN

The dishonesty and brawling in play seen so constantly in the street wherever children gather may be corrected by ethical argument, but a much quicker teacher is that practice which gives the boy a taste of the other thing—an athletic contest won fairly and squarely by sheer clean powers of body and mind.

WILLIAM MAXWELL

On January 9, Frank Farrell, "the poolroom king," and Bill Devery, a former police captain tied to Tammany Hall, purchased the Baltimore Orioles for $18,000. They moved the franchise to New York and renamed the team the Highlanders, forerunners of the Yankees. Hilltop Park, the club's home field, was built in six weeks along Broadway between 165th and 168th Streets; its capacity was 16,000, plus standing room for 15,000. Clark Griffith was the manager. On April 22, the Highlanders lost their first game, falling to the Senators, 3–1, in Washington; in their first home game, on April 30, they beat the Senators, 6–2, before 16,243. In the first game between Boston and New York on May 7, the Pilgrims (forerunners of the Red Sox) topped the Highlanders, 6–2.

. . .

The Inter-Settlement Athletic Association was founded, fostering competition in basketball and boxing for boys, most of them Jewish, from the Henry Street Settlement, University Settlement, and other settlement houses.

. . .

The nation's first squash courts opened at the New York Athletic Club.

. . .

Jamaica Race Track opened on April 27. It closed in 1959, replaced by Rochdale Village.

. . .

Jamaica Race Track. (Queens Borough Public Library, Long Island Division, Post Card Collection)

The Greater New York Irish American Athletic Club was founded. Naturally, the club admitted Jewish athletes.

. . .

In his 1903 Winton, Horatio Nelson Jackson completed the first cross-country automobile trip, arriving in Manhattan at 4:30 A.M. on July 26: 63 days, 12 hours, 30 minutes after leaving San Francisco.

. . .

On August 8, a week after pitching and winning both games of a doubleheader, Joe "Iron Man" McGinnity of the Giants again won both games of a twin bill, beating the Dodgers, 6–1 and 4–3. In the second game, he even stole home.

. . .

Over a 30-mile course off Sandy Hook on September 3, the New York Yacht Club's *Reliance* defeated Sir Thomas Lipton's *Shamrock III* for the third consecutive time to defend the America's Cup. On Memorial Day in 1959, *Shamrock III*'s mast was installed as a flagpole in front of the Brooklyn Public Library at Grand Army Plaza.

. . .

Walter Travis won the United States Men's Amateur Golf Championship at the Nassau Country Club in Glen Cove on September 5.

. . .

On September 7, Brooklyn and New York played a home-and-home doubleheader. In the morning, the Giants beat the Dodgers, 6–4, at Washington Park; that afternoon, the Dodgers prevailed at the Polo Grounds, 3–0.

. . .

August Belmont II, chairman of the Jockey Club, announced on September 28 that he was retiring from active racing and would sell his horses, while retaining his breeding stable: "I have not the time to devote to my racing stable at present. I rarely have a chance to see my horses run, and I have so many corporate interests that require my attention that a big racing stable becomes a positive care to me instead of a pleasure." He remained head of the Jockey Club.

∎ ∎ ∎

A crowd of about 3,000 attended the reopening of Hamilton Fish Park, at East Houston and Stanton Streets, on October 3. Opened in 1900, the park was under the supervision of the Outdoor Recreation League, an organization formed in 1898 to foster recreation in immigrant neighborhoods and generously supported by wealthy patrons.

∎ ∎ ∎

On December 13, the Dodgers traded shortstop Bill Dahlen to the Giants for two marginal players. Dahlen said, "It has always been my ambition to play in New York City. Brooklyn is all right, but if you're not with the Giants you might as well be in Albany."

∎ ∎ ∎

Luther Gulick founded the Public Schools Athletic League to provide organized competition for boys in baseball and track and field. The PSAL's motto was "Duty, Thoroughness, Patriotism, Honor, and Obedience." Andrew Carnegie, John D. Rockefeller, and J. Pierpont Morgan provided financial support, and A. G. Spalding, the baseball pioneer turned sporting goods manufacturer, donated the trophies. School Superintendent William Maxwell said,

The substitution of controlled athletics for uncontrolled, erratic contests is different only in degree from substituting pure, clean valuable exercises and sport for the undesirable amusements to which a city subjects a child. The city child has naturally little that encourages the healthy, young animal growth. The crowded conditions, the absence of convenient playing places, the inhibition of many games in the street because of their danger to pedestrians and property, all make more alluring abnormal methods of passing the time, or

Outdoor gymnasium for boys at Hamilton Fish Park. (New York City Parks Photo Archive)

rather wasting it. . . . The dishonesty and brawling in play seen so constantly in the street wherever children gather may be corrected by ethical argument, but a much quicker teacher is that practice which gives the boy a taste of the other thing—an athletic contest won fairly and squarely by sheer clean powers of body and mind. The league is to encourage these things.

On December 26, the PSAL held its first games at Madison Square Garden, attracting 1,040 participants and 9,000 spectators. Flushing High School won the first boys' basketball championship.

∎ ∎ ∎

Bernarr Macfadden, the "Father of Physical Culture," founded the Coney Island Polar Bears Club. The members swim every Sunday from October through April, but hundreds attend the club's annual New Year's Day plunge.

1904

Hermann Helms, chess editor of the *Brooklyn Eagle*, began to publish the *American Chess Bulletin*, continuing until his death in 1963.

∎ ∎ ∎

In Brooklyn, the Sunday School Athletic League was organized, with participation limited to boys attending Sunday school.

▪ ▪ ▪

At Baltusrol Golf Club on September 10, H. Chandler Egan won the United States Men's Amateur Golf Championship.

▪ ▪ ▪

The Giants won the National League pennant with a 106–47 record, the best in franchise history. The Highlanders met the Boston Pilgrims on the last day of the season at Hilltop Park for the American League pennant. The Pilgrims won when Jack Chesbro, winner of 41 games, threw a wild pitch—a spitball. He returned to the bench and broke down in tears. An editorial in the *New York Times* opined: "Though the metropolitan fan may be temporarily distressed and even impoverished, the metropolitan philosopher will be ashamed to begrudge Boston one championship out of two. Her necessity is greater than ours." John McGraw refused to play the Pilgrims for "the championship of the world." In mid-season, he had said, "The American League management

has been crooked more than once. . . . My team will have nothing to do with the American League."

▪ ▪ ▪

William K. Vanderbilt and the Long Island Automobile Club initiated the Vanderbilt Cup Race in Nassau County in October. The race was discontinued after four spectators were killed and 20 injured in 1910.

▪ ▪ ▪

On October 15, about 20,000 attended the final day of thoroughbred racing at Morris Park, the venerable race track that had opened in 1889.

▪ ▪ ▪

The Explorers Club was founded. Members are scientists and explorers, and they have sponsored expeditions on land, sea, and air. Their home is a townhouse at 46 East Seventieth Street.

1905 ....

On February 13, the Westminster Kennel Club staged the largest dog show in the world to that time; 1,752 dogs were entered.

Vanderbilt Cup Race in Jericho, 1904. (Suffolk County Historical Society, Hal B. Fullerton Collection)

Spectators along the route of the Vanderbilt Cup Race, 1904. (Suffolk County Historical Society, Hal B. Fullerton Collection)

Finish line of the Vanderbilt Cup Race in Westbury, 1904. (Suffolk County Historical Society, Hal B. Fullerton Collection)

Entrance to the grandstand from the paddock at Belmont Park. (Queens Borough Public Library, Long Island Division, Post Card Collection)

Belmont Park. (Queens Borough Public Library, Long Island Division, Post Card Collection)

. . .

The National Association of Colored Professional Clubs of the United States and Cuba was founded, with traveling baseball teams based in the metropolitan area, each named the Giants, including the Brooklyn Royal Giants, owned by black businessman John W. Connors.

. . .

Former bantam- and featherweight champion Terry McGovern, "the Brooklyn Terror," was voluntarily committed to a sanitarium in Stamford, Connecticut, for "nervous exhaustion" and alcoholism on April 17. He fled back to Brooklyn his first day, but was committed again in late 1906.

. . .

About 40,000 attended the opening of Belmont Park on May 4. August Belmont's colt Blandy won the first race, and in the Metropolitan, Sysonby and Race King finished in a dead heat. The Belmont Stakes has been run at the track annually except from 1963 to 1968, when the race moved to Aqueduct Racetrack while Belmont's grandstand was rebuilt. The official drink of the Belmont Stakes, at least since 1998, is the Belmont Breeze (Seagram's 7, Harvey's Bristol Cream, lemon juice, simple [or sugar] syrup, orange juice, cranberry juice, and 7-Up, with a strawberry and lemon garnish). Before 1998, it was the White Carnation (Vodka, peach schnapps, orange juice, soda, and a splash of cream over crushed ice, with an orange slice garnish). The official songs of the Belmont Stakes are the traditional "The Sidewalks of New York" and the ubiquitous "New York, New York."

. . .

Morris Park reopened on May 20 as the first venue in the country operated specifically for automobile racing. David Hennen Morris, one of the owners, was also president of the Automobile Club of America. Wall Street broker J. Horace Harding became the vice president of the new enterprise, the Morris Park Motor Club. On the inaugural day of racing, Louis Chevrolet broke the world record for the mile, covering the distance in $52\,4/5$ seconds behind the wheel of a 90-horsepower Fiat. On June 10, again at Morris Park, he lowered his record to $52\,1/5$ seconds. On July 3, Webb Jay, driving a 20-horsepower White steam car, reduced the mark to $49\,3/5$ seconds, the first time the record was held by vehicle not powered by gasoline. The next day, he lowered it to $48\,4/5$ seconds.

On May 21, the transatlantic race for the Kaiser's Cup, sponsored by the New York Yacht Club, began in New York Harbor. Wilson Marshall's 185-foot schooner *Atlantic*, built at the Townsend & Downsey shipyard in the city, won in the record time of 12 days, 4 hours, 1 minute, 19 seconds. Charlie Barr was the skipper.

Giants hurler Christy Mathewson tossed his second no-hitter, a 1–0 victory over the Chicago Cubs, on June 13. Mathewson went 31–9, with a 1.28 ERA, during the season. With a record of 105–48, the Giants won the National League pennant for the second straight year. At the Polo Grounds before 24,187 fans on October 14, the Giants beat the Philadelphia Athletics, 2–0, to take the World Series in five games. Christy Mathewson threw three complete-game shutouts and did not allow a runner to reach third base.

On October 14, Pauline Mackay won the United States Women's Amateur Golf Championship, held at the Morris County Golf Club in Morristown, New Jersey, for the second time.

With the stated purpose of "athletics for all girls," a separate division of the PSAL was established under Elizabeth Burchenal.

1906

The Great Kills Yacht Club was founded on Staten Island.

The *New York World* sponsored field days across the city for elementary school boys and continued to do so for many years. A. G. Spalding donated the Play Ball trophy, presented to the best elementary school baseball team in the city.

At Englewood Golf Club in New Jersey on July 14, Eben Byers won the United States Men's Amateur Golf Championship.

1907

The Brighton Beach Bath and Racquet Club opened. It closed in 1997 and housing rose on the site.

The Brighton Beach Race-Course closed. It had opened in 1879.

The Westminster Kennel Club awarded Best in Show for the first time.

Driving a 35-horsepower Renault, Maurice Bernin won a 24-hour automobile race at Morris Park on September 7, covering 1,081 miles at an average speed of 45 miles an hour.

1908

Baseball never had no "fadder"; it jest growed.

HENRY CHADWICK

Employees of John Wanamaker & Company, a department store (Broadway and Ninth Street), founded the Millrose Athletic Association, taking the name from Robert Wanamaker's country house, and staged the first Millrose Games, now the oldest indoor track and field meet in the United States.

English-born Henry Chadwick died at age eighty-three in his Brooklyn home on April 20. The first baseball editor in the country, Chadwick developed the box score and the batting average. His monument in Green-Wood Cemetery is inscribed "Father of Base Ball" and features a bronze mitt, a catcher's mask, and crossed bats; four bases mark his plot. He was the baseball and cricket editor of the *Brooklyn Eagle* from 1856 to 1894 and in 1862 wrote the first baseball report in the *New York Herald*. He covered the sport for the *New York World* for 13 years and the *Sun* for six years, and was the editor of the *Spalding Baseball Guide* from 1881 to his death. In a 1904 interview, he remarked, "Baseball never had no 'fadder'; it jest growed."

The first stock car road race was staged in Westchester on April 24, attracting tens of thousands of spectators. Twenty-two cars entered, and 18 finished. The 32-mile loop began at Briarcliff Manor and went through Pines Bridge, Mount Kisco, and Armonk. Driving a 50-horsepower Isotta-Frascini, Louis Strang won the 240-mile race in 5 hours, 14 minutes, 13 $\frac{1}{5}$ seconds, averaging 46 miles an hour, with a top speed of 75. One experienced automobile man remarked, "Beyond doubt it was the most successful race ever held, but I hope to goodness they'll never try to hold another over this course." En route to the event, thirty drivers were arrested in the Bronx for speeding. (Was this the first speed trap?)

On May 2, lyricist Jack Norworth and composer Albert Von Tilzer registered the copyright of their new song, "Take Me Out to the Ball Game." Norworth had been inspired by a sign at the Polo Grounds announcing the day's ball game.

On June 11, Governor Charles Evans Hughes, an uncompromising opponent of gambling, signed the Agnew-Hart Act, which banned wagering at racetracks and elsewhere. Investment in New York's horse-racing industry was estimated at $81 million at the time.

In the first game of a doubleheader at the Polo Grounds on the Fourth of July, George Leroy "Hooks" Wiltse of the Giants pitched a 10-inning no-hitter for a 1–0 victory over the Phillies. The only man to reach base was a hit batsman with two out in the bottom of the ninth (and he should have been called out on strikes on the previous pitch!).

Kid Elberfeld became player-manager of the Highlanders, replacing Clark Griffith, whose record was 419–370 (.531). The team finished last.

At the Garden City Golf Club on September 19, Jerome Travers defeated Max Behr, 8 and 7, to win the 36-hole United States Men's Amateur Golf Championship.

On September 23, in a crucial game against the Cubs, who led the Giants by one game in the standings, nineteen-year-old rookie Fred Merkle failed to touch second base as the potential winning run scored. Cubs manager Frank Chance called for a play at second, but the crowd on the field made it impossible. Still, umpire Hugh O'Day called Merkle out and declared a 1–1 tie, with the game to be replayed after the season if the teams were tied, which is what happened. "Merkle's Boner" loomed even larger on October 8, when the Cubs beat Christy Mathewson, 4–2, at the Polo Grounds to win the playoff game for the National League pennant.

Fans at the Polo Grounds on October 8, 1908, for the one-game playoff for the National League pennant. (Library of Congress, George Grantham Bain Collection, Prints and Photographs Division)

Long Island Motor Parkway. (Queens Borough Public Library, Long Island Division, Illustrations Collection)

Entrants running in the Brooklyn Marathon, February 12, 1909. (Library of Congress, George Grantham Bain Collection, Prints and Photographs Division)

After the Vanderbilt Cup Race in October, the Long Island Motor Parkway, the nation's first limited-access road, opened to the public; construction had begun in June. By 1911, this private toll road extended from Creedmoor in Queens to Lake Ronkonkoma in Suffolk County; it was abandoned when Grand Central Parkway opened in the 1930s.

1909

On January 12, 10 women motorists completed a two-day ride and return from New York to Philadelphia, finishing in front of the Plaza Hotel. Their top speed was almost 30 miles an hour.

◦ ◦ ◦

For the third consecutive year, Champion Warren Remedy, a smooth fox terrier, won Best in Show at the Westminster Dog Show, a triumph never equaled.

◦ ◦ ◦

The Brooklyn Marathon was staged with 164 runners on February 12, starting in the Thirteenth Regiment Armory in Bedford-Stuyvesant (Sumner and Jefferson Avenues), down Ocean Parkway to Sea Gate, and back to the armory. About 250,000 spectators lined the route, and 8,000 jammed the armory. James A. Clark of the Xavier Athletic Club won in 2 hours, 46 minutes, 52³/₅ seconds.

◦ ◦ ◦

On April 15, opening day at the Polo Grounds, Red Ames of the Giants held the Superbas hitless through nine innings, only to yield one hit in the tenth and surrender three runs in the thirteenth for a 3–0 loss.

◦ ◦ ◦

At Verona Lake in New Jersey, Charles M. Daniels of the New York Athletic Club set a new record for the mile swim: 26 minutes, 19.6 seconds.

◦ ◦ ◦

The Motor Racing Association converted the old Brighton Beach Race-Course into the Brighton Beach Motordrome and opened with a two-day speed carnival on July 30. On October 15, a crowd of 10,000 was on hand for the start of a 24-hour

Automobile racers at the Brighton Beach Motordrome, 1909. (Queens Borough Public Library, Long Island Division, Ephemera Collection)

Fanciful view of aircraft above the Hudson River near Grant's Tomb during the Hudson-Fulton Celebration. (Jeffrey A. Kroessler)

race. Louis Chevrolet, driving a Buick, covered the first 100 miles in 1 hour, 46 minutes, 19.2 seconds, a new record. Driving a Lozier, Ralph Mulford won the race, completing a record 1,196 miles.

■ ■ ■

As part of the Hudson-Fulton Celebration, the nation's first indoor aeronautic exposition opened at Madison Square Garden on September 25. On the September 29, Wilbur Wright took off from an improvised field on Governors Island for the first airplane flight over water. He buzzed the Statue of Liberty and the *Lusitania* on his three flights that day. Not so fortunate were the two dirigibles competing for a $10,000 prize offered by the *New York World*; both crashed into the Hudson River.

■ ■ ■

On September 29, 16 cars entered the Long Island Automobile Derby and raced over a 22.75-mile course in Riverhead. Ralph De Palma won the 227-mile event, driving a Fiat. Behind the wheel of a Buick, Louis Chevrolet averaged 70 miles an hour during a 113.5-mile run. Herbert Lytle crashed during the race and was seriously injured; his mechanic, James Bates, was killed. (Mechanics accompanied the drivers in the cars.)

■ ■ ■

The Dodgers acquired outfielder Zack Wheat, one of the best players of the era. During his 18 years with Brooklyn, he set team records for games played (2,322), at bats (8,859), doubles (464), triples (171), and hits (2,804).

1910—1919

Even as amateur and professional sports became more fully integrated into the urban scene, New York State still endeavored to impose controls or prohibitions. The Agnew-Perkins Act, passed in 1910, made racetrack owners liable for gambling on their premises and quickly shut down all racetracks in the state. Some hosted automobile races and air shows, attracting impressive crowds. A judge ruled in the track owners' favor three years later, and thoroughbred racing returned. Prizefighting had been all but absent in the state since 1900, but the legislature legalized the sport in 1911, only to again impose a ban in 1917, reflecting the nation's moralistic temper during World War I. After the war, however, the city finally legalized Sunday baseball. Tex Rickard, probably the most influential sports promoter in the city's history, staged his first boxing matches at Madison Square Garden, which also hosted the Millrose Games for the first time. The West Side Tennis Club in Forest Hills Gardens, Queens, one of the best-known and classiest sports venues in the world, opened; it hosted men's and women's championships from 1914 to 1977. Professional basketball was born, and the barnstorming Original Celtics soon represented the city's dominance.

In baseball, the Highlanders became the Yankees, and the Giants won four pennants, but no World Series. The Federal League challenged major league baseball, and dozens of players defected, but the league lasted for only two seasons. It was the decade of Frank Chase, the first baseman for the Yankees and Giants long suspected of working with gamblers and the go-between in the Black Sox scandal of 1919, which almost destroyed the game. Not even baseball was immune from the corrupting influence of gamblers.

1910

Keep your eye clear, and hit 'em where they ain't.
WEE WILLIE KEELER

The Westminster Dog Show featured Fire Department dalmatians for the first time. The winner was Mike, of Engine Company 8 on Fifty-first Street.

On March 9, first baseman Hal Chase was named the Highlanders' first captain, a position he held through 1912. On September 26, the team dismissed manager George Stallings and announced

Running of the Suburban Handicap, Sheepshead Bay Race Track. (Queens Borough Public Library, Long Island Division, Post Card Collection)

that Chase would take over for the remainder of the season and the following year. Stallings had accused Chase of not giving the team his best effort, but team owner Frank Farrell sided with his player over his manager. In actuality, the sure-fielding Chase was long suspected of associating with gamblers—committing intentional errors and throwing games.

□ □ □

The Department of Parks established the Bureau of Recreation and stationed 30 playground leaders across the city.

□ □ □

The athletic department at Barnard College added baseball to the list of approved sports, but fielded a team for only a few years.

□ □ □

Dan Whalen, Joe Manning, and Eddie Manning organized the New York Bloomer Girls, a barnstorming women's baseball team based on Staten Island.

□ □ □

The Agnew-Perkins Act made racetrack owners liable for wagering on their premises, knowingly or not, effectively ending thoroughbred racing in the state until 1913, when a judge ruled that track proprietors had to have actually permitted gambling.

□ □ □

On August 19, at Sheepshead Bay Race Track, 5,000 spectators attended the first day of an aviation meet and saw—for the first time in America!—four airplanes aloft simultaneously, piloted by Glenn Curtiss, J. C. Mars, Eugene Ely, and J. A. D. McCurdy.

□ □ □

Driving a Stearns, Alfred Poole and Cyrus Patschke won the 24-hour race at the Brighton Beach Motordrome on August 20, covering a record 1,253 miles. On September 5, Barney Oldfield, driving a 200-horsepower Benz, set a new record for the mile on a circular track: 49.8 seconds.

□ □ □

Beginning on October 13, the Giants and Highlanders met for a postseason best-of-seven series for the championship of the city. Christy Mathewson won three games and saved a fourth as the Giants won in six; attendance topped 100,000. After this final season with the Giants, the team he had broken in with in 1892, Wee Willie

Keeler retired. The first player to wear the uniform of all three New York teams, and a future Hall of Famer, Keeler had a lifetime batting average of .341. Asked the secret of his success at the plate, he famously remarked, "Keep your eye clear, and hit 'em where they ain't."

▫ ▫ ▫

Driving an Alco, Harry F. Grant won the Vanderbilt Cup Race in the record time of 4 hours, 15 minutes, 58 seconds, finishing 25 seconds ahead of Joe Dawson in a Marmon. An estimated 275,000 spectators lined the course along the Long Island Motor Parkway and Old Country Road from Westbury to Hicksville. One driver and his mechanic died in a wreck, and Louis Chevrolet smashed into a car of spectators, killing his mechanic.

▫ ▫ ▫

The second International Aviation Tournament opened at Belmont Park on October 22. Two days later, 10,000 spectators witnessed an unprecedented 10 aircraft aloft at once. On October 29, English airman Claude Grahame-White won the Gordon Bennett International Aviation Cup in a 100-horsepower Bleriot monoplane, covering the 62.1-mile course in 1 hour, 1 minute, 4.74 seconds. The next day, American John B. Moisant beat Grahame-White by 42.5 seconds in a race around

Start of the Vanderbilt Cup Race, 1910. (Queens Borough Public Library, Long Island Division, Post Card Collection)

Mechanics changing a tire on Harry F. Grant's Alco during the Vanderbilt Cup Race, 1910. (Queens Borough Public Library, Long Island Division, Post Card Collection)

the Statue of Liberty and back for $10,000. A crowd of 25,000 jammed the grandstand.

▫ ▫ ▫

At Sheepshead Bay Race Track on October 25, a crowd of 5,000, including hundreds of African Americans, saw champion driver Barney Oldfield, driving a 60-horsepower Knox, easily beat heavyweight boxing champion Jack Johnson in two 5-mile heats. Afterward, Oldfield said, "I did not enter into the race against Johnson for gold or glory, but to eliminate from my profession an invader who might cause me trouble in a year or so if I ignored him now. If Jeffries had fought Johnson five years ago when the white man was in his

Player-manager Hal Chase of the Highlanders and manager John McGraw of the Giants before the start of their post-season series at the Polo Grounds, October 1910. (Library of Congress, George Grantham Bain Collection, Prints and Photographs Division)

Five airplanes aloft simultaneously at the International Aviation Tournament at Belmont Park, October 1910. (Nassau County Museum Collection, Long Island Studies Institute, Hofstra University)

Claude Grahame White and his monoplane at the International Aviation Tournament at Belmont Park, October 1910. (Nassau County Museum Collection, Long Island Studies Institute, Hofstra University)

prime, he would not have had to return to the ring and suffer the Reno defeat." Oldfield went on, "There is no reason why Johnson should not develop into a good driver, with track experience and a high-powered racing car. I am getting old, and it was much wiser for me to win from him today than to take a chance on losing to him a year or two hence, and his ambition and persistency would certainly have caused him to get to the top if I had ignored him."

■ ■ ■

Jack Golomb founded the Everlast Company in the Bronx to manufacture swimwear. Everlast began to make boxing equipment—headgear, gloves, and bags—in 1917. Jack Dempsey won the heavyweight championship in 1919 using Everlast gloves, cementing the company's reputation.

1911 . . . .

Mathewson pitched against Cincinnati yesterday. Another way of putting it is that Cincinnati lost a game of baseball.

The first statement means the same as the second.

DAMON RUNYON, *NEW YORK AMERICAN*, JULY 16, 1911

Spectators outside Belmont Park during the International Aviation Tournament, October 1910. (Nassau County Museum Collection, Long Island Studies Institute, Hofstra University)

It was grand. I didn't feel like ever coming to earth again.

HARRIET QUIMBY

Nat Strong organized the Inter-City Baseball Association to handle local bookings for barnstorming semi-pro teams, especially black teams, eventually monopolizing bookings at several semi-pro ballparks. Strong was also an agent of the A. G. Spalding & Brothers sporting goods company, supplying balls and equipment to the teams.

▪ ▪ ▪

On March 21, representatives of the Coney Island Jockey Club (Sheepshead Bay Race Track), the Westchester Racing Association (Belmont Park), the Saratoga Racing Association (Saratoga Race Course), the Queens County Jockey Club (Aqueduct Racetrack), the Empire City Racing Association (Empire City Race Track), and the Metropolitan Jockey Club (Jamaica Race Track) announced that there would be no thoroughbred racing in 1911 because of the so-called Directors Liability law (Agnew-Perkins Act):

> [R]ace track directors cannot possibly prevent betting, for which under the law they may be held criminally liable. . . . The tracks about New York have conducted racing at big pecuniary loss since the adoption of the first of Gov. Hughes's anti-racing measures in 1908, and they have been willing to keep on for the good of racing and the improvement of the breed of horses if nothing more than the pecuniary sacrifices were asked. But to subject the Directors to the chance of imprisonment for permitting alleged violations of the law of which they cannot possibly have knowledge, much less prevent, is putting a severe trial up to them that they should be asked to bear.

▪ ▪ ▪

New York and Philadelphia ballplayers at the Polo Grounds after the fire, April 14, 1911. (Library of Congress, George Grantham Bain Collection, Prints and Photographs Division)

The Polo Grounds burned on April 14. The Highlanders agreed to share Hilltop Park with the Giants until the stands were rebuilt. The Giants returned to the rebuilt Polo Grounds on June 28 and defeated Boston, 3–0, behind Christy Mathewson. Team owner John T. Brush named the field Brush Stadium, but fans and the press persisted in using the old name.

▪ ▪ ▪

Jess McMahon, a white boxing promoter, organized the Lincoln Giants, a black baseball team. At Olympic Field (136th Street and Fifth Avenue), they took on semi-pro teams and barnstorming major leaguers, compiling a 108–12 record in their first season. The team disbanded around 1930.

▪ ▪ ▪

Colonial Park opened in Harlem. Redesigned by the Works Progress Administration during the New Deal, it was renamed for Jackie Robinson in 1978.

▪ ▪ ▪

At an airfield in Garden City on August 1, Harriet Quimby became the first woman to earn a pilot's license from the Aero Club of America. At the Staten Island Fair at Dongan Hills on September 4, she piloted a monoplane in a night flight and received $1,500. After she landed, her mother said, "You were

Harriet Quimby and Shakir S. Jerwan preparing to take off in a Bleriot monoplane in Garden City. (Queens Borough Public Library, Long Island Division, Joseph Burt, Sr., Photographs)

up there just seven minutes, and I think that I would have come up after you if you had remained in the air any longer." Quimby replied, "Oh, mother, you'll get used to it all right. It was grand. I didn't feel like ever coming to earth again."

‣ ‣ ‣

On August 29, the Frawley Act went into effect. After eight years of almost no legal boxing and three years of club-sponsored bouts, New York again legalized prizefights open to the public. The law permitted 10-round bouts regulated by a state athletic commission.

‣ ‣ ‣

Calbraith Perry Rodgers and his *Vin Fiz* at Sheepshead Bay Race Track before his transcontinental flight. (Nassau County Museum Collection, Long Island Studies Institute, Hofstra University)

About 10,000 witnessed the finals of the first inter-park athletic contests at Tompkins Square Park (Seventh to Tenth Streets, between Avenues A and B).

‣ ‣ ‣

Attempting to complete a transcontinental flight in less than 30 days to claim a $50,000 prize offered by William Randolph Hearst, Calbraith Perry Rodgers took off on September 17 from Sheepshead Bay Race Track in a Wright biplane called the *Vin Fiz* (after a new grape soda, made by the sponsor). After numerous crash landings, he landed in Pasadena, California, on November 5.

‣ ‣ ‣

The Giants won the National League pennant, but lost the World Series to the Philadelphia Athletics in six games.

‣ ‣ ‣

On October 14, Margaret Curtis won her third United States Women's Amateur Golf Championship, held at Baltusrol Golf Club in Springfield, New Jersey, for the second time.

‣ ‣ ‣

At Celtic Park in Sunnyside, Queens, on October 22, P. J. McDonald of the Irish-American Athletic Club set the world's record for the 24-pound shot put: 38 feet, 10 $^{11}/_{16}$ inches.

‣ ‣ ‣

In October, heavyweight Jim Flynn, "the Pueblo Fireman," beat Carl Morris, a much-hyped fighter from the West, at Madison Square Garden. Before the bout, sportswriter—and former western

Christy Mathewson warming up before the World Series between the Giants and the Athletics. (Library of Congress, George Grantham Bain Collection, Prints and Photographs Division)

P. J. McDonald setting the world shot-put record at Celtic Park in Sunnyside, October 22, 1911. (Library of Congress, George Grantham Bain Collection, Prints and Photographs Division)

Thomas McLaughlin leading Jim Thorpe in the 1,500-meter race during the Olympic pentathlon qualifying trials at Celtic Park in Sunnyside, May 18, 1912. Thorpe finished first overall. (Library of Congress, George Grantham Bain Collection, Prints and Photographs Division)

lawman—William Barclay "Bat" Masterson exposed a scheme for Flynn to throw the fight for $7,500. As a result, the match was clean.

1912

On May 18, the tryout to select the eastern representative for the Olympic pentathlon trials was held at Celtic Park in Sunnyside. Jim Thorpe was the winner of the five-event contest: 200 meters, 1,500 meters, broad jump, discus, and javelin.

Hawaiian-born Olympic champion Duke Kahanamoku gave a swimming and surfing exhibition on the beach at Rockaway. A section of Shorefront Parkway at Beach Thirty-eighth Street was renamed Duke Kahanamoku Way in the 1990s.

Christy Mathewson gained his 300th victory, beating the Chicago Cubs, 3–2, on June 13.

On June 29, the Stadium Motordrome in Brighton Beach, with a one-third-mile saucer track, opened for motorcycle racing. A crowd of 10,000 was on hand for the start of the 24-hour motorcycle race on September 20. The team of Billy Shields and George Lockner rode a record 67.33 miles in the first hour, eventually winning the event in the new world's record of 1,374 miles in 21 hours of actual racing.

In the first game of a doubleheader in Philadelphia on September 6, Jeff Tesreau of the Giants hurled a no-hitter to beat the Phillies, 3–0.

On October 5, the Dodgers lost to the Giants, 1–0, in their last game in Washington Park, their home field since 1898. The same day, the Yankees played their last game at Hilltop Park, beating the Washington Senators, 8–6, before 5,000 fans. Hilltop

Opening day at Washington Park, 1912, the final season the Dodgers played there. (Queens Borough Public Library, Long Island Division, Joseph Burt, Sr., Photographs)

Park was demolished in 1914; Columbia Presbyterian Hospital rose on the site.

· · ·

The Giants again won the National League pennant. On October 16, in the eighth game of the World Series (one game ended in a tie), the Boston Red Sox beat the Giants, 3–2, when center fielder Fred Snodgrass dropped an easy fly ball, allowing two runs to score in the tenth inning; Christy Mathewson would have had the 2–1 victory. Second baseman Larry Doyle of the Giants was voted the National League's Most Valuable Player.

1913

On February 21, the Appellate Division of the New York State Supreme Court ruled that oral betting at racetracks was within the law and that owners and directors could not be held liable for the actions of their patrons unless they had direct knowledge of the actions, clearing the way for the return of the Sport of Kings to the Empire State.

· · ·

On April 9, the Phillies beat the Dodgers, 1–0, before 10,000 fans in their first game at Ebbets Field. (In an exhibition game on April 5, the Dodgers had beaten the Yankees on Charles Dillon "Casey" Stengel's inside-the-park homer.) Construction of the $750,000 ballpark had begun on March 5, 1912.

· · ·

The Highlanders were officially renamed the Yankees before the season. They played the first of 10 seasons in the Polo Grounds, paying the Giants an annual rent of $55,000. In their first game, on April 17, they lost to the Senators, 9–3.

· · ·

Beginning on May 31, Morris Park was auctioned off for building lots.

· · ·

At Belmont Park on June 13, Prince Eugene took the Belmont Stakes (run for the first time since 1910), the eighth horse trained by James Rowe Sr. to win the race. Rowe also had won the race twice as a jockey, in 1872 and 1873.

· · ·

Mayor William Gaynor sponsored "Safe and Sane" games on the Fourth of July in public parks and pools.

· · ·

On August 6, John Henry Mears arrived at the office of the *Evening Sun*, having completed his 21,066-mile journey around the world in 35 days, 21 hours, 43 minutes. He had begun his record-breaking trip, which he estimated to have cost $800, on July 2.

· · ·

At the Garden City Golf Club on September 6, Jerome Travers won his fourth United States Men's Amateur Golf Championship.

· · ·

The Giants won their third straight National League pennant, but lost the World Series to the Athletics in five games. During an unpleasant exchange at a postseries party, John McGraw fired his friend and third base coach, Wilbert Robinson. On November 17, the Dodgers hired Robinson as manager to replace Bill Dahlen. The team soon became known as the Robins.

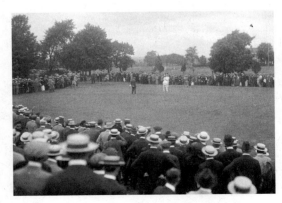

Players competing at the United States Men's Amateur Golf Championship at the Garden City Golf Club. (Queens Borough Public Library, Long Island Division, Joseph Burt, Sr., Photographs)

Giants manager John McGraw and Dodgers manager Wilbert Robinson, 1915. (Library of Congress, George Grantham Bain Collection, Prints and Photographs Division)

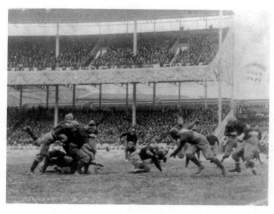

The Army-Navy Game being played at the Polo Grounds, 1916. (Library of Congress, George Grantham Bain Collection, Prints and Photographs Division)

▪ ▪ ▪

On November 29, the Army-Navy Game was played at the Polo Grounds for the first time. (The stadium hosted the contest nine times between 1913 and 1927.) President Woodrow Wilson and his entire cabinet were among the 42,000 fans who saw Army triumph, 22–9.

1914

The Millrose Games were staged at Madison Square Garden for the first time. (Previously, the event was held in armories in New York and Brooklyn.) Over the years, this became the winter's premier indoor track meet, attracting international stars.

▪ ▪ ▪

The Original Celtics, a barnstorming professional basketball team, was founded. The team played until 1942 and boasted such basketball pioneers as Joe Lapchick and Nat Holman.

▪ ▪ ▪

Frank J. Marshall was named one of the original five grand masters of chess (along with Emanuel Lasker, José Raúl Capablanca, Alexander Alekhine, and Siegbert Tarrasch) in St. Petersburg, Russia.

▪ ▪ ▪

The Federal League, founded to rival the National and American Leagues, began play. Robert Ward, owner of Ward's Bakery Company, organized the Brooklyn Tip-Tops, named for his best-selling bread in the borough. In their first game at Washington Park, on May 11, the Tip-Tops lost to the Pittsburgh Rebels, 2–0.

▪ ▪ ▪

Before 10,000 in Pawtucket, Rhode Island, on May 16, the Brooklyn Field Club, champion of the National Association Football League, defeated the Brooklyn Celtics of the New York State Amateur Foot Ball League, 2–1, to capture the first National Challenge Cup. The soccer tournament attracted forty clubs from the eastern United States.

▪ ▪ ▪

With Nat Strong as his silent partner, Max Rosner founded the Bushwick Baseball Club. On May 24, Rosner and several of his players were arrested for having violated the Sunday blue laws after plainclothes policemen had been denied admission to the "free" game unless they bought a program (ball clubs used that ruse to get around the law). At the Long Island City Courthouse, Judge Miller said that whether admission had been charged was not the issue. He asked Rosner whether the public had been disturbed. Rosner answered "no." Case dismissed.

The Mosholu Golf Course, designed by John Van Kleek, opened in the Bronx.

At the Stadium Motordrome on June 13, Brooklyn's George Sperl set a new motorcycle record for 10 miles, covering the distance in 7 minutes, 46.4 seconds.

In a polo match played before 35,000 at the Meadow Brook Club in Westbury on June 16, England bested the United States, 4 to 2 3/4, to capture the International Challenge Cup, first presented by the Westchester Polo Club of Newport in 1884.

The first municipal playground in Queens opened in Ashmead Park in Jamaica.

The outbreak of World War I forced the cancellation of the America's Cup series between the New York Yacht Club and Sir Thomas Lipton's *Sham-*

rock IV. The defender would have been either *Resolute* or *Vanitie*.

At the new West Side Tennis Club in Forest Hills, Australasia (Australia and New Zealand) captured the Davis Cup, 3–2, on August 15.

Shortstop Roger Peckinpaugh became captain of the Yankees, an honor he held until traded to the Senators in January 1922. On September 16, the twenty-three-year-old Peckinpaugh was named player-manager to finish out the season, the youngest manager in major league history.

John O'Brien of Brooklyn organized the Interstate Pro Basketball League, the city's first. In 1915, he became president of the league and in 1921 organized the Metropolitan Basketball League, which he merged into the American Basketball League in 1928. O'Brien remained president of the ABL until it folded after the 1951/1952 season. He was enshrined in the Naismith Memorial Basketball Hall of Fame in 1961.

At a packed Madison Square Garden on November 21, the team of Alf Goullet and Alfred Grenda, both Australians, won the six-day bicycle race, riding 2,758 miles plus one lap in 142 hours (7 miles farther than the mark set in 1913).

1915

There is no charity in baseball. I want to win the pennant every year.

JACOB RUPPERT

On January 11, Colonel Jacob Ruppert and Colonel Tillinghast L'Hommedieu Huston purchased the Yankees for $460,000. Ruppert once remarked, "There is no charity in baseball. I want to win the

Polo match between England and the United States at the Meadow Brook Club, Westbury. (Queens Borough Public Library, Long Island Division, Joseph Burt, Sr., Photographs)

pennant every year." The Yankees wore their legendary pinstripes for the first time on April 22.

＊＊＊

At the Polo Grounds on April 15, left-hander Rube Marquard of the Giants pitched a no-hitter to beat the Dodgers (or Robins), 2–0. Marquard had jumped to the Federal League the previous season.

＊＊＊

Pitching for the Red Sox against the Yankees at the Polo Grounds on May 6, Babe Ruth hit his first major league home run. The Yanks won, 4–3.

＊＊＊

On May 18, about 4,100 women attended Suffrage Day at the Polo Grounds and saw the Cubs beat the Giants, 1–0.

＊＊＊

Frank J. Marshall, American chess champion from 1909 to 1936, founded Marshall's Chess Divan at Keen's Chop House (72 West Thirty-sixth Street). This became the Marshall Chess Club, which later purchased a townhouse at 135 West Twelfth Street.

＊＊＊

In College Point, Queens, the American Hard Rubber Company built Ahrco Field on the site of Donnelly's picnic park (115th Street and Fourteenth Avenue). The field hosted amateur soccer and football games and semi-pro baseball teams.

＊＊＊

For the first time, the Men's National Singles Championship, forerunner of the United States Open, was held at the West Side Tennis Club in Forest Hills. The tournament had been held at the Newport Casino since 1881 and, except for 1921 to 1923, remained at Forest Hills for six decades.

＊＊＊

The Sheepshead Bay Speedway, a 2-mile wooden oval with 17-degree banked turns, opened in

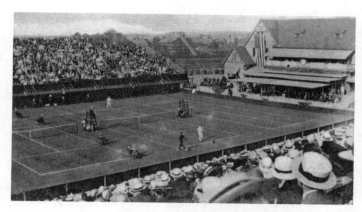

The United States Men's National Singles Championship being played at the West Side Tennis Club in Forest Hills. (Queens Borough Public Library, Long Island Division, Post Card Collection)

September. On September 27, Harry F. Grant crashed while racing at 90 miles an hour; he died 10 days later. The speedway closed in 1919.

＊＊＊

On September 30, the Tip-Tops played their final game at Washington Park, losing to the Buffalo Bisons, 3–2. The Federal League folded in December, dropping an antitrust suit against the major leagues in return for financial compensation.

＊＊＊

At the National Horse Show at Madison Square Garden on November 6, Marion duPont of Virginia

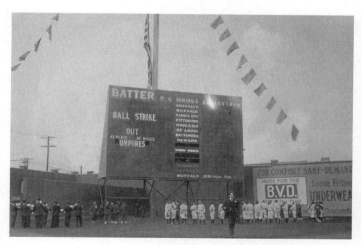

Opening day for the Brooklyn Tip-Tops against the Buffalo Bisons at Washington Park, April 10, 1915, for the second and last season of the Federal League. (Library of Congress, George Grantham Bain Collection, Prints and Photographs Division)

Casey Stengel, Jimmy Johnston, Hy Myers, and Zach Wheat at Ebbets Field before the World Series. (Library of Congress, George Grantham Bain Collection, Prints and Photographs Division)

was the first woman to ride astride her mount instead of sidesaddle.

1916

On January 17, Rodman Wanamaker hosted a luncheon at the Taplow Club that led to the formation of the Professional Golfers Association; it was incorporated on April 10, with 82 members. In the first PGA Championship, at the Siwanoy Country Club in Bronxville on October 14, Jim Barnes of England defeated Jock Hutchinson Sr. of St. Andrews, Scotland, on the thirty-sixth hole, winning $500, a diamond-studded gold medal, and possession of the sterling silver Rodman Wanamaker Trophy. World War I forced the cancellation of the event in 1917 and 1918.

• • •

The Millrose Games initiated the Wanamaker 1.5-mile race; it became the famous Wanamaker Mile in 1926.

• • •

At Madison Square Garden on March 25, a crowd of 13,000, including about 200 women, saw heavyweight champion Jess Willard win a 10-round

decision over Frank Moran. This was promoter Tex Rickard's first event at the Garden.

• • •

A crowd of 25,000 was on hand at the Sheepshead Bay Speedway for a 150-mile race on May 13. Driving his Delage at 104 miles an hour, Carl Limberg crashed, killing himself and his mechanic, R. Pollotti.

• • •

The Giants won 26 straight games, a major league record.

• • •

The Dodgers won the National League pennant and appeared in the World Series for the first time. They fell to the Red Sox, losing the fifth and final game on October 12 by a score of 4–1. Babe Ruth was a pitching star for Boston, winning 2–1 in 14 innings on October 9. Ruth began a streak of 29 scoreless innings in World Series play; Whitey Ford broke Ruth's record in 1961.

• • •

The Isaac L. Rice Stadium was dedicated in Pelham Bay Park. Julia Rice, the widow of the founder and president of the Electric Storage Battery Company, donated $1 million for the 5,000-seat facility, designed by Herts & Tallant. In 1989, it was demolished and the site was renamed the Aileen B. Ryan Recreation Field.

Isaac L. Rice Stadium in Pelham Bay Park, Bronx. (Lehman College, Bronx Chamber of Commerce Collection)

1917

The trouble with this legislature is that it is run by long-haired men and short-haired women.

JAMES J. "JIMMY" WALKER

The Kingsbridge Armory opened in the Bronx, with the world's largest indoor drill floor at the time. Now a city landmark, it has hosted sporting events ranging from automobile races to track meets.

- - -

George Mogridge became the first Yankee to hurl a no-hitter, beating the Red Sox, 2–1, at Fenway Park on April 24.

- - -

On May 10, the New York State legislature voted to repeal the Frawley Act and again ban boxing in New York, effective November 15. State Senator James J. "Jimmy" Walker grumbled, "The trouble with this legislature is that it is run by long-haired men and short-haired women." Governor Charles Whitman, a Republican, signed the act on May 19.

- - -

At the Manhattan Athletic Club on May 28, challenger Benny Leonard (born Benjamin Leiner on the Lower East Side) knocked out Freddie Welsh of Britain in the ninth round to claim the world's lightweight championship. Leonard held the crown for a remarkable seven and a half years.

- - -

At Ebbets Field on August 22, the Dodgers beat the Pirates, 6–5, in 22 innings, the longest game in National League history to that time.

- - -

John McGraw and Christy Mathewson were arrested at the Polo Grounds on a Sunday for playing a charity game to raise funds for the Sixty-ninth Regiment, which was about to head overseas. City magistrate Francis X. McQuade dismissed the charges, and then led the campaign to legalize Sunday baseball. He later became part owner of the team.

- - -

The Giants won the National League pennant, but lost to the Chicago White Sox in the World Series in six games. In the final game, on October 15, the Giants failed to cover home as Eddie Collins raced around the bases for the winning run.

- - -

On October 25, Miller Huggins became manager of the Yankees. William "Wild Bill" Donovan had piloted the club for three seasons, compiling a record of 220–239–6.

1918

On February 22, former bantam- and featherweight champion Terry McGovern, "the Brooklyn Terror," died of pneumonia at age thirty-seven. A few years before, his former manager, Sam Harris, had arranged a benefit for the broken fighter, raising $13,000 to buy a house for him and his family.

- - -

The St. Albans Golf Club opened in southeastern Queens. During World War II, it became a naval hospital.

- - -

José Raúl Capablanca of Cuba won the international chess tournament, held in New York.

- - -

Shipyards in Brooklyn; Staten Island; Newburgh, New York; Kearny, New Jersey; and New London, Connecticut, sponsored baseball teams in the Shipbuilding League. Many ballplayers went into shipyards to receive draft deferments for working in a vital defense industry.

- - -

Max Rosner's semi-pro Bushwicks made Dexter Park in Woodhaven (Jamaica Avenue and Elderts Lane) their home field.

Entrance to Dexter Park in Woodhaven, 1923. (Queens Borough Public Library, Long Island Division, Eugene Armbruster Photographs)

■ ■ ■

On June 6, in his first at bat at Ebbets Field after being traded from Brooklyn to Pittsburgh in the off-season, Casey Stengel was soundly booed. In response, he doffed his cap and a sparrow flew out.

■ ■ ■

Because of the war, the Dodgers recorded their lowest season attendance at Ebbets Field (83,831), and the Giants attracted a record low at the Polo Grounds (258,618).

Casey Stengel at Ebbets Field, while still with the Dodgers, 1916. Note his checkered uniform. (Library of Congress, George Grantham Bain Collection, Prints and Photographs Division)

1919 ....

On January 14, Charles A. Stoneham purchased the Giants from the estate of John T. Brush for over $1 million, the highest price paid for a team in baseball history to that point. City magistrate Francis X. McQuade and manager John McGraw were minority partners, with 10 percent between them.

■ ■ ■

Built for carriages, and opened in 1898, the Harlem Speedway opened to automobiles.

■ ■ ■

On April 29, the Board of Aldermen voted 64–0 to permit professional baseball games to be played on Sundays (after 2:00 P.M.). Mayor John F. Hylan signed the long-overdue act a few days later. On May 4, the Giants beat the Phillies, 4–1, at the Polo Grounds in the first legal professional Sunday baseball game. State Senator Jimmy Walker had introduced the enabling legislation.

■ ■ ■

On April 30, Brooklyn and Philadelphia played a 20-inning game, to a 9–9 tie, each team scoring 3 runs in the nineteenth inning. Incredibly, both pitchers went the distance: Burleigh Grimes for the Dodgers and Joe Oeschger for the Phillies.

■ ■ ■

At Belmont Park, Sir Barton won the Belmont Stakes and became the first horse to win the Triple Crown.

■ ■ ■

Locked in a tight pennant race, the Giants met the Cincinnati Reds in three straight doubleheaders at the Polo Grounds between August 15 and 18; the Giants lost four and never got close again. Errors by usually sure-handed first baseman Hal Chase during this series furthered suspicions that he was throwing games. Chase had long associated with gamblers, and questions dated back to his time with the Yankees and Reds. He was later revealed as a go-between in the Black Sox scandal later in the year.

▫ ▫ ▫

At the Engineers Country Club in Roslyn on September 20, Englishman Jim Barnes won the second PGA Championship, defeating Scotsman Fred McLeod on the thirty-first hole, 6 and 5. Barnes had won the inaugural PGA tournament in 1916.

▫ ▫ ▫

Against the Yankees at the Polo Grounds on September 24, Babe Ruth of the Red Sox hit his twenty-eighth home run to set a new single season record.

▫ ▫ ▫

On September 28, the Giants beat the Phillies, 6–1, in only 51 minutes, the shortest major league game on record.

▫ ▫ ▫

Marshall Stillman's Movement, a gym where boys could get off the streets and learn to box, opened in a storefront at 125th Street and Seventh Avenue in Harlem. Professionals soon adopted the place for training, and in the 1920s Stillman's Gym moved to Eighth Avenue between Fifty-fourth and Fifty-fifth Streets. Many champions and challengers who were fighting at nearby Madison Square Garden worked out at Stillman's, famously dubbed by sportswriter A. J. Liebling "the University of Eighth Avenue."

1920—1929

The 1920s was perhaps the most glorious decade for sport in the city's history. Ironically, it was also the decade of Prohibition, with beer exiled from all venues. The Yankees acquired Babe Ruth; Yankee Stadium opened; and the team won its first world championship and became a dynasty. Lou Gehrig started his consecutive-game streak. Tex Rickard opened the third Madison Square Garden and introduced professional hockey, while establishing the Garden as the international center of boxing. The white Original Celtics and the black New York Renaissance Big Five fostered greater public interest in basketball, barnstorming across the region and dominating the national scene. Sports that had been strictly upper-class pursuits—polo, tennis, and golf—captured the public imagination and attracted impressive crowds and media coverage. Why the general public cared about sports whose pursuit was far beyond their means is perhaps odd, but every sport generated celebrities during the 1920s. Bill Tilden won six straight men's singles titles at Forest Hills; Jack Dempsey dominated the heavyweight ranks, and the Lower East Side's Benny Leonard retired as undefeated lightweight champion; Gertrude Ederle set swimming records locally before conquering the English Channel; and Manhattan-born Italian American Gene Sarazen rose to the top in professional golf. Even in chess, the city was home to three grand masters: Frank J. Marshall, José Raúl Capablanca, and Edward Lasker. Oddly, the Roaring Twenties also saw quixotic efforts to ban sports on Sundays.

1920

On January 5, Red Sox owner Harry Frazee, a Broadway producer and Park Avenue resident, sold Babe Ruth to the Yankees for $125,000 and a $350,000 loan. According to Frazee, "Ruth had become simply impossible and the Boston Club could no longer put up with his eccentricities. While Ruth without question is the greatest hitter that the game has ever seen, he is likewise one of the most selfish and inconsiderate men that ever wore a baseball uniform." Ruth hit his first home run as a Yankee on May 1, a shot that cleared the roof of the Polo Grounds, in a 6–0 win over his former team. He hit 54 home runs (breaking his own record of 29), drove in 137 runs, and hit .376. The Yankees became the first team in baseball history to draw over 1 million fans in a season

(1,289,422), more than doubling the previous year's attendance. Boston endured "the curse of the Bambino" until 2004.

▫ ▫ ▫

At Braves Field, Brooklyn and Boston played a 26-inning, 1–1 tie game. Both pitchers went the distance—Leon Cadore for the Dodgers and Joe Oeschger for the Braves—and neither yielded a hit over the last six frames. Umpires called the game on account of darkness, with Brooklyn's second baseman, Ivy Olson, asking for one more inning to equal three full games.

▫ ▫ ▫

On May 24, Governor Al Smith signed State Senator Jimmy Walker's boxing bill, creating the State Boxing Commission and mandating licensing for all involved—fighters, managers, and promoters. The law also permitted judges to decide fights that went the full 15 rounds, called for medical supervision of all bouts, standardized gloves, and compelled a champion to defend his title within six months. The governor had told Walker that he would sign the bill only if he secured the signatures of 100 clergymen, adding pointedly, "Protestant." More than 1,000 telegrams landed on the governor's desk, thanks to Walker's supporter and boxing fan Anthony J. Drexel Biddle, who recently had donated $500,000 to the Bible Society.

▫ ▫ ▫

The Queensboro Arena, an outdoor boxing venue seating about 7,000, opened adjacent to the Astoria elevated line near Queens Plaza; the arena was expanded to seat 16,000 in 1924. The site had been Schwalenberg's picnic grounds, and boxing matches had been fought in the clubhouse since 1911. It was demolished in 1950.

▫ ▫ ▫

On June 12, Samuel D. Riddle's Man o' War (a product of August Belmont's stable) won the Belmont Stakes in the world-record time of 2 minutes,

Man o' War and his groom. (Author's collection)

14 1/5 seconds (over the Belmont Course, not the main track). Against only one challenger, he went off at 1–20 odds and won by half a furlong—20 lengths. Before 25,000 at Aqueduct Racetrack on July 10, Man o' War defeated Harry Payne Whitney's John P. Grier by two lengths in the $6,000 Dwyer Stakes, a match race for three-year-olds, and set the new world record for the mile and a furlong: 1 minute, 49 1/5 seconds.

▫ ▫ ▫

Tex Rickard signed a 10-year lease for Madison Square Garden on July 12.

▫ ▫ ▫

In the first America's Cup defense in 17 years, and the final series staged in New York Harbor, the New York Yacht Club's *Resolute* bested Sir Thomas Lipton's *Shamrock IV*, representing the Royal Ulster Yacht Club. *Shamrock IV* won the first two races, but the defender took the last three, winning the final race by 13 minutes, 5 seconds (19 minutes, 45 minutes adjusted time) on July 27. After the fifth race, Lipton said, "I am very sorry, but the best boat won. We did our best, and we have been beaten fair and square."

▫ ▫ ▫

On August 16, in the fifth inning at the Polo Grounds, Yankee hurler Carl Mays beaned Cleveland Indians shortstop Ray Chapman, fracturing his skull. Chapman died the next day. This is the only on-field fatality in major league history.

▫ ▫ ▫

Charles "Chick" Evans Jr. won the United States Men's Amateur Golf Championship at the Engineers Country Club in Roslyn on September 11. The 12,000 spectators overwhelmed the course.

▫ ▫ ▫

Behind hard-hitting outfielder Zack Wheat, pitchers Rube Marquard and Burleigh Grimes ("master of the aqueous toss," or spitball), and manager Wilbert Robinson—all future Hall of Famers—the Dodgers faced the Indians in the World Series. In game five, played on October 10, Cleveland's Elmer Smith hit the first grand slam in a World Series game, and Bill Wambsganss completed the only unassisted triple play in World Series history. Two days later, the Indians beat the Dodgers, 3–0, to take the best-of-nine series, five games to two.

▫ ▫ ▫

On October 29, the Yankees introduced Red Sox manager Ed Barrow as their new business manager, a key to building the first Yankee dynasty. On December 15, the Yankees acquired pitcher Waite Hoyt from Boston in an eight-player deal.

▫ ▫ ▫

In a sold-out Madison Square Garden on December 14, heavyweight champion Jack Dempsey knocked out challenger Bill Brennan. With his $35,000 share, Brennan opened a speakeasy, and in 1924 he was gunned down by bootleggers.

▫ ▫ ▫

At Madison Square Garden on December 22, Joe Lynch took a 15-round decision from Pete Herman for the world bantamweight championship. Herman had held the title for almost four years.

1921 ....

There's only one Big Apple. That's New York.

JOHN J. FITZGERALD

Fans waiting outside Ebbets Field before the start of the World Series, October 5, 1920. (Library of Congress, George Grantham Bain Collection, Prints and Photographs Division)

On February 6, the Yankees paid $675,000 for 11.6 acres at 161st Street and River Avenue in the Bronx, just across the Harlem River from the Polo Grounds. Work began on the $2.5 million stadium on May 6, 1922.

▫ ▫ ▫

At Madison Square Garden on March 17, middleweight champion Johnny Wilson (born John Panica in Harlem) retained his title with a 15-round decision over Mike O'Dowd.

Yankee Stadium under construction. (The Bronx County Historical Society)

- - -

The professional American Soccer League was organized with seven teams in the New York metropolitan area, including the New York Field Club and Todd Shipyards in Brooklyn. The Brooklyn Wanderers joined the league the next season and remained active until the ASL disbanded in 1933.

- - -

Members of the New York Athletic Club founded Winged Foot Golf Club and purchased property in Mamaroneck. Although never officially part of the NYAC, the name honors the club's logo. Designed by A. W. Tillinghast, the golf course opened in June 1923; it has hosted the United States Open five times (1929, 1959, 1974, 1984, and 2006).

- - -

In the first game of a national championship series on April 16, the New York Whirlwinds defeated the Original Celtics, 40–29, at the Seventy-first Regiment Armory (Park Avenue at Thirty-fourth Street) before 11,000, the largest crowd to see a basketball game in the city to date. At the Sixty-ninth Regiment Armory (Lexington Avenue at Twenty-fifth Street) on April 20, the Original Celtics defeated the Whirlwinds, 26–24, before about 8,000. With no third game, the teams were declared co-champions.

- - -

Horse-racing scribe John J. Fitzgerald of the *New York Morning Telegraph* first used the phrase "Big Apple" to describe New York. He claimed to have heard the term among black stable hands at a New Orleans racetrack in 1920. In 1924, he titled his column "Around the Big Apple with John J. Fitzgerald": "The Big Apple. The dream of every lad that ever threw a leg over a thoroughbred and the goal of all horsemen. There's only one Big Apple. That's New York."

- - -

On May 30, Walter J. Martin of the Bronx won the annual 10-mile City Hall to Coney Island walking race, sponsored by the Walkers Club of America. Starting with a 17-minute handicap, he covered the distance in the actual time of 1 hour, 38 minutes, 33 seconds.

- - -

Grey Lag won the mile-and-three-furlong Belmont Stakes in the record time of 2 minutes, 14$^4/_5$ seconds over Belmont Park's main track on June 11. For the first time, the race was run counter-clockwise instead of clockwise, in the English fashion.

- - -

On July 2, before a crowd of 90,000 at Tex Rickard's Stadium in Jersey City, New Jersey, Jack Dempsey battered Georges Carpentier in four rounds to defend his world heavyweight title. Gate receipts of $1.6 million made this the first million-dollar bout. Radio station WJZ in Newark broadcast the action, the first sporting event broadcast over radio. Major J. Andrew White, editor of *Wireless Age*, relayed the action by telephone from ringside to J. O. Smith, broadcasting from a temporary studio in a railroad yard.

- - -

In a rematch at Ebbets Field before 20,000 fans on July 25, Pete Herman regained the world bantamweight crown from Joe Lynch, who had taken the title from Herman on December 22, 1920. During the bout, gunmen robbed the box office and escaped with the receipts.

- - -

At the West Side Tennis Club in Forest Hills on September 5, the United States defeated Japan, 5–0, to win the Davis Cup.

- - -

On September 5, at Boyle's Thirty Acres in Jersey City, Johnny Wilson defeated Bryan Downey for the middleweight title.

- - -

Ichiya Kumagae of Japan and Bill Johnston of the United States before their Davis Cup match at the West Side Tennis Club in Forest Hills. (Library of Congress, George Grantham Bain Collection, Prints and Photographs Division)

At the final swim meet of the outdoor season at the Brighton Beach Baths on September 25, competitors set five world's records for women and one for men. Gertrude Ederle swam on three of the record-setting relay teams.

▫ ▫ ▫

In the Professional Golfers Association Championship at Inwood Country Club on Long Island on October 1, Walter Hagen bested Jim Barnes, 3 and 2.

▫ ▫ ▫

During the season, Babe Ruth passed Roger Connor (138 homers, mostly with the Giants) to become the all-time home run leader. On October 2, the final day of the season, Ruth hit his record 59th home run (162 total) as the Yankees beat the Red Sox, 7–6. The Yankees won their first American League title, and the Giants won the National League pennant, so all the World Series games were played at the Polo Grounds. The Giants triumphed, five games to three, taking the final game, 1–0, on October 13. In the fourth game, Ruth became the first Yankee to homer in the World Series. Each member of the Giants received $5,265; the Yankees, $3,510. On October 5, a World Series game was broadcast over the radio for the first

Babe Ruth in the dugout at the Polo Grounds, 1921. (Library of Congress, George Grantham Bain Collection, Prints and Photographs Division)

time. Station KDKA in Pittsburgh carried the game live, and WBZ and WJZ relayed the action by telephone to their studio in Newark, where Tommy Cowan re-created the game for listeners.

▫ ▫ ▫

On October 25, sixty-seven-year-old sportswriter William Barclay "Bat" Masterson died at his typewriter in the office of the *Morning Telegraph*. Tex Rickard and Damon Runyon served as honorary pallbearers at his funeral, and he is buried in Woodlawn Cemetery in the Bronx.

▫ ▫ ▫

Following Sunday games between the Original Celtics and the Italian Catholic Club played at 143–145 West Fourteenth Street and at Madison Square Garden on November 20, 12 basketball players were arrested for having interfered with "the religious liberty of the community." In dismissing the charges on December 17, city magistrate George

W. Simpson quoted Jesus in Mark 2:27: "The Sabbath was made for man and not man for the Sabbath." Simpson continued:

> I am satisfied that basketball is a clean sport, conducive to recreation, relaxation and refreshment; as conducted in the premises under observation in this case there was no disorder, nor was the peace of the Sabbath day disturbed in any way, nor was the religious liberty of the community affected or interfered with. No strained construction should be given to the statutes so as to prohibit indoor basketball, because if the statutes were construed as the prosecution contends many symphony concerts, musicales and organ recitals on Sunday would be criminal, which they are not.

• • •

John O'Brien of Brooklyn founded the Metropolitan Basketball League with six teams: the Greenpoint Knights of St. Anthony, the West Brooklyn Assumption Triangles, the Brooklyn Big Five, the Brooklyn Dodgers (or Visitations), the New York MacDowell Lyceum Macs, and the Paterson (New Jersey) Legionnaires. The Dodgers won the first championship by default when the Macs went on strike.

• • •

Before only 3,000 spectators at the Polo Grounds on December 3, Jim Thorpe's Cleveland Tigers defeated Charlie Brickley's Giants, 17–0, in the first American Professional Football Association game in the city. (The association was renamed the National Football League in 1922.) This Giants team folded after one brief season.

• • •

On December 5, baseball commissioner Kenesaw Mountain Landis suspended Babe Ruth, Bob Meusel, and William Piercy until May 20, 1922, and fined each his World Series earnings ($3,262.62 for Ruth and Meusel, $100 less for Piercy) for having defied his authority by barnstorming after the series.

1922 ....

Backed by Tex Rickard, Nat Fleischer launched the *Ring*, "The Bible of Boxing." The first issue appeared on February 15, and the publication awarded its first championship belt to Jack Dempsey. Fleischer remained editor and publisher until September 1972.

• • •

The New York Celtics won the Eastern League championship, defeating the Trenton Royal Bengals by two games to one. The Celtics joined the Metropolitan Basketball League the next season, but dropped out before the championship series.

• • •

The upper deck of the Polo Grounds was completed, increasing capacity to 55,000.

• • •

At the Polo Grounds on May 7, Jess Barnes of the Giants threw a no-hitter to beat the Phillies, 6–0. He faced the minimum, 27 batters; one man walked, but was erased in a double play.

• • •

After Roger Peckinpaugh was traded to the Washington Senators, the Yankees named Babe Ruth as team captain. He and Bob Meusel did not play until May 20, however, having been suspended by commissioner Kenesaw Mountain Landis for barnstorming after the 1921 World Series. At the Polo Grounds on May 25, Ruth was called out while trying to stretch a single into a double. Enraged, he threw a handful of dirt at the umpire and was immediately ejected. In the dugout, Ruth became furious at the taunts of a fan, climbed over the railing, and chased the man through the stands. Afterward, Ruth said, "They can boo and hoot me all they want. That doesn't matter to me. But when a fan calls me insulting names from the grand-stand and becomes abusive I don't intend to stand for it. This fellow today, whoever he was, called me a 'low-down bum' and other names that got me mad, and when I went after him he ran." Ruth lost his captaincy as a result.

▪ ▪ ▪

On May 30, the Empire City Wheelmen sponsored a revival of the Coney Island handicap, a 25-mile race for amateurs along Ocean Parkway. Joseph Schaefer of the Acme Wheelmen set a new course record of 1 hour, 54 seconds (actual time), but George Hess won based on the handicap.

▪ ▪ ▪

The New York Velodrome (225th Street and Broadway), which cost $250,000 to build, opened with 14,000 on hand on May 30.

▪ ▪ ▪

After the Yankees acquired third baseman Joe Dugan from the Red Sox a one-sided deal on July 24, commissioner Landis ruled that no trades could be made after June 15 unless the players cleared waivers.

▪ ▪ ▪

Before 50,000 spectators at Boyle's Thirty Acres in Jersey City on July 27, lightweight champion Benny Leonard defended his crown against Lew Tendler with a close 12-round decision. Receipts totaled $327,565, the richest lightweight bout to date; promoter Tex Rickard cleared more than $90,000.

▪ ▪ ▪

On August 1, fifteen-year-old Gertrude Ederle beat 51 other women to win a 3.5-mile swim from Manhattan Beach to Brighton Beach, finishing in 1 hour, 1 minute, 34 3/5 seconds. She defeated Helen Wainwright, the American all-around champion, and Hilda James of England, Europe's best. After the race, James said, "The best girl won, of that I am sure." Between 1921 and 1925, Ederle held 29 national and world records; at the

Gertrude Ederle. (Queens Borough Public Library, Long Island Division, Illustrations Collection)

Summer Olympic Games in 1924, in Paris, she won a gold medal in the 4 × 100-meter freestyle relay and bronzes in the 100- and 400-meter freestyle.

▪ ▪ ▪

In the second competition for the Walker Cup (named for George Herbert Walker, former president of the United States Golf Association and donor of the trophy, and grandfather of President George Herbert Walker Bush), which pit amateur golfers from the United States against amateurs from Great Britain, the Americans prevailed at the National Golf Links in Southampton, Walker's home club, on August 29.

▪ ▪ ▪

Behind Bill Tilden's surprisingly tough five-set singles victory, the United States defeated Australia, 4–1, to defend the Davis Cup at the West Side Tennis Club on September 5.

▪ ▪ ▪

Max Rosner and Nat Strong purchased Dexter Park from the William Ulmer Brewery for $200,000 on September 30. The 9.9-acre grounds featured a carousel, dance hall, bowling alley,

Bill Tilden playing in the Davis Cup match at the West Side Tennis Club in Forest Hills, 1921. (Library of Congress, George Grantham Bain Collection, Prints and Photographs Division)

shooting gallery, and restaurant in addition to the ball field. For the next season, they completely rebuilt the ballpark, adding more seats, refreshment stands, and locker rooms.

· · ·

For the second consecutive year, the Giants and the Yankees met at the Polo Grounds in the World Series. John McGraw's Giants swept the series in five games (one ended in a tie), taking the final game, 5–3, on October 8. This was the first World Series broadcast in its entirety over the radio; sportswriter Grantland Rice provided the play-by-play for the Westinghouse Network.

· · ·

Mickey Walker, "the Toy Bulldog," took the welterweight title from Jack Bitton in a 15-round decision at Madison Square Garden on November 1.

· · ·

On December 16, promoter Nat Strong, owner of the Brooklyn Royal Giants, organized the Mutual Association of Eastern Colored Baseball Clubs to arrange bookings in the metropolitan area; the

six-team league also included the Lincoln Giants of New York. It operated until 1928.

1923 ....

I'll put this one up so close to the hole that it will break Walter's heart.

GENE SARAZEN

This is the way old Casey Stengel ran yesterday afternoon running his home run home.

This is the way old Casey Stengel ran running his home run home to a Giant victory by the score of 5 to 4 in the first game of the World Series of 1923.

This is the way old Casey Stengel ran running his home run home when two were out in the ninth inning and the score was tied, and the ball still bounding inside the Yankee yard.

This is the way—

His mouth wide open.

His warped old legs bending beneath him at every stride.

His arms flying back and forth like those of a man swimming with the crawl stroke.

His flanks heaving, his breath whistling, his head far back.

Yankee infielders passed by old Casey as he was running his home run home, say Casey was muttering to himself, adjuring himself to greater speed as a jockey mutters to his horse in a race, saying, "Go on, Casey, go on."

The warped old legs, twisted and bent by many a year of baseball campaigning, just barely held out under Casey until he reached the plate, running his home run home.

Then they collapsed.

DAMON RUNYON, DESCRIBING CASEY STENGEL'S INSIDE-THE-PARK HOME RUN IN THE WORLD SERIES, *NEW YORK AMERICAN*, OCTOBER 10, 1923

Governor Al Smith named James A. Farley to the State Boxing Commission. The governor asked, "What do you know about boxing?" "Nothing at all," Farley answered.

◦ ◦ ◦

Following a game at Madison Square Garden on February 18 between the Original Celtics and the New Jersey Camdens attended by 2,000 fans, announcer Joseph J. Humphreys, play-by-play man John Whittley, ticket seller Thomas J. Jordan, and ticket taker James Cash were arrested for having violated the blue laws. Theodore Gillman, chairman of the New York Sabbath Committee, part of the "blue law crusade" of the Lord's Day Alliance, had filed the complaint. The Original Celtics won 204 games and lost seven during the year, but the Kingston-Paterson Legionnaires of the Metropolitan Basketball League defeated them, three games to two, for the unofficial world basketball championship.

◦ ◦ ◦

Yankee Stadium, "The House That Ruth Built," opened on April 18, with 74,217 in attendance. With a capacity of 60,000, more than double that of the average ballpark, the Stadium was the largest in the nation, the first with three tiers; and the first not called field, park, or grounds. Governor Al Smith threw out the first ball. The Yankees beat the Red Sox, 4–1, and, naturally, Babe Ruth hit the first home run. The field featured a short porch in right field—a 43-inch-high fence, 290 feet from home—for his benefit.

◦ ◦ ◦

The Giants home games were broadcast on the radio for the first time, with Graham McNamee at the microphone.

◦ ◦ ◦

American chess champion Frank J. Marshall defended his title for the only time in his 30-year reign. In a match begun in March—with play in Chicago, Cleveland, Baltimore, and, finally, the

Manager Miller Huggins and owner Jacob Ruppert at the opening of Yankee Stadium, April 18, 1923. (The Bronx County Historical Society)

Marshall Chess Club—he defeated Edward Lasker, 5–4, with nine drawn games. Marshall won the last game at his home club on May 12.

◦ ◦ ◦

Yankee Stadium was the site of a professional boxing card for the first time on May 12. The Stadium had a hydraulic lift under second base for the boxing ring. Former heavyweight champion Jess Willard defeated Floyd Johnson by an eleventh-round technical knockout, and Luis Ángel Firpo, "the Wild Bull of the Pampas," knocked out Jack McAuliffe in the third round. On July 23, over 58,000 crowded the Stadium for the first championship bout there, seeing lightweight champion Benny Leonard win a 15-round decision over Lew Tendler. Over half a century, Yankee Stadium was the scene of at least 46 boxing cards, including 31 championship bouts. Joe Louis fought there 11 times, the most of any boxer.

The New York Bloomer Girls baseball team defeated the Philadelphia Girls Athletic Club, 21–13, in an inter-city challenge.

On July 15, twenty-one-year-old amateur Bobby Jones won the U.S. Open at Inwood Country Club, defeating Robert A. Cruickshank in the 18-hole playoff round by two strokes on the final hole.

Built in only four months for $150,000, the West Side Tennis Club's concrete 13,000-seat stadium opened in Forest Hills on August 11. A crowd of 5,000 attended the first event, the inaugural Wightman Cup match, pitting the best women players from the United States against those from Great Britain. Hazel Hotchkiss Wightman donated the trophy as a counterpart to the men's Davis Cup. Helen Wills won the first match, defeating Kitty McKane in straight sets; the Americans won, 7–0. The matches alternated between Forest Hills and Wimbledon until 1947, and then rotated to other venues. The Wightman Cup was not contested after 1989, with the United States holding a 51–10 advantage.

Harry Greb took the world middleweight crown from Johnny Wilson in a 15-round decision before 11,000 spectators at the Polo Grounds on August 31. The bout was broadcast over WEAF, with Graham McNamee announcing. WEAF became NBC's flagship station; WFAN now broadcasts on the frequency, AM 660.

Sheepshead Bay Race Track, the last in Brooklyn, was auctioned off for building lots on September 1.

On September 3, the American team, with Bill Tilden, defeated Australia, 4–1, to defend the Davis Cup; 13,000 attended the matches at the West Side Tennis Club.

In front of 90,000 fans at the Polo Grounds on September 14, heavyweight champion Jack Dempsey knocked out Luis Ángel Firpo, only 57 seconds into the second round. Dempsey knocked down the challenger seven times in the first round, but Firpo then bashed him through the ropes; Dempsey barely staggered back into the ring at the count of nine (helped by sportswriters in the front row). Promoter Tex Rickard claimed that the gate totaled $1,250,000.

In an 8–3 Yankee victory at Fenway Park on September 27, Lou Gehrig hit the first of his 493 career home runs.

In the PGA Championship at the Pelham Country Club on September 29, Gene Sarazen (born Eugene Saracini in Manhattan) and Walter Hagen tied after 36 holes. On the second playoff hole, with his first shot lying in the deep rough, Sarazen said to onlookers, "I'll put this one up so close to the hole that it will break Walter's heart." He did, and it did, giving Sarazen his second straight PGA victory.

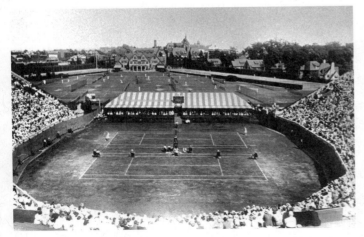

Spectators crowd the stadium to watch a tournament at the West Side Tennis Club in Forest Hills, 1931. (Nassau County Museum Collection, Long Island Studies Institute, Hofstra University)

■ ■ ■

In their first game at Baker Field, Columbia University defeated Ursinus College, 13–0, on September 29. Financier George F. Baker had donated $700,000 to the university to acquire the site at the northern tip of Manhattan (218th Street and Broadway).

■ ■ ■

The German American Soccer League was organized with five clubs: S.C. New York, Wiener Sport Club, D.S.C. Brooklyn, Hoboken F.C., and Newark S.C.; the next year Swiss F.C., Elizabeth S.C., Eintracht S.C., and Germania S.C. joined. It became the German American Football Association in 1927, and in 1977 was renamed the Cosmopolitan Soccer League. In 2006, there were 77 clubs in nine divisions.

■ ■ ■

For the third consecutive year, the Yankees and Giants met in the World Series, the first played in Yankee Stadium. On October 13, the Yanks took the sixth game, 6–4, for their first world championship. Babe Ruth hit three home runs in the series; Casey Stengel was in center field for the Giants and, in the first game, hit the first World Series homer at the Stadium. The games were broadcast live, with Graham McNamee behind the mike. McNamee announced every World Series through 1935 and later wrote:

> You must make each of your listeners, though miles from the spot, feel that he, or she, too, is there with you in the press stand, watching the movements of the game, the color, and flags; the pop bottles thrown in the air; the straw hat demolished; Gloria Swanson arriving in her new ermine coat; McGraw in his dugout, apparently motionless but giving signals all the time; the pitcher beginning to waver; and two figures far off against the left field fence, where another pitcher is preparing to come to the relief of his faltering comrade.

In 1927, Ring Lardner quipped, "I don't know which game to write about; the one I saw or the one I heard Graham McNamee announce."

■ ■ ■

Babe Ruth was the American League's Most Valuable Player, leading the league with 41 home runs, 131 RBIs, a .393 batting average, and a .764 slugging percentage.

■ ■ ■

In a match race before 45,000 at Belmont Park on October 20, Harry Sinclair's three-year-old colt Zev beat Benjamin Irish's English Derby winner Papyrus by five lengths. Perhaps it was the unfamiliar mud track, or the wrong shoes, but some attributed Papyrus's performance to his being denied his usual post-workout bucket of beer because of Prohibition.

■ ■ ■

Bob Douglas had organized the Spartan Braves, a black basketball team, in 1922. In 1923, he secured Harlem's Renaissance Ballroom (138th Street and Seventh Avenue) as the team's home court and changed the name to the New York Renaissance Big Five, generally called the Rens. In their first home game, on November 3, they defeated the Collegiate Big Five, 28–22. The original Rens included Clarence "Fats" Jenkins, James "Pappy" Ricks, Hilton Slocum, Leon Monde, Frank "Strangler" Forbes, Hy Monte, Zack Anderson, and Harold Mayers. Douglas owned and coached the Rens until they disbanded in 1949; their final record was 2,318–381 (.859).

1924

In a rematch before 11,093 at Madison Square Garden on January 18, middleweight champion Harry Greb again won a 15-round decision over former champion Johnny Wilson.

■ ■ ■

The Brooklyn Visitations won both halves of the season to claim the Metropolitan Basketball League championship.

▪ ▪ ▪

Sporting a 134–6 record, the Original Celtics defeated the Cleveland Rosenblums, 25–17, for the unofficial world basketball championship.

▪ ▪ ▪

An international chess tournament featuring 11 masters from around the world ran from March 16 to April 17 in the Japanese Room of the Hotel Almanac (Broadway at Seventy-first Street). Emanuel Lasker of Germany won; José Raúl Capablanca finished second; Alexander Alekhine, third; and Frank J. Marshall, fourth.

▪ ▪ ▪

At the Garden City Golf Club on September 13, the United States defeated Great Britain for its third consecutive Walker Cup triumph.

▪ ▪ ▪

The Giants won their fourth straight National League pennant, but lost the World Series to the Senators, dropping the seventh game in 12 innings, 4–3, on October 10.

▪ ▪ ▪

Before 60,000 at the Polo Grounds on October 18, Notre Dame defeated Army, 13–7. About the Notre Dame backfield, Grantland Rice wrote, "Outlined against a blue-gray October sky, the Four Horsemen rode again. In dramatic lore, they are known as Famine, Pestilence, Destruction, and Death. These are only aliases. Their real names are Stuhldreher, Miller, Crowley, and Layden."

1925

Charlie wouldn't want anyone to miss a Dodger–Giant series just because he died.

WILBERT ROBINSON

In New York, an empty store with two chairs in it is worth that much.

TIM MARA

On January 15, Benny Leonard announced his retirement after holding the world lightweight title for seven and a half years:

I am retiring from boxing for the love of my mother, who has begged me not to fight again. . . . During the last three years I fought my biggest ring battles. I fought Jack Britton, Lew Tendler twice, Richie Mitchell, Pinkey Mitchell, Rocky Kansas twice, Sailor Friedman, Joe Welling, Pal Moran, Ever Hammer, Charlie White—all the real contenders. I fought everybody the public demanded me to meet. I beat them all in my class. Nobody can say Benny Leonard didn't give all the boys a chance at the title.

▪ ▪ ▪

A crowd of 2,000 packed Rose Hill Gymnasium, on the campus of Fordham University, for its opening on January 16. Fordham defeated Boston College, 46–16; Frankie Frisch, the "Fordham Flash," second baseman for the Giants, refereed. Still in use 85 years later, it is the oldest Division I basketball court.

▪ ▪ ▪

Everlast, the Bronx-based manufacturer of sporting gear, introduced elastic-waist boxing trunks, which soon replaced the leather-belted trunks.

▪ ▪ ▪

Paavo Nurmi of Finland was awarded the first Outstanding Performer trophy at the Millrose Games on January 28. He won the Wanamaker 1.5-mile race in 6 minutes, 39 $2/5$ seconds, bettering the old mark by 2 $2/5$ seconds and setting his fourteenth and fifteenth world's records since arriving in the United States. At the New York Athletic

Club meet at Madison Square Garden on February 14, he ran the 2-mile in 8 minutes, 58¹/₅ seconds, the fastest time ever.

◻ ◻ ◻

On March 7, Bobby Walthour Jr. and Freddie Spencer won the last six-day bicycle race held in the old Madison Square Garden, taking the $10,000 first prize. They covered 2,397 miles before capacity crowds.

◻ ◻ ◻

A group of Germans and Hungarians purchased a 4-acre parcel in Maspeth, Queens, and built Metropolitan Oval, now the oldest soccer field in continuous use in the United States.

◻ ◻ ◻

The Brooklyn Visitations defeated the Kingston-Passaic Colonials, two games to one, for the Metropolitan Basketball League championship. The Original Celtics then took two straight from the Visitations to claim the unofficial world championship.

◻ ◻ ◻

At Madison Square Garden on March 20, Charley Phil Rosenberg from Harlem won a 15-round decision over defending bantamweight champion Eddie "Cannonball" Martin, an Italian American from Brooklyn.

◻ ◻ ◻

Charles Ebbets died on April 18. In his honor, the Dodgers refused to cancel their game at Ebbets Field. As manager Wilbert Robinson put it, "Charlie wouldn't want anyone to miss a Dodger–Giant series just because he died." The Giants won, 7–1. Ebbets is buried in Green-Wood Cemetery.

◻ ◻ ◻

The Clearview Golf Club opened in Bayside, Queens. Willie Tucker designed the course, which required the removal of some 2,000 trees, many of them first growth.

◻ ◻ ◻

Charles Ebbets, ca. 1910. (Library of Congress, George Grantham Bain Collection, Prints and Photographs Division)

On May 5, the second Madison Square Garden, designed by Stanford White, held its final event, a boxing match. The occasion attracted many celebrities, including Mr. and Mrs. Jack Dempsey, Jimmy Walker, Bernard Gimbel, and John Ringling. Announcer Joseph J. Humphreys said, "We mourn our loss but we take with us fragrant memories," and then read an ode to the old place: "Temple of Fistiana."

◻ ◻ ◻

Lou Gehrig took over at first base for the Yankees from Wally Pip on June 1, beginning a streak of 2,130 consecutive games that ended on May 2, 1939. Babe Ruth played his first game of the season that day, having suffered a physical collapse in the spring. On July 23, Gehrig hit the first of his career record 23 grand slams in an 11–7 win over the Senators.

◻ ◻ ◻

Before challenging the English Channel, seventeen-year-old Gertrude Ederle completed a 21-mile swim from the Battery to Sandy Hook in 7 hours, 11 minutes, 30 seconds on June 15.

◻ ◻ ◻

On June 25, Gene Sarazen won the U.S. Open at the Fresh Meadows Country Club.

◻ ◻ ◻

Before more than 50,000 at the Polo Grounds on July 2, Harry Greb successfully defended his middleweight title with a 15-round decision over welterweight champion Mickey Walker.

□ □ □

At the West Side Tennis Club, Bill Tilden won the Men's National Singles Championship for the sixth straight year, beating Bill Johnston, 4–6, 11–9, 6–3, 4–6, 6–3. The two met in the finals six times, with Tilden winning five.

□ □ □

On October 7, Giant great Christy Mathewson died of tuberculosis in Saranac Lake, New York. The Christian Gentleman, or Big Six (for his height), was gassed in World War I and never fully recovered. He briefly coached the Giants after the war, but retired in 1920. He first pitched for New York in 1901, was a 30-game winner in three straight seasons, threw no-hitters in 1901 and 1905, and hurled three shutouts in the 1905 World Series. John McGraw said, "There was never another pitcher like Mathewson, and I doubt there ever will be."

□ □ □

At Yankee Stadium on October 17, before 80,000, the largest crowd to see a football game in the city to date, Army beat Notre Dame, 27–0, ending the 16-game winning streak of Knute Rockne's Fighting Irish. The teams clashed at the Stadium annually until 1946. At the Polo Grounds on November 28, Army beat Navy, 10–3, before 70,000 fans.

□ □ □

For $500, bookmaker Tim Mara bought a franchise in the National Football League, which had been founded as the American Professional Football Association in 1920. He reportedly remarked, "In New York, an empty store with two chairs in it is worth that much." The New York Giants lost their first three games, but finished with a record of 8–4 under coach Bob Folwell. On October 18, they fell to the Frankford Yellow Jackets, 14–0, before 27,000 in their first home game at the Polo Grounds. Jim Thorpe, age thirty-eight, began the

season with the Giants, but they released him after that game. On December 6, a crowd of 70,000 filled the Polo Grounds to watch Harold "Red" Grange and the Chicago Bears beat the Giants, 19–7. (Grange took home $30,000 for the afternoon.) Following the game, three persons were arrested for having violated the blue laws on a complaint by Daniel J. Burns, secretary of the Lord's Day Alliance. Magistrate James M. Barrett dismissed the charges, noting that of the 70,000 who had attended the game, only Burns filed a complaint: "That is just about the ratio between those who want Sunday sports and those who do not— 70,000 to 1."

□ □ □

A semi-pro team defeated the Babe Ruth All-Stars at Ahrco Park in College Point, Queens, on October 25, the same day that the Lou Gehrig All-Stars defeated the Jamaica Cardinals at the Jamaica Oval.

□ □ □

With 15,000 on hand, Tex Rickard opened the third Madison Square Garden (Forty-ninth Street and Eighth Avenue) on Saturday, November 28, with bicycle racing. Before the start of the six-day bicycle race the next night, the police issued summonses for violations of the blue laws. The event started on schedule. The Garden's official opening was a game between the New York Americans, the city's first professional hockey team, and the Montreal Canadiens on December 15; Montreal

The third Madison Square Garden. (Author's collection)

won, 3–1. (William B. "Big Bill" Dwyer had purchased the Hamilton Tigers and moved them to the city as the Americans.) The crowd of 17,000 included Mayor John F. Hylan and Mayor-elect Jimmy Walker. Rickard remarked how he loved "seeing the evening dress, the ladies, the big people out there."

On December 6, 10,000 attended the first basketball games played at Madison Square Garden. In the first game, St. John's Prep of Brooklyn defeated St. Benedict's Prep of Newark, 53–14. In the second game, the Original Celtics defeated the Palace Club of Washington, D.C., 35–31. Following the game, several players were arrested on a complaint by the Lord's Day Alliance for having violated the blue laws. Magistrate Jean Norris fined the players $10 each. The alliance defended its action by claiming that "it is not an issue of sports on Sunday—it is a question, 'was the law violated? If so why, then, was it not enforced?'"

When the Harlem-based New York Renaissance were refused admission to the new American Basketball League, the Original Celtics declined to join.

Joseph Hubertus Pilates arrived in New York from Germany and opened his gym, offering his own unique exercise techniques.

1926

Schuyler Van Vechten Hoffman and other lawyers and businessmen founded the Downtown Athletic Club, an elite membership organization and the original home of the Heisman Trophy.

Before more than 20,000 at Madison Square Garden on February 26, challenger Theodore "Tiger" Flowers won a 15-round split decision over Harry Greb for the middleweight crown. In a rematch at the Garden on August 19, Flowers again won a 15-round split decision over Greb.

Isaac T. Flatto opened Ridgewood Grove Sporting Club, a boxing venue. Located at St. Nicholas Avenue and Palmetto Street, it was turned into a supermarket in 1956.

In the first championship series of the American Basketball League, the Brooklyn Arcadians lost to the Cleveland Rosenblums in three straight. The Greenpoint Knights defeated the Yonkers Indians, two games to one, to become the champions of the Metropolitan Basketball League.

Nineteen-year-old Maureen Orcutt won the first of 10 Women's Metropolitan Amateur Golf Championships; she won her last in 1968 at age sixty-one. She won the Women's New Jersey Association championship 10 times, six New Jersey Amateurs titles, and five Metropolitan Seniors championships. She was also among the first female sports journalists, writing for the New York Journal, the New York Evening World, Golf Illustrated, National Golf Review, and, for 35 years, the New York Times.

The Belmont family gave a Tiffany-designed solid-silver bowl as a permanent trophy for the Belmont Stakes. The owner of the winning horse receives a smaller version. Crusader, son of Man o' War, won in a downpour on June 12.

At Ebbets Field on July 16, Jack Delaney defeated Paul Berlenbach for the light heavyweight title.

On August 6, nineteen-year-old Gertrude Ederle became the first woman to swim the English Channel, accomplishing the feat in 14 hours, 31 minutes—bettering the previous record by 2 hours.

Gertrude Ederle swimming the English Channel. (Queens Borough Public Library, Long Island Division, Illustrations Collection)

(She had failed the year before after swimming 23 miles in 8 hours, 43 minutes.) She received a ticker-tape parade up Broadway on August 27.

• • •

In the first game of a doubleheader against the Braves at Ebbets Field on August 15, the Dodgers put three men on third base—Dazzy Vance, Chick Fewster, and Babe Herman—resulting in a most unusual double play. Still, Brooklyn won both games.

• • •

On August 16, the state License Committee refused to permit Jack Dempsey to fight Gene Tunney unless he first faced Harry Wills, a black contender, as demanded by the State Athletic Commission. Promoter Tex Rickard then moved the bout to Philadelphia, where Tunney took the title from Dempsey.

• • •

Joseph Alexander replaced Robert Folwell as coach of the football Giants. The team finished with a 8-4-1 record.

• • •

At the West Side Tennis Club on September 16, Henri Cochet of France defeated Bill Tilden, 6–8, 6–1, 6–3, 1–6, 8–6, ending Tilden's six-year reign as the United States singles champion. Two French

players battled in the final on September 18, with Jean René Lacoste besting Jean Borotra in straight sets; it was the first time that two foreign players met in the final in the tournament's 45-year history.

• • •

In the United States Men's Amateur Golf Championship at Baltusrol Golf Club in Springfield, New Jersey, on September 18, George Von Elm won a surprise victory over the United States and British Open champion Bobby Jones, 2 and 1.

• • •

On September 25, Walter Hagen won the PGA Championship, beating Leo Diegel, 5 and 3, at the Salisbury Country Club (now the Red Course at Eisenhower Park) in Nassau County.

• • •

The Yankees lost the seventh game of the World Series to the St. Louis Cardinals on October 10. Grover Cleveland Alexander struck out Tony Lazzeri with the bases loaded to end the seventh inning and preserve a 3–2 Cardinal win. (Alexander had

The PGA tournament at the Salisbury Country Club, September 1926. (Queens Borough Public Library, Long Island Division, Joseph Burt, Sr., Photographs)

The PGA tournament at the Salisbury Country Club, September 1926. (Queens Borough Public Library, Long Island Division, Joseph Burt, Sr., Photographs)

pitched nine innings the day before.) The game ended with Babe Ruth caught stealing second in the bottom of the ninth. Ruth had hit three homers in the fourth game.

■ ■ ■

The Brooklyn Lions played their first and only season in the NFL, finishing with a 3–8 record. In the inaugural season of the American Football League, the New York Yankees finished with a record of 9–5 under coach Ralph Scott, with Red Grange at running back. The team and the league folded in 1927, but the Yankees reemerged in the NFL in 1927 and 1928. The Brooklyn Horsemen were briefly in the AFL, going 1–3 under coach Bob Berryman.

■ ■ ■

The Rangers took the ice for the first time on November 16, defeating the Montreal Maroons, 1–0, at Madison Square Garden. Despite an agreement that the New York Americans would be the only hockey team at the Garden, Tex Rickard purchased an expansion franchise in the National Hockey League for $50,000, specifically to play there. They were called Tex's Rangers.

1927 ....

What was I supposed to do, mail him a letter?

JACK DEMPSEY

How to hit home runs: I swing as hard as I can, and I try to swing right through the ball. . . . The harder you grip the bat, the more you can swing through the ball, and the farther the ball will go. I swing big, with everything I've got. I hit big or I miss big. I like to live as big as I can.

BABE RUTH

At the Hotel Pennsylvania on January 7, Willie Hoppe defeated Eric Hagenlacher to regain the balkline billiard championship. In another three-day championship match at the Hotel Pennsyl-

vania in December, three-time billiard champion Jack Schaefer defeated Welker Cochran to regain the championship.

■ ■ ■

On February 4, the State Athletic Commission stripped Charley Phil Rosenberg of his bantamweight title when he failed to make weight for a match against Busby Graham; they fought anyway, Rosenberg winning a 15-round decision. The commission then suspended Rosenberg and his manager, Harry "Champ" Segal, over questionable influences—gamblers—in that fight.

■ ■ ■

An international grand-master chess tournament ran at the Hotel Manhattan Square from February 19 to March 25, featuring Frank J. Marshall of the United States, José Raúl Capablanca of Cuba, Alexander Alekhine of France, Aron Nimzowitsch of Denmark, Milan Vidmar of Yugoslavia, and Rudolf Spielmann of Austria. Capablanca won a decisive victory.

■ ■ ■

The Brooklyn Visitations took three straight from the Paterson Crescents for the Metropolitan Basketball League title. The Original Celtics, having joined the American Basketball League to replace the Brooklyn Arcadians, defeated the Cleveland Rosenblums, 35–32, on April 9 to sweep the best-of-five series for the championship.

■ ■ ■

Sportswriter Paul Gallico of the *Daily News* organized the city's first Golden Gloves tournament. On March 28, 21,500 fans filled Madison Square Garden, and 8,000 more were turned away, the largest crowd to see an indoor boxing event in the city to date.

■ ■ ■

On May 20, Charles Lindbergh took off from Roosevelt Field in Garden City for the first nonstop solo flight across the Atlantic. He received a joyous ticker-tape parade up the Canyon of Heroes after his return to the United States on June 11.

∎ ∎ ∎

The North Hills Golf Club opened in Douglaston, Queens. The firm of William H. Tucker & Son designed the course.

∎ ∎ ∎

The Yankees led the American League from opening day and went on to defeat the Pittsburgh Pirates in four straight in the World Series behind "Murderers' Row": Babe Ruth, Lou Gehrig, Tony Lazzeri, and Bob Meusel. They won a record 110 games, which stood until the Cleveland Indians won 111 in 1954, which in turn stood until the Yankees won 114 in 1998. Babe Ruth hit his 60th home run of the season off Tom Zachary of the Washington Senators on September 30. (The Yanks won, 4–2.) His record stood until Roger Maris hit 61 in 1961. Lou Gehrig was named Most Valuable Player, with 47 home runs, 175 RBIs, a .373 average, and a .765 slugging percentage.

∎ ∎ ∎

In the last victory of his career, thirty-two-year-old Jack Dempsey knocked out twenty-four-year-old Jack Sharkey before 77,283 at Yankee Stadium on July 21. As Sharkey turned to the referee to complain about a low blow, Dempsey knocked him out with a right. Asked about it later, Dempsey answered, "What was I supposed to do, mail him a letter?" The fight grossed $1 million.

∎ ∎ ∎

At Madison Square Garden on October 7, Tommy Loughran won a 15-round decision to take the light-heavyweight crown from Mike McTigue. Before 12,000 at the Garden on December 12, Loughran won a 15-round decision over National Boxing Association titleholder Jimmy Slattery to claim the undisputed world championship.

∎ ∎ ∎

On December 11, the Giants defeated Red Grange and the Yankees at Yankee Stadium, 13–0, to win their first NFL title with an 11–1–1 record. (There was no championship game.) Coach Earl Potteiger's team scored 213 points and allowed only 20. After moving over from the AFL, the Yankees finished with a record of 7–8–1.

1928

On January 6, three weeks after winning the light-heavyweight title, Tommy Loughran won a 15-round decision over challenger Leo Lomski before 15,000 at Madison Square Garden, despite twice being knocked down for a nine-count. On June 2, Loughran outpointed challenger Pete Latzo before 10,000 spectators at Ebbets Field.

∎ ∎ ∎

Finishing 40–9 in their first full season in the American Basketball League and beating the Philadelphia Warriors in two straight for the Eastern Division title, the Original Celtics defeated the Fort Wayne Hoosiers, 27–26, at Arcadia Hall in Brooklyn on March 25 to take the championship, three games to one. They then faced the New York Renaissance for the unofficial world championship, taking that series, two games to one.

∎ ∎ ∎

In the second period of the second game of the Stanley Cup finals against the Montreal Maroons on April 7, Ranger goalie Lorne Chabot was hit in the eye by the puck. With no other goalie available, Lester Patrick, the forty-four-year-old coach who had retired as a player seven years before, put on the pads and held the Maroons to one goal. The Rangers won, 2–1, in overtime. They borrowed goalie Joe Miller from the New York Americans for the rest of the series. At the Montreal Forum on April 14, the Rangers won, 2–1, to take the series, three games to two, and become the first American team to win the Stanley Cup.

∎ ∎ ∎

In an amateur bout on April 11 at St. Anthony's Boxing Club, at 840 Manhattan Avenue in Greenpoint, nineteen-year-old Joseph Michallick knocked out nineteen-year-old Julius Rubin. Rubin never regained consciousness and died of a cerebral hemorrhage the next day.

◾ ◾ ◾

The Gaelic Athletic Association began to host hurling and Irish football at Gaelic Park in the Bronx (240th Street and Broadway). Manhattan College took over the facility in 1991 and installed artificial turf. The GAA continued to use the field.

◾ ◾ ◾

Harold S. Vanderbilt donated the Vanderbilt Trophy, with a $100,000 trust fund, for a bridge tournament. He won the trophy himself in 1932 and 1940. Since 1958, the trophy has been awarded during the Spring North American Championships.

◾ ◾ ◾

At Yankee Stadium on July 26, Gene Tunney recorded an eleventh-round technical knockout over Tom Heeney of New Zealand, and then retired as heavyweight champion. Tunney took home a $500,000 purse. With tickets priced from $5 to $40, reduced to $3 as the day approached, only 50,000 attended, and promoter Tex Rickard claimed that he had lost $100,000. Fifty radio stations in the United States and 21 in Britain carried the fight.

◾ ◾ ◾

The Yankees beat the Cardinals to sweep the World Series for the second consecutive year. Babe Ruth hit three home runs in the fourth game (as he had in the 1926 series) and had a .625 batting average; Lou Gehrig had four homers, nine RBIs, and a .545 average; Waite Hoyt won two games.

◾ ◾ ◾

On October 6, a record crowd of 40,000 thronged International Field at the Meadow Brook Club in Westbury for the championship polo match between the United States and Argentina. Behind

Thomas Hitchcock Jr. in action at the Meadow Brook Club, Westbury. (Nassau County Museum Collection, Long Island Studies Institute, Hofstra University)

captain Thomas Hitchcock Jr., the Americans won, 13–7.

◾ ◾ ◾

The Metropolitan Basketball League, founded in 1921, suspended operations. Resurrected in 1931, it disbanded in 1933.

◾ ◾ ◾

Behind tailback Ken Strong, the New York University football team suffered only four losses from 1926 to 1928. Strong later played professional football with the Staten Island Stapletons, the Giants, and the New York Yankees; he scored 17 points for the Giants in the 1934 NFL championship game. He was elected to the Pro Football Hall of Fame.

◾ ◾ ◾

Notre Dame beat previously undefeated Army, 12–6, at Yankee Stadium. With the Fighting Irish trailing 6–0 at halftime, coach Knute Rockne told his team, "Win one for the Gipper." (Twenty-five-year-old George Gipp had died of pneumonia eight years earlier.)

◾ ◾ ◾

The Yankees folded after going 4–8–1 in their second season in the NFL.

On December 20, Viola Gentry flew a biplane above Roosevelt Field for 8 hours, 6 minutes, 37 seconds, setting the first women's endurance record. Gentry became a charter member of the International Women's Pilots Association, or the Ninety-Nines.

- - -

Beginning on Christmas Day, the Noun and Verb Rodeo was staged at the Seventy-first Regiment Armory. Eleven women and 24 men entered the talking marathon. Contestants had to speak non-stop for four days, with only three 30-minute breaks every 24 hours. After four days, only two competitors remained: Howard Williams (a well-known flagpole sitter) and Betty Wilson (a young lifeguard). Having lost $10,000 on the venture (the expected crowds stayed away), promoter Milton Crandall declared a tie and stated that neither contestant had won the $1,000 prize.

1929 ....

Famed boxing promoter and sports impresario Tex Rickard died on January 6. Summing up his life, he once said, "I always took a chance."

- - -

In the first NHL championship series between two American teams, the Boston Bruins beat the Rangers in two straight games for the Stanley Cup.

- - -

In a series for the unofficial world basketball championship, the Original Celtics took three straight from the New York Renaissance.

- - -

The Yankees wore numbers on their uniforms for the first time, including Babe Ruth's immortal 3 and Lou Gehrig's 4.

- - -

Left-hander Carl Hubbell of the Giants hurled a no-hitter to beat the Pirates, 11–0, at the Polo Grounds on May 8. This was the last no-hitter by a New York Giants pitcher.

- - -

At Yankee Stadium on May 19, two people were killed when the standing-room crowd rushed for cover during a sudden rainstorm.

- - -

In near darkness on June 24, Columbia University's Varsity Eight prevailed in the choppy Hudson River, beating the University of Washington by two and a half lengths over a 4-mile course; four of the starting nine boats sank. About 125,000 spectators watched the races from the shore or in boats. This was Columbia's second Intercollegiate Rowing Championship in three years.

- - -

After a practice round at Winged Foot Golf Club in preparation for the U.S. Open, and then a round at the Queens Valley Golf Club, where he shot a course record 71, Bobby Jones had his clubs stolen from his car in Manhattan. The clubs, including his prized putter, Calamity Jane, were soon recovered. On June 30, Jones won a 36-hole playoff over professional Al Espinosa, 141–164, to capture the U.S. Open.

- - -

Before a crowd of 25,000 at Yankee Stadium on July 18, Tommy Loughran defended his light-heavyweight title for the final time, outpointing James Braddock. Loughran then retired as undefeated light-heavyweight champion to pursue the heavyweight crown.

- - -

Governor Franklin D. Roosevelt presided at the opening of Jones Beach State Park on August 4. In 1930, the first full season, the park welcomed 1.5 million visitors. Jones Beach is without doubt Robert Moses's greatest achievement and was the pattern for his redesign of the Rockaways, Coney Island, South Beach, and Orchard Beach while New York City parks commissioner.

Jones Beach, ca. 1930. (Nassau County Museum Collection, Long Island Studies Institute, Hofstra University)

At League Park in Cleveland on August 11, Babe Ruth hit his 500th home run, his 30th of the season, but the Yankees lost to the Indians, 6–5. This was Miller Huggins's last year as manager; Art Fletcher took over for the last 11 games of the season as the Yankees finished with an 88–66 record. Over his 12 years at the helm, Huggins compiled a record of 1,067–719 (.597), winning six pennants and three World Series.

Bill Tilden won his seventh and last men's singles title at Forest Hills at the West Side Tennis Club, defeating fellow American Francis Hunter in five sets.

In September, Fay Gillis parachuted to safety when her flight instructor lost control of his biplane above Curtiss Field in Valley Stream. While not the first woman parachutist, Gillis was cele-

brated in all the newspapers. She received her pilot's license on October 5. On October 9, Gillis wrote to each of the other 117 women licensed pilots and proposed that they form the International Women's Pilots Association. Amelia Earhart was

Eight of the Ninety-Nines at Curtiss Field, Valley Stream: (*left to right*) Mona Holmes, Mary Samson, Elvy Kalep, Ruth Elder, Mrs. John Remey, Amelia Earhart, Eleanor Smith Sullivan, and Viola Gentry. (Nassau County Museum Collection, Long Island Studies Institute, Hofstra University)

elected the first president and suggested their name—the Ninety-Nines, for the number of charter members.

▫ ▫ ▫

Le Roy Andrews became coach of the football Giants. The team finished the season with a record of 13–1–1, outscoring the opposition, 312–86.

▫ ▫ ▫

The Staten Island Stapletons played their first season in the NFL. (The team had begun as the Brooklyn Lions in 1926, and then were the New York Yankees in 1927 and 1928.) With Ken Strong in the backfield, they finished with a 3–4–3 record under coach Doug Wycoff. The team folded after the 1932 season, with a final record of 14–22–9.

1930—1939

The decade of the Great Depression was also a dynamic time for sports (and not merely because Prohibition ended in 1933). Under Robert Moses, the Department of Parks built or renovated dozens of playgrounds and in 1936 opened 11 pools, all built with federal funds. The Olympic swimming and diving trials were held in the new Astoria Pool, and the track and field trials at Triborough Stadium, a new municipal stadium on Randall's Island. To protest Germany's racist and anti-Semitic laws, basketball players at Long Island University refused to take part in the trials for the Berlin Games, and Marty Glickman was denied his chance at a gold medal in track. In baseball, the Yankees won five world championships as Babe Ruth's era ended and Joe DiMaggio's began. The Giants won the Fall Classic once, but lost to the Yankees twice. The Dodgers were terrible. Under Steve Owen, the football Giants reached the title game twice, and Fordham, New York University, and even Columbia were national powers. A series of colorful heavyweights generated terrific interest in boxing, culminating in two historic bouts at Yankee Stadium between Joe Louis and Max Schmeling—one man symbolizing the contradictions of race in America, and the other embodying Hitler's racist ideology. A team of New Yorkers won three consecutive world chess championships for the United States. The city's three baseball clubs began to regularly broadcast games over the radio—bringing sports into every neighborhood; transcending race, class, and ethnicity; and garnering fans from unexpected quarters. In 1939, television arrived, and, not surprisingly, the cameras immediately focused on sporting events.

1930

I had a better year than he did.

BABE RUTH

Asked about his salary of $80,000 being higher than President Herbert Hoover's salary of $75,000, Babe Ruth answered, "I know, but I had a better year than he did."

▪ ▪ ▪

On May 6, the Yankees acquired Red Ruffing, another Hall of Fame pitcher, from the Boston Red Sox. Ruffing won 20 games in four consecutive seasons with the Yanks.

▪ ▪ ▪

With Earle Sande up, Gallant Fox, trained by Jim Fitzsimmons, won the Belmont Stakes on June 7, capturing the Triple Crown.

▫ ▫ ▫

At Yankee Stadium on June 12, 79,222 were on hand for the heavyweight title fight between Max Schmeling and Jack Sharkey. (Gene Tunney had relinquished the crown on July 31, 1928.) After landing a low blow in the fourth round that left Schmeling writhing in pain, Sharkey was disqualified and Schmeling was awarded the decision. The event netted $150,000 for the Free Milk Fund for Babies.

▫ ▫ ▫

On July 5, about 15,000 fans attended a doubleheader between the New York Lincoln Giants and the Baltimore Black Sox, the first Negro League games played at Yankee Stadium. Staged as a benefit for the Brotherhood of Sleeping Car Porters, the day also featured running races; Bill "Bojangles" Robinson won a 100-meter race, running backward.

▫ ▫ ▫

At Dexter Park in Woodhaven on July 23, a crowd of 4,500 enjoyed the first professional night game in the metropolitan area. The visiting Springfields (named for their home field, Springfield Oval [Steinway Street and Thirty-fifth Avenue]) defeated the Bushwicks, 5–2.

▫ ▫ ▫

Lou Little (born Luigi Piccolo) became the football coach at Columbia University. He retired in 1956, having led the Lions to 110 victories.

▫ ▫ ▫

Thomas A. Armour won the Professional Golfers Association Championship at the Fresh Meadows Country Club on September 13, besting Gene Sarazen on the thirty-sixth hole.

▫ ▫ ▫

In the first America's Cup defense staged off Newport, Rhode Island, rather than in New York Harbor, the New York Yacht Club's *Enterprise* defeated Sir Thomas Lipton's *Shamrock V* in four straight races in September. *Enterprise* had lighter duraluminum spars; *Shamrock V* used traditional wood. After pursuing his life's ambition for 31 years, Sir Thomas declared, "I will not challenge again. We cannot win. Although they have beaten me, I could not have had better and fairer sportsmen to race against. You cannot blame them for doing their very best to win."

▫ ▫ ▫

In September, the 38-story Art Deco home of the Downtown Athletic Club was dedicated. The building housed a swimming pool, squash and handball courts, a gym, dining facilities, a miniature golf course, and rooms for members.

▫ ▫ ▫

Giants first baseman Bill Terry batted .401, the last National Leaguer to top .400.

▫ ▫ ▫

In their first season in the National Football League, the Brooklyn Dodgers finished with a 7–4–1 record under coach Al Jolley. In their second season, under LeRoy Andrews, the Dodgers finished second, with a 13–4 mark, .004 behind the Green Bay Packers (10–3–1). In 1945, they merged with the Boston Yanks and then folded; their final record was 60–100–9.

▫ ▫ ▫

The Yankees finished third, with a record of 86–58, in Bob Shawkey's single season as manager. On October 14, Joe McCarthy became manager and remained at the helm for 15 years.

▫ ▫ ▫

Celtic Park, the venerable athletic complex in Sunnyside, Queens, closed. The Celtic Park Apartments rose on the site.

▫ ▫ ▫

Constantine "Cus" D'Amato and Jack Barrow opened the Empire Sporting Club at the Gramercy

Gym on Fourteenth Street. D'Amato trained future champions Floyd Patterson, Mike Tyson, and José Torres there.

▪ ▪ ▪

In a charity game to raise funds for unemployment relief, the Giants defeated Knute Rockne's Notre Dame All-Stars, 22–0, before 50,000 fans at the Polo Grounds on December 14. Notre Dame featured the celebrated "Four Horsemen" of 1924 and members of the unbeaten 1929 team. The event raised $112,000.

1931

Steve Owen became coach of the Giants. He retired in 1953 with a record of 155–108–17 (.589), having led his teams to the NFL championship game eight times, winning twice.

▪ ▪ ▪

Behind captain George Gregory, a 6-foot, 4-inch center, Columbia University won its first Eastern Intercollegiate League championship. Gregory became the first black All-American basketball player.

▪ ▪ ▪

The Brooklyn Visitations bested the Fort Wayne Hoosiers, four games to two, for the American Basketball League championship. The league suspended operations after the season, but resumed in 1933.

▪ ▪ ▪

Jacob Ruppert bought the Newark Indians of the International League. Renamed the Bears, they remained the Yankees' top farm team until 1949.

▪ ▪ ▪

An international chess tournament ran from April 18 to May 3 at the Hotel Almanac in Lake Hopatcong, New Jersey. Former world champion José Raúl Capablanca won, and Isaac Kashdan, champion of the Manhattan Chess Club, was second. In

Prague on July 26, the American team—Frank J. Marshall, United States champion; Arthur Dake, Marshall Chess Club champion; Isaac Kashdan; Al Horowitz of Brooklyn; and Herman Steiner, also of New York—won the International Chess Federation's tournament for the world chess championship and took home the Hamilton-Russell Trophy. (The Soviet Union did not participate.) The Marshall Chess Club dedicated its new home, at 23 West Tenth Street, on December 20 with a dinner honoring the championship team.

▪ ▪ ▪

Freeport Municipal Stadium opened. Over the years, the venue hosted baseball, midget racing, and stock car racing. It closed in 1983 and was demolished a few years later.

▪ ▪ ▪

The Glasgow Celtics and the Hakoah All-Stars of the American Soccer League played a 1–1 tie game at the Polo Grounds on June 14 in front of 20,000 fans. Two weeks later, in the first soccer game played at Yankee Stadium, the Celtics defeated the Yankees, a merger of the Fall River Marksmen of Massachusetts and the New York Soccer Club, 4–1.

▪ ▪ ▪

Clair F. Bee became head basketball coach at Long Island University. He retired in 1952 with a record of 357–79. Originator of the 1–3–1 defense, Bee was enshrined in the Naismith Memorial Basketball Hall of Fame in 1968.

▪ ▪ ▪

On October 31, Max Carey replaced Wilbert Robinson as manager of the Dodgers—and, finally, the name Robins was retired.

▪ ▪ ▪

John Philip Sousa's last march, "The Circumnavigator's March," was performed for the first time on December 10 at a meeting of the Circumnavigators Club. Sousa himself was a member.

1932 ....

We wuz robbed!

JOE JACOBS

On January 23, the Brooklyn chapter of the Base Ball Writers Association of America selected Dodgers, the popular choice, as the official name of the National League team from the Borough of Churches.

. . .

The Rangers fell to the Maple Leafs, 6–4, in Toronto on April 9, losing the Stanley Cup finals in three straight.

. . .

On April 11, Mayor Jimmy Walker, Queens Borough President George U. Harvey, and former heavyweight champion and Bayside resident James J. "Gentleman Jim" Corbett took part in the groundbreaking for the Madison Square Garden Bowl (Northern Boulevard, between Forty-third and Forty-eighth Streets). The open-air arena, with seating for 72,000 on wooden bleachers, was intended for boxing, football, cycling, and track, but hosted only boxing. The first event was the heavyweight title fight between champion Max Schmeling and challenger Jack Shar-

key on June 21; a near-capacity crowd was on hand, with tickets priced from $2.30 to $23. Sharkey won a 15-round split decision. Schmeling's manager, Joe Jacobs, immediately shouted into the radio microphone, "We wuz robbed!" The arena became known as the "Jinx Bowl" because no champion successfully defended his title there.

. . .

In the resurrected Metropolitan Basketball League, the Brooklyn Visitations (the only team remaining from the first season) defeated the Brooklyn Jewels, two games to one, for the championship.

. . .

Businessman James "Soldier Boy" Semler and entertainer Bill "Bojangles" Robinson, backed by Nat Strong, founded the New York Black Yankees. The team joined the Negro National League in the middle of the 1936 season. The Black Yankees played their home games at Dexter Park; Freeport Municipal Stadium; Hinchcliffe Stadium in Paterson, New Jersey; and Triborough Stadium on Randall's Island before landing at Yankee Stadium in 1946 and 1947. In 1948, the team moved to Red Wing Stadium in Rochester, New York, and folded after the season.

. . .

The first of five public golf courses opened at Bethpage State Park on Long Island. Redesigned by A. W. Tillinghast, the Green Course had been the Lenox Hills Country Club. The Blue and Red Courses opened in 1935, and the famed Black Course in 1936, all designed by Tillinghast. The Yellow Course, designed by Alfred Tull, opened in 1958.

. . .

On June 3, Yankees first baseman Lou Gehrig hit four consecutive home runs against the Philadelphia Athletics in a 20–13 Yankee win.

. . .

After 30 years at the helm, John McGraw, in ill health, resigned as manager of the Giants on June 3.

Madison Square Garden Bowl, between Northern Boulevard (*bottom*) and the Long Island Rail Road tracks. (*Queensborough*, Queens Borough Public Library, Long Island Division)

Clubhouse at Bethpage State Park. (Queens Borough Public Library, Long Island Division, Post Card Collection)

Golf tournament at Bethpage State Park. (Queens Borough Public Library, Long Island Division, Post Card Collection)

Bill Terry was named his replacement. McGraw won 10 pennants and three World Series, with a final record of 2,583–1,791 (.591). Known as Little Napoleon, he holds the major league record for times thrown out of a game: 131. He died at age sixty on February 25, 1934.

□ □ □

Gene Sarazen won the United States Open at the Fresh Meadows Country Club on June 25. He had been club pro there from 1925 to 1931, but resigned because no club pro had ever won the event on his home course.

□ □ □

The New York Bloomer Girls defeated the Philadelphia Girls Athletic Club, 14–5, for the Eastern Female Baseball Championship. On August 22,

the team lost to the Cos Cob Club, 11–6, ending a 20-year unbeaten streak against all-woman teams.

□ □ □

The Bronx Bombers swept the Chicago Cubs in the World Series, scoring 37 runs and amassing 45 hits. In the third game, Babe Ruth called his shot, pointing to the seats where he would hit a home run. (Or did he? Frank Crosetti later suggested Ruth was only responding to taunts from the Cubs' dugout.) Gehrig followed Ruth's blast with his own homer; he hit .529, with three homers and eight RBIs.

□ □ □

Before 6,000 fans at Madison Square Garden on October 13, Eligio "Kid Chocolate" Sardinias won the featherweight title with a twelfth-round technical knockout over Brownsville's Lew Feldman. On December 9, again at the Garden, he defended his crown with a 15-round decision over Fidel Labarba. Labarba had injured his left eye during training, and the retina was permanently torn during the bout.

□ □ □

The Staten Island Stapletons of the NFL folded after the season, with a cumulative record of 14–22–9.

1933

On January 2, at Miami's inaugural Festival of Palms, precursor to the Orange Bowl, the University of Miami upset Manhattan College, 7–0.

□ □ □

At Madison Square Garden on February 10, heavyweight Primo Carnera knocked out Ernie Schaaf in the thirteenth round. The crowd of 20,000 booed the seemingly light punch, but Schaaf did not recover. He died of a blood clot on his brain four days later. Charles Norris, the chief medical examiner, determined that Schaaf had had an inflamed brain before he stepped into the ring that night.

⬛ ⬛ ⬛

Led by Nat Holman and Joe Lapchick, the Original Celtics beat the New York Renaissance and ended the Rens' 88-game winning streak. Still, the Rens beat the Celtics seven times that season and claimed the title of the world's best basketball team. Over the next four seasons, under owner and coach Bob Douglas, the Rens built a .906 winning percentage (473–49) with the same seven players: Clarence "Fats" Jenkins, Bill Yancey, John "Casey" Holt, James "Pappy" Ricks, Eyre "Bruiser" Saitch, Charles "Tarzan" Cooper, and Wee Willie Smith.

⬛ ⬛ ⬛

The Brooklyn Jewels defeated the Union City Reds in the final championship series of the Metropolitan Basketball League.

⬛ ⬛ ⬛

The Rangers beat the Maple Leafs, 1–0, on April 13 to take the Stanley Cup in four games.

⬛ ⬛ ⬛

To encourage home attendance during the tight years of the Great Depression, the Dodgers, Giants, and Yankees began a five-year ban on live radio broadcasts of their games.

⬛ ⬛ ⬛

Henrietta Sumner won the Annette Gipson All-Women Air Race on June 4, flying from Floyd Bennett Field, in Brooklyn, to Valley Stream and back in 17 minutes, 9 seconds.

⬛ ⬛ ⬛

Before 60,000 at Yankee Stadium on June 8, Max Baer, with a Star of David on his trunks, knocked out Max Schmeling in the tenth round. After a round in which he absorbed a terrific punch from Schmeling, Baer said, "I see three of him." Jack Dempsey, acting as his second, replied, "Hit the one in the middle."

⬛ ⬛ ⬛

Jack Dempsey with Max Baer after Baer defeated Max Schmeling, June 8, 1933. (Author's collection)

In London on June 23, the American chess team, led by Frank J. Marshall—with Isaac Kashdan, Reuben Fine, and Albert Simonson of New York and Arthur Dake of Oregon—successfully defended its world championship title.

⬛ ⬛ ⬛

On June 29, at Madison Square Garden Bowl before 40,000, challenger Primo Carnera (260 pounds) knocked out heavyweight champion Jack Sharkey (201 pounds) in the sixth round. It was Sharkey's first and only title defense. Carnera was the first Italian to wear the heavyweight crown.

⬛ ⬛ ⬛

For the first time since August 2, 1931, a span of 308 games, the Yankees were shut out, losing to Lefty Grove and the Athletics, 7–0, on August 3. Lou Gehrig played his 1,308th consecutive game on August 17, breaking Everett Scott's record.

⬛ ⬛ ⬛

At the Women's National Singles Championship at the West Side Tennis Club in Forest Hills on August 26, Helen Wills Moody lost a match for the first time since 1926, falling to Helen Jacobs, 8–6, 3–6, 3–0. (In no match since 1927 had Jacobs won a set from Moody.) In the third set, Moody informed the umpire that she could not continue, later saying, "I felt as if I were going to faint because of pain in my back and hip and a complete numbness of my right leg. The match was long and by defaulting I do not wish to detract from the excellence of Miss Jacobs's play." The previous Sunday, Moody had lost a set to Betty Nuthall, the first set she had lost in the United States since 1926.

□ □ □

The New York Bloomer Girls, founded in 1910, disbanded after the season, a victim of the Depression. Margaret Nabel had been the baseball team's manager since the early 1920s.

□ □ □

On October 1, about 25,000 fans at Yankee Stadium watched Babe Ruth take the mound and pitch a complete game to defeat the Red Sox, 6–5. He struck out none, walked three, and yielded 12 hits in his final appearance as a pitcher, a position he had not played in years. Naturally, he also hit a home run.

□ □ □

On July 2, left-hander Carl Hubbell of the Giants had pitched an 18-inning shutout to beat the St. Louis Cardinals, 1–0. The Giants won the National League pennant and faced the Washington Senators in the World Series. In game four on October 6, Hubbell pitched an 11-inning complete game for a 2–1 victory, recording 15 strikeouts and a 0.00 ERA in his two series starts. The Giants took the final game the next day, 4–3, on Mel Ott's home run in the tenth inning. With a record of 23–12, a 1.66 ERA, 156 strikeouts, and 10 shutouts, Hubbell was voted the National League's Most Valuable Player.

□ □ □

Backed by Damon Runyon and other sportswriters, Mike Jacobs formed the Twentieth Century Sporting Club to promote boxing matches. By the late 1930s, he virtually controlled the sport, in partnership with Madison Square Garden.

□ □ □

Thomas Lockhart, a promoter of amateur hockey games on Sunday afternoons at Madison Square Garden (25 cents admission), organized the Eastern Amateur Hockey League with three local teams: the St. Nicholas Hockey Club, the New York Athletic Club, and the Crescent Athletic–Hamilton Club of Brooklyn. The schedule listed 48 games, but with only 16 open dates at the Garden, Lockhart recorded many phantom results.

□ □ □

At Wrigley Field on December 17, the Chicago Bears defeated the Giants, 23–21, in the first championship game between the winners of the Eastern and Western Divisions of the NFL. Each member of the Bears received $210.34; the Giants, $140.22.

1934 ....

If they're ready for the fastball and don't get it, they can adjust to the breaking ball. But with a screwball, it isn't the break that fools the hitter, it's the change of speed. They don't time it. They couldn't time the screwball. They were all out in front of it.

CARL HUBBELL

Is Brooklyn still in the league?

BILL TERRY

Columbia University upset Stanford University in the Rose Bowl, 7–0.

□ □ □

On February 23, Casey Stengel was named manager of the Dodgers, succeeding Max Carey, whose record over two seasons was 146–161 (.476). He lasted for three seasons, finishing sixth, fifth, and seventh—with a record of 208–251 (.453).

□ □ □

Sportswriter Stan Lomax joined WOR radio for a nightly 15-minute sports show. He left the station in 1977, but took his show first to WNYC, and then to WBAI. He retired from the airwaves in 1981.

□ □ □

Barney Ross won a 15-round split decision over welterweight champion Jimmy McLarnin at Madison Square Garden Bowl on May 28. In a rematch on September 17 before 25,000, again at the Jinx Bowl, McLarnin won a split decision to reclaim the crown from Ross. The charity bout benefited the Christmas and Relief Fund of the *New York American.*

▪ ▪ ▪

A doubleheader between the Dodgers and the Giants on May 30 brought out the largest crowd recorded at Ebbets Field: 41,209.

▪ ▪ ▪

Before 56,000 at Madison Square Garden Bowl on June 14, challenger Max Baer dethroned heavyweight champion Primo Carnera with an eleventh-round knockout. On the undercard that night, James J. Braddock began his comeback by knocking out John "Corn" Griffin.

▪ ▪ ▪

In the All-Star Game at the Polo Grounds on July 10, Carl Hubbell of the Giants struck out in succession Babe Ruth, Lou Gehrig, Jimmie Foxx, Al Simmons, and Joe Cronin—all future Hall of Famers. Said Hubbell, "If they're ready for the fastball and don't get it, they can adjust to the breaking ball. But with a screwball, it isn't the break that fools the hitter, it's the change of speed. They don't time it. They couldn't time the screwball. They were all out in front of it." Still, the American League prevailed, 9–7.

▪ ▪ ▪

On July 27, the New York State Athletic Commission, the powerful governing body of boxing, rejected the application of Vera De Grasse for a license as manager for her brother, Pete De Grasse. Voicing opposition to women being involved in the sport, the commission also announced that it would not renew the license of Lena Levy, sister of King Levinsky.

▪ ▪ ▪

In front of 5,000 spectators at Dyckman Oval (104th Street and Nagle and Tenth Avenues) on August 30, Alberto Arizmendi of Mexico won a 15-round decision over Mike Belloise of the Bronx for the featherweight crown.

▪ ▪ ▪

In the America's Cup defense off Newport, Harold S. Vanderbilt's *Rainbow* defeated Thomas Octave Murdoch Sopwith's *Endeavour.* With Sopwith, a British aircraft manufacturer, as helmsman, *Endeavour* won the first two races, but *Rainbow* won the next four, taking the final race on September 25. President Franklin Delano Roosevelt, himself a sailor, watched the first two contests from Vincent Astor's yacht *Nourmahal.*

▪ ▪ ▪

Asked about the rival Dodgers early in the season, Giants manager Bill Terry answered, "Is Brooklyn still in the league?" But at the Polo Grounds on September 29 and 30, Casey Stengel's team took the last two games of the season to deny the Giants the pennant. The Giants had led the league since June 8 and enjoyed a seven-game advantage on September 7, but lost their last five games and finished two back.

▪ ▪ ▪

Babe Ruth and Lou Gehrig led the Yankees on a goodwill tour of Japan after the season. Ironically, Ruth's last game in pinstripes was played in Japan.

▪ ▪ ▪

In October, world-class figure skater Maribel Vinson became the first woman sports reporter at the *New York Times.*

▪ ▪ ▪

Dangling dates at Madison Square Garden, Thomas Lockhart convinced the four-team Tri-State Hockey League—the Bronx Tigers, Atlantic City Sea Gulls, Hershey B'ars, and Baltimore Orioles—to join his Eastern Amateur Hockey League. Lockhart remained president of the

EAHL and its successor, the Eastern Hockey League, until 1972.

• • •

On December 9, a crowd of 35,059 braved the 9-degree temperature at the Polo Grounds to watch the NFL title game. In what became known as the "sneaker game," the Giants scored 27 points in the fourth quarter to defeat the Bears, 30–13. To cope with the icy field, the Giants had borrowed basketball sneakers from Manhattan College. Former New York University All-America Ken Strong scored 17 points, a title game record. Each member of the Giants received $621; the Bears, $414.02.

• • •

On December 29, 16,188 attended the first college basketball games at Madison Square Garden, an event organized by sportswriter Ned Irish. In the first game, Westminster College beat St. John's University, 37–33; New York University then defeated Notre Dame, 25–18.

1935 ....

Nat Strong died on January 10. He had operated semi-pro baseball teams and controlled bookings in the metropolitan area for three decades. For years, he reserved Dexter Park on Memorial Day, July Fourth, and Labor Day for Negro League doubleheaders. Nat Strong, Inc., continued under Bill Leuschner.

• • •

At the Westminster Dog Show at Madison Square Garden on February 13, Mrs. Sherman Hoyt took her standard poodle, Champion Nunsoe Duc de la Terrace of Blakeen, to the Best in Show award, the first woman handler to do so.

• • •

Jack Dempsey opened a restaurant on Eighth Avenue, opposite Madison Square Garden. It later moved to 1619 Broadway, between Forty-ninth

Jack Dempsey's Restaurant, at Fiftieth Street and Eighth Avenue, opposite Madison Square Garden. (Author's collection)

and Fiftieth Streets. He closed the establishment in 1974.

• • •

In front of reporters and with the Sultan of Swat at his side, Yankees owner Colonel Jacob Ruppert gave Babe Ruth his unconditional release on February 26.

• • •

The Brooklyn Visitations won the American Basketball League championship over the New York Jewels, three games to two.

• • •

The Yankees named Lou Gehrig as team captain on April 21, and he remained captain until his death.

• • •

The *New York Times* began a weekly bridge column by Albert H. Morehead; it became a daily feature in 1959.

• • •

Abe Manley and his wife, Effa, formed the Brooklyn Eagles in the Negro National League. Mayor Fiorello La Guardia threw out the first ball for the team's inaugural home game at Ebbets Field; the Eagles lost to the Homestead Grays, 21–7. Lacking fan support, the Eagles moved to Newark the next year, merging with the Newark Dodgers.

· · ·

The New York Cubans, a baseball club, was organized out of the Cuban All-Stars barnstorming teams. The Cubans disbanded after the 1936 season, re-formed in 1939, joined the Negro American League in 1949, and folded in 1950.

· · ·

On May 3, twenty-four-year-old Samuel Reshevsky of the Marshall Chess Club won the international masters tournament in England. He had come to New York from Poland in 1920.

· · ·

In their third title fight in a year, Barney Ross recaptured the welterweight crown from Jimmy McLarnin in a unanimous decision before 40,000 spectators at the Polo Grounds on May 28. Jack Dempsey was the referee. The event raised $27,921 for the Milk Fund for Babies.

· · ·

In a steady rain on June 8, 25,000 saw Omaha, son of Triple Crown winner Gallant Fox, win the Belmont Stakes and capture the Triple Crown. Jim Fitzsimmons trained both sire and son.

· · ·

Challenger James J. Braddock took a 15-round decision from heavyweight champion Max Baer in front of 30,000 at Madison Square Garden Bowl on June 13. Two years before, Braddock had been washed up and on relief in New Jersey. Damon Runyon dubbed him "Cinderella Man." Afterward, Braddock told reporters, "I'm glad I won, because it will please the wife and kids. I've got the prettiest kids in the world, and tonight I can go home to them and say, 'Your daddy is champ.'"

· · ·

The Kissena Park Golf Course opened in Flushing, Queens. Designed by John Van Kleek, it is the shortest course in the city at 4,665 yards; it was redesigned by Stephen Kay in the 1990s. Also, the 18-hole pitch-and-putt course opened at Jacob

Riis Park, another improvement implemented under Robert Moses.

· · ·

In his first fight in New York, twenty-year-old Joe Louis, the "Brown Bomber," scored a sixth-round technical knockout over former heavyweight champion Primo Carnera before 60,000 at Yankee Stadium on June 25. The Milk Fund received part of the gate. On September 24, in front of 88,150—the biggest crowd ever for a boxing match at the Stadium—Louis knocked out former champion Max Baer in the fourth round.

· · ·

Herschel "Rip" Day, an athletic promoter in Harlem, founded the Brown Bombers, a professional football team (the name honored Joe Louis); its home field was Dyckman Oval. Under head coach Frederick D. "Fritz" Pollard, a former NFL player and coach, the team took on white squads and went 35–38. Despite the team's more than respectable record, no players were recruited by NFL clubs, and it folded in the 1940s.

· · ·

On July 14, the 225 caddies at the Dyker Beach Golf Course went on strike, demanding an increase from 75 cents to $1 a round. Within two weeks, the young men were back at work, without their raise.

· · ·

In Warsaw on August 31, the American chess team, led by Frank J. Marshall—with Isaac Kashdan, Reuben Fine, Abraham Kupchik, Al Horowitz, and Arthur Dake—again won the International Chess Federation tournament.

· · ·

A crowd of 18,000 attended the United States Open Polo Championship at International Field at the Meadow Brook Club in Westbury on September 21. Greentree (John Hay "Jock" Whitney, Tommy Hitchcock Jr., Gerald Balding, and G. H. "Pete" Bostwick) defeated Aurora (Jimmy Mills,

Thomas Hitchcock Jr. at the Meadow Brook Club, Westbury. (Nassau County Museum Collection, Long Island Studies Institute, Hofstra University)

Member of the New York Rovers at Madison Square Garden, 1942. (Queens Borough Public Library, Long Island Division, Frederick J. Weber Photographs)

Seymour Knox, Ebby Gerry, and Billy Post), 7–6, in overtime.

□ □ □

Olin J. Stephens designed the New York 32 for the New York Yacht Club. The Henry B. Nevins Shipyard on City Island, in the Bronx, built 20 of the one-design racing boats for club members.

□ □ □

The Downtown Athletic Club awarded the first Heisman Trophy (named for John W. Heisman, the club's athletic director), for the nation's best college football player, to Jay Berwanger of the University of Chicago. The sculptor was Frank Eliscu; the model was New York University footballer Ed Smith.

□ □ □

After fielding a team off and on since 1893, St. Francis College dropped football.

□ □ □

The New York Rovers joined the Eastern Amateur Hockey League and remained in the league until 1952. They were league champions in 1939, 1942, and 1950.

□ □ □

The Detroit Lions beat the Giants, 26–7, in the NFL championship game in Detroit on December 15.

1936 ....

The Long Island University Blackbirds boycotted the Olympic trials, held at Madison Square Garden, to protest American participation in the Berlin Games. Remembering their stand 60 years later, Leo Merson, one of three Jewish players on the team, said, "It was emotional, it was traumatic, it was a lost opportunity, but we thought it had to be done. And I'm not sorry." On December 30, LIU's 43-game winning streak ended with a 45–41 loss to Stanford.

□ □ □

At the Broadway Arena in Brooklyn on March 17, lightweight Lou Ambers knocked out twenty-two-year-old Tony Scarpati of Brooklyn in the seventh round. (Scarpati had won the Golden Gloves featherweight title in 1931.) Scarpati fell into a coma and died three days later. On April 7, Ambers returned to the Broadway Arena to fight Pete Mascia on a benefit card for Scarpati's family; a crowd of 3,066 attended that night, but the event raised only $1,684.

▪ ▪ ▪

The Philadelphia Sphas (South Philadelphia Hebrew Association) dethroned the Brooklyn Visitations as champions of the American Basketball League, four games to three.

▪ ▪ ▪

The Pell Golf Course in the Bronx was redesigned by John Van Kleek and renamed the Pelham Golf Course. The Split Rock Golf Course, constructed with funds from the Works Progress Administration, opened immediately adjacent.

▪ ▪ ▪

Real-estate developers Klein & Jackson acquired the Old Country Club in Flushing for $450,000 on April 30.

▪ ▪ ▪

On May 3, Joe DiMaggio had three hits in his first game as a Yankee as the Bronx Bombers beat the St. Louis Browns, 14–5. On July 7, he became the first rookie to start in an All-Star Game.

▪ ▪ ▪

In a match fraught with symbolism, former heavyweight champion Max Schmeling of Germany

knocked out Joe Louis in the twelfth round before a packed Yankee Stadium on June 19. For some, Schmeling's victory confirmed the Nazi ideology of Aryan supremacy.

▪ ▪ ▪

Immediately before the Louis–Schmeling bout, boxing promoter and former deputy boxing commissioner Tom O'Rourke died of a heart attack in Schmeling's dressing room. The eighty-two-year-old O'Rourke promoted matches at the Polo Grounds and managed bantamweight champion George Dixon and welterweight champion Joe Wolcott; earlier, he had run four clubs that could legally stage boxing matches under the old Horton Act: the Broadway, the Lenox, the Madison Square, and the Coney Island Athletic Clubs.

▪ ▪ ▪

It was a big year for swimming pools. The Department of Parks, under Robert Moses, opened 11 over about eight weeks, and Mayor Fiorello La Guardia was on hand for each dedication. Hamilton Fish Pool (Pitt and Houston Streets) opened on June 24; the Olympic team trained there before the 1952 Helsinki Games. The opening of Thomas Jefferson Pool (East 112th Street and First Avenue) on June 27 attracted a crowd of 10,000. Astoria Pool in Astoria Park, the largest of the 11, opened on July 2, just in time to host the Olympic swimming and diving trials; it also was the site of the trials for the 1964 Tokyo Games. Joseph H. Lyons Pool on Staten Island (Pier 6 and Victory Boulevard) opened on July 7; La Guardia called the facility "a monument to the progressive government which would not and could not see unemployed men on the breadline." Highbridge Pool (West 173rd Street and Amsterdam Avenue) opened on July 14. Sunset Pool in Brooklyn (Seventh Avenue, between Forty-first and Forty-fourth Streets) opened on July 20. In the Bronx, Crotona Pool (173rd Street and Fulton Avenue) opened on July 24. The McCarren Park Play Center in Greenpoint (Lorimer Street, between Bayard Street and

Split Rock Golf Course. (Lehman College, Bronx Chamber of Commerce Collection)

Astoria Pool. (New York City Parks Photo Archive)

Driggs Avenue) opened on July 31; it closed in 1984 and suffered a disastrous fire in 1987. Betsy Head Pool in Brownsville (Boyland, Livonia, and Dumont Avenues), an expansion and modernization of a facility built in 1915, opened on August 6. On August 8, 25,000 attended the dedication of Colonial Park Pool in Harlem (West 146th Street and Bradhurst Avenue); it was later renamed the Jackie Robinson Pool. Finally, about 40,000 attended the opening of the Red Hook Pool (Bay Street, between Clinton and Henry Streets) on August 17.

■ ■ ■

The Olympic track and field trials were held at Triborough Stadium on Randall's Island before capacity crowds on July 11 and 12. During the games, American officials bumped Marty Glickman and Sam Stoller (the only two Jews on the track team) from the 400-meter relay, replacing them with Jesse Owens and Ralph Metcalfe. Bronx-born Glickman, a star athlete for the Grand Street Boys Club and Syracuse University, believed that Avery Brundage did not want to further embarrass Adolf Hitler by having Jews beat his Aryans. Glickman went on to become the consummate New York sports announcer, calling

games for the Knicks, Jets, and Giants and for local colleges.

■ ■ ■

Enhanced with sand shipped by barge from the Rockaways, Orchard Beach opened on July 25. The landscape architect was Gilmore Clarke, and Aymar Embury II designed the bathhouse and pavilion. The complex was completed in 1938.

■ ■ ■

Olympic track and field trials at Triborough Stadium on Randall's Island, July 1936. (New York City Parks Photo Archive)

Orchard Beach. (Lehman College, Bronx Chamber of Commerce Collection)

On Staten Island, the Children's Aid Society's Goodhue Center Pool, built by the WPA, opened on August 13.

▪ ▪ ▪

Before 30,000 at Yankee Stadium on August 18, Joe Louis knocked out former heavyweight champion Jack Sharkey in the third round of a nontitle bout.

▪ ▪ ▪

On September 3, at Madison Square Garden, Lou Ambers won the lightweight crown with a 15-round decision over Tony Canzoneri. On the same card, featherweight champion Mike Belloise of the Bronx knocked out challenger Dave Crowley of England in the ninth round.

▪ ▪ ▪

With a sweep of the Cleveland Indians, 11–3 and 12–9, on September 9, the Yankees clinched their eighth pennant, finishing 19 1/2 games ahead of the Detroit Tigers, the widest margin in team history. The Giants won the National League flag. The Yankees won the World Series in six games. Lou Gehrig was named the American League's Most Valuable Player for the second time, and Carl Hubbell won his second National League Most Valuable Player Award.

▪ ▪ ▪

At the Garden City Golf Club on September 19, John W. Fischer defeated Jock McLean on the thirty-seventh hole to win the United States Men's Amateur Golf Championship.

▪ ▪ ▪

On October 4, the Dodgers fired manager Casey Stengel after three mediocre seasons. Burleigh Grimes was named his successor on November 5.

▪ ▪ ▪

George Preston Marshall revived the Vanderbilt Cup Race with a new course at Roosevelt Raceway. Driving an Alfa Romeo, Tazio Nuvolari won the 300-mile event on October 12.

▪ ▪ ▪

St. John's University purchased the Hillcrest Golf Club (Union Turnpike and Utopia Parkway) for its new campus but construction did not begin until 1953.

▪ ▪ ▪

In the first season of the American Football League, the New York Yanks went 5–3–2 under coach Jack McBride, and the Brooklyn Tigers went 0–6–1 under coach Mike Palm. In 1937, the Tigers moved to Rochester.

▪ ▪ ▪

In soccer, D.S.C. Brooklyn won the National Amateur Cup.

Track and grandstand built for the Vanderbilt Cup Race at Roosevelt Raceway, 1936. (Nassau County Museum Collection, Long Island Studies Institute, Hofstra University)

Hillcrest Golf Club, 1927. New suburban homes are encroaching on the course. (Queens Borough Public Library, Long Island Division, Eugene Armbruster Photographs)

◦ ◦ ◦

On Thanksgiving Day, New York University upset powerful Fordham University, 7–6, before 50,000 fans at Yankee Stadium. This was the last game played by Vincent Lombardi, Fordham class of 1937, one of the "Seven Blocks of Granite."

◦ ◦ ◦

With 29,545 on hand at the Polo Grounds on December 13, the Green Bay Packers defeated the Boston Redskins, 21–6, in the NFL title game. Redskins owner George Marshall, disgusted by the lack of fan support in Boston, had refused to host the championship game and moved the team to Washington, D.C., the next season.

◦ ◦ ◦

The skating rink at Rockefeller Center opened on Christmas Day. Omero C. Catan, "Mr. First," was the first paying patron, although twelve-year-old Elinor Weiler took the ice for an exhibition waltz with an eighty-eight-year-old man before the public was admitted.

1937 ....

What'd dem bums do today?

ANONYMOUS CABDRIVER

Peter Robert Gagliardi (also known as Bobby Gleason) opened Gleason's Gym in the Bronx at 434 Westchester Avenue (between 149th Street and Third Avenue). When the building was slated for demolition in 1974, the gym moved to 252 West Thirtieth Street in Manhattan, and then to 83 Front Street in Brooklyn in 1984. For many years, Gleason's was a popular training ground for aspiring and established boxers, including Jake La-Motta, Mike Belloise, Phil Terranova, and Benny "Kid" Paret.

◦ ◦ ◦

In a nontitle bout before only 7,000 at Madison Square Garden on March 12, Henry Armstrong knocked out Mike Belloise to bolster his claim to the world featherweight crown. (Neither fighter came in under the class weight of 126.) On August 10, the New York State Athletic Commission declared the title vacant because Belloise was ill; in truth, he had not fought at that weight since becoming champion nearly a year earlier. The commission agreed to recognize the winner of the fight between Armstrong and Peter Sarron on October 29. Before 14,000 at the Garden, Armstrong knocked out Sarron in the sixth round to claim the title, recognized by both the New York State Athletic Commission and the National Boxing Association. This was the first night of boxing at the Garden under promoter Mike Jacobs. Known as Hurricane Hank and Homicide Hank, Armstrong fought 27 times in 1937. He relinquished the featherweight crown as undefeated champion in December 1938.

◦ ◦ ◦

Amateur golf champion Maureen Orcutt joined the sports department of the *New York Times*, covering women's golf and writing a regular column, "Women in Sports." She retired in 1972.

◦ ◦ ◦

Max Rosner, owner of the Bushwicks, and Bill Leuschner of Nat Strong, Inc., organized the

Metropolitan Baseball Association for semi-pro teams in the Greater New York area. Teams had to have a quality home field with lights for night games. Because of the ban on night games during World War II, the association was suspended, but re-formed in 1946.

■ ■ ■

The right field grandstand at Yankee Stadium was extended, and the original wooden bleachers were replaced with concrete stands, increasing capacity from 62,000 to 71,699.

■ ■ ■

On April 15, the Detroit Red Wings defeated the Rangers, 3–0, to take the Stanley Cup in five games.

■ ■ ■

Before 11,000 at Madison Square Garden on May 7, Lou Ambers defended his lightweight crown with a 15-round decision over Tony Canzoneri. Ambers had beaten Canzoneri for the title on September 3, 1936.

■ ■ ■

On May 27, Giant ace Carl Hubbell beat the Cincinnati Reds, 3–2, for his 24th straight victory, a major league record. (He lost his next start, on May 31, to the Dodgers, 10–3.) His streak had begun on July 17, 1936.

■ ■ ■

Sports cartoonist Willard Mullin of the *World-Telegram* created a new symbol for the Dodgers—the Bum. He got the idea when a cabby who picked him up outside Ebbets Field asked, "What'd dem bums do today?"

■ ■ ■

Heavyweight champion James J. Braddock failed to appear for the weigh-in on June 3 for a scheduled title bout against Max Schmeling at Madison Square Garden Bowl. Braddock was training in Michigan to face Joe Louis in Chicago. The New York State Athletic Commission fined and suspended both Braddock and his manager, Joe Gould.

Promoter Mike Jacobs (*center*) announcing a bout between heavyweight champion James J. Braddock (*left*) and Max Schmeling (*right*). Jacobs subsequently had Braddock back out of the match in order to fight Joe Louis. (Museum of the City of New York, *Look* Collection)

Schmeling said, "The ruling is a joke. . . . The commission should have declared the championship vacated. I certainly did not expect them to name me champion, and I would not have had it that way."

■ ■ ■

On June 5, War Admiral, son of Man o' War, won the Belmont Stakes in a record 2 minutes, 28³/₅ seconds, bettering his sire's mark by ¹/₅ second, to capture the Triple Crown.

■ ■ ■

Driving for the German company Auto Union, Bernd Rosemeyer won the 300-mile Vanderbilt Cup Race before 70,000 at Roosevelt Raceway on July 5; his top speed was 159 miles an hour. The event was never staged again.

■ ■ ■

The new bathhouse, designed by Aymar Embury II, opened at Jacob Riis Park.

■ ■ ■

On August 5, defending the America's Cup off Newport, Harold S. Vanderbilt's *Ranger* (designed by Olin J. Stephens) defeated the English challenger, Thomas Octave Murdoch Sopwith's *Endeavour II*, for the fourth straight time.

■ ■ ■

Jacob Riis Park, 1946. (Queens Borough Public Library, Long Island Division, Queens Chamber of Commerce Collection)

Fred Frankhouse of the Dodgers hurled a no-hitter against the Reds on August 27. The umpires called the game with two out in the bottom of the eighth on account of rain.

◻ ◻ ◻

For the second straight year, Joe McCarthy's Yankees beat Bill Terry's Giants, with slugging first baseman Mel Ott, in the World Series. Lefty Gomez bested Carl Hubbell in the first game and won the fifth and final game. Joe DiMaggio led the American League with a career-high 46 homers and 167 RBIs that season.

◻ ◻ ◻

About 35,000 were at the Polo Grounds on September 23 for the Carnival of Champions, four title bouts promoted by Mike Jacobs. Welterweight champion Barney Ross decisioned Ceferino Garcia of the Philippines; lightweight champion Lou Ambers defeated Pedro Montañez of Puerto Rico; Fred Apostoli scored a technical knockout over middleweight champion Marcel Thil of France; and Harry Jeffra won a decision over bantamweight champion Sixto Escobar of Puerto Rico.

◻ ◻ ◻

At the Polo Grounds on October 17, the football teams of Fordham and the University of Pittsburgh battled to a scoreless tie, the third straight year they played to 0–0.

1938 ....

At the insistence of National League president Ford Frick, the Dodgers hired Larry MacPhail as executive vice president on January 19, with full control over personnel and operations. One of his first decisions was to change the team's colors from green to blue.

◻ ◻ ◻

At Madison Square Garden on February 23, heavyweight champion Joe Louis knocked out Nathan Mann in the third round.

◻ ◻ ◻

Victory Lanes opened at Castleton Corners on Staten Island. The victim of high taxes and the smoking ban, the bowling alley closed in 2003.

◻ ◻ ◻

The Metropolitan Basketball Writers Association organized the first National Invitational Tournament for college basketball teams. Before 14,497 fans at Madison Square Garden on March 16, Temple University defeated the University of Colorado, 60–36, for the first championship.

◻ ◻ ◻

The Jersey Reds defeated the New York Jewels in six games for the American Basketball League championship.

◻ ◻ ◻

An all-time-record crowd of 83,533 (81,891 paid) attended a doubleheader at Yankee Stadium on May 30; 511 fans received refunds because there was no room. The Yankees swept the Red Sox, 10–0 and 5–4

◻ ◻ ◻

Before 30,000 at Madison Square Garden Bowl on May 31, featherweight champion Henry Armstrong wrested the world welterweight title from Barney Ross in a 15-round decision. The Jinx Bowl continued to bedevil champions.

◻ ◻ ◻

On June 15, in the first night game at Ebbets Field, Johnny Vander Meer of the Reds beat the Dodgers,

6–0, with his second consecutive no-hitter, the only pitcher to accomplish that feat.

▪ ▪ ▪

Before a capacity crowd at Yankee Stadium on June 22, heavyweight champion Joe Louis knocked out Max Schmeling at 2 minutes, 4 seconds of the first round, the swiftest knockout in the Brown Bomber's career. While many saw this as a contest between Nazi Germany and democratic America, Schmeling and Louis bore no personal animosity and remained lifelong friends.

▪ ▪ ▪

In July, Parks Commissioner Robert Moses published *The Future of Jamaica Bay*, criticizing the Sanitation Department's plans to dump garbage there. Moses suggested that the bay was better suited for recreation and urged protecting it from development. After World War II, Moses had sewage-treatment plants built to improve the bay's water quality and added recreational facilities.

▪ ▪ ▪

After filing for a nonstop flight to Long Beach, California, Douglas Corrigan took off from Floyd Bennett Field at 5:15 A.M. on July 17. He disappeared in a cloudbank, and 28 hours, 13 minutes, and 3,150 miles later landed in Dublin. He asked the airport workers, "Just got in from New York. Where am I?" Wrong Way Corrigan became a folk hero, celebrated on August 5 with a ticker-tape parade up Broadway.

▪ ▪ ▪

On July 30, baseball commissioner Kennesaw Mountain Landis suspended Yankee outfielder Jake Powell for 10 days for remarks he had made in a radio interview in Chicago the day before. He claimed to be a police officer in Dayton, Ohio, in the off-season (which was not true) and said that he had fun "cracking niggers over the head."

▪ ▪ ▪

Don Budge, in the far court, facing Charles Hare of Great Britain for the Men's National Singles Championship at the West Side Tennis Club in Forest Hills, September 1938. (Nassau County Museum Collection, Long Island Studies Institute, Hofstra University)

The Queens Valley Golf Club, near Kew Gardens, was sold to developers for $750,000 on August 15. It had opened in 1922.

▪ ▪ ▪

At a packed Madison Square Garden on August 17, Henry Armstrong, already holding the featherweight and welterweight titles, won an unpopular split decision over Lou Ambers to claim the lightweight (135 pounds) championship, becoming the first fighter to hold three titles simultaneously.

▪ ▪ ▪

At the West Side Tennis Club on September 24, Don Budge defeated Gene Mako, 6–3, 6–8, 6–2, 6–1, in the Men's National Singles Championship, becoming the first man to hold the Australian, French, British, and American championships simultaneously.

▪ ▪ ▪

The Yankees—powered by Lou Gehrig, Joe DiMaggio, Bill Dickey, Joe Gordon, Frank Crosetti, and Tommy Henrich—swept the Cubs in the World Series. Red Ruffing won two complete games, and Lefty Gomez and Monte Pearson won the other two.

· · ·

Shortstop Leo Durocher, thirty-two years old, was named manager of the Dodgers on October 12, replacing Burleigh Grimes (131–171, .434).

· · ·

Before 6,000 at St. Nicholas Arena (Sixty-sixth Street and Columbus Avenue) on October 17, Joey Archibald won a 15-round decision over former champion Mike Belloise to claim the featherweight title vacated by Henry Armstrong.

· · ·

Caroline Marshall, wife of American chess champion Frank J. Marshall, organized the first United States Women's Chess Championship; it was held at Rockefeller Center.

· · ·

Dyckman Oval was demolished.

· · ·

With 15,725 on hand at Madison Square Garden on November 25, Henry Armstrong defended his welterweight title with a 15-round decision over Ceferino Garcia.

· · ·

In the title game before 48,120 fans at the Polo Grounds on December 11, the Giants defeated the Packers, 23–17, on a pass from quarterback Ed Danowski to fullback Hank Soar, who dragged defenders into the end zone for the winning score. After his football career, Soar became a respected major league umpire and was at first base for Don Larsen's perfect game in the 1956 World Series.

1939 ....

Fans, for the past two weeks you have been reading about the bad break I got. Yet today, I consider myself the luckiest man on the face of the earth.

LOU GEHRIG

Before 17,350 at Madison Square Garden on January 25, heavyweight champion Joe Louis defended his title for the fifth time, stopping challenger John Henry Lewis at 2 minutes, 29 seconds of the first round. Lewis was recognized as the world light-heavyweight champion everywhere except New York State because he refused to fight the top challenger, Tiger Jack Fox.

· · ·

On February 4, Glenn Cunningham won the Wanamaker Mile at the Millrose Games for a record sixth time in seven years. Since the early 1930s, the race had gone off at 10:00 P.M., originally to be broadcast live over Ted Husing's radio show. In 2007, it moved to 9:00 P.M. for television.

· · ·

Brooklyn's undefeated James Madison High School won the Public Schools Athletic League basketball championship. The team's five starters and the sixth man all played in the pros: Stanley Waxman, Larry Baxter, Fuzzy Levane, Freddie Lewis, and the Rader twins: Lennie and Howie.

· · ·

At Madison Square Garden on March 22, Long Island University defeated Loyola of Chicago, 44–32, to win the National Invitational Tournament. Bradley University upset St. John's University, 40–35, for third place.

· · ·

The New York Jewels took three straight from the Jersey Reds to win the American Basketball League title.

· · ·

The New York Renaissance finished its season with a record of 110–7. In the world's basketball championship in Chicago, the Rens defeated the New York Yankees, 30–21; the Harlem Globetrotters (a Chicago team), 27–23; and, in the title game on March 28, the Oshkosh All-Stars, 34–25.

· · ·

Glenn Cunningham winning the 1,500-meter race at the Olympic trials at Triborough Stadium on Randall's Island, July 1936. (Alajos Schuszler/New York City Parks Photo Archive)

On March 31, at Madison Square Garden, welterweight champion Henry Armstrong defeated Davey Day.

▪ ▪ ▪

At 12:40 A.M. on April 3, in the eighth minute of the third overtime period in the seventh game of the Stanley Cup semifinals, Mel Hill of the Boston Bruins scored to beat the Rangers, 4–3, at Boston Garden. The Rangers had lost the first three games of the series, the first two in overtime on sudden-death goals by Hill.

▪ ▪ ▪

The Dodgers broke with the Yankees and Giants and ended their five-year ban on live radio broadcasts of their games. WOR paid $77,000 to carry the Dodger games, and Larry MacPhail brought in Red Barber, the Reds broadcaster. The Yankees hired Mel Allen and Arch McDonald that season. Except for his years in the military, Mel Allen remained the voice of the Yankees until 1964.

▪ ▪ ▪

Lou Gehrig played his last game for the New York Yankees on April 30. After 2,130 consecutive games, the thirty-five-year-old first baseman took

himself out of the lineup on May 2 "for the good of the team." Babe Dahlgren replaced him in the game against the Tigers in Detroit (the Yankees won, 22–2). The Iron Horse explained to the press, "I haven't been a bit of good to the team since the season started. It would not be fair to the boys, to Joe or to the baseball public for me to try going on. In fact, it would not be fair to myself. It's tough to see your mates on base, have a chance to win a ball game, and not be able to do anything about it." He was diagnosed with amyotrophic lateral sclerosis, known since as Lou Gehrig's Disease. On July 4, 62,000 attended Lou Gehrig Appreciation Day at Yankee Stadium; the Yankees retired his number, 4, the first number to be retired in American professional sports. Gehrig said to the crowd:

Fans, for the past two weeks you have been reading about the bad break I got. Yet today, I consider myself the luckiest man on the face of the earth. I have been in ballparks for seventeen years, and I have never received anything but kindness and encouragement from you fans. Look at these grand men. Which of you wouldn't consider it the highlight of his career just to associate with them for even one day? Sure I'm lucky. Who wouldn't consider it an honor to have known Jacob Ruppert? Also, the builder of baseball's greatest empire, Ed Barrow? To have spent six years with that wonderful little fellow, Miller Huggins? Then to have spent the next nine years with that understanding leader, that smart student of psychology, the best manager in baseball today, Joe McCarthy? Sure I'm lucky. When the New York Giants, a team you would give your right arm to beat, and vice versa, sends you a gift—that's something. When everybody down to the groundskeepers and those boys in white coats remember you with trophies—that's something. When you have a wonderful mother-in-law who takes sides with you in squabbles with her own daughter—that's something. When you have a father and a mother who work all their lives so you can have an education and build your body—it's a blessing. When you have a wife who has been a tower of strength and shown more courage than you dreamed existed—that's the finest I know. So I close in saying I may have had a tough break, but I have an awful lot to live for.

He ended his 13-year career with 1,995 RBIs, a .340 batting average, and 493 home runs. Gehrig, the "Pride of the Yankees," died on June 2, 1941.

Sporting events were televised for the first time. On May 17, W2XBS, NBC's experimental television station, broadcast a baseball game between Princeton and Columbia at Baker Field (Columbia lost, 2–1), with Bill Stern doing the play-by-play. The transmitter atop the Empire State Building beamed the game to receivers at Radio City and the World's Fair. Three days later, the first event was televised from Madison Square Garden, part of a six-day bicycle race. On August 26, NBC broadcast the first major league baseball game, a doubleheader between the Dodgers and the Reds at Ebbets Field. Red Barber called the game, and the three radio sponsors—Wheaties, Ivory Soap, and Mobil gasoline—had a single commercial between half-innings. On October 22, in the first Sunday television broadcast, the Brooklyn Dodgers and Philadelphia Eagles played the first televised professional football game. The following Saturday evening, W2XBS broadcast boxing from the Ridgewood Grove Sporting Club. There were about 1,000 sets in the city by the end of the year.

At the Meadow Brook Club on June 11, the American team of Michael Phipps, Tommy Hitchcock Jr., Stewart Inglehart, and Winston Guest defeated the British, 9–4, taking the International Polo Challenge Cup series by 2–0.

Swimming champions Eleanor Holm, Johnny Weissmuller, and Buster Crabbe performed at Billy Rose's Aquacade at the World's Fair. The first woman swimmer selected for three Olympics (1928, 1932, and 1936), Brooklyn-born Holm had been thrown off the 1936 team for drinking champagne and breaking curfew on the ship carrying the team to Europe.

Michael Phipps in action at the Meadow Brook Club, 1934. (Nassau County Museum Collection, Long Island Studies Institute, Hofstra University)

The Aquacade, built as the New York State Pavilion for the 1939 World's Fair. (Author's collection)

Eleanor Holm and Johnny Weismuller at the Aquacade, 1939. (Queens Borough Public Library, Long Island Division, World's Fair Collection)

■ ■ ■

In a referendum on June 20, New Jersey voters overwhelmingly approved an amendment to the state constitution to permit pari-mutuel betting on horse races, returning the Sport of Kings to the Garden State after 42 years.

■ ■ ■

At Yankee Stadium on July 11, 62,892 saw Joe DiMaggio hit a home run and lead the American League to a 3–1 victory in the All-Star Game. Manager Joe McCarthy started six of his Yankees: Joe Gordon at second base, Red Rolfe at third base, DiMaggio in center field, George Selkirk in left field, Bill Dickey catching, and Red Ruffing on the mound. "You have to play your best men," he said.

■ ■ ■

Henry Picard defeated Byron Nelson on the first playoff hole to capture the PGA Championship at the Pomonok Country Club in Queens on July 15.

■ ■ ■

At Yankee Stadium before 29,088 on August 22, Lou Ambers regained the lightweight crown with a controversial decision over Henry Armstrong, who battered Ambers throughout the fight but was penalized five rounds for low blows. It was Armstrong's first loss in 47 bouts over three years.

■ ■ ■

The Yankees beat the Reds, 7–4, in 10 innings on October 8 for their second consecutive sweep of the World Series and unprecedented fourth straight world championship. Rookie outfielder Charlie Keller hit .438 in the series. Joe DiMaggio was named the American League's Most Valuable Player.

■ ■ ■

At Madison Square Garden on September 20, Joe Louis knocked out challenger Bob Pastor in the eleventh round to retain his heavyweight crown.

■ ■ ■

On October 2, at Madison Square Garden, challenger Ceferino Garcia won the middleweight championship with a seventh-round knockout of Fred Apostoli.

■ ■ ■

On December 10, the Giants lost the NFL title game to the Packers, 27–0, in Milwaukee.

1940—1949

During World War II, many athletes served in the armed forces; some professional teams folded, and others merged. Still, all sports continued, albeit at a diminished level. Attendance rebounded to new heights in the postwar years, and the rapid growth of television fueled popular interest, bringing sports into living rooms and corner taverns. Overall, New York teams enjoyed significant success during the 1940s. The Rangers won the Stanley Cup in 1940 (their last for more than half a century); the Giants appeared in the title game of the National Football League three times; and after the war, the Yankees of the new All-America Football Conference were immediately successful. The Yankees won five pennants and four World Series championships, beating the now competitive Dodgers in 1941, 1947, and 1949. Jackie Robinson broke baseball's color line in 1947. His arrival did not herald a flood of black ballplayers, however; only in 1949 did the Giants integrate, the second National League team to do so. The Basketball Association of America was founded in 1946, becoming the National Basketball Association in 1949; the Knickerbockers filled their roster with local talent. Joe Louis defended his heavyweight crown throughout the decade, retiring in 1948. But it became clear that the fight game was not entirely honest, as even top-ranked pros were linked to fixed fights. St. John's University emerged as a power in college basketball; Army and Notre Dame met annually at Yankee Stadium in some of the most hard-fought football games ever played, but that series ended in 1946. As New York City grew after the war, many private golf courses in Queens succumbed to real-estate development. Finally, Toots Shor opened his famous saloon in Midtown Manhattan; for three decades, it was the premier hangout for players, writers, celebrities, and fans.

1940

In a split decision, heavyweight champion Joe Louis defeated Arturo Godoy of Chile before 15,000 spectators at Madison Square Garden on February 9. On March 29, again at the Garden, Louis knocked out Johnny Paychek in the second round. Before only 27,786 at Yankee Stadium on June 20, the champ knocked out Godoy in the eighth round.

■ ■ ■

The first hockey game was televised on February 25, a contest between the Rangers and the Montreal Canadiens at Madison Square Garden. On February 28, in the first televised basketball game, again at the Garden, Fordham lost to the University of Pittsburgh, 57–37 (for the nineteenth time in 20 contests at the Garden); New York University beat Georgetown in the other game played that night.

□ □ □

Toots Shor opened his legendary restaurant at 51 West Fifty-first Street; it soon became the watering hole of choice among athletes and sportswriters. When a midnight curfew was imposed during the war, Toots declared, "A bum who can't get drunk by midnight ain't tryin'."

□ □ □

The Rangers defeated the Toronto Maple Leafs to win the Stanley Cup, taking the sixth game by a score of 3–2 in overtime on April 13. Alex Shibicky, Mac Colville, and Neil Colville were known as the "Bread Line" (as in the "bread and butter" of the offense).

□ □ □

After voters approved a constitutional amendment in November 1939 to allow pari-mutuel wagering at racetracks, the New York State legislature passed the Dunnigan-Penny Act in March. The pari-mutuel system set the odds on the "tote," based on the pool of bets. This supplanted the bookmakers setting their own odds. On April 15, pari-mutuel wagering debuted at Jamaica Race Track.

□ □ □

On April 30, James "Tex" Carleton of the Dodgers threw a no-hitter, beating the Reds, 3–0, in Cincinnati as Brooklyn tied the modern record of nine straight wins to start a season. (They lost the next day.)

□ □ □

At 1 minute, 29 seconds of the third round, challenger Lew Jenkins knocked out world lightweight champion Lou Ambers at Madison Square Garden on May 10. Before 11,343 at the Garden on December 19, Sammy Angott won a 15-round decision over Jenkins to take the crown.

□ □ □

On May 23, at Madison Square Garden, only 7,587 watched Ken Overlin take the middleweight title from Ceferino Garcia with a unanimous 15-round decision.

□ □ □

In the first night game at the Polo Grounds, the Giants defeated the Boston Braves, 8–1, before 22,260 fans on May 24.

□ □ □

George Morton Levy organized the Old Country Trotting Association and opened Roosevelt Raceway (the half-mile oval had been used for automobile races) for 27 nights of racing beginning on September 2; a crowd of about 5,000 wagered $40,742 the first night. The first brief season attracted 75,000 trotting fans who wagered $1.2 million. Roosevelt Raceway enjoyed great success into the 1970s but closed in 1988, unable to compete with the new track at the Meadowlands in New Jersey.

□ □ □

Toots Shor (*center*) with guests at his legendary restaurant. (Museum of the City of New York, *Look* Collection)

Roosevelt Raceway. (Queens Borough Public Library, Long Island Division, Post Card Collection)

At Winged Foot Golf Club on September 14, Richard Chapman defeated weekend golfer W. B. Duff McCullough, 11 and 9, to win the United States Men's Amateur Golf Championship.

‧ ‧ ‧

With 12,000 on hand at Madison Square Garden on October 4, challenger Fritzie Zivic won a 15-round decision to dethrone welterweight champion Henry Armstrong.

‧ ‧ ‧

The American Professional Football League was formed on August 5. The New York franchise was called the Yankees. In their opening game at Yankee Stadium on October 6, the Yanks fell to the Columbus Bullies, 23–13, before only 5,312 spectators. The team finished with a 4–5 record under coach Jack McBride. On December 9, sportsman Douglas Grant Hertz, owner of the Pegasus Club, a polo and riding club in Rockleigh, New Jersey, purchased the franchise.

‧ ‧ ‧

The University of Missouri football team trounced visiting New York University, 33–0, on November 2. Leonard Bates, NYU's star running back, did not make the trip, as NYU honored Missouri's policy of prohibiting black players from participating in sports with whites. On October 18, 2,000 students had demonstrated before the administration building to protest the university's cowardly decision. As for Bates, he explained in a letter to students that the "gentlemen's agreement" had been explained to him when he enrolled, adding, "My major concern had been to gain a college education. Football is secondary."

‧ ‧ ‧

Breweries in Brooklyn produced a record 3.4 million gallons of beer, eclipsing the 1907 record of 2.5 million gallons.

1941

He can run, but he can't hide.

JOE LOUIS

On New Year's Day, Texas A&M beat Fordham in the Cotton Bowl, 13–12.

The Fordham Rams playing at Triborough Stadium on Randall's Island, 1940. (Max Ulrich/New York City Parks Photo Archive)

■ ■ ■

The ice-skating and roller-skating rinks in the New York City Building at the World's Fair opened on January 12. The facility was jammed to capacity, and thousands were turned away on opening day.

■ ■ ■

Before 23,190 at Madison Square Garden (an estimated 5,000 fans were turned away) on January 18, Fritzie Zivic defended his welterweight title with a twelfth-round knockout of Henry Armstrong, from whom he had wrested the crown on October 4, 1940.

■ ■ ■

Heavyweight champion Joe Louis knocked out Clarence "Red" Burman in the fifth round at Madison Square Garden on January 31, before a crowd of 18,061.

■ ■ ■

In February, New York University again bowed to a policy of racial segregation by keeping three black athletes out of an intercollegiate track meet at Catholic University in Washington, D.C. In March, the university suspended seven students—Argyle Stoute, Anita Krieger, Jean Borstein, Evelyn Maisel, Naomi Bloom, Mervyn Jones, and Robert Schoenfeld—for having led protests against NYU's policy of respecting the "gentlemen's agreement." In February 2001, NYU honored those seven students, but did not actually apologize. A university spokesman said, "We can't put ourselves in their shoes, and we can't turn back the hands of time. Fundamentally, what we want to do is embrace these members of our community and hold them up as models of people who fight for an important cause. I would call it an acknowledgement of good work and courage." Not that NYU had anything to apologize for.

■ ■ ■

At Mayor Fiorello La Guardia's urging, the city outlawed pinball machines. The City Council finally rescinded the ban in 1976.

∎ ∎ ∎

After defeating the Brooklyn Celtics, three games to one, for the American Basketball League title, the Philadelphia Sphas beat the Original Celtics, 48–38, on March 2, snapping their 60-game winning streak and taking the $1,000 prize in an invitational tournament in Cleveland. In the consolation game, the New York Renaissance defeated the Detroit Eagles, 49–45.

∎ ∎ ∎

On March 21, after six competitive seasons, Long Island University announced that it was dropping football "until world conditions stabilize," according to Dean Metcalfe. The university never reinstated the sport.

∎ ∎ ∎

Long Island University won the National Invitational Tournament at Madison Square Garden, defeating Ohio University, 56–42.

∎ ∎ ∎

At Madison Square Garden on May 9, challenger Billy Soose won a 15-round decision over Ken Overlin to take the middleweight title. In a demonstration of RCA's new television technology, 1,400 invited guests watched the fight on the large screen at the New Yorker Theater.

∎ ∎ ∎

Joe DiMaggio's record 56-game hitting streak began on May 15; it ended in Cleveland before 67,000 on July 17. The Yankees still won the game, 4–3. DiMaggio finished the season with a .357 batting average and a league-leading 125 RBIs. He was named the American League's Most Valuable Player for the second time, beating out Ted Williams, who led the league with a .406 average and 37 homers; one Boston sportswriter intentionally left Williams off his ballot.

∎ ∎ ∎

Running at 1–4 odds, Eddie Arcaro rode Whirlaway to victory in the four-horse-field Belmont Stakes on June 7, capturing the Triple Crown.

∎ ∎ ∎

On June 18, Joe Louis fought Billy Conn at the Polo Grounds before 54,487 for his eighteenth title defense. Conn controlled the fight until Louis landed a knockout punch in the thirteenth round. Before the bout, Louis remarked of the younger challenger, "He can run, but he can't hide." On the chilly night of September 29, Louis knocked out Lou Nova in the sixth round before 56,549 at the Polo Grounds.

∎ ∎ ∎

W. D. Griffith, president of the American Professional Football League, suspended Yankees owner Douglas G. Hertz on August 24 for having failed to fulfill his obligations to the league. On September 13, a syndicate headed by William D. Cox bought the franchise. The team was renamed the Americans. Still under coach Jack McBride but fielding almost entirely different players, the team finished the season with a 5–2–1 record.

∎ ∎ ∎

With a 6–0 win over the Braves on September 25, the Dodgers clinched their first pennant in 21 years. Leo Durocher's club featured future Hall of Famers Pee Wee Reese, Billy Herman, and Joe "Ducky" Medwick, as well as fan favorites Pete Reiser (who led the National League with a .343 average to become the youngest ever batting champion), Dolph Camilli, Cookie Lavagetto, and spitballer Hugh Casey. The Yankees won the American League flag. On October 5, in game four of the World Series, the Dodgers led 4–3 in the ninth, one out away from evening the series at two games apiece. Tommy Henrich, "Old Reliable," struck out swinging against Casey, but Mickey Owen dropped the third strike, allowing Henrich to reach first. DiMaggio followed with a hit, and Charlie Keller drove them in with a double, leading to a 7–4 Yankee win. The Yankees took the fifth and deciding game the next day, 3–1.

∎ ∎ ∎

On December 21, the Giants lost the National Football League title game to Sid Luckman (Erasmus Hall High School and Columbia University) and the Chicago Bears, 37–9, before only 13,341 fans at Wrigley Field.

1942

On New Year's Day, Fordham beat the University of Missouri, 2–0, in the Sugar Bowl.

Before about 20,000 at Madison Square Garden on January 9, Joe Louis scored a first-round knockout over Buddy Baer, younger brother of former champion Max Baer. The event was a benefit for the Navy Relief Society, which aided sailors' families. At a benefit for the Army Emergency Relief Fund on March 27 at the Garden, Private Joe Louis knocked out challenger Abe Simon in the sixth round. The champ's entire purse went to the fund (and for years, the IRS hounded Louis to pay taxes on those donated winnings, driving him into penury).

In the pole vault at the Millrose Games, Cornelius Warmerdam became the first athlete to clear 15 feet indoors.

Because of the war, Manhattan College dropped intercollegiate football.

In the second All-Star Game played at the Polo Grounds, the American League beat the National League, 3–1, on July 6. Manager Joe McCarthy used only two pitchers, Spud Chandler and Al Benton, of his Yankees.

At Yankee Stadium on October 5, the St. Louis Cardinals beat the Yankees, 4–2, to take the World Series in five games, the only time Joe DiMaggio's team lost the Fall Classic. Yankee second baseman Joe Gordon was named the American League's Most Valuable Player.

Branch Rickey, long-time executive with the Cardinals, became president and general manager of the Dodgers on October 29, replacing Larry MacPhail, who had accepted a military commission.

Before the start of the National Hockey League season, the Americans, the city's first professional hockey team, disbanded. The Amazing Amerks, or Starshirts, had played as the Brooklyn Americans the previous season.

On December 18, before 18,817 at Madison Square Garden, Beau Jack knocked out Tippy Larkin in the third round to claim the lightweight title.

1943

In the semifinals of the National Collegiate Athletic Association basketball tournament at Madison Square Garden on March 24, Georgetown upset New York University, 55–36. Behind Hy Gotkin and Harry Boykoff (former teammates at Thomas Jefferson High School in Brooklyn) and Fuzzy Levane, St. John's University defeated the University of Toledo, 48–27, to win the National Invitational Tournament at Madison Square Garden on March 29. In a Red Cross charity game pitting the winners of the NCAA and the NIT at the Garden on April 1, Wyoming beat St. John's, 52–47, in overtime.

In his first title defense, lightweight champion Beau Jack lost a 15-round decision to Bob Montgomery, a 13–5 underdog, before 18,343 spectators at Madison Square Garden on May 21. In a rematch at the Garden on November 19, he regained the crown with a 15-round decision over Montgomery.

Running at odds of 1–20, Count Fleet won the three-horse-field Belmont Stakes by 30 lengths in 2 minutes, 28$\frac{1}{5}$ seconds, capturing the Triple Crown, on June 5. Asked why he had not pushed his horse to break Bolingbroke's track record of 2 minutes, 27$\frac{3}{5}$ seconds, jockey Johnny Longden replied, "It's a long summer. We're trying to beat horses. Why run against the clock and risk injury, when the colt can breeze and sweep all before him?"

• • •

Because wartime gasoline rationing made transporting horses difficult, the Empire City Racing Association shifted its summer meeting from Yonkers to Jamaica Race Track. From July 29 through Labor Day, the Empire City Race Track hosted a joint trotting meet of the state's four trotting associations, which staged races at Saratoga, Hamburg, Goshen, and Old Westbury. (Empire City had been built as a trotting track in 1899, but was used almost exclusively for thoroughbred racing.) On August 11, the Hambletonian, the premier race for three-year-olds previously run at Goshen, was run at Empire City before 12,407 spectators who wagered $353,443. Ben White drove Volo Song to victory in the three-heat race.

• • •

During the first game of the World Series on October 5, Lieutenant Jack W. Watson, a twenty-one-year-old from Indianapolis, buzzed Yankee Stadium three times in his B-17 Flying Fortress, surprising the crowd and Yankee starter Spud Chandler. On October 11, the Yanks took the fifth and final game from the Cardinals, 2–0, winning the series even though Joe DiMaggio, Phil Rizzuto, and Red Ruffing were in the military. Chandler won the first and last games, giving up only one earned run in 18 innings; he was voted the American League's Most Valuable Player. In 1943, the Yankees recorded their lowest attendance at the Stadium: 645,006.

• • •

After finishing with identical 6–3–1 records in the Eastern Division of the NFL, the Giants and the Washington Redskins met in a playoff game at the Polo Grounds on December 19, the third week in a row that the teams played each other. (The Giants had taken the first two to force the playoff.) Washington prevailed, 28–0, before 42,800 fans.

1944

In their third and final bout, Bob Montgomery regained the world lightweight championship from Beau Jack in a split decision before 19,066 at Madison Square Garden on March 3.

• • •

Under coach Joe Lapchick, St. John's University again won the NIT at Madison Square Garden, upsetting DePaul University, 47–39, before 18,374 on March 26 (the only time a team won the tournament in successive years). Hy Gotkin, Bill Kotsores, Wade Dyum, Ray Wertis, and Ivy Summer were the starting five. In a Red Cross charity game pitting the winners of the NCAA tournament and the NIT at the Garden on March 30, the University of Utah beat St. John's, 42–36.

• • •

The Rangers finished with the worst record in franchise history: 6–39–5.

• • •

The Brooklyn Dodgers of the NFL were renamed the Tigers.

• • •

Grand master and longtime American chess champion Frank J. Marshall died at age sixty-seven on November 9.

• • •

Pete Cawthon, coach of the Brooklyn Tigers, with Bill Brown (*center*) and Bob Masterson (*right*). (Museum of the City of New York, *Look* Collection)

S. C. Eintracht of Astoria won the National Amateur Cup, representing national soccer supremacy.

- - -

The Green Bay Packers beat the Giants, 14–7, in the NFL title game before a crowd of 46,016 at the Polo Grounds on December 17. Veteran Mel Hein, always playing all 60 minutes on both sides of the ball, anchored the Giants team patched together during the war.

1945 ....

Mr. Rickey, do you want a ballplayer who's afraid to fight back?

I want a ballplayer with guts enough not *to fight back.*

EXCHANGE BETWEEN JACKIE ROBINSON AND BRANCH RICKEY

Dan Topping, Del Webb, and Larry MacPhail bought the Yankees from the estate of Jacob Ruppert for $2.8 million on January 25.

- - -

On January 29, Brooklyn gamblers Henry Rosen and Harvey Stemmer were arrested after five members of the Brooklyn College basketball team admitted to having received $1,000 to throw a game against the University of Akron scheduled for the Boston Garden two nights later. The players also said that they were to throw a game against St. Francis College scheduled for Madison Square Garden in February. The players—Bernard Barnett, Lary Pearlstein, Robert Leder, Jerry Greene, and Stanley Simon—were not charged.

- - -

Red Smith's column "Views of Sport" began in the *New York Herald Tribune*. After the newspaper's demise in 1967, Smith moved to the *New York Times*.

- - -

At Madison Square Garden on March 22, Bowling Green State University beat St. John's University, 57–44, in the semifinals of the NIT, foiling the Redmen's bid for a third straight title. Oklahoma A&M defeated New York University, 49–45, for the NCAA basketball championship before a packed house at the Garden on March 27.

- - -

On April 10, the Brooklyn Tigers and the Boston Yanks of the NFL merged. They played all their home games in Boston, except for a game against the Giants at Yankee Stadium. In December, Dan Topping, owner of the Tigers, withdrew from the league and obtained a franchise in the new All-America Football Conference, giving the league instant credibility. His New York Football Yankees would play at the Stadium.

- - -

On August 20, Tommy Brown of the Dodgers—all of seventeen years, eight months, and fourteen days—became the youngest player to hit a home run in the majors when he connected off Preacher Roe of the Pittsburgh Pirates at Ebbets Field.

. . .

Branch Rickey had his legendary meeting with Jackie Robinson in the Dodgers office in downtown Brooklyn on August 28. After Rickey described what Robinson should expect from opposing players and fans, Robinson asked, "Mr. Rickey, do you want a ballplayer who's afraid to fight back?" Rickey replied, "I want a ballplayer with guts enough *not* to fight back." On October 23, the Montreal Royals, Brooklyn's top farm club, announced that Robinson would play for them in the 1946 season.

. . .

Beginning on September 1, the United States and the Soviet Union began a four-day chess match via radio between New York and Moscow. The Americans competed from the Henry Hudson Hotel (Fifty-seventh Street and Ninth Avenue). The Soviets triumphed, 15½–4½. The American team was composed predominantly of members of the Marshall and Manhattan Chess Clubs, including United States champion Arnold S. Denker.

. . .

In soccer, S. C. Eintracht of Astoria again won the National Amateur Cup.

. . .

On November 19, Mayor Fiorello La Guardia's Committee on Baseball—with Dr. John H. Johnson as chairman, Larry MacPhail of the Yankees, and Branch Rickey of the Dodgers—issued a report that urged the end of the color line in the sport: "The only equitable solution to this problem is that individuals be treated alike and with relation to their abilities throughout organized baseball. [Integration] is a problem for each club to undertake individually, but a problem which can no longer be deferred or avoided. . . . [G]ood sports-

manship alone, as well as the moral principles involved, would demand that they not be excluded."

1946 ....

To be a great sports writer a man must hold himself pretty much aloof from the characters of the games with which he deals before his sympathy for them commences to distort his own viewpoint. There is nothing more engaging than an engaging rogue and there are many engaging rogues in professional sports. I fear I knew most of them, and that is not good for a sports writer.

DAMON RUNYON, "POSTSCRIPT ON SPORTS WRITING"

On January 30, the Fresh Meadows Country Club, once host of the Professional Golfers Association and United States Open tournaments, was sold to real-estate developers.

. . .

At a sold-out Madison Square Garden on March 29, middleweight Rocky Graziano (152 pounds) knocked out welterweight champion Marty Servo (144½ pounds) at 1 minute, 52 seconds of the

Clubhouse and practice green at the Fresh Meadows Country Club. (Queens Borough Public Library, Long Island Division, Frederick J. Weber Photographs)

Middleweight Rocky Graziano knocking out welterweight champion Marty Servo at Madison Square Garden, with referee Arthur Donovan moving in to stop the fight. (Museum of the City of New York, *Look* Collection)

second round. Before 39,827 at Yankee Stadium on September 27, middleweight champion Tony Zale knocked out Graziano in the sixth round. In 1947, Graziano won a rematch in Chicago. (The New York State Athletic Commission refused to sanction the bout because Graziano had not reported a bribe offer for a cancelled fight.) Zale took the third bout in Newark on July 16, 1948. According to Red Smith, "Ask any fight buff of the 1940's to name the most memorable series fought in his time and without hesitation he will say the Zale–Graziano battles of 1946, 1947, 1948."

■ ■ ■

For the first time, all Yankee games—home and away—were broadcast live on the radio. General manager Larry MacPhail also sold the television rights to the DuMont Television Network for $75,000.

■ ■ ■

Playing for the Montreal Royals, Jackie Robinson made his debut in organized baseball on April 18 against the Jersey City Giants before a capacity crowd of 25,000 at Roosevelt Stadium in Jersey City. Robinson had four hits, including a home run; scored four runs; and had three RBIs and two stolen bases.

■ ■ ■

On May 24, Larry MacPhail forced Joe McCarthy to resign as manager of the Yankees "due to illness." Catcher Bill Dickey took over the team. McCarthy had led the Yankees to eight pennants and seven world championships in 15 seasons, with a .627 winning percentage.

■ ■ ■

The mobile starting gate was introduced at Roosevelt Raceway on May 24. Based on an idea by starter Steve Phillips and built for $63,000 by Republic Aircraft, the gate ensured fair starts and eliminated tedious restarts, making the trotters much more popular.

■ ■ ■

On May 28, Charles E. Wilson, president of General Electric, threw out the ceremonial first ball for the first night game at Yankee Stadium. The Washington Senators beat the Yankees, 2–1.

■ ■ ■

Running at odds of 7–5, Assault beat six other horses to win the Belmont Stakes and capture the Triple Crown on June 1.

■ ■ ■

The New York Black Yankees of the Negro National League played their home games in Yankee Stadium. According to witnesses, Josh Gibson hit a ball over the left field roof, the only player to do so.

■ ■ ■

Yankee Stadium, with the new lights installed. (Lehman College, Bronx Chamber of Commerce Collection)

The new Monmouth Park Racetrack in Ocean-port, New Jersey, opened on June 19, 53 years after the original course closed.

Before 45,266 at Yankee Stadium on June 19, Joe Louis scored an eighth-round knockout over Billy Conn. This was the first heavyweight title fight to be televised. On September 18, again at the Stadium, a crowd of 38,494 saw the champ knock out challenger Tami Mauriello of the Bronx in the first round.

Ted Bishop won the United States Men's Amateur Golf Championship over Smiley Quick on the thirty-seventh hole at Baltusrol Golf Club in Springfield, New Jersey, on September 14.

In the Negro League World Series, the Newark Eagles defeated the mighty Kansas City Monarchs in seven games.

The Yankees drew more than 2 million fans (2,265,512) to the Stadium for the first time. The Dodgers also set a franchise attendance record: 1,796,824.

In the first playoff series in National League history, the Cardinals took two straight from the Dodgers, winning the second game, 8–4, at Ebbets Field on October 3. The Dodgers scored three runs in the ninth and had the bases loaded with one out, but Eddie Stanky and Howie Schultz struck out.

Big George Mikan of the Minneapolis Lakers grabbing a rebound against the Knicks at Madison Square Garden, 1948. (Museum of the City of New York, *Look* Collection)

The Basketball Association of America was founded, with Maurice Podoloff as president; in 1949, it merged with the National Basketball League to form the National Basketball Association. The New York Knickerbockers played their first game in the 11-team league on November 1, beating the Toronto Huskies, 68–66. The original Knicks, led by coach Neil Cohalan, included Ossie Schectman (LIU), Sonny Hertzberg (City College), Nat Militzok (Hofstra), Ralph Kaplowitz (NYU), Hank Rosenstein (City College), Dick Murphy (Manhattan), Tommy Byrnes (Seton Hall), Bobby Mullens (Fordham), Bud Palmer (Princeton), Stan Stutz (Rhode Island), and Leo Gottlieb (DeWitt Clinton High School). Ossie Schectman scored the first basket in the league's history. Marty Glickman called that historic game on radio. The Knicks split their home games between Madison Square Garden and the Sixty-ninth Regiment Armory (Lexington Avenue at Twenty-fifth Street).

□ □ □

Before 70,000 in their final meeting at Yankee Stadium, undefeated Army and undefeated Notre Dame played to a scoreless tie on November 9. Behind Doc Blanchard and Glenn Davis—Mr. Inside

and Mr. Outside, the Touchdown Twins—Army had been the national champion in 1944 and 1945. Notre Dame took the title in 1946 after Army struggled to beat Navy.

□ □ □

The Kingsbridge Armory in the Bronx hosted indoor automobile races for the first time on December 4; midget racers speeded around a one-fifth-mile oval. Racing continued until 1962.

□ □ □

Damon Runyon, the "Chronicler of Broadway," died on December 10; Eddie Rickenbacker scattered his ashes from an airplane above Broadway. Runyon had joined William Randolph Hearst's *New York American* as a sportswriter in 1911. Known for his wonderfully humorous short stories featuring the gamblers, horseplayers, and mugs who frequented Times Square, including "Baseball Hattie," he also penned sports verse, such as "That Handy Guy Named Sande" (about jockey Earle Sande) and "All Horse Players Die Broke." In "Postscript on Sports Writing," he wrote: "The race is not always to the swift, nor the battle to the strong, but that's the way to bet."

□ □ □

Before 58,346 fans at the Polo Grounds on December 15, Sid Luckman and the Bears defeated the Giants in the NFL title game, 24–14. Before the game, gamblers offered fullback Merle Hapes and quarterback Frank Filchock of the Giants $2,500, plus a personal bet of $1,000, to match the point spread. The players were subsequently banned.

□ □ □

At Madison Square Garden on December 20, Sugar Ray Robinson of Harlem won the vacant world welterweight title with a unanimous fifteen-round decision over Tommy Bell.

□ □ □

In the inaugural season of the AAFC, the New York Yankees finished with a record of 10–3–1 and won the Eastern Division under coach Ray Flaherty; the Brooklyn Dodgers went 3–10–1 under coach Mal Stevens and then Cliff Battles. In the championship game in Cleveland on December 22, the Browns defeated the Yankees, 14–9.

▪ ▪ ▪

A bout between middleweights Rocky Graziano and Ruben Shank scheduled for December 27 was cancelled after Graziano complained of back pain. In truth, Graziano had been offered a $100,000 bribe to throw the fight; he did not report it because, as he later told Manhattan district attorney Frank S. Hogan, he would be "double-crossing persons" who had bet on his opponent. His rematch against Tony Zale, scheduled for Madison Square Garden, was moved to Chicago.

1947

The Giants held spring training in Phoenix, Arizona, for the first time, the second team in the so-called Cactus League. On March 8, they lost their first exhibition game to Bob Lemon and the Cleveland Indians, 3–1, in Tucson.

▪ ▪ ▪

A week after his Golden Gloves bout, Anthony Sconzo Jr. died of a subdural hemorrhage. This was the first fatality since the Golden Gloves began in 1927.

▪ ▪ ▪

Basketball pioneer Joe Lapchick, head coach at St. John's University for 11 years and a member of the Original Celtics, became head coach of the Knicks on March 31, replacing Neil Cohalan, who had guided the team to a third-place finish. Lapchick had been offered the job the previous year, but had turned it down and suggested Cohalan.

▪ ▪ ▪

On April 9, four days before opening day, baseball commissioner Albert B. "Happy" Chandler suspended Dodger manager Leo Durocher for one year for having associated with gamblers and engaged in other activities detrimental to baseball.

Jackie Robinson dancing off first base at Ebbets Field, 1949. (Museum of the City of New York, *Look* Collection)

Clyde Sukeforth was named interim manager until Burt Shotten took over.

▪ ▪ ▪

Jackie Robinson made his major league debut on opening day at Ebbets Field, April 15. About 14,000 black fans attended, but the ballpark was only two-thirds full. In the *Daily News*, sportswriter Jimmy Cannon opined, "He will never make the grade," calling him "a 1,000-to-one shot." Despite the racial taunts from opposing players and fans, Robinson played inspired baseball and was named the National League's Rookie of the Year. (How much easier would Robinson's season have been had the feisty Durocher been manager?) The Dodgers staged Jackie Robinson Day on September 23; master of ceremonies Bill "Bojangles" Robinson quipped, "I'm sixty-nine years old and never thought I'd live to see Ty Cobb in Technicolor." On August 26, Dan Bankhead of the Dodgers became the first black pitcher in the major leagues. He homered in his first at bat, but the Pirates hammered him for six runs in three and one-third innings.

▪ ▪ ▪

Refereeing his seventh bout of the night at St. Nicholas Arena on April 18, fifty-one-year-old Benny Leonard, undefeated world lightweight champion from 1917 to 1925, suffered a cerebral hemorrhage and died in the ring.

□ □ □

On April 27, Babe Ruth Day, the Sultan of Swat's number, 3, was retired. He said to the capacity crowd: "Thank you very much, ladies and gentlemen. You know how bad my voice sounds. Well, it feels just as bad. You know, this baseball game of ours comes up from the youth. That means the boys. And after you're a boy and grow up to play ball, then you come to the boys you see representing the clubs today in your national pastime. The only real game in the world, I think, is baseball."

□ □ □

In a soccer exhibition, Hapoel of Tel Aviv beat the New York Stars, 2–0, before more than 53,000 at Yankee Stadium on May 4.

□ □ □

A crowd of 74,747, the highest attendance for a single game at Yankee Stadium, saw the Yankees defeat the Boston Red Sox, 9–3, on May 26.

□ □ □

On July 29, a crowd of 38,402 attended the Negro League All-Star Game at the Polo Grounds, where the American League bested the National League, 8–2.

□ □ □

Parks Department employee Holcombe Rucker founded a summer basketball league in Harlem. The games moved to a park at 155th Street and Eighth Avenue in 1965, officially renamed Holcombe Rucker Park in 1974, nine years after his death. Over the years, the tournament has attracted top college and professional players, including Wilt Chamberlain, Julius Erving, Bill Bradley, Malik Sealy, and Connie Hawkins, as well as such local playground legends as Joe "The Destroyer" Hammond, Earl "The Goat" Manigault, and Herman "The Helicopter" Knowings.

□ □ □

Guy Lombardo's *Tempo VI* speeding past his East Point House restaurant in Freeport. (Author's collection)

Driving *Miss Peps V*, Danny Foster won the International Gold Cup for speedboats on August 10. A 3-mile oval course was set in Rockaway Inlet, from Beach 123rd to Beach 148th Streets. Representing the South Shore Yacht Club in Freeport, bandleader Guy Lombardo, the defending champion, finished third overall; his boat, *Tempo VI*, broke down during the third and final 30-mile heat. An estimated 400,000 people watched from shore or from boats.

□ □ □

The Dodgers surpassed their previous season's record attendance, drawing 1,807,526 to Ebbets Field, the highest in franchise history. The Giants also set an attendance mark at the Polo Grounds: 1,600,793.

□ □ □

The United States successfully defended the Davis Cup, defeating Australia, 4–1, at Forest Hills on September 1. In the crucial fourth match, Ted Schroeder defeated Dinny Pails, 6–3, 8–6, 4–6, 9–11, 10–8, in a nearly three-hour contest. Because of blisters, Schroeder played barefoot from the thirteenth game of the second set into the final set.

□ □ □

On September 28, the New York Cubans defeated the Cleveland Buckeyes, 6–5, to take the Negro League World Series in five games. The Cubans split their home games in the series between the Polo Grounds and Yankee Stadium, but drew poorly.

□ □ □

The Yankees hosted baseball's first Old-Timers' Day at the Stadium on the last day of the season, September 28, to benefit the Babe Ruth Foundation. The crowd of just over 25,000 saw Ty Cobb, Tris Speaker, Cy Young, Earle Combs, Waite Hoyte, Lefty Gomez, Bob Meusel, Jimmy Foxx, Chief Bender, and others take the field in uniform.

▪ ▪ ▪

The Yankees and the Dodgers met in the first World Series to be televised. With two out in the ninth in game four on October 3, Cookie Lavagetto of the Dodgers stroked a pinch-hit double to break up Bill Bevens's bid for a no-hitter and beat the Yankees, 3–2. In the sixth game, Al Gionfriddo made a terrific catch to rob Joe DiMaggio of a homer. On October 6, the Yankees won the seventh game, 5–2, thanks to the relief pitching of Joe Page, who gave up one hit over five innings. After the game, Larry MacPhail announced that he was selling his third of the team to his partners, Dan Topping and Del Webb. He then fired George Weiss, director of the Yankees' farm system, but Topping hired him back the next day. MacPhail left baseball for good. Joe DiMaggio was named the American League's Most Valuable Player for the third time, again beating out Ted Williams, winner of the Triple Crown. Again, a Boston sportswriter pointedly left Williams off his ballot.

▪ ▪ ▪

Queens College fielded a women's basketball team for the first time.

▪ ▪ ▪

At Madison Square Garden on November 14, light-heavyweight Billy Fox scored a fourth-round technical knockout over Jake LaMotta. Many at ringside thought the outcome peculiar, and years later LaMotta admitted that he had thrown the fight in return for a shot at the middleweight title.

▪ ▪ ▪

Japanese American Wataru Misaka, a 5-foot, 7-inch point guard out of the University of Utah,

played three games for the Knicks, scoring seven points before his release on November 24. (The Knicks had drafted him after Utah upset Kentucky at Madison Square Garden.)

▪ ▪ ▪

Before a crowd of 18,194 at Madison Square Garden on December 5, Joe Louis, floored twice, won a 15-round split decision over Jersey Joe Walcott, as many fans booed the result.

▪ ▪ ▪

In the AAFC, the Yankees went 11–2–1 to again win the Eastern Division; Spec Sanders rushed for 1,431 yards, the only 1,000-yard rusher in the league's short history. In the AAFC championship game, before 61,879 at Yankee Stadium on December 14, the Browns again defeated the Yankees, 14–3.

1948 ....

I didn't get the job through friendship. The Yankees represent an investment of millions of dollars. They don't hand out jobs like this just because they like your company. I know I can make people laugh, and some of you think I'm a damn fool. I got the job because the people here think I can produce for them.

CASEY STENGEL

On January 6, Branch Rickey bought the Brooklyn Dodgers franchise in the AAFC and changed the team colors from black, gold, and white to Dodger blue and white. Under coach Carl Voyles, the team finished with a 2–12 record.

▪ ▪ ▪

At the Sixty-ninth Regiment Armory on March 20, the intercollegiate three-weapon championship (foil, épée, and saber) was resumed after a five-year hiatus. City College won behind Bronx-born Albert Axelrod, who took first in the foil and finished second in the épée; New York University, champion every year but one from 1935 to 1942,

Trainer Jimmy Jones leading Citation, with Eddie Arcaro aboard, at the Belmont Stakes, June 12, 1948. (Bob and Adam Coglianese Photographs, Mike Sirico, photographer)

finished second. At the Naval Academy on April 3, CCNY won the NCAA fencing championship, as Axelrod won the national foil title.

▫ ▫ ▫

In the NIT championship game, New York University lost to Saint Louis University, 65–52.

▫ ▫ ▫

In the World Professional Basketball Tournament before 16,892 at Chicago Stadium on April 11, the Minneapolis Lakers defeated the New York Renaissance, 75–71, for the title.

▫ ▫ ▫

Clair F. Bee, coach of the Long Island University basketball team, published the first of his Chip Hilton sports stories, *Touchdown Pass*. Bob Davis, a Seton Hall basketball player, was Bee's model for the fictional Chip Hilton. He wrote 23 stories in all, his last published in 1965.

▫ ▫ ▫

Ernie Harwell joined the Dodgers' broadcasting team.

▫ ▫ ▫

On June 12, Eddie Arcaro rode Citation to a six-length victory in the Belmont Stakes for his second Triple Crown.

▫ ▫ ▫

Babe Ruth made his last appearance at Yankee Stadium on June 13 for the Stadium's twenty-fifth anniversary. After a long bout with cancer, the fifty-two-year-old Ruth died on August 16. His body was laid out in the rotunda, and thousands of fans lined up to pay their respects. For many years, Ruth had lived at 110 Riverside Drive.

▫ ▫ ▫

In his final title defense, Joe Louis knocked out Jersey Joe Walcott in the eleventh round before 42,667 spectators at Yankee Stadium on June 25.

▫ ▫ ▫

Unable to work under Branch Rickey, Leo Durocher shocked fans on July 16 when he quit as manager of the Dodgers, a post he had held for eight and a half seasons, to take over the rival Giants, replacing Mel Ott, the all-time National League home run leader at the time (511). Burt Shotten returned to manage Brooklyn.

▫ ▫ ▫

Only 17,928 fans attended the Negro League All-Star Game at Yankee Stadium on August 24; the National League beat the American League, 6–1. In a Negro League game at the Polo Grounds, Luke Easler of the Homestead Grays became the first player to hit a home run into the center field bleachers, 450 feet from home plate.

▫ ▫ ▫

At the West Side Tennis Club on September 6, the United States completed a 5–0 sweep of Australia to retain the Davis Cup.

Leo Durocher and the umpires. (Museum of the City of New York, *Look* Collection)

On September 9, at the Polo Grounds, Rex Barney of the Dodgers hurled a no-hitter to beat the Giants, 2–0.

Before 19,272 at Roosevelt Stadium in Jersey City on September 21, challenger Marcel Cerdan of France knocked out titleholder Tony Zale in the twelfth round for the middleweight championship.

On October 12, Yankees president George Weiss named Casey Stengel, whom he had known since 1916, as manager. Stengel said, "I didn't get the job through friendship. The Yankees represent an investment of millions of dollars. They don't hand out jobs like this just because they like your company. I know I can make people laugh, and some of you think I'm a damn fool. I got the job because the people here think I can produce for them."

Owner Effa Manley disbanded the Newark Eagles after vainly trying to prevent major league teams from raiding the Negro Leagues after the color line was broken. Founded in Brooklyn in 1936, the Eagles boasted Hall of Famers Larry Doby, Monte Irvin, Ray Dandridge, Leon Day, and Willie Wells, as well as Don Newcombe. Effa Manley died on April 16, 1981, and was elected to the Baseball Hall of Fame in 2006.

1949

In order to be good at chess, you had to play in New York City. I played for ten cents an hour on 42nd Street. I loved the game and continued to play despite admonitions to the contrary.

LARRY EVANS

On January 4, Manhattan district attorney Frank S. Hogan announced the arrest of four Brooklyn gamblers—Joseph Aronowitz, Jack Levy, Philip Klein, and William Rivlin—for having attempted to bribe the captain of the George Washington University basketball team, David Shapiro, before a game against Manhattan College at Madison Square Garden. Shapiro had worked with the D.A.'s office for months.

On January 21, the NFL permitted Ted Collins to move his Boston Yanks to New York, sharing the Polo Grounds with the Giants; they were renamed the Bulldogs on February 1. In June, Collins turned down offers from local television stations to broadcast the games because he believed that would cut into the paid attendance. The team went 1–10–1 under thirty-three-year-old coach Charley Ewart, the lone victory coming over the Giants.

The New York Renaissance disbanded. Under founder and coach Bob Douglas, the barnstorming

Rens notched a record of 2,588–539 (.828). The team had won 88 straight games in 86 days in 1932 and 1933, and had gone 112–7 in 1939. Douglas was the first black man to be enshrined in the Naismith Memorial Basketball Hall of Fame, and in 1963 the team was so honored: Charles "Tarzan" Cooper, John "Casey" Holt, Clarence "Fats" Jenkins, James "Pappy" Ricks, Eyre "Bruiser" Saitch, Wee Willie Smith, and Bill Yancy.

▫ ▫ ▫

Mike Jacobs dissolved his Twentieth Century Sporting Club and sold his interests to James D. Norris, president of Madison Square Garden, and Arthur M. Wirtz, Norris's partner in the Detroit Olympia and Chicago Stadium. With Joe Louis as a junior partner, they organized the International Boxing Club, which staged 80 percent of all title fights between 1949 and 1953. Indicted as a monopoly, it was broken up by the United States Supreme Court in 1959.

▫ ▫ ▫

Alfred O. Hoyt and his partners purchased the Empire City Race Track in Yonkers, mostly idle since World War II, for $2.4 million on March 8. They modified the thoroughbred track for night harness racing.

▫ ▫ ▫

The Giants signed Monte Irvin and Hank Thompson, becoming the second National League team to integrate. Two years later, seven of the eight black ballplayers in the league were with the Dodgers or the Giants.

▫ ▫ ▫

Russ Hodges became the radio announcer for the Giants and remained the voice of the Giants for 22 years. Every Giant homer brought his call, "Bye-bye baby!" Curt Gowdy joined Mel Allen in the Yankees' broadcast booth. Gowdy recalled, "Timing, organization, reading a commercial—I had so many bad habits, but Mel's polish helped me learn."

Mel Allen speaking into the microphone, Curt Gowdy to his left, in the broadcast booth at Yankee Stadium. (Museum of the City of New York, *Look* Collection)

▫ ▫ ▫

On July 12, the American League beat the National League, 11–7, in the only All-Star Game played at Ebbets Field. Jackie Robinson, Roy Campanella, and Don Newcombe of the Dodgers and Larry Doby of the Indians were the first black players to appear in the game. Lou Boudreau, manager of the American League, added DiMaggio to his squad even though he had been out with a heel spur until June 28. "Joe DiMaggio is Joe DiMaggio," he explained.

▫ ▫ ▫

In the national chess tournament in Fort Worth, Texas, on July 30, nineteen-year-old Arthur Bisguier, champion of the Manhattan Chess Club, successfully defended his national junior title; seventeen-year-old Larry Evans, champion of the Marshall Chess Club, was second.

▫ ▫ ▫

In a title bout before only 16,630 at Yankee Stadium on August 10, heavyweight champion Ezzard Charles scored a technical knockout over

Gus Lesnevich when the challenger could not come out for the eighth round. Charles's purse was $18,598. In a nontitle bout at the Stadium on August 24, 28,812 fans watched welterweight champion Sugar Ray Robinson of Harlem score a seventh-round TKO over middleweight Steve Belloise of the Bronx.

▪ ▪ ▪

At Winged Foot Golf Club on August 20, the United States defeated Great Britain and Ireland to again win the Walker Cup.

▪ ▪ ▪

At Forest Hills on August 28, the United States defeated Australia 4–1 to retain the Davis Cup.

▪ ▪ ▪

Each year from 1949 to 1953, Bridgehampton hosted a road race over a 4-mile course along Ocean Road, Bridge Lane, Main Street, and Sagponack Road. Bridgehampton first hosted automobile races from 1915 to 1921.

▪ ▪ ▪

Trailing the Red Sox by one game on October 1, the Yankees took the final two games at Yankee Stadium to win the pennant. The Dodgers also captured the pennant on the last day of the season, beating the Phillies, 9–7, in 10 innings at Shibe Park. (On September 24, the Dodgers had their highest home attendance for a night game, 35,583, for a game against the Phillies.) Both pennant winners finished with a record of 97–57. In the first game of the World Series, Allie Reynolds bested Don Newcombe, 1–0, behind Tommy Henrich's home run leading off the ninth, the first walk-off homer in series history. The Yankees took the series in five games.

▪ ▪ ▪

Suspended in 1946 for having jumped to the Mexican League, Giants outfielder Daniel L. Gardella sued the Giants, baseball commissioner Albert B. Chandler, and organized baseball over the reserve clause in October 1947. His suit was dismissed in

Pomonok Country Club. (Queens Borough Public Library, Long Island Division, Eugene Armbruster Photographs)

federal court, but reinstated by a court of appeals. On October 7, he dropped the suit after obtaining his release from the Giants and signing with the Cardinals.

▪ ▪ ▪

The Pomonok Country Club, host of the PGA Championship in 1939, closed on November 19. Local 3 of the International Brotherhood of Electrical Workers purchased the property for $1,238,172 and built Electchester, a 2,100-unit apartment complex for union members. Pomonok Houses, a Housing Authority project, went up on another part of the golf course.

▪ ▪ ▪

S. C. Eintracht of Astoria won the National Amateur Cup for the third time.

▪ ▪ ▪

The Yankees and the Dodgers of the AAFC merged for the league's final season. Playing at Yankee Stadium, the team went 8–4 under coach Norman "Red" Strader and assistant coach Carl Voyles. In their final game, on December 4, the Yankees fell to the San Francisco 49ers in the semifinals of the playoffs, 17–7. The AAFC folded on December 9; the stronger franchises were absorbed by the NFL, but the Yankees dissolved.

□ □ □

A story by Ed Reid in the *Brooklyn Eagle* on December 11 revealed widespread police protection of sports bookmakers. A grand jury was immediately impaneled.

□ □ □

In a heavyweight bout at Madison Square Garden on December 30, Rocky Marciano (born Rocco Francis Marchegiano) knocked out twenty-year-old Carmine Vingo of the Bronx in the sixth round. Vingo remained unconscious for over an hour and was carried by stretcher to St. Clare's Hospital, two blocks from the Garden. A priest attending the fight administered last rights before Vingo came to. He remained hospitalized until February 10, 1950.

1950—1959

The 1950s were the glory years of New York baseball—and the end of an era. The Yankee dynasty continued uninterrupted as Joe DiMaggio retired and Mickey Mantle arrived; the Bronx Bombers won eight pennants and five world championships. The Dodgers appeared in the World Series four times, winning Brooklyn's one and only championship in 1955. The Giants, with the phenomenal Willie Mays, won two pennants and one World Series. But after the 1957 season, the Dodgers and Giants left for California. Television contributed to the demise of the semi-pro teams that had drawn loyal crowds, as sons and daughters abandoned the old neighborhoods for the greener pastures of suburbs. The National Football League championship game of 1958, between the Giants and the Colts—"the greatest game ever played"—brought professional football greater legitimacy, and television gave it broader visibility. Althea Gibson of Harlem became the first black woman to win at Forest Hills and Wimbledon. Belmont Park, Aqueduct Racetrack, and Roosevelt Raceway modernized, although Jamaica Race Track closed. But boxing and basketball revealed the seamier side of sports, the ever-present influence of gamblers. The courts finally broke Madison Square Garden's monopoly on boxing, exposing sordid links to organized crime. College basketball's point-shaving scandal broke the hearts of many New Yorkers, sports fans or not, as players from City College, Long Island University, Manhattan College, New York University, and other schools were implicated. If there ever was a golden age of college basketball in the city, it was certainly over.

1950

On March 4, for the second time, Columbia beat Holy Cross to end the Crusaders' 26-game winning streak. (They had done it the first time on December 17, 1947.) Guard Bob Cousy of St. Albans, Queens, led Holy Cross.

▪ ▪ ▪

Under coach Nat Holman, City College defeated heavily favored Bradley University, 69–61, in the National Invitational Tournament on March 18. In the National Collegiate Athletic Association tournament 10 days later, CCNY again beat Bradley, 71–68. Both games were played at Madison Square Garden.

▪ ▪ ▪

City College basketball team, November 22, 1950: coach Nat Holman speaking to his players (*clockwise from right*) Edward Warner, Ronnie Nadel, Alvin Roth, Arnie Smith, Floyd Layne, and Ed Roman. (Queens Borough Public Library, Long Island Division, *New York Herald-Tribune* Morgue)

After radio play-by-play man Ernie Harwell moved from the Dodgers to the Giants, the Dodgers brought in Bronx-born Vin Scully to join Red Barber and Connie Desmond in the broadcast booth. Harwell left the Giants for the Detroit Tigers in 1953.

On April 23, the Rangers lost the seventh game of the Stanley Cup finals to the Detroit Red Wings in double overtime, 4–3.

The Queensboro Arena in Long Island City was demolished. For years, Isaac T. Flatto's Ridgewood Grove Sporting Club had leased the venue for outdoor boxing matches in the summer.

On April 27, a crowd of 21,181 attended the first night of harness racing at Yonkers Raceway, wagering $688,009. The track had begun as the Empire City Race Track in 1900. Renovated at a cost of $1.5 million, Yonkers had a capacity of 35,000, with parking for 8,800 cars.

Wall Speedway opened off Route 34 in Monmouth County, New Jersey. The short track (less than 1 mile) closed in 2008, the victim of encroaching real-estate development and declining local interest, as well as the availability of NASCAR events on television.

On June 23, the Yankees and Tigers combined for a record eleven home runs. The Yanks hit six, but Detroit won the game, 10–9.

Arthur Bisguier, the twenty-year-old former champion of the Manhattan Chess Club, won the United States Chess Federation's open championship on July 22.

For the third consecutive year, the Americans and Australians contended for the Davis Cup at Forest Hills. This time, the Australians prevailed, 4–1, on August 27.

On August 28, Althea Gibson, born in South Carolina and raised in Harlem, became the first black player to take part in the national championships at the West Side Tennis Club.

A crowd of 5,100 attended the first night of roller derby at Dexter Park in Woodhaven on September 5. (Only 3,000 had seen the Bushwicks split a doubleheader the day before, Labor Day, against the Baltimore Elite Giants, champions of the Negro American League.) Over 15 nights, roller derby brought in 63,472 spectators.

In their third featherweight title bout, former champion Sandy Saddler of Harlem and titleholder Willie Pep met at Yankee Stadium on September 8. Trailing badly, Saddler scored a technical knockout in the eighth round, when Pep dislocated his shoulder and could not continue.

On September 15, bookmaker Harry Gross was arrested in his suite in the Towers Hotel in Brooklyn Heights. Based in Inwood on Long Island, his operation took in as much as $50,000 a day. Initially uncovered by the *Brooklyn Eagle*, the scandal brought down Mayor William O'Dwyer and set off a widespread investigation of police corruption.

Before only 22,357 at Yankee Stadium on September 27, heavyweight champion Ezzard Charles scored a unanimous 15-round decision over thirty-six-year-old Joe Louis, who returned to the ring a year and a half after retiring. (Over 11 years, Louis defended his title 25 times.) For this comeback fight, Louis took home more than $100,000; Charles, about $57,000.

Tied for first, the Dodgers and the Phillies met at Ebbets Field on the final day of the season, October 1. The Phillies won in 10 innings, 4–1. The Yankees then defeated Gene Mauch's "Whiz Kids," in four straight in the World Series. Joe DiMaggio won the second game with a home run in the tenth; rookie Whitey Ford won the first of his record 10 World Series games. Shortstop Phil Rizzuto, the "Scooter," was voted the American League's Most Valuable Player.

On October 26, Walter O'Malley bought out Branch Rickey for $1,050,000. (The $50,000 went to William Zeckendorf, who had offered to buy Rickey's share of the Dodgers if O'Malley did not.) O'Malley became president of the team, and so much did he dislike Rickey that mere mention of his name in Dodger offices brought a $1 fine. Despite winning two pennants in three and a half seasons, Burt Shotton was let go as Dodger manager because he was Rickey's man, and Charlie Dressen was brought in.

Dodgers President Branch Rickey. (Museum of the City of New York, *Look* Collection)

The Knicks signed their first black player, Nathaniel "Sweetwater" Clifton, a veteran of the New York Renaissance and the Harlem Globetrotters. He played with the team through 1957.

The New York Bulldogs (originally the Boston Yanks) of the National Football League were renamed the Yanks. In 1952, the team moved to Dallas and became the Texans.

Ending the season with a 10–2 record, tied with the Browns, the Giants lost a one-game playoff for the Eastern Division title in Cleveland, 8–3, on December 17.

Mayor Vincent Impellitteri opened the Wollman Memorial Rink in Central Park on December 21. The ice-skating rink was a gift from Kate Wollman in memory of her parents and four brothers.

1951 ....

We, you and I, have flunked. We have not done the job that was expected of us in training the young people. I am not bitter. I am hurt, hurt desperately. When I was told that three of my boys had sold themselves, it was a deep bereavement. I am not ashamed to say that I wept. It was then that something died within me.

CLAIR F. BEE

I was glad I won but I was sorry I had to do it to him.

ROCKY MARCIANO

With 11,504 on hand at Madison Square Garden on January 12, heavyweight champion Ezzard Charles knocked out challenger Lee Oma in the tenth round.

▪ ▪ ▪

On February 18, gambler Salvatore T. Sollazzo and three members of the City College basketball team were arrested for point shaving. At the arraignment, chief magistrate John M. Murtagh, a City College graduate, said that Sollazzo "appears to have corrupted these young men and brought disgrace on a great institution." Between 1947 and 1950, 86 games had been fixed, involving 32 players from seven schools: City College, Long Island University, New York University, Manhattan College, the University of Kentucky, Bradley University, and the University of Toledo. The scandal emerged when Junius Kellogg, a Manhattan College sophomore from Portsmouth, Virginia, and the school's first black scholarship player, told coach Kenny Norton that Henry Poppe, Manhattan's co-captain the previous year, had offered him $1,000. Norton sent Kellogg to Manhattan district attorney Frank S. Hogan. Kellogg later played for the Harlem Globetrotters, but was crippled in an automobile accident in 1954. City College suspended coach Nat Holman for two seasons, but he eventually was reinstated. (Could such an astute basketball man not have suspected that his players were shaving

points?) In November, Sollazzo pleaded guilty to 30 of 32 counts of bribery and conspiracy and received a sentence of eight to 16 years. Also convicted were Eddie Gard (LIU), up to three years in the state penitentiary; Sherman White (LIU), one year in the workhouse; and Edward Warner and Alvin Roth (both CCNY) and Harvey "Connie" Schaff (NYU), six months in the workhouse. Nine other players received suspended sentences: Adolph Bigos, Dick Feurtado, Nathan Miller, and LeRoy Smith of LIU, and Irwin Dambrot, Floyd Layne, Herbert Cohen, Ed Roman, and Norman Mager of CCNY. Barred from the National Basketball Association, Warner, Layne, and Roman played in the Eastern League. Warner later served time for attempting to sell heroin, but then became a high school basketball referee; Roman earned a doctorate in adolescent psychology; and, ironically, Layne was the City College basketball coach in the 1970s and 1980s.

▪ ▪ ▪

In the wake of the point-shaving scandal, Long Island University dropped men's basketball. Addressing fellow coaches soon afterward, coach Clair F. Bee said, "We, you and I, have flunked. We have not done the job that was expected of us in training the young people. I am not bitter. I am hurt, hurt desperately. When I was told that three of my boys had sold themselves, it was a deep bereavement. I am not ashamed to say that I wept. It was then that something died within me."

▪ ▪ ▪

At the Golden Gloves, sixteen-year-old Floyd Patterson won the middleweight championship. He had been training at Constantine "Cus" D'Amato's Gramercy Gym since he was fourteen. The next year, he won a gold medal at the Summer Olympic Games in Helsinki.

▪ ▪ ▪

Under first-year coach Lou Rossini, Columbia finished with a record of 21–0; sophomore forward Jack Molinas of the Bronx, a graduate of

The Bushwicks playing at Dexter Park in Woodhaven, April 1946. (Queens Borough Public Library, Long Island Division, Borough President of Queens Collection)

Stuyvesant High School, sparked the Lions. In the first round of the NCAA basketball tournament, Columbia lost to Illinois, 79–71. Rossini left in 1958 to coach at New York University, finishing with a 117–71 record over eight seasons. Thoroughly corrupt, Molinas was the central figure in the point-shaving scandals of the late 1950s.

◾ ◾ ◾

With attendance at semi-pro baseball games dropping, Max Rosner's Bushwicks played their final season at Dexter Park. Rosner reconfigured the field to make a one-third-mile track for midget-auto racing. The races continued through 1955. Rosner died on November 28, 1953.

◾ ◾ ◾

Riverhead Raceway opened for stock car racing. The dirt track was a quarter-mile banked oval with a figure-eight course. It was paved with asphalt in 1955.

◾ ◾ ◾

On April 17, Yankee rookie Mickey Mantle made his debut, hitting a single in four at-bats, as the Yanks

Max Rosner (*fourth from left*) on opening Day at Dexter Park, 1950. (Queens Borough Public Library, Long Island Division, Illustrations Collection)

Mickey Mantle at the annual Welcome Home Dinner for the Yankees at the Hotel Concourse Plaza after their home opener, April 17, 1951. (Lehman College, Bronx Chamber of Commerce Collection)

beat the Boston Red Sox, 5–0. Bob Sheppard made his debut as the public-address announcer at Yankee Stadium on the same day, and he remained the stadium's announcer for more than half a century.

■ ■ ■

After defeating the Boston Celtics and the Syracuse Nationals in the NBA playoffs, the Knicks fell to the Rochester Royals in the finals. They dropped the first three games, won the next three, and lost game seven, 79–75, on April 21 in Rochester. (Game five was their first win in Rochester.)

■ ■ ■

Before only 3,594—the smallest crowd to see a professional boxing match in the history of Madison Square Garden—challenger James Carter of the Bronx stopped champion Ike Williams in the fourteenth round to take the world lightweight crown on May 25.

■ ■ ■

On May 28, nineteen-year-old Giant rookie Willie Mays got his first major league hit, a home run off left-hander Warren Spahn of the Boston Braves

that cleared the roof of the Polo Grounds. In the locker room after the game, Spahn remarked, "Gentlemen, for the first sixty feet, that was a helluva pitch." Mays was named the National League's Rookie of the Year.

■ ■ ■

Scheduled for the Polo Grounds but postponed by rain, a bout between Joe Louis and Lee Savold moved to a packed Madison Square Garden on June 15. Louis scored a sixth-round knockout. The fight was not broadcast on radio or television, but was shown on closed-circuit television in eight movie theaters in six cities, drawing 22,000 fans.

■ ■ ■

At the Manhattan Chess Club on June 17, Samuel Reshevsky of New York won the 11-game Wertheim Memorial Tournament with an 8–3 record, defeating the world's best players—outside the Soviet orbit, that is.

■ ■ ■

In a nontitle bout at Yankee Stadium on June 27, light-heavyweight Bob Murphy stopped Jake LaMotta, attempting to move up a weight class after losing the middleweight title. LaMotta could not answer the bell in the eighth round. The fight was shown on closed-circuit television to capacity crowds in 11 movie theaters in eight cities.

■ ■ ■

On July 12, right-hander Allie Reynolds threw a no-hitter to beat Bob Feller and the Cleveland Indians, 1–0. Gene Woodling homered for the only run. On September 28, Reynolds threw his second no-hitter of the season, beating the Red Sox, 8–0, in the first game of a doubleheader as the Yankees swept Boston to clinch the pennant.

■ ■ ■

Larry Evans, a nineteen-year-old City College student, won the United States Chess Federation's open championship on July 21 in Fort Worth, Texas. In August, Evans won the national championship at the Hotel Empire in Manhattan. He later remarked, "In order to be good at chess, you had to play in New York City. I played for ten cents an hour on 42nd Street. I loved the game and continued to play despite admonitions to the contrary."

▪ ▪ ▪

On August 29, welterweight Roger Donoghue knocked out twenty-year-old George Flores in the eighth round at Madison Square Garden. Taken to the hospital, Flores died of a cerebral hemorrhage four days later. Flores's family sued the New York State Athletic Commission because he had averaged two fights a month for nearly two years. The suit failed, but the commission ruled that henceforth boxers must sit out for 30 days following a knockout. Donoghue donated his purse from his next fight to the Flores family, but fought only three times after the fatal bout.

▪ ▪ ▪

On September 12, two months after losing his middleweight title to English boxer Randy Turpin in London, Sugar Ray Robinson knocked out Turpin in the tenth round to regain his crown in front of 61,370 at the Polo Grounds and many thousands more in movie theaters in several cities, watching the match on closed-circuit television.

▪ ▪ ▪

On August 11, the Giants were 13½ games behind the Dodgers, but the teams ended the season tied and met in a best-of-three series for the pennant. In the bottom of the ninth in the third game, on October 3, third baseman Bobby Thomson hit a three-run shot off Ralph Branca to win the game, 5–4. Radio announcer Russ Hodges shouted into the microphone, "The Giants win the pennant! The Giants win the pennant!" But the "Miracle of Coogan's Bluff" was perhaps less than miraculous. A half century later, it was revealed that the Giants had secreted a telescope in the center-field scoreboard to steal the catcher's signs. In the World Series, the Yankees defeated Leo Durocher's club in six games. In his last at bat, Joe DiMaggio hit a double; he retired after the season. Catcher Yogi Berra was the American League's Most Valuable Player for the first time, and catcher Roy Campanella of the Dodgers won his first National League Most Valuable Player Award. After the season, DiMaggio led an all-star squad on a goodwill tour of Japan, going 13–1–1.

▪ ▪ ▪

At Madison Square Garden on October 26, thirty-seven-year-old Joe Louis suffered the second knockout of his career, falling to Rocky Marciano in the eighth round. (The first had been at the hands of Max Schmeling on June 19, 1936.) "He hits harder than Schmeling," said Louis after the fight. "That Schmeling must have hit me a hundred times. I went out from exhaustion more than anything else. It took Marciano only two good shots to do it." This was Louis's final fight. After the fight, Marciano said, "I was glad I won but I was sorry I had to do it to him."

▪ ▪ ▪

The German-Hungarian S.C. of the city's long-established German American Football Association won the National Amateur Cup and the National Open Challenge Cup (for any soccer team, amateur or professional), to reign supreme in American soccer.

▪ ▪ ▪

Bill Cook, captain of the Rangers from 1926 to 1937, was named coach of the Rangers on December 6. Dismissed during the 1953 season, his record was 34–59–24, a .393 winning percentage.

1952 ....

Giles E. Miller, a thirty-one-year-old Texas textile manufacturer, paid the NFL $100,000 for the New York Yanks franchise on January 29. The team became the Dallas Texans for the 1952 season, and then the Baltimore Colts.

▪ ▪ ▪

Sugar Ray Robinson. (Museum of the City of New York, *Look* Collection)

The University of Kansas defeated St. John's University, 80–63, for the NCAA men's basketball championship.

In the best-of-three first round of the NBA playoffs, the Knicks—with Matt Zaslofsky, Harry Gallatin, Ernie Vandeweghe, and the McGuire brothers, Al and Dick—beat the Celtics, taking the third game, 88–87, in double overtime at the Boston Garden on March 26. They then defeated the Syracuse Nationals, three games to one. An overcapacity crowd of 5,200 packed the Sixty-ninth Regiment Armory for the final game. In the finals, the Knicks fell to the Lakers, dropping the seventh game, 82–65, in Minneapolis on April 25.

In May, the DuMont Television Network began airing *Boxing from Eastern Parkway*. Ted Husing was the announcer; Chris Schenkel took over in March 1953. In May 1954, the show moved to ABC and broadcast from St. Nicholas Arena. Schenkel also became the television announcer for the football Giants.

At Ebbets Field on June 19, Carl Erskine hurled a no-hitter to beat the Chicago Cubs, 5–0.

In a sweltering Yankee Stadium before 47,983 fans on June 25, middleweight champion Sugar Ray Robinson tried for a third title, but he could not answer the bell for the fourteenth round against light-heavyweight champion Joey Maxim. The ringside temperature of 104 also felled referee Ruby Goldstein.

On July 3, the S.S. *United States* sailed from New York on its maiden voyage and set a record for a transatlantic crossing: 3 days, 10 hours, 40 minutes.

The Yankees beat the Dodgers in the World Series, taking the seventh game, 4–2, on October 7. Dodger first baseman Gil Hodges went hitless; Mickey Mantle collected 10 hits, with two homers; and Allie Reynolds won the first and last games and earned a save in game six.

On Staten Island, Sunset Lanes in New Springville and Colonial Lanes in Clifton opened. The former bowling alley closed in 1994; the latter, in 2000.

A year after the college basketball point-shaving scandal, Ned Irish, president of Madison Square Garden, organized the Garden's first Holiday Festival, an eight-team tournament held in December. In the final, Utah State University topped Manhattan College (a program tainted by the scandal), 59–57.

1953 ....

It's too hot for a sermon. Go home, keep the commandments, and say a prayer for Gil Hodges.

FATHER HERBERT REDMOND

On January 10, after a weeklong, 256-hand tournament at the Sherry-Netherland Hotel, the United States defeated Sweden in contract bridge by 8,260 points to capture the Bermuda Bowl. The American team included Samuel Stayman, B. Jay Becker, Theodore Lightner, and George Rapee, all of New York, and John R. Crawford of Philadelphia.

◻ ◻ ◻

In the NIT championship game, Seton Hall defeated St. John's, 58–46.

◻ ◻ ◻

In the NBA playoffs, the Knicks beat the Baltimore Bullets in two straight in the first round, and then eliminated the Celtics, three games to one. In the finals, the Knicks again fell to the Lakers, losing the fifth and final game, 91–84, at the Sixty-ninth Regiment Armory on April 10.

◻ ◻ ◻

The Staten Island Little League opened its first season on May 16. In Queens, the Elmjack Little League was founded.

◻ ◻ ◻

On a hot Sunday in May, Father Herbert Redmond of St. Francis Church in Brooklyn said to his flock, "It's too hot for a sermon. Go home, keep the commandments, and say a prayer for Gil Hodges." Hodges had gone 0 for 21 in the World Series in 1952, and his slump continued into the 1953 season.

◻ ◻ ◻

On May 23, an estimated 50,000 enthusiasts attended the final road race at Bridgehampton. The feature event, the 100-mile Bridgehampton Cup Race, was stopped after eight laps after four spectators were injured in the second accident of the day. During the trials the day before, driver Robert Wilder had been killed at the Sagg Pond Bridge. The Town of Southampton subsequently banned road races. The Bridgehampton Road Racers Corporation was founded to construct a racetrack.

◻ ◻ ◻

The United States national soccer team lost to England, 6–3, before only 7,271 fans at Yankee Stadium on June 8.

◻ ◻ ◻

In front of 27,435 at the Polo Grounds on June 22, thirty-eight-year-old Archie Moore defended his light-heavyweight title with a third-round knockout of twenty-six-year-old Carl "Bobo" Olson.

◻ ◻ ◻

The Yankees, still not integrated, did not call up first baseman Vic Power from their top farm team, the Kansas City Blues, even though he led the American Association with a .349 batting average. Yankee co-owner Dan Topping said, "I am told that Power is a good hitter but a poor fielder," adding that "a player's race never will have anything to do with whether he plays for the Yankees." The Puerto Rican–born Power later collected seven Gold Gloves. Interviewed in retirement, Power said, "Maybe the Yankees didn't want a black player who openly dated light-skinned women, or who would respond with his fists when white pitchers threw beanballs at him."

◻ ◻ ◻

At the Polo Grounds before 44,562 on September 24, heavyweight champion Rocky Marciano defeated challenger Roland LaStarza of the Bronx; referee Ruby Goldstein stopped the fight in the eleventh round. This was Marciano's forty-fifth consecutive victory and the first heavyweight title fight between two white men since the bout between James J. Braddock and Max Baer on June 13, 1935.

◻ ◻ ◻

Before the World Series, Dodger announcer Red Barber refused to accept the salary that the sponsor offered and demanded the right to negotiate his contract. Walter O'Malley simply replaced him with Vin Scully. On October 28, Barber resigned as the team's radio and television voice (he cost too much for O'Malley's tight wallet, anyway) and signed to broadcast Yankee games over WPIX.

Scully became the voice of the Dodgers and moved to Los Angeles with the team.

■ ■ ■

The Dodgers won the pennant with a 103–49 record, but lost to the Yankees in the World Series in six games, a remarkable fifth straight world championship for the Bronx Bombers. In game three, Carl Erskine fanned 14 Yankees. Mickey Mantle went down four times. Billy Martin drove in the tie-breaking runs in the bottom of the ninth to win the last game. Roy Campanella was the National League's Most Valuable Player for the second time.

■ ■ ■

At a packed Madison Square Garden on October 21, Bobo Olson won a unanimous decision over Randy Turpin for the vacant middleweight crown.

■ ■ ■

On November 24, Walter Alston replaced Charlie Dressen (298–166, .642) as manager of the Dodgers. Dressen left because Walter O'Malley had offered him only a one-year contract. For his entire tenure, through 1976, Alston had only one-year contracts.

■ ■ ■

After 23 years as head coach of the Giants, fifty-five-year-old Steve Owen stepped down on December 13 to take a position in the front office. His record was 155–108–17, with two NFL championships (1934 and 1938) and eight Eastern Division titles (1933, 1935, 1939, 1941, 1944, and 1946). He never had a formal contract, only a "verbal deal" with the Maras. On December 15, the team promoted assistant coach Jim Lee Howell (who was also the coach at Wagner College) to head coach. Vincent Lombardi signed as backfield coach on December 28.

1954 ....

On January 9, basketball commissioner Maurice Podoloff suspended rookie Jack Molinas of the Fort Wayne Pistons for having bet on NBA games. The suspension became a permanent ban, although Molinas did play in the highly competitive Eastern Basketball League. In 1961, Judge Irving Kaufman finally dismissed Molinas's suit challenging the NBA's reserve clause.

■ ■ ■

Behind Bob Cousy, the East beat the West, 98–93, in overtime in the first NBA All-Star Game, held at Madison Square Garden on January 21. The winners received $150; the losers, $50.

■ ■ ■

Bill Gallo's first sports cartoon appeared in the *Daily News* in April. He began to work at the newspaper after graduating from high school in 1941 and rejoined the staff after serving with the Marines during World War II.

■ ■ ■

Before 47,585 at Yankee Stadium on June 17, heavyweight champion Rocky Marciano won a unanimous 15-round decision over former title holder Ezzard Charles. In a rematch before only about 25,000 at the stadium on September 17, Marciano knocked out Charles in the eighth round for his forty-seventh straight victory as a professional and his forty-first knockout.

■ ■ ■

Ed Furgol won the United States Open at Baltusrol Golf Club.

■ ■ ■

In the World Series, the Giants faced the Indians, winners of a record 111 games. In the first game, at the Polo Grounds on September 29, with the score tied 2–2 in the eighth, Willie Mays made "the catch," running down a 462-foot shot off the bat of Vic Wertz in deep center field. Pitcher Don Liddle had been brought in to face that one batter and, when manager Leo Durocher took him out, said, "I got my man." In the bottom of the tenth, Dusty Rhodes homered off Bob Lemon for a 5–2 win. The Giants took the series in four straight.

Willie Mays was the National League's Most Valuable Player, and, for the second time, Yogi Berra was the Most Valuable Player in the American League.

◾ ◾ ◾

The Dodgers signed eighteen-year-old left-hander Sandy Koufax, a graduate of Lafayette High School in Brooklyn, on December 23.

1955 ....

On January 14, in a weeklong tournament at the Beekman Hotel, Great Britain defeated the United States in contract bridge by 5,420 points to capture the Bermuda Bowl.

◾ ◾ ◾

The New York Racing Association took over the operation of Belmont Park, Aqueduct Racetrack, and Saratoga Race Course.

◾ ◾ ◾

The NBA All-Star Game was held at Madison Square Garden for the second straight year. The East beat the West, 100–91, before 13,148 fans.

◾ ◾ ◾

Elston Howard, the first black player on the Yankees, had an RBI single in his first at-bat in the majors on April 14. The Yanks lost the game to the Red Sox, 8–4.

◾ ◾ ◾

On May 21, after a long tussle, the Department of Parks finally permitted the Rockaway Little League to use a ball field during the day when adult leagues were not playing. A Queens Parks official said, "If we lose the grass, we lose the grass."

◾ ◾ ◾

Riding 3–20 favorite Nashua, Eddie Arcaro won the Belmont Stakes for the sixth time on June 11, matching James McLaughlin, who had ridden six winners between 1882 and 1888.

◾ ◾ ◾

A crowd of 33,003 showed up for Pee Wee Reese Night at Ebbets Field on July 22, the night before the shortstop's thirty-seventh birthday. Reese anchored Brooklyn's infield during the 1940s and 1950s, when the team won eight pennants. He received a freezer full of groceries and a new Chevrolet.

◾ ◾ ◾

At the West Side Tennis Club, Australia swept the United States, 5–0, to capture the Davis Cup on August 28.

◾ ◾ ◾

The Dodgers clinched the pennant on September 8, beating the Milwaukee Braves, 10–2. In the World Series, they (finally!) defeated the Yankees for Brooklyn's first and only world championship. Left-hander Johnny Podres was the Most Valuable Player, winning the seventh game, 2–0, on October 4; Pee Wee Reese, the only man remaining from the 1941 team, fielded a grounder for the final out. Yogi Berra was named the Most Valuable Player in the American League for the third time, and Roy Campanella was the National League's Most Valuable Player for the third time. After the season, the Yankees embarked on a goodwill tour of Hawaii and Japan, compiling a 15–0–1 record and drawing 500,000 fans.

Yankees embarking on a goodwill tour of Hawaii and Japan after the 1955 season. Towering over Yogi Berra (*left*) is Don Larsen, while manager Casey Stengel stands with hands folded in the center of the group. (Lehman College, Bronx Chamber of Commerce Collection)

Rocky Marciano, in white trunks, battling Archie Moore at Yankee Stadium, September 21, 1955. (Museum of the City of New York, *Look* Collection)

- - -

Before 61,574 at Yankee Stadium on September 21, heavyweight champion Rocky Marciano knocked out thirty-eight-year-old light-heavyweight champion Archie Moore in the ninth round. It was Marciano's fourth fight at the Stadium and the final fight of his career. He retired undefeated, the only heavyweight champion to do so.

- - -

On September 24, Leo Durocher resigned as manager of the Giants. His record was 637–523 (.549), with two pennants and one World Series triumph in eight seasons. Bill Rigney took over.

- - -

Members of the Columbia University crew team painted a 60-foot white *C* on a 90-foot rock above the Harlem River; it was repainted in Columbia blue in 1986.

- - -

Triborough Stadium on Randall's Island was renamed for the city's former director of recreation, John J. Downing.

- - -

In soccer, S.C. Eintracht (based at Astoria's Eintracht Oval) won the National Open Challenge Cup.

1956

With the team at .500, Knicks coach Joe Lapchick resigned. His record was 326–247 (.569), and he had taken the team to the NBA finals in 1951, 1952, and 1953. Former Knick player Vince Boryla took over on February 11. In 1957, Lapchick returned to St. John's University, where he won two more NIT championships.

- - -

On February 14, Anne Hone Rogers became the first professional woman handler to take a dog to Best in Show at the Westminster Dog Show. The winner was a toy poodle, Champion Wilber White Swan, or, more familiarly, Peanuts.

- - -

Connie Desmond, longtime radio voice of the Dodgers, resigned on August 9.

- - -

On August 15, the Giants beat the Dodgers, 1–0, on a home run by Willie Mays in a night game before 26,385 at Roosevelt Stadium in Jersey City. This was the last of seven games the Dodgers played there; attendance totaled 148,371, an average of 6,000 more a game than they drew at Ebbets Field.

- - -

The Yankees released shortstop Phil Rizzuto on August 25, Old-Timers' Day, to clear a roster spot for Enos "Country" Slaughter. On orders from Ballantine Beer, sponsor of the Yankee broadcasts, Rizzuto joined Mel Allen and Red Barber in the broadcast booth, bumping veteran announcer Jim Woods, who moved to the Giants.

- - -

In the midst of the pennant race, on September 25, Sal "The Barber" Maglie of the Dodgers (when with the Giants, he was arguably the most hated man in Brooklyn for his notorious brushback pitches) hurled a no-hitter, beating the Phillies, 5–0. Brooklyn won its second straight pennant. Again, New York and Brooklyn faced off in the World Series. In game five, at Yankee Stadium on October 8, Don Larson pitched the only perfect game in World Series history, beating the Dodgers, 2–0. The Yankees took the seventh game, 9–0. Mickey Mantle won the Triple Crown—with 52 home runs, a .353 batting average, and 130 RBIs—and was voted the American League's Most Valuable Player. Dodger pitcher Don Newcombe won the National League's Most Valuable Player and Cy Young awards.

▫ ▫ ▫

The Dodgers traded Jackie Robinson to the Giants for Dick Littlefield and cash on December 13. He retired instead and accepted an executive position with Chock Full o' Nuts. During his 10 seasons with the Dodgers, Robinson led Brooklyn to six pennants and a world championship. To mark the fiftieth anniversary of his rookie season, all major league teams retired his number, 42.

▫ ▫ ▫

On December 29, with the temperature at 10 degrees, the Giants destroyed the Chicago Bears, 47–7, in the NFL title game before 56,836 shivering fans at Yankee Stadium. (This was their first season at the Stadium, after 31 years at the Polo Grounds.) This great Giants team had Charley Conerly at quarterback; Mel Triplett, Frank Gifford, and Alex Webster in the backfield; and Kyle Rote at wide receiver, while Roosevelt Grier, Andy Robustelli, and Sam Huff were on defense.

1957 ....

Acquiring land for sale to Walter O'Malley is not a public purpose and would be a scandalous procedure anyway.

ROBERT MOSES

Don Larsen pitching the only perfect game in a World Series, October 8, 1956. (Museum of the City of New York, *Look* Collection)

At Madison Square Garden on January 2, Gene Fullmer won a 15-round decision over middleweight champion Sugar Ray Robinson. According to the *New York Times*, "The fight was a bitter, savage one, in which the 18,134 observers took great delight."

▫ ▫ ▫

In the six-day, 224-hand contract bridge tournament for the Bermuda Bowl at the Biltmore Hotel, Italy defeated the United States by 10,150 points on January 12. Charles Goren led the American team. For the first time, part of the tournament was televised over WOR; the players sat in a soundproof glass booth dubbed the "fishbowl" as the action was described to the audience.

▫ ▫ ▫

Fourteen-year-old Bobby Fischer of Brooklyn won the United States Chess Championship at the Manhattan Chess Club, which he had joined two years before.

. . .

North Carolina won the NCAA basketball championship. Coach Frank McGuire and seven players, including the starting five, were all from New York City. They beat Wilt Chamberlain and the University of Kansas in triple overtime.

. . .

On May 11, the Staten Island Little League dedicated Hy Turkin Field, named for the late *Daily News* sportswriter.

. . .

On the night of May 16, Yankees Hank Bauer, Billy Martin, Whitey Ford, and Mickey Mantle were involved in a brawl at the Copacabana. Martin was soon traded to the Kansas City Athletics. Yogi Berra later testified, "Nobody never hit nobody."

. . .

Gallant Man won the Belmont Stakes in the record time of 2 minutes, 26³/₅ seconds on June 15.

. . .

At Winged Foot Golf Club on June 29, Betsy Rawls won the United States Women's Open Golf Championship when Jackie Pung, the apparent winner, was disqualified because of an incorrect scorecard.

. . .

After winning the women's singles title at Wimbledon, Althea Gibson received a ticker-tape parade up Broadway, a luncheon at the Waldorf-Astoria, and a party at her home (135 West 143rd Street). On September 8, she defeated Louise Brough, 6–3, 6–2, to win the Women's National Singles Championship at Forest Hills. Vice President Richard Nixon presented the trophy.

. . .

At Yankee Stadium on July 23, welterweight champion Carmen Basilio won a 15-round split decision over Sugar Ray Robinson to take the middleweight crown.

. . .

On the night of July 29, before only 18,101 (13,305 paid) at the Polo Grounds, heavyweight champion Floyd Patterson knocked out Tommy "Hurricane" Jackson in the tenth round.

. . .

On August 1, Roosevelt Raceway reopened after a $20 million expansion, designed by Arthur Froelich. There were dining facilities for 1,700 in the

Borough President Albert Maniscalco (*behind the plate*) and Buddy Cusack (*far right*), founder of the Staten Island Little League, at the dedication of Hy Turkin Field, May 11, 1957. (College of Staten Island, Archives and Special Collections)

Façade of the redesigned grandstand at Roosevelt Raceway. (Queens Borough Public Library, Long Island Division, Postcard Collection)

The last Brooklyn Dodgers team at Ebbets Field, 1957. (Queens Borough Public Library, Long Island Division, Illustrations Collection)

five-story grandstand, and parking for 15,000 cars.

． ． ．

Unhappy with Ebbets Field, Walter O'Malley tried to pressure the city into subsidizing a new stadium at Flatbush and Atlantic Avenues in downtown Brooklyn. Robert Moses opposed the idea: "Acquiring land for sale to Walter O'Malley is not a public purpose and would be a scandalous procedure anyway." Moses offered Flushing Meadows, but O'Malley refused and announced that he was moving the team to Los Angeles. Only 6,702 loyalists attended the last game played at Ebbets Field on September 24. Who could blame the angry Dodger fans for staying away? The Dodgers beat the Pittsburgh Pirates, 2–0, as organist Gladys Gooding played "Am I Blue?," "After You're Gone," "Que Sera, Sera," "Don't Ask Me Why I'm Leaving," "Thanks for the Memories," and, finally, "Auld Lang Syne." The Giants played their last game at the Polo Grounds on September 29 before 11,606 faithful, losing to the Pirates, 9–1. Horace Stoneham took his team to San Francisco.

． ． ．

Opening day at the Bridgehampton Race Circuit, September 28, drew 7,500 fans. The winning automobile from the 1908 Vanderbilt Cup Race, Peter Helck's Locomobile, took the ceremonial first lap around the 2.85-mile track. Charles Wallace won in a Porsche 550RS, averaging 85.73 miles an hour. The track remained active until 1999.

． ． ．

The Braves beat the Yankees, 5–0, on October 10 to take the World Series in seven games. Braves left-hander Lew Burdette won three games, the last two by shutouts, and Braves rookie Henry Aaron hit safely in each game. Again, Mickey Mantle was named the Most Valuable Player in the American League.

． ． ．

Long Island University again fielded a basketball team, having dropped the sport in 1951 in the wake of the point-shaving scandal.

1958 ....

At Madison Square Garden on January 9, Oscar Robertson of the University of Cincinnati scored

56 points against Seton Hall University to establish a new Garden record. Cincinnati won the game by a score of 118–54.

▪ ▪ ▪

Driving home from his liquor store, at 134th Street and Seventh Avenue in Harlem, late on January 27, Dodger catcher Roy Campanella skidded into a tree near his Glen Cove home; the accident left him paralyzed from the shoulders down. He died on June 26, 1993.

▪ ▪ ▪

On March 21, Manhattan district attorney Frank S. Hogan launched an investigation into the connection between organized crime and professional boxing at Madison Square Garden. On April 18, James D. Norris, president of the International Boxing Club, which was based at the Garden, resigned. After testifying before a grand jury, Billy Brown (born Dominick Mordini) resigned as matchmaker for the IBC on May 23. An associate of mobster Frankie Carbo, a notorious member of Murder, Inc., Brown had controlled the bouts televised on Wednesday and Friday nights since 1952.

▪ ▪ ▪

After taking the Knicks to their second consecutive last-place finish, coach Vince Boryla resigned on April 5. Three days later, Fuzzy Levane, former All-American at St. John's under Joe Lapchick, was named head coach

▪ ▪ ▪

Joe Kleinerman and others founded the Road Runners Club of America and, a few months later, the New York Road Runners Club, with 33 charter members.

▪ ▪ ▪

After defending her women's singles title at Wimbledon, Althea Gibson successfully defended her singles title at the West Side Tennis Club on September 7, defeating Darlene Hard, 3–6, 6–1, 6–2.

▪ ▪ ▪

Jack Curran replaced Lou Carnesecca as boys' basketball coach at Archbishop Molloy High School in Briarwood, Queens, and remained for over 50 years. His teams won five city basketball championships and 17 Catholic High School Athletic Association baseball championships.

▪ ▪ ▪

Avenging their loss the previous year, Casey Stengel's Yankees beat the Braves in the World Series, taking the seventh game, 6–2, on October 9 after being down three games to one. Bob Turley was the pitching star for the Yanks, winning games five and seven and earning the save in game six; infielder Gil McDougald provided sparkling defense; and Elston Howard, Moose Skowron, and Hank Bauer produced at the plate.

▪ ▪ ▪

In a snowstorm at Yankee Stadium before 63,192 fans on December 14, Pat Summerall kicked a 49-yard field goal with 2 minutes, 7 seconds remaining to lift the Giants over the Browns, 13–10, and force a one-game playoff with Cleveland the next week for the Eastern Conference title. Again with over 60,000 at the Stadium, the Giants shut out the Browns, 10–0 (the first time Cleveland had been blanked in 101 games, dating back to a 6–0

Dodger catcher Roy Campanella at Ebbets Field, 1953. (Museum of the City of New York, *Look* Collection)

loss to the Giants in 1950), to win the conference. In the championship game before 64,185 at Yankee Stadium on December 28—"the greatest game ever played"—the Baltimore Colts kicked a field goal to tie the game with 7 seconds left, and then defeated the Giants, 23–17, on Alan Ameche's 1-yard run in the first sudden-death-overtime game in NFL history.

1959

On January 12, the United States Supreme Court affirmed the 1957 decision by Judge Sylvester J. Ryan of the United States Court for the Southern District of New York that James D. Norris and Arthur M. Wirtz's International Boxing Club violated the Sherman Antitrust Act by monopolizing fights at Madison Square Garden, Yankee Stadium, the Polo Grounds, St. Nicholas Arena, Chicago Stadium, the Detroit Olympia, and the Arena in St. Louis, as well as the nationally televised fights on Wednesday and Friday nights (the case had been brought in 1952). Writing for the 5–3 majority, Associate Justice Tom C. Clark stated, "The choice given a contender was clear, i.e. to sign with the appellants [Norris and Wirtz] or not to fight.... An event could not be staged in any of those arenas, the most fruitful in the nation, without their consent." The ruling required Norris and Wirtz to divest their holdings in Madison Square Garden. On February 18, Judge Ryan approved the sale of their 219,350 shares for $3,948,300 to the Graham-Paige Corporation, Irving Mitchell Felt, president. On February 23, Norris and Wirtz formed National Boxing Enterprises, Inc., as a subsidiary of their Chicago Stadium Corporation; Truman Gibson, former head of the IBC, was a director.

At the Millrose Games, John Thomas became the first athlete to clear 7 feet in the high jump.

In the Skylight Room of the Statler Hilton Hotel on February 16, Italy defeated the United States and Argentina in contract bridge to win the Bermuda Bowl.

Tim Mara, founder of the New York Giants of the NFL and a charter member of the Pro Football Hall of Fame, died at age seventy-one on February 16. He had begun as a runner for bookmakers in Manhattan and established himself at Belmont Park by 1921. He had bought the Giants franchise in 1925 for $500. His sons, Jack and Wellington, had helped run the team for many years.

At Madison Square Garden on March 21, St. John's University defeated Bradley, 76–71, for its third NIT championship. New York University defeated Providence College, 71–57, for third place.

Toots Shor closed his original restaurant at 51 West Fifty-first Street. Yogi Berra once famously remarked, "Toots Shor's is so crowded nobody goes there anymore."

In the first round of the NBA playoffs, the Knicks fell to the Syracuse Nationals in two straight games.

At Winged Foot Golf Club on June 14, Billy Casper won the U.S. Open with a score of 282, a stroke ahead of Bob Rosburg.

Before 30,000 at Yankee Stadium, challenger Ingemar Johansson of Sweden floored defending heavyweight champion Floyd Patterson seven times in the third round before referee Ruby Goldstein stopped the fight.

On Staten Island, Columbian Lanes opened. The bowling alley closed in 1999.

Eddie Arcaro aboard Devil Diver at Jamaica Race Track, May 24, 1945. (Queens Borough Public Library, Long Island Division, Illustrations Collection)

▫ ▫ ▫

On July 27, attorney William A. Shea announced the formation of the Continental League, with franchises in New York, Houston, Denver, Toronto, and Minneapolis–St. Paul. Branch Rickey was the president. This potential competition forced baseball owners to grant the city a new National League franchise two years after the Dodgers and Giants left.

▫ ▫ ▫

The final day of racing at Jamaica Race Track was August 5. Rochdale Village, the largest cooperative-housing complex in the city, rose on the site.

▫ ▫ ▫

On August 31, Australia defeated the United States to take the Davis Cup. 3–2. This was the last time the event was held at the West Side Tennis Club in Forest Hills.

▫ ▫ ▫

The Staten Island Little League's Hy Turkin Field hosted the Eastern Regional Little League tournament.

▫ ▫ ▫

Aqueduct Racetrack reopened on September 14, after a $33 million makeover by architect Arthur Froelich. With a capacity of 80,000, it was the largest sports venue in the world in terms of acreage, although most of it was for parking. A crowd of 42,473 attended opening day. Eddie Shoemaker won the first race riding Four Lanes.

▫ ▫ ▫

The Original Celtics were enshrined in the Naismith Memorial Basketball Hall of Fame. Founded before World War I, the team re-formed in 1918,

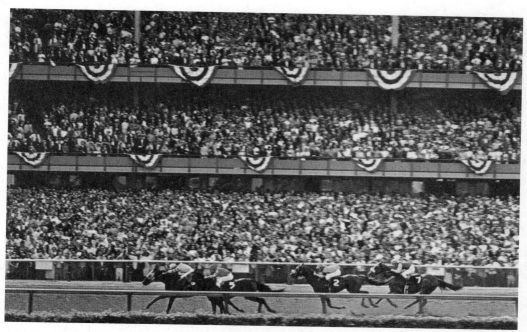

Opening day at renovated Aqueduct Racetrack, September 14, 1959. (Queens Borough Public Library, Long Island Division, Queens Chamber of Commerce Collection)

going 65–4 that first season. Their home court was the Central Opera House. They won the Eastern League championship in 1921 behind Nat Holman, later the coach at City College; Joe Lapchick, later the coach at St. John's University and of the Knicks, also played for the team.

□ □ □

Facing a 10-count indictment in the Court of General Sessions in Manhattan, Frankie Carbo, the "boxing commissioner of the underworld," pleaded guilty to conspiracy, undercover managing, and undercover matchmaking and was sentenced to two years in prison on October 30. He had begun his career with Murder, Inc., in the 1930s under Louis "Lepke" Buchalter, and by the late 1940s he was, in the words of the prosecutor, "prime minister of the boxing racket."

□ □ □

Richie Guerin scored a franchise-record 57 points at Madison Square Garden as the Knicks beat the Syracuse Nationals, 152–121, on December 11.

□ □ □

Guard Carl Braun was named player-coach of the Knicks on December 18, replacing Fuzzy Levane.

□ □ □

In Baltimore on December 27, the Colts defeated the Giants for the NFL championship, 31–16. The Associated Press named Giant quarterback Charlie Conerly the Most Valuable Player in the league.

1960—1969

The 1960s accelerated the transition from local loyalties and venues in neighborhoods across the region, New York's traditional sporting scene, to a concentration on a few professional teams. Ebbets Field and the Polo Grounds were demolished, and the fourth Madison Square Garden opened, sadly replacing magnificent Pennsylvania Station. The Giants reached the National Football League title game early in the decade, but swiftly declined. The rival American Football League was born with the decade; the original Titans became the Jets and, behind glamorous quarterback Joe Namath, won Super Bowl III. The Yankee dynasty collapsed, but the Mets were born. Casey Stengel's 1962 Amazin' Mets were the worst team ever; under Gil Hodges they won the World Series in 1969. The Knicks began the decade as an embarrassment, but were the best team in the National Basketball Association by decade's end. The American Basketball Association arrived with the charter franchise New Jersey Americans, who moved to Long Island and became the Nets. New York University and St. John's University continued to enjoy success on the hardcourt, but the 1960s also saw an-other point-shaving scandal. Amid the decade's confrontational racial climate, army lieutenant Arthur Ashe became the first black player to win the men's singles title at the United States Open, and the New York State Athletic Commission stripped Muhammad Ali of his heavyweight crown for having refused to be inducted into the military during the Vietnam War (unlike Joe Louis in World War II). In a final display of dominance, the Garden hosted the bouts to determine a new heavyweight champion.

1960

Bill Gallo succeeded Leo O'Mealia as the sports cartoonist of the *Daily News*.

▪ ▪ ▪

On January 1, the New York Titans of the American Football League (formed on August 14, 1959) signed their first player, wide receiver Don Maynard. Released by the Giants after one season in 1958, the press called him an "NFL reject." He retired after 13 seasons, having caught 633 passes for 11,834 yards (18.7-yard average) and 88 touchdowns.

▪ ▪ ▪

In a game against Bobby Hull and the Chicago Blackhawks on February 17, Ranger goalie Gump Worsley was injured and thirty-five-year-old Joe Schaefer, the team statistician and an amateur goalie, put on the pads. (At the time, teams suited up only one goalie, with an emergency goalie in the stands available for either team.) The Rangers were leading, 1–0, but lost the game, 5–1. On March 8, 1961, Schaefer again filled in after Worsley was injured. The score was 1–1, but the Blackhawks prevailed, 4–3, on a shot deflected off a defender. Schaefer had 27 saves.

. . .

The demolition of Ebbets Field began on February 23; a housing project rose on the site. The crew painted the wrecking ball white with red stitching. (It was later used on the Polo Grounds.) The eight light towers were moved to Downing Stadium on Randall's Island.

. . .

With a record of 421–190 over a 43-year career, Nat Holman retired as the basketball coach at City College. His team won the National Invitational Tournament and the National Collegiate Athletic Association championship in 1950, but the next year several of his players were involved with gamblers in a point-shaving scandal. Holman died on February 12, 1995, at age ninety-eight.

. . .

New York University lost to Ohio State in the semifinals of the NCAA basketball tournament.

. . .

At St. Nicholas Arena on June 6, lightweight Benny Gordon knocked out Tommy Pacheco in the tenth round. Pacheco never regained consciousness and died two days later. He had submitted documents claiming to be twenty-one, but he was only eighteen and thus ineligible to fight a 10-round bout.

. . .

On June 14, testifying before Senator Estes Kefauver's Subcommittee for Antitrust and Monopoly, which was investigating professional boxing, Jake LaMotta admitted that he had taken a dive against Billy Fox on November 14, 1947, in return for a shot at the middleweight crown.

. . .

Before 31,892 at the Polo Grounds on June 20, twenty-five-year-old Floyd Patterson knocked out heavyweight champion Ingemar Johansson in the fifth round, becoming the first man to regain the heavyweight title. "It was worth losing the title for this," he said. "This is easily the most gratifying moment of my life. I'm champ again, a real champ this time."

. . .

In the second All-Star Game of the year (from 1959 to 1962, there were two All-Star Games a season), the National League beat the American League, 6–0, before only 38,362 at Yankee Stadium on July 13.

. . .

Kelso ran three historic races at Aqueduct Racetrack, with Eddie Arcaro in the irons each time. On July 16, the gelding ran the fastest mile of any three-year-old in the history of New York racing:

Eddie Arcaro aboard Kelso. (Bob and Adam Coglianese Photographs)

1 minute, 34¹/₅ seconds. On September 14, he won the Discovery Handicap, running the fastest mile and an eighth ever at the track: 1 minute, 48²/₅ seconds. And on October 29, Arcaro rode Kelso to a three-and-a-half-length victory in the 2-mile Jockey Club Gold Cup, setting an American track record: 3 minutes, 19²/₅ seconds. Kelso was named Horse of the Year.

□ □ □

At the Summer Olympic Games in Rome, thirty-nine-year-old Albert Axelrod won the bronze medal in foil; the City College graduate competed in the event in every Olympics from 1952 to 1968.

□ □ □

A year after closing his original saloon, Toots Shor reopened at 33 West Fifty-second Street. "I think I got the best joint in America," he said, "because to me, New York is America."

□ □ □

Wearing blue-and-gold uniforms, the Titans took the field on a rainy September 11 before 10,200 (5,727 paid) at the Polo Grounds and beat the Buffalo Bills, 27–3. The team finished with a 7–7 record under coach Sammy Baugh. On October 9, Titans offensive guard Howard Glenn died of a cerebral hemorrhage after a game against the Houston Oilers.

□ □ □

The Yankees clinched the pennant on September 25 with a 4–3 win over the Boston Red Sox, Casey Stengel's tenth and last flag with the Yankees. In the bottom of the ninth of game seven of the World Series, against the Pittsburgh Pirates, on October 13, second baseman Bill Mazeroski homered off Ralph Terry to beat the Yankees, 10–9. Roger Maris was voted the American League's Most Valuable Player. On October 18, the Yankees dismissed Stengel; over 12 seasons, he had led the team to seven world championships and only once finished with fewer than 90 wins, leaving with a re-

Roger Maris, 1960. (Museum of the City of New York, *Look* Collection)

cord of 1,149–696, a winning percentage of .623. Casey said, "Mr. Topping and Mr. Webb paid me off in full and told me my services were no longer desired because they want to put in a youth program as an advance way of keeping the club going. That was their excuse, the best they've got." He later remarked, "I'll never make the mistake of being seventy again." Ralph Houk succeeded the Old Professor.

1961

Brooklyn-born Allie Sherman became head coach of the Giants on January 10, having been assistant

Allie Sherman, head coach of the New York Giants, with his staff, 1961. (Lehman College, Bronx Chamber of Commerce Collection)

coach under Jim Lee Howell for two seasons. Howell had built a 53–27–4 record and reached the National Football League championship game three times, winning in 1956.

* * *

At the New York Athletic Club track and field meet at Madison Square Garden on February 17, eighteen-year-old Valeri Brumel of the Soviet Union cleared 7 feet, 3 inches in the high jump, besting world-record holder John Thomas of Boston University. At the same meet, Ralph Boston set a new indoor broad-jump mark at 26 feet, 1¾ inches, and Wilma Randolph set a world indoor mark of 6.8 seconds for the 60-yard dash. At the Amateur Athletic Union's seventy-third annual indoor meet on February 25 before 16,243—a record crowd for a track meet at the Garden—Brumel again bested Thomas and tied his meet record of 7 feet, 2 inches. Boston set another broad-jump record: 26 feet, 6½ inches. At the Knights of Columbus track meet on March 3, their third contest at the Garden in three weeks, Brumel won again and set a world indoor record, clearing 7 feet, 3½ inches, with the New York crowd cheering him on.

* * *

On March 17, Manhattan district attorney Frank S. Hogan arrested gamblers Aaron Wagman and Joseph Hacken for having bribed basketball players at the University of Connecticut and Seton Hall University. In the wake of the scandal, Seton Hall stepped back from big-time basketball, declining to participate in tournaments and playing home games only on campus, not in public arenas like Madison Square Garden. In June, it was revealed that Columbia University sophomore Fred Portnoy had accepted money from gamblers; he was expelled, but received immunity from prosecution for testifying. The point-shaving scandal reached 38 players in 22 colleges over the previous five seasons.

* * *

The Knicks drafted Tony Jackson of St. John's University, but because Frank Hogan included Jackson's name among players who had failed to report an attempted bribe, basketball commissioner Maurice Podoloff banned him. Jackson never played in the National Basketball Association, but did play in the American Basketball League and in 1967 joined the New Jersey Americans of the American Basketball Association.

* * *

Emile Griffith knocked out Benny "Kid" Paret of Cuba in the thirteenth round to gain the world welterweight title at Madison Square Garden on April 1. Before a crowd of 6,072 at the Garden on September 30, Paret regained the crown in a controversial split decision over Griffith.

* * *

After finishing with a 21–58 record, the Knicks dismissed coach Carl Braun. On May 8, they hired Eddie Donovan, a graduate of St. Francis Prep in Brooklyn (now in Queens).

* * *

At St. Nicholas Arena on May 29, featherweight Anselmo Castillo of Puerto Rico knocked out José Rigores of Cuba. Rigores died of his injuries on June 3. In an amateur bantamweight fight at the same venue on November 16, Ben Hurst knocked out nineteen-year-old Cookie Ronan. Ronan died three days later of a subdural hematoma, the third death at the arena in a year and a half.

* * *

The South Shore Swimming Club opened in Tottenville, Staten Island, in July.

* * *

Mickey Wright won the United States Women's Open Golf Championship at Baltusrol Golf Club.

* * *

Both let go by the Yankees after the 1960 season, George Weiss and Casey Stengel were reunited with the Mets. Weiss became team president, and on September 29 Stengel signed a one-year contract as manager. (Weiss had tapped him to manage the Yankees in 1949.) Stengel became the only man to wear the uniform of all four New York clubs: the Giants, Dodgers, Yankees, and Mets. In the National League's first expansion draft on October 10, the Mets picked catcher Hobie Landrith of the San Francisco Giants first. As Stengel explained, "You've got to have a catcher or you'll have all passed balls." They also selected Dodgers Gil Hodges and Roger Craig and former Dodger, current Cub, Don Zimmer.

· · ·

With Eddie Arcaro up, Kelso—running at 1–2 odds—won the Woodward Stakes at Belmont Park on September 30 by eight lengths, tying the track record for the mile and a quarter at 2 minutes. Kelso was again voted Horse of the Year. Arcaro rode the gelding to victory 12 times in 14 races and said that he had "never ridden a better horse."

· · ·

At Yankee Stadium on October 1, the last day of the season, Roger Maris hit his 61st home run to surpass Babe Ruth's single-season record of 60. Until suffering a late-season injury, Mickey Mantle had kept pace, finishing with 54 homers. Because Ruth had set his mark in a 154-game season and Maris in a 162-game season, baseball commissioner Ford Frick originally wanted to put an asterisk in the record book, but that never happened.

· · ·

In the World Series, the Yankees beat the Cincinnati Reds in five games. Roger Maris won game three with a ninth-inning homer; Whitey Ford won two games, not yielding a run in 14 innings. Again, Maris was voted the American League's Most Valuable Player.

· · ·

On October 28 was the groundbreaking for the Mets' new stadium in Flushing Meadows–Corona Park. Construction took 29 months, and the Mets had to play for two seasons at the Polo Grounds. (Before welcoming the Mets, the Polo Grounds hosted stock car races.)

· · ·

The Long Island Ducks joined the Eastern Hockey League; their home rink was the Long Island Arena in Commack. The team, and league, folded in 1973.

· · ·

New York Hungaria S.C. won the National Open Challenge Cup. Several players from the Hungarian national team had fled Hungary after the failed uprising in 1956, including the Geza brothers: goalkeeper Heni and defender Nikolas. Hungaria became the dominant soccer team in the area.

· · ·

Stillman's Gym at Eighth Avenue, between Fifty-fourth and Fifty-fifth Streets, was demolished to make way for an apartment building. "The University of Eighth Avenue," as A. J. Liebling called it, was the gym of choice for boxers fighting at Madison Square Garden.

Boxers sparring at Stillman's Gym, 1952. (Museum of the City of New York, *Look* Collection)

Only 15,123 attended the first Gotham Bowl at the Polo Grounds on December 9; Baylor University downed Utah State University, 24–9. The next year, only 6,166 tickets were sold for the Miami-Nebraska matchup at Yankee Stadium (Nebraska won, 36–34), and the bowl died.

The Kate Wollman Memorial Rink opened on December 22 in Prospect Park. Dreadfully designed and sited, it obliterated a picturesque lakefront (as did the ice-skating rink in Central Park).

On December 31, the Packers dominated the Giants, 37–0, in the NFL title game, held in Green Bay. Wide receiver Kyle Rote retired after the season, holding team records for receptions (300), receiving yards (4,795), and touchdown receptions (52). Rote was also the first president of the NFL Players Association.

1962

They have shown me ways to lose I never knew existed.

CASEY STENGEL

It was my job to set the broadcast policy. I told our broadcast team, "This is a very inept group of players, and we're not going to hide their ineptness. We're also not going to make fun of them." We simply described what they did, and what they did was hilarious.

LINDSEY NELSON

On February 18, Italy won the world contract bridge championship and kept the Bermuda Bowl. During the 10-day event, the 550-seat theater at the Barbizon Plaza Hotel was filled; the action was displayed on the large "Bridgerama" board on stage.

Playing before 4,124 fans at the Sports Arena in Hershey, Pennsylvania, on March 2, the Knicks lost to the Philadelphia Warriors, 169–147, as Wilt Chamberlain scored an NBA-record 100 points. Richie Guerin of the Knicks tallied a mere 39 points.

The venerable National Invitational Tournament allowed the National Collegiate Athletic Association to select teams for its tournament first, beginning the decline of the NIT. In the NIT championship game, St. John's University lost to the University of Dayton, 73–67.

In their third match in a year, Emile Griffith met Benny "Kid" Paret at Madison Square Garden on March 24 for the welterweight crown. In the twelfth round, Griffith unleashed a torrent of blows on a defenseless Paret, stopping only when referee Ruby Goldstein intervened. Paret never regained consciousness and died on April 3. At the weigh-in, the fighters nearly had come to blows after Paret called Griffith a *maricón*.

Jimmy Caras defeated Willie Mosconi in a pocket billiards match at the New York Athletic Club for a $3,500 prize. The match was taped for ABC's *Wide World of Sports*.

On April 7, Roger Angell published his first piece about baseball in the *New Yorker*, "The Old Folks Behind Home," a description of spring training in Florida. His 1972 collection, *The Summer Game*, covered the seasons from 1962 to 1971. He continued to write about baseball for the rest of his life.

The Mets took the field for the first time on April 11 in St. Louis, losing to the Cardinals, 11–4. Their opening day lineup was Richie Ashburn (center field), Felix Mantilla (shortstop), Charlie Neal (second base), Frank Thomas (left field), Gus Bell (right field), Gil Hodges (first base), Don Zimmer (third base), Hobie Landrith (catcher), and Roger Craig (pitcher). Gil Hodges hit the first home run for the Mets in that game, the 362nd of his career (moving him ahead of Joe DiMaggio for eleventh on the all-time list). At their home opener at the Polo Grounds on Friday, April 13, the Mets lost to the Pirates, 4–3. The Mets set a record for futility in their debut season, losing 120 games, with a team batting average of .240 and an ERA of 5.04. Manager Casey Stengel summarized the situation:

> We come in there and you never seen anything like it in your life. I find I got a defensive catcher, only he can't catch the ball. The pitcher throws. Wild pitch. Throws again. Passed ball. Oops. The ball drops out of the glove. And all the time I am dizzy on account of these runners running around in circles on me and so forth. Makes a man think. You look up and down the bench and you have to say to yourself, "Can't anybody here play this game?"

The Mets original broadcasting team of Lindsey Nelson (known for his outlandish sport coats), Ralph Kiner, and Bob Murphy worked together until 1978.

▪ ▪ ▪

On May 17, Manhattan district attorney Frank S. Hogan announced the indictment of former Columbia All-American and NBA player Jack Molinas for conspiracy to bribe 22 athletes from 12 universities in a point-shaving scheme affecting 25 games. Ultimately, the scandal involved 49 players from 25 colleges in 18 states. Molinas was sentenced to 10 to 15 years in Sing-Sing; he served four.

▪ ▪ ▪

Rocky Graziano, Emile Griffith, Archie Moore, and other champions were on hand for the final night of boxing at St. Nicholas Arena on May 28. Since opening in 1906, the venue at Sixty-sixth Street and Columbus Avenue had hosted at least 15,000 fights.

▪ ▪ ▪

On June 17, New York Hungaria S.C. defeated the San Francisco Scots, 3–0, to win its fourth consecutive National Open Challenge Cup—its fifth in six years.

▪ ▪ ▪

Rookie shortstop Tom Tresh of the Yankees started in the All-Star Game.

▪ ▪ ▪

Clyde "Bulldog" Turner replaced Sammy Baugh as coach of the New York Titans; over two seasons, Baugh's record was 14–14.

▪ ▪ ▪

A group of teenagers organized the first East Coast Surfing Championships at Gilgo Beach on Long Island, held on September 7, advertised only by word of mouth. The event was staged there in 1963, but in 1965 moved to Virginia Beach.

▪ ▪ ▪

On September 10, Australian Rod Laver bested fellow Aussie Roy Emerson to win the Men's National Singles Championship at Forest Hills, becoming only the second man to complete the Grand Slam. (Don Budge had done it in 1938.)

▪ ▪ ▪

The Yankees beat the San Francisco Giants in the World Series, taking the seventh game, 1–0, on October 16. With two men in scoring position and two outs in the bottom of the ninth, Willie McCovey hit a sharp liner into the glove of second baseman Bobby Richardson to end the game. Mickey Mantle was named the American League's Most Valuable Player.

On October 28, Giant quarterback Y. A. Tittle passed for 505 yards and seven touchdowns, and Del Schofner caught 11 passes for 269 yards, to beat the Washington Redskins, 49–34.

On November 16, Wilt Chamberlain of the Warriors scored a Madison Square Garden–record 73 points in a 127–111 win over the Knicks. (Elgin Baylor of the Lakers had scored 71 points at the Garden in 1960.)

At Yankee Stadium on December 30, the Packers defeated the Giants in the NFL championship game, 16–7.

1963

Hermann Helms, the dean of American chess writers, died in his Brooklyn home at age ninety-three on January 6. His weekly column ran in the *Brooklyn Eagle* from 1893 to 1955, when the paper folded, and then in the *World Telegram and Sun* until his death.

By a 20–2 vote on January 15, the City Council named the Mets' new stadium in Flushing Meadow Park for William A. Shea, the attorney who had secured the National League franchise for New York.

On March 28, Sonny Werblin, Townsend B. Martin, Donald C. Lillis, Philip H. Iselin, and Leon Hess bought the Titans for $1 million. On April 15, they renamed the team the Jets and hired Weeb Ewbank as general manager and head coach. The new green-and-white uniforms matched the colors of Hess's gas stations.

Eddie Donovan coached the Knicks to the worst record in franchise history: 21–59 (.263). The previous season, they had finished with a record of 21–58 (.266).

The North Hills Golf Club became a municipal golf course and was renamed Douglaston Park; it opened to the public on April 27.

The Kissena Park Velodrome (officially, the Siegfried Stern Memorial Track) opened, and the Kissena Park Cycling Club was founded.

The Olympic cycling trials being held at the Kissena Park Velodrome, 1964. (New York City Parks Photo Archive)

Because construction of Shea Stadium was so far behind schedule, the Mets played at the Polo Grounds for a second year. The Mets thirty-nine-year-old first baseman, Gil Hodges, retired as a player on May 22 to manage the Washington Senators. He finished with 370 career home runs and 14 grand slams, a National League record. On June 14, Duke Snider hit his 400th home run as the Mets beat the Reds, 4–3, in Cincinnati. In the first Mayor's Trophy Game on June 20, the Mets defeated the Yankees, 6–2, before 50,742 fans at Yankee Stadium. (Earlier that day, the Yanks had beaten the Senators.) At the Polo Grounds on June 23, Mets outfielder Jimmy Piersall hit his 100th career home run and celebrated by running the bases backward. On August 9, the Mets beat the Chicago Cubs, 7–3, on Jim Hickman's ninth-inning grand slam, ending Roger Craig's record-tying losing streak at 18 games. In the last major league game played at the Polo Grounds, the Phillies defeated the Mets, 5–1, on September 18. The Mets finished the season with a record of 51–111.

The Mid-Island Little League of Staten Island became New York State champions.

The Yankees again won the pennant, but the Los Angeles Dodgers swept the World Series. In the first game, on October 2, Sandy Koufax struck out 15 Yankees. Catcher Elston Howard was voted the American League's Most Valuable Player.

On October 24, at age thirty-eight, Yogi Berra retired as a player and succeeded Ralph Houk as manager of the Yankees. He left the game with the most home runs by a catcher (313) and the most hits in the World Series (71).

Tim Mara, founder and original owner of the Giants, was inducted into the Pro Football Hall of Fame as a charter member.

Sportswriter A. J. Liebling died on December 28. He had started with the *New York World*, and then wrote for the *New Yorker*. In 1956, the boxing pieces he wrote between 1951 and 1955 were collected in *The Sweet Science* (a term he credited to the early-nineteenth-century English writer Pierce Egan), which in 2002 *Sports Illustrated* selected as the best sports book ever published.

The Giants lost the NFL title game for the third year in a row, falling to the Bears, 14–10, in Chicago on December 29. The Giants did not play for the championship again for another 23 years. Giant quarterback Y. A. Tittle threw a record 36 touchdown passes and was voted the NFL's Most Valuable Player.

1964

On January 1, London-born Alan Truscott became the second bridge editor at the *New York Times*, succeeding Albert H. Morehead. He held the position until his death in 2005.

At Madison Square Garden on March 17, Boys High defeated Benjamin Franklin High School, 70–59, for its fifth Public Schools Athletic League basketball title since 1957. It was the eighteenth consecutive playoff appearance for Benjamin Franklin under coach Bill Spiegel without a championship. (The school had won four titles before 1947.) After the game, Boys High retired Eldridge Webb's number, 31. According to referee Tom Michael, "After Boys High won, bottles came down from the old balcony, then the problem spread into the street outside the Garden where the real

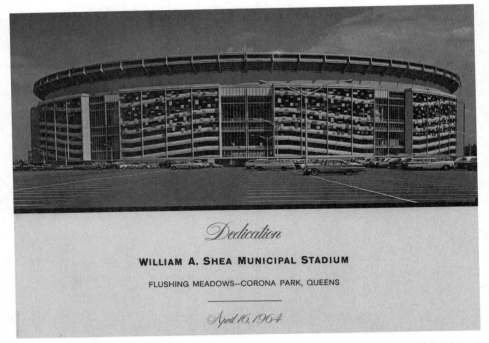

Dedication

WILLIAM A. SHEA MUNICIPAL STADIUM

FLUSHING MEADOWS—CORONA PARK, QUEENS

April 16, 1964

Program for the dedication of William A. Shea Stadium, Department of Parks and Recreation, April 16, 1964. (Queens Borough Public Library, Long Island Division, Ephemera Collection)

riot was." The PSAL championship game did not return to the Garden until 1989.

◻ ◻ ◻

Demolition of the Polo Grounds began on April 10 for a public-housing project.

◻ ◻ ◻

Bill Mazur began hosting the first sports talk-radio program on WNBC-AM. Known for his mastery of sports trivia, Mazur was the sportscaster for WNEW (Channel 5) for almost 20 years, originating the pioneering show *Sports Extra*, which aired on Sunday nights.

◻ ◻ ◻

A crowd of 50,312 fans attended the first game at Shea Stadium on April 17. The Mets lost to the Pirates, 4–3; Willie Stargell christened the ballpark with the first homer. Mr. Met, the first human mascot for any major league team, debuted on opening day. On May 31, the Mets and the Giants played the longest doubleheader on record, a 9-hour, 52-minute affair. The Giants won the nightcap, 8–6, after 23 innings that lasted for 7 hours and 23 minutes. On Father's Day, Jim Bunning of the Phillies threw a perfect game against the Mets; Bunning was a special guest on *The Ed Sullivan Show* that night. The All-Star Game was played at Shea for the only time on July 7, with second baseman Ron Hunt the first Met to start; the National League won, 7–4, drawing even with the American League for the first time since the series began.

◻ ◻ ◻

The Marine Park Golf Course in Brooklyn, designed by Robert Trent Jones, opened on a former landfill.

◻ ◻ ◻

Emile "The Cat" Francis became general manager of the Rangers. A year later, he dismissed coach Red Sullivan and took over the job himself.

◻ ◻ ◻

From April to August, the trials for the Summer Olympic Games, in Tokyo, were held in venues

The Olympic rowing trials being held at Orchard Beach in Pelham Bay Park. (New York City Parks Photo Archive)

across the city, in conjunction with the World's Fair. Cycling was held in the Kissena Park Velodrome; fencing and boxing at the fairgrounds; swimming and diving at Astoria Pool, as in 1936; track and field at Downing Stadium on Randall's Island, as in 1936; rowing and canoeing at Orchard Beach; volleyball at Queens College; and basketball at St. John's University.

▪ ▪ ▪

The Beatles played two sold-out concerts at Forest Hills Stadium in August.

▪ ▪ ▪

In August, Dan Topping and Del Webb sold 80 percent of the Yankees to the Columbia Broadcasting System (retaining 10 percent each) for $11.2 million. Completed on November 2, the deal ushered in a decade of decline for the franchise. Webb sold his 10 percent share to CBS in March 1965.

▪ ▪ ▪

On August 29, the Mid-Island Little League of Staten Island won the Little League World Series, defeating Monterrey, Mexico, 4–0, behind Danny Yacarino, who hurled a no-hitter and hit a home run.

▪ ▪ ▪

In the first AFL game held at Shea Stadium, the Jets defeated the Denver Broncos, 30–6, before 52,663 fans (a record attendance for the AFL) on the night of September 12.

▪ ▪ ▪

At Aqueduct Racetrack on October 12, a crowd of 43,142 saw Going Abroad, Ray Broussard up, win the Manhattan Handicap in 2 minutes, 26⅕ seconds, an American record for the mile and a half on a dirt track.

▪ ▪ ▪

The Yankees won the pennant with a 99–63 record under manager Yogi Berra. They lost the World Series to the Cardinals in seven, dropping

The Jets playing the Denver Broncos in their first home game at Shea Stadium, September 12, 1964. (New York City Parks Photo Archive)

the deciding game, 7–5, on October 15. Mickey Mantle ended his World Series career with a record 40 RBIs and 18 home runs, and Whitey Ford set records with 10 wins and 94 strikeouts. For the World Series, the Yankees replaced Mel Allen, the voice of the Yankees since 1939, with Phil Rizzuto. (Each team provided one announcer, and the sponsor and Major League Baseball provided the others.) Allen was fired after the season. A day after the series ended, the Yankees fired Berra and, in a stunning move, hired Johnny Keane, who had resigned as manager of the Cardinals on the same day that Berra was let go. (Keane had spent 35 years in the Cardinal organization.)

□ □ □

On November 23, the Milwaukee Braves sold left-hander Warren Spahn to the Mets, who gave him a franchise-high $70,000 contract. Spahn went 4–12 in 1965, losing 11 straight before his release in July.

□ □ □

The Wagner College football team completed its first undefeated season.

□ □ □

A year after reaching the NFL championship game, the Giants finished with a record of 2–12. Quarterback Y. A. Tittle retired after the season.

□ □ □

Running back Matt Snell of the Jets was voted the AFL's Rookie of the Year.

1965

On January 2, a day after a losing effort against the University of Texas in the Orange Bowl, quarterback Joe Namath of the University of Alabama snubbed the NFL to sign with the New York Jets. (He had actually signed before the bowl game.) His three-year, $427,000 deal included a new Lincoln Continental. In 2007, Namath finally completed the requirements for his bachelor's degree.

◼ ◼ ◼

On January 2, St. John's University defeated top-ranked Michigan, 75–74, to win the Holiday Festival at Madison Square Garden. On March 20, St. John's defeated top-seeded Villanova University, 55–51, to win its fourth NIT championship under coach Joe Lapchick. This was Lapchick's final game. In the consolation game, Army beat New York University, 75–74.

◼ ◼ ◼

With the team at 12–26, and after finishing last in the Eastern Division the previous three seasons, the Knicks dismissed Eddie Donovan on January 3 and replaced him with Harry "The Horse" Gallatin as head coach. The Knicks' top draft pick in 1948, Gallatin had played with the team from 1949 to 1957 and was an NBA all-star from 1951 to 1957. Donovan's winning percentage of .302 (84–194) is the lowest among all Knick coaches, but he became general manager and put together the franchise's championship teams. "Building a ball club is like putting together a puzzle until all the parts fits," he said. In the next draft, the Knicks selected Bill Bradley, Dave Stallworth, and Dick Van Arsdale.

◼ ◼ ◼

In front of a turn-away crowd of 12,500 at the University of Maryland's Cole Fieldhouse on January 30, DeMatha Catholic High School of Hyattsville, Maryland, defeated Lew Alcindor (later Kareem Abdul-Jabbar) and Power Memorial Academy,

46–43, ending Power's record 71-game winning streak and giving Alcindor the only loss in his high school career; he was held to 16 points. On March 7, Power trounced Rice High School, 73–41, for a third straight Catholic High School Athletic Association championship. In the fourth quarter, Alcindor broke the city schoolboy scoring record of 2,063 shared by Tom Stith of St. Francis Prep and Jim McNamara of St. Agnes Boys High School, finishing with 2,067. Alcindor's teams won 78 of 79 games.

◼ ◼ ◼

Knicks center Willis Reed, drafted out of Grambling State University, was named the NBA's Rookie of the Year.

◼ ◼ ◼

Challenger José Torres won the light-heavyweight title with a ninth-round technical knockout of Willie Pastrano at Madison Square Garden on March 30. On the same card, Emile Griffith defended his welterweight crown with a 15-round decision over Jose Stable.

◼ ◼ ◼

Red Barber, Jerry Coleman, Phil Rizzuto, and Joe Garagiola were the Yankees' broadcast crew.

◼ ◼ ◼

Manager Casey Stengel recorded his 3,000th victory as a manager as the Mets beat the Giants, 7–6, on April 24. (His career record as manager of the Dodgers, Braves, Yankees, and Mets was 1,926–1,867 [.508]; he notched 1,063 victories managing five minor league teams.) On July 14, Stengel broke his hip leaving a party at Toots Shor's to honor participants in the next day's Old-Timers' Game; he officially retired a few weeks later. His record with the Amazin' Mets was 175–404 (.302). Wes Westrum became manager.

◼ ◼ ◼

Parks employee Holcombe Rucker moved his indoor basketball league to a park on 155th Street and Eighth Avenue (now named for him). Top pros and college players competed with the city's best street players.

. . .

On August 15, the Beatles performed before a capacity crowd at Shea Stadium, the first rock concert held in a ballpark in the city. (They had given two concerts at the West Side Tennis Club in Forest Hills in 1964.) They played a 28-minute set on a stage constructed at second base, but few heard a note because of the screaming audience. They returned to Shea the next year.

. . .

The Ukrainian S.C. of New York won the National Open Challenge Cup.

. . .

William Dobbs, hunt master for the Meadow Brook Hunt (established 1881) explained how difficult fox hunting had become on Long Island: "You could chase a fox for hours without coming across any buildings or roads. Now we have one or two families of foxes living in the remaining wooded areas, roughly from Westbury to Cold Spring Harbor. It sometimes takes an hour and a half to flush one and all we get out of it is a 15-minute chase. The minute a fox crosses a road the hounds lose their scent." The club dissolved soon after.

. . .

In their first meeting in New York since 1946, Notre Dame beat Army, 17–0, before a crowd of 61,000 at Shea Stadium on October 9.

. . .

On November 29, with the team at 6–15 and last in the Eastern Division, the Knicks fired Harry Gallatin and named Dick McGuire as head coach.

1966 . . . .

I don't know what the paid attendance is today—but whatever it is, it is the smallest crowd in the history of

the Stadium . . . and this smallest crowd is the story, not the ball game.

RED BARBER

Jets quarterback Joe Namath passed for 2,220 yards and 18 touchdowns and was voted the AFL's Rookie of the Year.

. . .

In the NIT championship game at Madison Square Garden, New York University lost to Brigham Young University, 97–84.

. . .

At Madison Square Garden on April 25, Emile Griffith won a unanimous 15-round decision over defending champion Dick Tiger to claim the middleweight crown. In the ninth round, Tiger was knocked down for the first time in his career.

. . .

After finishing in sixth place in 1965, their worst showing in 40 years, and starting the season 4–16, the Yankees fired manager Johnny Keane on May 7 and brought back Ralph Houk. Keane's record was 81–101. Under Houk, the Yankees finished last, the first time they had landed in the cellar since 1908.

. . .

On May 21, light-heavyweight champion José Torres won a 15-round decision over Wayne Thornton in the first boxing match at Shea Stadium, and the first professional fight held outdoors in the city since the bout between Floyd Patterson and Ingemar Johansson at the Polo Grounds on June 20, 1960.

. . .

On September 19, CBS bought out Dan Topping's 10 percent share to gain complete control of the Yankees. Mike Burke replaced Topping as team president. On October 13, the team hired Lee MacPhail, son of former Yankee owner Larry MacPhail, as general manager. MacPhail had been general manager of the newly successful Baltimore Orioles.

Red Barber broadcasting a Brooklyn Dodgers game, 1949.
(Museum of the City of New York, *Look* Collection)

With the Yankees mired in last place, only 413 paid to see them lose to the Chicago White Sox, 4–1, on a cold and dreary September 22. Broadcaster Red Barber asked the director for a shot of the empty stands, but was refused. He then said, "I don't know what the paid attendance is today—but whatever it is, it is the smallest crowd in the history of the Stadium . . . and this smallest crowd is the story, not the ball game." Over breakfast four days later, Mike Burke fired the Old Redhead. He broadcast his last game on September 29. Barber had called Yankees games for 13 years and had been the voice of the Dodgers for 15 years before that.

Richard Dattner's first Adventure Playground opened in Central Park at West Sixty-eighth Street in the fall; another opened near East Seventy-second Street in 1970. In the 1990s, the Central Park Conservancy tried to destroy Dattner's design in favor of "safer," less adventurous adventure playgrounds.

At Madison Square Garden on December 16, Dick Tiger won a unanimous 15-round decision over José Torres to claim the light-heavyweight crown.

The Giants endured their worst season, finishing with a record of 1–12–1 under coach Allie Sherman.

1967

At Madison Square Garden on March 22, Muhammad Ali defended his heavyweight crown for the ninth time, knocking out Zora Folley in the seventh round. It was the last heavyweight-title bout in the third Garden.

In the playoffs, the Knicks were eliminated by the Boston Celtics, three games to one.

Mike Burke hired theater organist Eddie Layton to play between innings at Yankee Stadium. Layton initially refused on the grounds that he knew nothing about baseball and lived out in Queens. The team volunteered to provide a limousine, and Layton performed at every home game until 2003, in later years lending a touch of class and civility to the cacophony of canned noise.

At Madison Square Garden on April 17, Nino Benvenuti of Italy won a 15-round decision over title-holder Emile Griffith to take the middleweight crown.

Hours after Muhammad Ali refused induction into the army on April 28, the New York State Athletic Commission suspended his boxing license and withdrew recognition of his heavyweight title. The World Boxing Association also stripped him of his crown.

• • •

In a closely fought bout at Madison Square Garden on May 16, Dick Tiger retained his light-heavyweight title with a 15-round decision over José Torres.

• • •

The Knicks drafted Walt Frazier of Southern Illinois University and Phil Jackson of the University of North Dakota, two more pieces of the puzzle.

• • •

Mickey Mantle hit his 500th home run as the Yankees beat the Orioles, 6–5, on May 14.

• • •

At Baltusrol Golf Club on June 18, Jack Nicklaus won the United States Open with a record 72-hole score of 275, four strokes ahead of Arnold Palmer.

• • •

Carlos Ortiz defended his lightweight title with a 15-round decision over Ismael Laguna at Shea Stadium on August 16.

• • •

On September 10, Billie Jean King defeated Ann Haydon Jones of England for her first women's singles title at Forest Hills; she also won in 1971, 1972, and 1974. In men's singles, John Newcombe defeated American Clark Graebner in straight sets to continue Australian dominance. From 1951 through 1974, Australians won 15 times; both finalists were Aussies 10 times, and only five times was an Aussie not in the finals.

• • •

In his rookie season, Tom Seaver won 16 games for the last-place Mets and was named to the All-Star team. On September 21, with 11 games remaining in the season, Mets manager Wes Westrum resigned; Salty Parker took over, finishing the season with a 4–7 record. Westrum's record was 142–237 (.375). On October 11, the Mets sent pitcher Bill Denehy and $50,000 to the Washington Senators to release Gil Hodges from the last year of his contract. Hodges then signed a three-year deal as the Mets' fourth manager.

• • •

Emile Griffith regained the middleweight title from Nino Benvenuti before only 20,000 at Shea Stadium on September 29.

• • •

Damascus beat Buckpasser (Horse of the Year, 1966) and Dr. Fager (Horse of the Year, 1968) by 10 lengths in the Woodward Stakes at Aqueduct Racetrack on September 30 and went on to be named Horse of the Year.

• • •

With his signature "Yesss!" for a basket, Marv Albert began to call Knicks games on the radio and remained the voice of the Knicks until 2004. A protégé of Marty Glickman, Albert announced his first Knicks game in 1963, when he was nineteen, filling in for Glickman. Albert also called Rangers games from 1965 through 1995.

• • •

The New Jersey Americans began play as a charter franchise in the ABA; Max Zaslofsky was the head coach for the first two seasons. In their first game, on October 23, the Americans fell to the Pittsburgh Pipers before 3,089 spectators on their home court in the Teaneck Armory. Ending the season tied with the Kentucky Colonels at 36–42, they forfeited the one-game play-in for the playoffs because a circus had left the armory in terrible condition.

• • •

In the first and only season of the United Soccer Association, the New York Skyliners (actually Cerro of Uruguay) finished with a 2–6–4 record and averaged 8,766 fans at Yankee Stadium. In the rival National Professional Soccer League, the New York Generals finished with a record of 11–8–13 and drew 4,234. After the season, the two leagues merged into the North American Soccer League, and the Skyliners folded.

◦ ◦ ◦

Wagner College completed another undefeated football season.

◦ ◦ ◦

In a 42–31 Jets victory over the Chargers in San Diego on December 24, Joe Namath passed for 343 yards to finish the season with 4,007, the only quarterback to pass for more than 4,000 yards in a 14-game season. For the first time, the Jets sold out all their home games at Shea Stadium.

◦ ◦ ◦

Columbia University enjoyed its last great basketball season in 1967/1968, winning the Holiday Festival and the Ivy League title and gaining a bid to the NCAA tournament.

◦ ◦ ◦

The Greek American A.C. won the National Open Challenge Cup.

◦ ◦ ◦

Chief scout William "Red" Holzman replaced Dick McGuire as head coach of the Knicks on December 27. McGuire had taken the team to the playoffs in the 1967/1968 season, but finished with an overall record of 75–103.

1968 ....

The NBA All-Star Game was held in Madison Square Garden on January 23. The record crowd of 18,422 saw the Eastern beat the Western Division, 144–124. The game had been scheduled to be played in the new Garden, but the arena was behind schedule. The last event held in the third Garden, on February 12 and 13, was the Westminster Dog Show.

◦ ◦ ◦

The fourth Madison Square Garden and its banal office tower were completed above Pennsylvania Station. Architect Charles Luckman responded to preservationists decrying the demolition of Penn Station: "Does it make any sense to preserve a building merely as a monument?" Ada Louise Huxtable, architecture critic of the *New York Times*, responded: "We will probably be judged not by the monuments we build, but by those we have destroyed." About the new structure, Huxtable remarked, "We want and deserve tin-can architecture in a tin-can culture." The first event held in the new Garden was a Salute to the USO, with Bob Hope and Bing Crosby, on February 11.

◦ ◦ ◦

The New York Athletic Club held its 100th annual track meet at Madison Square Garden on February 16. Sociologist Harry Edwards led about 2,000 demonstrators outside to protest the NYAC's policy of not admitting blacks as members while sponsoring them in Olympic sports. Aiming for a boycott of the upcoming Summer Olympics in Mexico City by black athletes, Edwards convinced several colleges to refuse to participate in the NYAC meet.

◦ ◦ ◦

In the first night of boxing at the new Madison Square Garden, on March 4, a crowd of 18,096 saw Joe Frazier stop Buster Mathias in the eleventh round to claim the heavyweight title stripped from Muhammad Ali by the New York State Athletic Commission. On the same card, middleweights Nino Benvenuti and Emile Griffith met for the third time; Benvenuti won a 15-round decision to reclaim the title.

◦ ◦ ◦

On March 9, the undefeated Boys High Kangaroos held on to defeat once-beaten DeWitt Clinton High School, 73–71, for the PSAL basketball championship. The game was played at Springfield Gardens High School in Queens—a neutral site—with attendance limited to about 800 students. WPIX televised the game.

▫ ▫ ▫

Lucille Kyvallos became the women's basketball coach at Queens College. From 1972 to 1978, her teams were ranked in the top 10, and Queens College reached the national championship game in 1973. She resigned in 1980.

▫ ▫ ▫

The gentlemanly Frank Messer replaced Joe Garagiola in the Yankees broadcast booth, working with Phil Rizzuto and Jerry Coleman, and later Bill White. He was moved from television to radio in 1985, and then let go after the season.

▫ ▫ ▫

In June, thirty-seven-year-old Bernard "Boom Boom" Geoffrion retired as a player and became coach of the Rangers. Three months into the season, he was gone and Emile Francis was back behind the bench.

▫ ▫ ▫

In July, the first annual tournament of the 111th Street Old Timers Stickball Organization was held in Harlem. The event continued for decades.

▫ ▫ ▫

In the men's singles finals at the West Side Tennis Club on September 9, army lieutenant Arthur Ashe defeated Tom Okker of the Netherlands, 14–12, 5–7, 6–3, 3–6, 6–3. It was the first United States Open to bring together the five major championships (men's and women's singles, men's and women's doubles, and mixed doubles) and to admit professionals. As an amateur, Ashe received only $20 a day for expenses.

▫ ▫ ▫

On September 20, Mickey Mantle hit his 536th and final home run, a solo shot off Jim Lonborg of the Red Sox; he retired after the season with 1,509 RBIs and a record 1,710 strikeouts. The Yankees retired his number, 7, at the Stadium on June 8, 1969.

▫ ▫ ▫

Owner Arthur Brown moved his New Jersey Americans to the Long Island Arena in Commack and renamed the team the Nets (as in the Mets and Jets).

▫ ▫ ▫

Mickey Rosario and his wife, Negra, started a boxing club in the hallway outside their apartment in the Wagner Houses (124th Street and First Avenue). The club, soon known as the Gladiators, moved to church basements and ultimately found a home in the Thomas Jefferson Recreation Center (112th Street and First Avenue). The club was evicted in 2002. Over the years, the Gladiators boasted many Golden Gloves champions, including Hector Camacho, and won the team trophy four years in a row in the 1970s.

▫ ▫ ▫

The Greek American A.C. repeated as the winner of the National Open Challenge Cup for soccer supremacy among professional and amateur teams.

▫ ▫ ▫

In the inaugural season of the North American Soccer league, the Generals finished with a 12–12–8 record. The team folded after the season, leaving the fledgling league without a New York franchise.

▫ ▫ ▫

In Oakland on November 17, the Jets were leading the Raiders, 32–29, with 1 minute, 5 seconds remaining when NBC-TV cut away from the game to broadcast *Heidi*, as scheduled, at 7:00 P.M. Oakland proceeded to score 14 points for a 43–32 victory, but none of the viewing public saw the finish. Fans' complaints flooded the NBC switchboard until the circuits blew.

▫ ▫ ▫

Knicks general manager Eddie Donovan traded center Walt Bellamy and guard Howard Komives to the Detroit Pistons for forward Dave De-

Busschere on December 19. Walt Frazier called him "the final piece of the puzzle." From 1969 through 1974, the Knicks were the winningest team in the NBA.

■ ■ ■

Before 62,627 at Shea Stadium on December 29, the Jets defeated the Oakland Raiders, 27–23, in the AFL championship game.

1969 ....

We're going to win Sunday. I guarantee it.

JOE NAMATH

On January 12, after brashly guaranteeing victory—"We're going to win Sunday. I guarantee it"—quarterback Joe Namath led the underdog Jets to a 16–7 win over the powerhouse Baltimore Colts in Super Bowl III, the first victory for the upstart AFL over the NFL. Four players—running back Bill Mathis, flanker Don Maynard, linebacker Larry Grantham, and punter Curley Johnson—remained from the original Titans.

■ ■ ■

Before 16,129 at Madison Square Garden on January 22, light-heavyweight champion Bob Foster floored Frankie DePaula three times in the first round. The referee stopped the fight at 2 minutes, 17 seconds, in accordance with New York's three-knockdown rule.

■ ■ ■

Nets coach Max Zaslofsky resigned on March 5, effective season's end. The team finished with the worst record in the ABA, 17–61 (.218). Roy Boe and partners bought the Nets for $1.1 million on May 26. Boe, who held 51 percent of the Nets, was the owner of the Long Island Bulls of the Atlantic Coast Football League, a Giants farm team. The Nets changed their home court from the Long Island Arena in Commack to the Island Garden in West Hempstead. On June 18, Lou Carnesecca

of St. John's University became head coach, vice president, and general manager, effective in 1970; until then, York Larese was interim coach.

■ ■ ■

In her first race at Aqueduct Racetrack, Barbara Jo Rubin rode Bravy Galaxy to a two-length victory on March 14. She was the first woman to win a pari-mutuel race in New York State. Another jockey in that race, Heliodoro Gustines, said of Rubin, "This girl is all right. She rode a very good race." The next day, she won again, riding May Berry to a three-length victory. Buddy Jacobson, the trainer of both horses, had given her the chance.

■ ■ ■

On March 20, Boys High, the nation's top-ranked high school basketball team, defeated Martin Van Buren High School, 85–72, for its second straight PSAL title. The game was played at Wingate High School, capacity 570; with a combined enrollment of 6,000 students, the schools were allotted 250 tickets each. Boys High had won 49 consecutive games before losing, 85–83, in an unauthorized game the previous Sunday to Rockwood Academy, a prep school in Lenox, Massachusetts, that had postgraduates on its squad.

■ ■ ■

In April, the defending champion Celtics eliminated the Knicks in the Eastern Division finals of the NBA.

■ ■ ■

Pete Rozelle, commissioner of the NFL, ordered Jets quarterback Joe Namath to sell his interest in Bachelors III, an East Side watering hole, because it attracted known gamblers.

■ ■ ■

In a 4–0 victory over the Cubs at Shea Stadium on July 9, Tom Seaver took a perfect game into the ninth inning, but gave up a single to Jimmy Qualls. Seaver had four one-hitters with the Mets, including another broken up in the ninth. On August 13, the Cubs were nine and a half games ahead of the Mets, but the Amazins steadily chipped away. With 58,436 fans at Shea for a crucial game against Chicago on September 9, a black cat wandered onto the field and circled Ron Santo in the on-deck circle. Thus cursed, the Cubs lost, 7–1, and finished nine games back. The Miracle Mets swept a doubleheader from the Montreal Expos at Shea on September 10 and moved into first place for the first time in franchise history. They clinched their first division title with a 6–0 win over the Cardinals on September 24. In the National League Championship Series, they swept the Atlanta Braves in three straight, and then faced the heavily favored Orioles in the World Series. In the third game, on October 14, the first ever played at Shea, centerfielder Tommie Agee made two spectacular catches and hit a home run. Manager Gil Hodges called Agee's seventh-inning grab, "Number one of any World Series catch I've seen." In the fifth and final game, on October 19, the Mets trailed 3–0 when Hodges ran onto the field and pointed to shoe polish on the ball to prove that Cleon Jones had been hit by the pitch. Donn Clendenon, acquired midseason from the Expos, followed with his third home run of the series to spark the Miracle Mets to a 5–3 triumph. First baseman Ed Kranepool and pitcher Al Jackson were the only players remaining from the 1962 season.

In an exhibition game before 70,874 at the Yale Bowl on August 17, the Giants and the Jets faced off for the first time. Joe Namath led the Super Bowl champions to a decisive 37–14 victory. On September 12, Alex Webster replaced Allie Sherman as coach of the Giants. Sherman had won three division titles in eight years with the Giants, but had not had a winning season since 1963. Unhappy fans had serenaded him with "Good-bye, Allie" (to the tune of "Good-night, Ladies") at home games throughout the 1968 season. His final record was 57–51–4. Under Webster, the team went 6–8.

The Greek American A.C. won the National Open Challenge Cup for the third straight year. New York soccer clubs had won the cup eight times since its inception in 1951.

The Jets finished with a 10–4 record, but lost to the Kansas City Chiefs, 13–6, in the AFL playoffs on December 20.

1970—1979

The 1970s were the only decade when New York City actually lost population. Even as rising crime, a contentious racial climate, and the city's near bankruptcy fostered a pervasive sense of decline, sports provided ample diversion and excitement. Where horse racing once was a vital urban sport, the only event to consistently capture the public's imagination was the Belmont Stakes, with the magnificent victory by Secretariat in 1973 and the intense rivalry between Affirmed and Alydar in 1978. The crowds declined at all tracks, hastened by the opening of Off-Track Betting. By mid-decade, the Yankees had a new owner, George Steinbrenner; a stadium rebuilt at public expense during the fiscal crisis; and a new dynasty based on free agency. The Mets began the 1970s as the world champions and reached the World Series in 1973, but then settled into mediocrity. The Knicks won two championships, and then faded, while the Nets came into their own. Behind Julius Erving, they won the American Basketball Association title, but traded him when his contract demands displeased team owners. Queens College was a power in women's basketball, playing the first collegiate women's game at Madison Square Garden. The professional Women's Basketball League, however, did not succeed. After many lackluster years, the Rangers returned to playoff form, and the expansion Islanders quickly became competitive. Neither the Jets nor the Giants shone, although Giants Stadium opened. Pelé signed with the Cosmos of the struggling North American Soccer League in 1975; his farewell two years later was in a sold-out Giants Stadium. To accommodate more spectators, the United States Open moved from the classy confines of Forest Hills to Flushing Meadows–Corona Park. The women's game came into its own, with Billie Jean King and Chris Evert dominating the courts. The New York City Marathon was inaugurated and became a five-borough, international showcase. In boxing, there were fewer championship bouts in the city, as Las Vegas emerged as the sport's new capital. Yankee Stadium hosted its final title fight, but the Garden was the site of the "Fight of the Century," the first meeting of Joe Frazier and Muhammad Ali.

1970

New York City's Off-Track Betting parlors opened. OTB simultaneously cut the handle (amount wagered) at local racetracks and lost money.

◦ ◦ ◦

At Madison Square Garden on February 16, Smokin' Joe Frazier scored a fifth-round victory over Jimmy Ellis to claim the undisputed heavyweight championship. Angelo Dundee, Ellis's manager, did not let his fighter respond to the bell.

◦ ◦ ◦

In March, Knicks general manager Eddie Donovan resigned to become vice president and general manager of the expansion Buffalo Braves.

◦ ◦ ◦

In the National Invitational Tournament championship game, St. John's University fell to Marquette University, 65–53.

◦ ◦ ◦

Tom Seaver, "Tom Terrific," struck out a major league–record 10 in a row and fanned a record-tying 19 in all as the Mets beat the San Diego Padres, 2–1, on April 22.

◦ ◦ ◦

After finishing the season with a 39–45 record, the Nets lost to the Kentucky Colonels in the first round of the American Basketball Association playoffs, dropping the seventh game, 112–101, in Louisville on April 29.

◦ ◦ ◦

Opening the season at 23–1, including 18 straight wins, a National Basketball Association record, the Knicks finished with the best record in franchise history, 60–22 (.732). In the playoffs, they beat the Baltimore Bullets in seven games and the Milwaukee Bucks in five. In the finals, they defeated the Los Angeles Lakers, with Wilt Chamberlain and Jerry West, for the NBA championship, taking the dramatic deciding game, 113–99, on May 8. Center Willis Reed injured his leg in game five and sat out the game-six loss. Minutes before the start of game seven, he limped onto the court, inspiring his teammates and the crowd at Madison Square Garden. He scored the game's first basket, and then Walt Frazier—"Clyde"—took over, finishing with 36 points and 19 assists. Reed was the Most Valuable Player of the All-Star Game, the league, and the finals. William "Red" Holzman was Coach of the Year.

◦ ◦ ◦

At Madison Square Garden on June 17, 18 former champions—including Georges Carpentier, Gene Tunney, and Jack Sharkey—gathered for a seventy-fifth-birthday tribute to Jack Dempsey. Dempsey said to the packed house, "When you're the champ, you never think about what it'll be like in the future. Over the years, it's been tremendously gratifying to know people still show an interest in me." On the boxing card that night, heavyweight Jerry Quarry knocked out Mac Foster.

◦ ◦ ◦

In the Rucker League championship game, Harlem legend Joe "The Destroyer" Hammond, playing only the second half, scored 50 points against Julius Erving. Hammond rejected a contract from the Lakers because he made more selling drugs, a career choice that landed him in prison.

◦ ◦ ◦

At the Amateur Fencers League of America tournament at the Hotel Commodore on July 5, forty-nine-year-old Albert Axelrod won his fourth national foil championship. (He also had won in 1955, 1958, and 1960.) In 1948, he had led City College to the National Team Foil Championship, and he was on every Olympic team from 1952 to 1968, winning the bronze medal at the Rome Games in 1960. "I have no purely defensive moves," he once explained. "In the classical style, the fencers move back and forth from the defensive to the offensive. The moves are based on a heavier weapon than is used today. I have integrated my counterattack into my attack."

◦ ◦ ◦

Professor Monroe Newborn of Columbia University staged the first chess tournament for computers at the New York Hilton before 300 spectators on August 31. Teams from Columbia, the University of Alberta, Northwestern University, Texas A&M, Bell Laboratories in New Jersey, and the Goddard Space Center competed in the four-day event, won by Northwestern.

▫ ▫ ▫

On September 13, New York fireman Gary Muhrcke won the first New York City Marathon, completing four 6-mile laps around the Park Drive in Central Park in 2 hours, 31 minutes, 39 seconds; he received a watch. Only 55 of the 127 starters finished. Nina Kuscsik, the lone woman, dropped out, but won in 1972 and 1973. Muhrcke later established the Super Runners chain.

▫ ▫ ▫

In the inaugural game on *Monday Night Football*, broadcast by ABC on September 21, Joe Namath and the Jets lost to the Browns, 31–21, in Cleveland. Howard Cosell was one of the announcers. The original agreement between the network and the league stated that home games in New York were to be avoided. (In the final *Monday Night Football* broadcast by ABC, on December 26, 2005, the Jets lost to the New England Patriots.) In their first regular season meeting, on November 1, the Giants defeated the Jets, 22–10, before a record crowd of 63,903 at Shea Stadium. (Earlier in the year, the National Football League and the American Football League had merged.)

▫ ▫ ▫

At Madison Square Garden on December 7, Muhammad Ali knocked out Oscar Bonavena of Argentina in the fifteenth round, setting up a title bout at the Garden against undefeated champion Joe Frazier.

1971

The North American Soccer League had awarded a New York franchise in December 1970, and on February 4 the team was officially named the Cosmos. (Meyer Diller, the soccer coach at Martin Van Buren High School, and Al Capelli, the track coach, had submitted the winning name in a contest that drew 3,000 entries.) The team, essentially an all-star squad of the German American Football Association, played its first game on April 17, defeating the St. Louis Stars, 2–1, before 3,701 at Busch Stadium. In their first home game, on May 5, the Cosmos beat the Washington Darts, 1–0, before 3,476 at Yankee Stadium. The Cosmos finished with a record of 9–10–5, but lost two straight to the Atlanta Chiefs in the first round of the playoffs.

▫ ▫ ▫

On March 2, the city announced a $24 million modernization of Yankee Stadium. (On the same day, the Board of Education voted to terminate the contracts of 6,500 employees, mainly teachers, to close a $40 million budget deficit.) The historic ballpark's distinctive architectural features were all but eliminated during the renovation. Work began in 1973, and costs ballooned to $110 million. The Yankees played at Shea Stadium for two seasons.

▫ ▫ ▫

In the battle of the unbeatens at a sold-out Madison Square Garden on March 8, Smokin' Joe Frazier floored former champion Muhammad Ali in the fifteenth round to retain the heavyweight crown with a unanimous decision. Famed announcer Don Dunphy called the fight at ringside. Each fighter took home $2.5 million, the richest purse ever, in what was immediately dubbed the "Fight of the Century."

▫ ▫ ▫

Coach Lou Rossini, who had guided New York University to three National Collegiate Athletic Association tournaments and four NIT bids over 13 seasons for a 185–137 record, resigned in March. In April, NYU dropped basketball for financial reasons.

Yankee Stadium before its renovation in the 1970s, with pillars obstructing some views. (Lehman College, Bronx Chamber of Commerce Collection)

On April 2, the Internal Revenue Service pad-locked Toots Shor's Restaurant at 33 West Fifty-second Street because he owed $269,516 in back taxes.

In their first season under Lou Carnesecca, the Nets finished with a 40–44 record. Rick Barry was second in the ABA in scoring, averaging 29.4 points a game. In the first round of the playoffs, the Nets fell to the Virginia Squires, dropping the sixth game, 118–114, at the Felt Forum in Madison Square Garden before 3,016 fans on April 10.

After beating the Atlanta Hawks in five games in the first round of the playoffs, the Knicks fell to the Baltimore Bullets, losing the seventh game, 93–91, at Madison Square Garden on April 19.

The New York Hota S.C. won the National Open Challenge Cup.

On December 20, the National Hockey League awarded a franchise for Long Island to Nets owner Roy Boe for $10 million ($4 million went to the Rangers for encroaching on their territory). The Islanders began play the next season.

Rick Barry of the Nets grabbing a rebound at Nassau Coliseum, March 31, 1972. Note the American Basketball Association's distinctive red, white, and blue ball. (Queens Borough Public Library, Long Island Division, Joseph A. Ullman Photographs)

1972 . . . .

In Bedford-Stuyvesant, James Searles organized the Brooklyn Elite Pool Checker Club "to elevate checkers to a level of respect equal to or greater than that of any other national or international pastime."

■ ■ ■

On February 17, the Nets signed center Jim Chones of undefeated Marquette University, ranked second in the nation, to a five-year, $1.5 million contract. Al McGuire, head coach at Marquette, urged Chones to sign and leave the team, even though he could not play until the next season.

■ ■ ■

Jean Ratelle of the Rangers broke his ankle on March 1, ending his season with a franchise record 109 points—46 goals and 63 assists—in only 63 games.

■ ■ ■

On April 3, Mets manager Gil Hodges died of a heart attack after playing 27 holes of golf; he was

forty-seven. Hodges had joined the Brooklyn Dodgers in 1947 and appeared in seven World Series and six All-Star Games. His record with the Mets was 339–309, a winning percentage of .523. Yogi Berra became manager. Shamefully, Hodges is not in the Baseball Hall of Fame.

■ ■ ■

Robert Douglas, founder and coach of the New York Renaissance, was enshrined in the Naismith Memorial Basketball Hall of Fame on April 20, the first black man so honored. The St. Kitts native lived at 45 West 135th Street.

■ ■ ■

In the NBA playoffs, the Knicks—now with Earl "The Pearl" Monroe joining Willis Reed, Walt Frazier, Bill Bradley, and Dave DeBusschere—won a tough first-round series over the Baltimore Bullets, four games to two, and then eliminated the Boston Celtics in five games. In the finals, they fell to the Lakers in five, losing the last game, 114–100, in Los Angeles on May 7.

■ ■ ■

In the Stanley Cup finals, the Rangers, behind goalie Eddie Giacomin, fell to Bobbie Orr and the Boston Bruins in six games, losing the final game, 3–0, at Madison Square Garden on May 11. This was the closest that coach Emile Francis came to winning the Stanley Cup.

■ ■ ■

At Winged Foot Golf Club on July 2, Susie Maxwell Berning came from behind to win her second United States Women's Open Golf Championship, taking home the $6,000 top prize.

■ ■ ■

On July 11, WNET broadcast the first game of the chess match between Bobby Fischer and Boris Spassky, taking place in Reykjavk, Iceland. Shelby Lyman was in the studio, and Edmar Mednis provided commentary from the Marshall Chess Club. The simple show—with Lyman standing in front of a large board and analyzing each move, for hours—soon attracted a million viewers each day, as PBS stations across the country picked up the program.

• • •

At Hofstra Stadium on August 26, 6,102 saw the Cosmos defeat the St. Louis Stars, 2–1, on Josef Jelinek's penalty kick with 4 minutes remaining for their first NASL championship. Striker Randy Horton led the league in scoring with nine goals and four assists. The Cosmos played at Hofstra in 1972 and 1973.

• • •

Before 17,378 at Madison Square Garden on September 20, Muhammad Ali beat thirty-seven-year-old former heavyweight champion Floyd Patterson. Referee Arthur Mercante stopped the fight in the seventh round after the ringside doctor examined Patterson's swollen eye.

• • •

On September 24, Joe Namath and Johnny Unitas set an NFL passing record with 872 combined yards. Namath threw a personal best 494 yards as the Jets beat the Baltimore Colts, 44–34.

• • •

The Yankees drew only 966,328 to Yankee Stadium, dipping below 1 million for the first time since World War II. The Mets drew 2.1 million fans to Shea.

• • •

In the first game in franchise history, the Islanders lost to the Atlanta Flames, 3–2, at Nassau Coliseum on October 7. Captain Ed Westfall scored the first goal for the Islanders. Phil Goyette was the coach.

• • •

Jackie Robinson died at age fifty-three on October 24. His funeral was at Riverside Church. In *I Never Had It Made*, his autobiography published a month later, he wrote: "I had to fight hard against loneliness, abuse and the knowledge that any mistake I made would be magnified because I was the only black man out there. Many people resented my impatience and honesty, but I never cared about acceptance as much as I cared about respect."

• • •

The Nets played their first season at Nassau Coliseum.

• • •

The New York Raiders joined the new World Hockey Association, playing at Madison Square Garden. Renamed the Golden Blades for the next season, the team still did not draw fans and was dissolved by the league in November 1973.

1973

We plan absentee ownership as far as running the Yankees is concerned. We're not going to pretend we're something we aren't. I'll stick to building ships.

GEORGE STEINBRENNER

Ya gotta believe!

TUG MCGRAW

On January 3, a syndicate formed by forty-two-year-old Cleveland businessman George Steinbrenner, owner of the American Ship Building Company and part-owner of the Chicago Bulls, purchased the Yankees for $10 million from CBS ($3.2 million less than CBS had paid for the team in 1964). Michael Burke, a member of the new ownership, would continue to run the club. "It's the best buy in sports today. I think it's a bargain," said Steinbrenner. The new owner renegotiated his lease with the city to permit the deduction of maintenance costs from the rent. After grossing $11.9 million in 1976, Steinbrenner calculated that the city owed the Yankees $10,000 (in the middle of the fiscal crisis!); under the old lease, the club would have paid the city $854,504.

Al Horowitz died at age sixty-five on January 18. A member of the world champion American chess teams of 1931, 1933, and 1935 and a three-time United States champion, Horowitz was also the chess columnist for the *New York Times* from 1962 to 1972.

On January 29, halfway through their first season, the Islanders fired Phil Goyette and installed Earl Ingarfield as coach. On June 10, the team named Al Arbour the new coach.

The NHL All-Star Game was held at Madison Square Garden for the first time on January 30. The East defeated the West, 5–4.

On February 1, the Jets hired Charley Winner to succeed Weeb Ewbank as head coach beginning with the 1974 season. He was an assistant coach under Ewbank in 1973, as the team finished with a record of 4–10. Over 11 seasons, Ewbank's record with the Jets was 71–77–6 (.480).

Queens College hosted the Association of Intercollegiate Athletics for Women basketball tournament. (The AIAW existed from 1972 to 1982.) In the championship game, before 3,000 on its home court on March 24, Queens fell to Immaculata College, 59–52.

In the top of the first at Fenway Park on opening day, April 6, Ron Bloomberg of the Yankees stepped up to bat as the first designated hitter in baseball history. He walked with the bases loaded. (The Yanks lost to the Red Sox, 15–5.) The bat went to Cooperstown.

On April 6, the Nets lost to the Carolina Cougars, 136–113, and were eliminated from the playoffs in five games. Nets guard Brian Taylor was the ABA's Rookie of the Year. After the season, Lou Carnesecca resigned as coach of the Nets and returned to St. John's.

In the Eastern Conference finals, the Knicks—Willis Reed, Earl Monroe, Walt Frazier, Bill Bradley, and Dave DeBusschere, with the invaluable Phil Jackson as the sixth man—bested the Celtics in a tough seven-game series, taking the deciding game, 94–78, at Boston Garden on April 29. In the finals, the Lakers took game one, but the Knicks won the next four, winning the last game, 102–93, in Los Angeles on May 10 for their second NBA championship.

Former Ranger Larry Popein became head coach on June 1, but lasted less than three months into the season. General manager Emile Francis again went behind the bench.

On June 9, Secretariat shattered the track record to win the Belmont Stakes by a stunning 31 lengths in 2 minutes, 24 seconds to take the Triple Crown. Ron Turcotte was the jockey.

Ron Turcotte riding Secretariat to a record 31-length victory in the Belmont Stakes, June 9, 1973. (Bob and Adam Coglianese Photographs)

. . .

On August 1, the Nets acquired Julius Erving from the Virginia Squires for forward George Carter and "a lot of cash." A Long Island native, Dr. J had asked to sign with the Nets in 1971 after his junior year at the University of Massachusetts, but coach Lou Carnesecca would not sign an undergraduate.

. . .

In the NASL semifinals on August 15, the Cosmos lost to the Dallas Tornado, 1–0.

. . .

In mid-August, Yogi Berra's Mets were in last place, 12 games under .500, but relief pitcher Tug McGraw rallied his teammates with his constant "Ya gotta believe!" They won the Eastern Division with a record of 82–79 (the worst record of any division winner in major league history). The pitching rotation of Tom Seaver, Jon Matlack, Jerry Koosman, and George Stone carried the team, while an aging Willie Mays, Rusty Staub, and Cleon Jones provided timely hitting. The Mets defeated the Cincinnati Reds in the National League Championship Series, three games to two. In game three, with the series tied one game apiece, Pete Rose slid hard into Mets shortstop Bud Harrelson to break up a double play, setting off a bench-clearing brawl. Roger Angell wrote: "First the benches emptied and then the bullpens, with the galloping Mets battalion led by—Ta Ra—Teddy R. McGraw." Fans showered Rose with objects from the stands, and the Mets almost forfeited the game when Reds manager Sparky Anderson responded by pulling his team from the field. In the World Series, the Mets lost to the Oakland Athletics in seven, dropping the deciding game, 5–2, on October 21.

. . .

Frustrated by George Steinbrenner's meddling, Yankee manager Ralph Houk resigned after the season. In two stints with the team (1961–1963, 1966–1973), his record was 944–806 (.539).

. . .

Sportswriter Jimmy Cannon died on December 5. Son of a Tammany Hall politician, he had dropped out of high school to work as a copyboy. A protégé of Damon Runyon, he joined the *New York American* as a sportswriter in 1936. After writing for *Stars and Stripes* during World War II, he joined the *New York Post* in 1946 and in 1959 moved to the *Journal-American* for $1,000 a week, making him the highest paid sportswriter in America. His column included bits that began "Nobody asked me, but . . ." He covered baseball and boxing exclusively and famously called boxing "the red light district" of sports. It was Cannon who wrote of Joe Louis, "He's a credit to his race—the human race."

. . .

At the Long Island Arena in Commack on December 8, the New York Chiefs defeated the Midwest Pioneers in the last official game of the International Roller Derby League (founded 1937). The teams skated an exhibition at Madison Square Garden the next night, and that was the end.

1974 ....

If you play 25 innings and win, you feel a lot better than when you play 25 innings and lose.

YOGI BERRA

After failing to obtain permission from the American League to sign Dick Williams of the Oakland Athletics, the Yankees named Bill Virdon as manager on January 3. Thus began George Steinbrenner's manager-go-round.

. . .

The New York Sets joined World Team Tennis, a new professional league, playing at Madison

Square Garden. Manuel Santana of Spain was the player-coach. The team became the Apples in 1977.

• • •

Working with physical-education teachers at Intermediate School 10, New York Police Department community affairs detective David A. Walker and his partner, detective Ulysses Williams, organized the first double Dutch tournament on February 14. Nearly 600 fifth through eighth graders participated. Walker then founded the American Double Dutch League.

• • •

The Yankees played their first game at Shea Stadium, beating the Cleveland Indians, 6–1, before 20,744 fans on April 6.

• • •

Denis Potvin of the Islanders, the first overall pick in the previous draft, won the Calder Trophy as the NHL's Rookie of the Year.

• • •

Behind second-year center John Gianelli, the Knicks beat the Capital Bullets in the first round of the playoffs in seven games, but then fell to the Celtics in the Eastern Conference finals in five.

• • •

Under first-year coach Kevin Loughery, the Nets and Julius Erving won their first ABA championship, beating the Utah Stars in five games. They won the final game, 111–100, at Nassau Coliseum on May 10. Dr. J was voted the ABA's Most Valuable Player.

• • •

Jack Dempsey closed his restaurant at 1619 Broadway, between Forty-ninth and Fiftieth Streets, in Times Square. Some time before, two would-be muggers, seeing an old man walking from the restaurant, jumped him. Dempsey recorded the last two knockouts of his career. His home was a penthouse at 211 East Fifty-third Street. He died on May 31, 1983.

• • •

The New York Stars took the field in the new World Football League; their home field was Downing Stadium on Randall's Island. With one game left in the 20-game season, the team relocated to Charlotte, North Carolina.

• • •

At Winged Foot Golf Club on June 16, Hale Irwin won the United States Open by two strokes, finishing 7 over par at 287.

• • •

Fifteen-year-old Nancy Lieberman of Far Rockaway High School was named to the United States women's basketball team.

• • •

The Cosmos made Downing Stadium their home field.

• • •

French high-wire artist Philippe Petit staged a 45-minute exhibition on a cable between the twin towers of the World Trade Center on August 7. Asked why he had engaged in the illegal stunt, Petit replied, "When I see three oranges, I juggle; when I see two towers, I walk."

• • •

Bill Arnsparger succeeded Alex Webster as head coach of the Giants. From 1969 to 1973, Webster's record was 29–40–1 (.420).

• • •

Jimmy Connors won his first United States Open singles title, defeating Ken Rosewall of Australia in straight sets.

• • •

On September 3, the Jets moved into their new training complex at Hofstra University, their home through 2008, when they moved to Florham Park, New Jersey.

• • •

On September 11, after 7 hours and 4 minutes, the St. Louis Cardinals finally beat the Mets, 4–3, in the twenty-fifth inning, one inning shy of the 26-inning 1–1 tie between the Brooklyn Dodgers and the Boston Braves in 1920, and 19 minutes short of the game between the San Francisco Giants and the Mets on May 31, 1964. Umpire Ed Sudol was behind the plate, as he had been in the 1964 game. A record 202 men came up to bat; Felix Millan and John Milner each batted 12 times. Manager Yogi Berra said, "If you play 25 innings and win, you feel a lot better than when you play 25 innings and lose."

▪ ▪ ▪

The Greek American A.C. won the National Open Challenge Cup.

▪ ▪ ▪

On New Year's Eve, the Yankees signed pitcher Jim "Catfish" Hunter to a five-year, $3.75 million contract, the biggest in baseball to that point. Hunter said, "To be a Yankee is a thought in everyone's head and in mine. Just walking into Yankee Stadium chills run through you. I believe there was a higher offer, but no matter how much money offered, if you want to be a Yankee, you don't think about it."

1975 ....

Before only 3,000 in San Diego on February 14, the Nets lost to the Conquistadors, 176–166, in quadruple overtime. Julius Erving played for all but 2 minutes and scored a career-high 63 points.

▪ ▪ ▪

In the first intercollegiate women's basketball game played at Madison Square Garden, Queens College lost to reigning national champion Immaculata College, 65–61, before 11,969 on February 22. The previous season, Queens had ended Immaculata's 35-game winning streak.

▪ ▪ ▪

In April, after a stint as vice president and general manager of the Buffalo Braves, Eddie Donovan returned to the Knicks as general manager. In the opening round of the playoffs, the aging

Knicks lost to the Houston Rockets, two games to one.

▪ ▪ ▪

Twenty-three-year-old sportswriter Mike Lupica joined the *New York Post*. He moved to the *Daily News* in 1977 and was still with the paper more than 30 years later.

▪ ▪ ▪

The Nets finished with their best record, 58–26 (.690), and again Julius Erving was named the ABA's Most Valuable Player. But in the opening round of the playoffs, after winning game one, the Nets lost four straight to the lowly St. Louis Spirits, dropping the last game, 108–107, at Nassau Coliseum on April 15. The Spirits (winning percentage, .381) had not won four straight all season.

▪ ▪ ▪

In their third season, the Islanders made the playoffs. They defeated the Rangers, two games to one, in the opening round, and then beat the Pittsburgh Penguins in seven, winning the deciding game, 1–0, on April 26—only the second team in professional sports history to come back from a 0–3 deficit in a seven-game series. Goalie Chico Resch stopped 30 shots in that game. In the semifinals, the Isles fell behind the Philadelphia Flyers, three games to none, but forced a game seven. Attempting to neutralize the Flyers' good-luck charm, Kate Smith, Ed Westfall presented her with a bouquet of roses before she sang "God Bless America." Philadelphia still won, 4–1.

▪ ▪ ▪

At a press conference at the 21 Club on June 10, the Cosmos signed thirty-four-year-old Brazilian superstar Pelé to a three-year, $4.7 million contract, the highest in any team sport. The Brazilian government tried to prevent Pelé from leaving the country, but Secretary of State Henry Kissinger suggested that it would be good for relations between Brazil and the United States. He joined the team on June 15 for a game against the Dallas

Tornado at Downing Stadium before 21,278, triple the usual attendance, and scored a goal in the 2–2 game. The arrival of Pelé gave the NASL instant credibility.

In a mile-and-a-quarter match race at Belmont Park on July 6, undefeated Ruffian was leading Foolish Pleasure when she snapped her right front leg below the ankle. "She don't gimme no warning," said jockey Jacinto Vásquez. "She just went. She was running on three legs." Ruffian was put down that night.

On July 21, Joe Torre of the Mets hit into four double plays, a record. Torre said, "I couldn't have done it without Felix Millan," who singled in front of him four times.

The Yankees dismissed manager Bill Virdon after a season and a half (142–124, .534) and hired Billy Martin for the first time on August 1. Martin had played second base on the great Yankee teams of the 1950s.

On August 6, the Mets fired manager Yogi Berra and tapped Roy McMillan to finish the season. Berra's record was 292–296 (.497). Under McMillan, the team finished with a 26–27 record. On October 3, Joe Frazier was signed as manager. He lasted not even a season and a half.

On October 6, twenty-five-year-old Diana Nyad swam 28 miles around Manhattan in 7 hours, 57 minutes, bettering an unofficial record set in 1927. The water temperature was 65 degrees.

In a blockbuster trade on November 7, the Rangers sent team captain and fan favorite Brad Park, Jean Ratelle, and Joe Zanussi to the Bruins for Phil Esposito and Carol Vadnais. Esposito led the Rangers in scoring for four seasons before retiring in

The Queens College women's basketball team playing the Chinese national women's team at Madison Square Garden, November 24, 1975. (Queens College)

1981. Drafted number two overall in 1966, Park had joined the Rangers in 1968 at age twenty (the team's first draft pick to actually play for them), and they made the playoffs each year with him playing defense.

With the team at 2–7 after a six-game losing streak, the Jets fired Charley Winner and made offensive coordinator Ken Shipp interim coach on November 19.

At Madison Square Garden on November 24, a crowd of 7,029, many of them Chinese Americans, saw the Chinese national women's basketball team defeat Queens College, 85–58. In the first game of the doubleheader, Adlai Stevenson High School of the Bronx defeated Walton High School, also of the Bronx, 31–29, the first girls' basketball game played at the Garden.

1976

I'm the straw that stirs the drink.

REGGIE JACKSON

On becoming the first Yankee captain since Lou Gehrig, catcher Thurman Munson said, "Maybe they made me captain because I've been here so long. If I'm supposed to be captain by example, then I'll be a terrible captain." After playing at Shea Stadium for two seasons, the Yankees returned to a renovated Yankee Stadium on April 15, defeating the Minnesota Twins, 11–4; Dan Ford of the Twins hit the first home run in the rebuilt ballpark. In the American League Championship Series, they beat the Kansas City Royals in five games for the pennant. In the dramatic fifth game, on October 14, first baseman Chris Chambliss led off the bottom of the ninth with a first-pitch home run for a 7–6 Yankee win. But in the World Series, the Yankees were swept by the Reds, the "Big Red Machine." Munson was voted the American League's Most Valuable Player.

▪ ▪ ▪

In the Stanley Cup playoffs, the Islanders swept the Vancouver Canucks in two straight games, then ousted the Buffalo Sabres in six, but fell to the Montreal Canadiens in five. Center Bryan Trottier won the Calder Trophy as the NHL's top rookie, and Denis Potvin won the first of three Norris Trophies as the top defenseman.

▪ ▪ ▪

After defeating the San Antonio Spurs in the semifinals in seven, the Nets took the Denver Nuggets in six for their second ABA championship. In the final game, at Nassau Coliseum on May 13, the Nets were down 80–58 but came back for a

Opening day at the rebuilt Yankee Stadium, April 15, 1976. (The Bronx County Historical Society)

112–106 victory. Coach Kevin Loughery's pressing defense turned the game around. For a third consecutive year, Julius Erving was voted the ABA's Most Valuable Player.

▪ ▪ ▪

Giorgio Chinaglia made his debut with the Cosmos on May 17, scoring twice and setting up Pelé with an assist in a 6–0 win over the Los Angeles Aztecs at Yankee Stadium. The team acquired Chinaglia from the Italian team Lazio for $500,000; he led the league in scoring with 19 goals and 11 assists. In the NASL playoffs on August 20, the Tampa Bay Rowdies eliminated the Cosmos, 3–1.

▪ ▪ ▪

At Nassau Coliseum on August 27, the New York Sets—with Billie Jean King, Virginia Wade, Phil Dent, and Sandy Mayer—defeated the San Francisco Golden Gaters, 91–57, for the World Team Tennis championship.

▪ ▪ ▪

The South Shore Little League of Staten Island became New York State champion.

▪ ▪ ▪

In the inaugural women's basketball competition at the Summer Olympic Games in Montreal, the United States took a silver medal to the Soviet Union's gold. Gail Marquis of Queens College and Nancy Lieberman of Far Rockaway High School were on the team.

▪ ▪ ▪

At Yankee Stadium on September 28, heavyweight champion Muhammad Ali won a unanimous decision over Ken Norton. At $2.5 million, this was the highest grossing fight ever held at the Stadium. It was also the last boxing card there. Since opening in 1923, the Stadium had hosted 31 title bouts; Joe Louis fought there 11 times, the most of any boxer.

▪ ▪ ▪

Julius Erving refused to report to training camp unless the Nets renegotiated the final four years

The New York Sets of World Team Tennis: (*rear, left to right*) Phil Dent, Virginia Wade, Fred Stolle, Billie Jean King, and Sandy Mayer; (*front*) Lindsey Beaven and Linda Siegelman. (June Harrison)

of his original seven-year, $1.9 million contract. A day before the season opened, team owner Roy Boe sold him to the Philadelphia 76ers for $3 million. Dr. J signed a six-year, $3.5 million deal with his new team. Several season-ticket holders sued the Nets, unsuccessfully.

▪ ▪ ▪

In their first game at Giants Stadium in East Rutherford, New Jersey, on October 10, the Giants lost to the Dallas Cowboys, 24–14. (The Giants had played at the Polo Grounds [1925–1955], Yankee Stadium [1956–1973], the Yale Bowl [1973–1974], and Shea Stadium [1975].) With the team at 0–7, Bill Arnsparger was fired on October 25 and Jim McVay became head coach. In two and a half seasons, the team went 7–28 (.200) under Arnsparger.

▪ ▪ ▪

With 2,002 entrants, the New York City Marathon wound through the five boroughs from the Verrazano Narrows Bridge to Central Park for the first time. Bill Rodgers won in 2 hours, 10 minutes, 9 seconds—3 minutes ahead of rival Frank Shorter—and he won in the next three years also. Miki Gorman finished first among the 88 women entered, at

Crowds lining First Avenue to watch the runners in the New York City Marathon, ca. 1978. (Author's collection)

2 hours, 39 minutes, 11 seconds, good for seventieth place overall.

• • •

To show that pinball is a game of skill and not of chance, Roger Sharpe gave a demonstration to the City Council, which then voted to rescind the ban on pinball imposed in 1941.

• • •

On November 29, the Yankees signed free agent outfielder Reggie Jackson to a five-year, $2.96 million contract. He had problems with manager Billy Martin from the start and alienated his teammates when he was quoted in *Sports Illustrated* in May 1977: "I'm the straw that stirs the drink."

• • •

On December 9, with the Jets at 3–10 and one game remaining, first-year coach Lou Holtz resigned. Mike Holovak took over for the last game on December 12, a 42–3 shellacking by the Cincin-

nati Bengals. That was Joe Namath's last game in a Jets uniform. (He played for the Los Angeles Rams the next season, and then retired.)

1977

There it is, ladies and gentlemen, the Bronx is burning.

HOWARD COSELL

Part-owner Leon Hess became acting president of the Jets. Walt Michaels was named head coach on January 5.

• • •

Legendary saloonkeeper Toots Shor died on January 23. He held season tickets for all the local teams (which the Internal Revenue Service acknowledged as a legitimate business expense for him), and his restaurant was the preferred watering hole for the sporting crowd from the 1940s into the 1960s. His first joint, at 51 West Fifty-first Street, lasted from 1940 to 1959; the second, at 33 West Fifty-second Street, opened in 1960 and was padlocked by the IRS in 1971; the third opened at 5 East Fifty-fourth in 1973. "I don't want to be a millionaire," he famously remarked. "I just want to live like one."

On March 9, the Knicks announced that Willis Reed would replace Red Holzman as head coach. Reed had retired as a player in 1975.

In the Stanley Cup playoffs, the Islanders eliminated the Chicago Blackhawks, and then swept the Buffalo Sabres before again falling to the Montreal Canadiens in the semifinals in six games. Mike Bossy, the first rookie to score more than 50 goals in a season, won the Calder Trophy.

Mystic and fitness guru Sri Chinmoy founded the Sri Chinmoy Marathon Team. In his words: "Run and become. Become and run. Run to succeed in the outer world. Become to proceed in the inner world." He died at his Jamaica, Queens, home at age seventy-six on October 11, 2007.

On May 19, about 15,000 attended the first night of racing at Parr Meadows, a quarter-horse track in Yaphank, Long Island. Ronald Parr intended the venue to be part of a larger residential and commercial development, but his financial and legal problems sank the project. The track closed on September 28.

When the team began the season at 15–30, the Mets fired Joe Frazier on May 31 and named Brooklyn-born Joe Torre as player-manager, the team's eighth manager in 16 years. Torre retired as a player. Frazier's record was 101–106 (.488).

On June 11, before 70,229, the second-largest crowd to attend the Belmont Stakes to date, Seattle Slew outran seven other horses to capture the Triple Crown, the first undefeated horse to do so.

Mets general manager M. Donald Grant perpetrated the "Midnight Massacre" on June 15, trading Tom Seaver, "The Franchise," to the Reds for Pat Zachry, Steve Henderson, Doug Flynn, and Dan Norman. Sportswriter Dick Young of the *Daily News* had called Seaver an "ingrate" for having pressed the team to renegotiate his contract. Fans began referring to Shea Stadium as "Grant's Tomb."

During a nationally televised game at Fenway Park on June 18, Yankee manager Billy Martin removed right fielder Reggie Jackson in the middle of an inning for not hustling. In the dugout, the two almost came to blows, but Yogi Berra and Elston Howard physically restrained Martin.

On July 19, Yankee Stadium was the site of the All-Star Game for the third time (1939 and 1960); the National League prevailed, 7–5.

At the Shinnecock Hills Golf Club on August 27, the United States defeated Great Britain and Ireland to retain the Walker Cup.

With Billie Jean King, Virginia Wade, Sandy Mayer, and Ray Ruffels, the New York Apples—formerly the Sets—defeated Chris Evert and the Phoenix Raquets, 55–39, for the World Team Tennis championship on August 27.

Denied entry into the U.S. Open in 1976, Renée Richards, formerly Richard Raskind, successfully sued the United States Tennis Association to be allowed to compete as a woman. She lost in the first round, but competed on the women's professional circuit for four years and was Martina Navratilova's coach for two years.

∎ ∎ ∎

After playing at Yankee Stadium, Hofstra University, and Downing Stadium, the Cosmos moved into Giants Stadium. Eddie Firmani became the new coach. The Cosmos signed Franz Beckenbauer, captain of West Germany's 1974 World Cup championship team, to a four-year, $2.8 million contract on May 25. They also signed Carlos Alberto, Pelé's longtime teammate in Brazil, on July 17. New Yorker Shep Messing was in goal. In their first playoff game, against the Fort Lauderdale Strikers, the Cosmos drew 77,691. In the NASL championship game, on August 28, the Cosmos defeated the Seattle Sounders, 2–1, on goals by Giorgio Chinaglia and Steve Hunt. In September, the Cosmos embarked on an Asian tour, playing in Japan, China, and India. At a sold-out Giants Stadium on October 1, Pelé closed his playing career in an exhibition game between the Cosmos and the Santos of Brazil, playing one half for each team.

∎ ∎ ∎

Muhammad Ali defended his heavyweight crown with a 15-round decision over Ernie Shavers before 14,613 at Madison Square Garden on September 29. Eva Shain was judging that night, the first woman to score a heavyweight-title fight.

∎ ∎ ∎

On October 9, the Knicks sent Walt Frazier to the Cleveland Cavaliers as compensation for signing Jim Cleamons. "Clyde" later became a Knicks broadcaster, noted for his tangled syntax. He once held team records for games, minutes, field goals, free throws, and points (14,617), and he still holds the team record for assists (4,791). The Knicks retired his number, 10, in 1979.

∎ ∎ ∎

For the second straight year, the Yankees beat the Royals in the ALCS in five games to win the pennant. In the World Series, they defeated the Los Angeles Dodgers in six, winning the last game, 8–4, on

Dedication of the William Red Holzman Gymnasium at Franklin K. Lane High School, November 17, 1977. Holzman is tossing up the first ball. (Queens Borough Public Library, Long Island Division, Joseph A. Ullman Photographs)

October 18. Reggie Jackson, "Mr. October," hit five home runs in the series, the last three on consecutive swings of the bat in the final game; Mike Torrez hurled two complete-game victories. Sparky Lyle became the first relief pitcher to win the Cy Young Award. During game two, the television camera zoomed in on a burning building near the Stadium, and Howard Cosell famously remarked, "There it is, ladies and gentlemen, the Bronx is burning."

∎ ∎ ∎

The Nets abandoned Long Island for New Jersey. For the next four seasons, the team's home court was the Rutgers Athletic Center in Piscataway.

∎ ∎ ∎

On November 17, the William Red Holzman Gymnasium was dedicated at Franklin K. Lane High School, Holzman's alma mater.

∎ ∎ ∎

Sunnyside Garden, a boxing arena on Queens Boulevard erected in the 1920s, was demolished on December 9.

1978 ....

15 Years of Lousy Football—We've Had Enough.

GIANTS FAN

A Golden Gloves bout, sponsored by the *Daily News*, at Sunnyside Garden, February 16, 1976. (Queens Borough Public Library, Long Island Division, Joseph A. Ullman Photographs)

At the Millrose Games on January 27, Franklin Jacobs, a sophomore at Fairleigh Dickinson University, cleared 7 feet, 7¼ inches to set the world indoor high-jump record, only half a inch short of the world outdoor record.

Retired firefighter Gary Muhrcke, winner of the first New York City Marathon in 1970, won the inaugural Empire State Building Run-Up on February 15. His sprint up the 1,575 steps to the eighty-sixth floor was controversial, however, as he was receiving a three-quarter disability pension from the Fire Department.

In the Yankees' home opener, on April 13, Reggie Jackson connected for a home run on his first swing of the bat. (In the last game of the World Series in 1977, he had hit homers on his last three swings at Yankee Stadium.) The fans celebrated by tossing the Reggie candy bars handed out as a promotion onto the field.

The Islanders fell to the Toronto Maple Leafs in the first round of the playoffs, losing the seventh game, 2–1, in overtime on April 29.

For the first time, there was a Triple Crown winner in consecutive years. In a five-horse field,

Affirmed, with Steve Cauthen up, nosed out Alydar, ridden by Jorge Velásquez, to win the Belmont Stakes on June 10. Alydar had finished a close second in the Kentucky Derby and the Preakness.

Affirmed (*right*) and Alydar battling down the stretch in the Belmont Stakes, June 10, 1978. (Bob and Adam Coglianese Photographs)

Affirmed nosing out Alydar at the wire in the Belmont Stakes. (Bob and Adam Coglianese Photographs)

On June 17, Yankee left-hander Ron Guidry struck out 18 batters in a 4–0 win over the California Angels, setting a single-game strike-out record for southpaws. He finished the season with a record of 25–3, the best ever for a Yankee pitcher; a 1.74 ERA; and nine shutouts, winning the Cy Young Award.

. . .

On June 25, the pool at the Aquacade in Flushing Meadows–Corona Park was named for Gertrude Ederle, the first woman to swim the English Channel. The Department of Parks and Recreation closed the pool in 1988 and in 1996 demolished the historic amphitheater, built for the 1939 World's Fair.

. . .

On July 24, after a disagreement with slugger Reggie Jackson over a missed sign, Yankee manager Billy Martin said of Jackson and George Steinbrenner, "The two of them deserve each other. One's a born liar; the other's convicted." (In 1974, Steinbrenner had entered a guilty plea for making illegal contributions to President Richard Nixon's reelection campaign.) The Boss dismissed Martin the next day and named Bob Lemon as manager.

At the time, the team was 10 games behind the Red Sox; in mid-August, the Yankees were 14 back. On September 7, they went to Fenway Park, trailing by four games, and won four straight: 15–3, 13–2, 7–0, and 7–4! Ending the season tied, the Yankees and the Red Sox met in a one-game playoff at Fenway Park on October 2. Shortstop Bucky Dent hit a three-run homer off Mike Torrez, and Jackson hit one out in the eighth, for a 5–4 victory. Facing the Royals for the third straight year, the Yankees took the ALCS in four games for the pennant. In the World Series, they defeated the Dodgers in six games after dropping the first two. Sparkling play by third baseman Graig Nettles and scoreless pitching by reliever Goose Gossage turned the series around.

. . .

The Cosmos averaged an attendance of nearly 47,856 for 15 home games at Giants Stadium and finished with a 24–6 record. After eliminating the Seattle Sounders, Minnesota Kicks, and Portland Timbers in the playoffs, they defeated the Tampa Bay Rowdies, 3–1, in the Soccer Bowl before nearly 75,000 fans at Giants Stadium on August 27.

. . .

The U.S. Open moved from the West Side Tennis Club in Forest Hills to Louis Armstrong Stadium (originally the Singer Bowl, built for the 1964 World's Fair) in Flushing Meadows–Corona Park. Jimmy Connors won his third men's title in straight sets over Bjorn Borg of Sweden, and Chris Evert won her fourth straight women's title in straight sets over Pam Shriver.

. . .

John Cook won the United States Men's Amateur Golf Championship at the Plainfield Country Club in New Jersey.

. . .

Broadcaster Lindsey Nelson left the Mets after the season. He had been with the club since 1962.

Gertrude Ederle and Queens Borough President Donald Manes renaming the pool at the Aquacade in Flushing Meadows–Corona Park, June 25, 1978. (Queens Borough Public Library, Long Island Division, Joseph A. Ullman Photographs)

Breaking ground for the Tennis Center at Flushing Meadows–Corona Park, the new home of the U.S. Open, on October 6, 1977, are Mrs. Louis Armstrong (*center*), Donald Manes (*left, looking up*), and comedian Alan King (*far right*). (Queens Borough Public Library, Long Island Division, Joseph A. Ullman Photographs)

Doubles partners Billie Jean King (*left*) and Martina Navratilova en route to victory at the U.S. Open, 1978. Each woman won the U.S. Open singles title four times. (June Harrison)

◘ ◘ ◘

The short-lived Women's Basketball League was founded. The New York Stars played the first season at Iona College in New Rochelle, and then at Madison Square Garden, but drew poorly and disbanded in 1980. The New Jersey Gems played at the Thomas Dunn Center in Elizabeth for the first two seasons, and then at the South Mountain Arena in West Orange in 1980/1981, the league's final season.

◘ ◘ ◘

Grete Waitz of Norway won the New York City Marathon for the first time. In all, she won the race nine times.

◘ ◘ ◘

Starting their second season under Willis Reed at 6–8, the Knicks brought back Red Holzman as head coach on November 11. Reed's record was 49–47.

◘ ◘ ◘

With 31 seconds remaining and having only to take a knee to seal a victory over the Philadelphia Eagles at Giants Stadium on November 19, quarterback Joe Pisarcik botched the handoff to fullback Larry Csonka. Defensive back Herman Edwards grabbed the ball and ran 26 yards into the end zone for a 17–12 Philadelphia win. "The Fumble" marked the low point in the team's fortunes. During a home game against the St. Louis Cardinals on December 10, a fed-up fan flew an airplane above Giants Stadium towing a banner: "15 Years of Lousy Football—We've Had Enough." (The Giants won the game, 17–0.) After the 6–10 season, the Giants fired head coach John McVay, and Andy Robustelli, director of operations, resigned. Over three seasons, McKay's record was 14–23 (.378).

◘ ◘ ◘

The Spalding sporting goods company discontinued the spaldeen, the beloved pink rubber ball sold in candy stores that was essential for stickball, stoopball, and punchball. The spaldeen was reintroduced in May 1999 as the Hi-Bounce Ball and in colors other than pink.

◘ ◘ ◘

Arizona State University beat Rutgers University in the first Garden State Bowl at Giants Stadium. The bowl was discontinued after four years.

◦ ◦ ◦

In the inaugural game of the Major Indoor Soccer League, the New York Arrows defeated the Cincinnati Kids, 7–2, before 10,386 fans at Nassau Coliseum on December 22. Pete Rose, part owner of the Cincinnati franchise, made the ceremonial first kick. Steve Zungul was named the game's Most Valuable Player.

1979

In a Golden Gloves heavyweight match at the Felt Forum in Madison Square Garden on January 30, Francis Ricotilli scored a second-round technical knockout over twenty-five-year-old Francisco Rodriguez. Rodriguez died of an enlarged heart a few hours after this bout, his first. Michael M. Baden, the chief medical examiner, said, "A person in this condition should not have been fighting. His heart was in such condition that it was subject to failure upon severe exertion." The malady could have been detected only by an X-ray, which was not required as part of the qualifying physical. This was the second fatality in the history of the Golden Gloves.

◦ ◦ ◦

At Madison Square Garden on February 11, the Soviet Union defeated the NHL all-stars, 6–0, to capture the Challenge Cup, two games to one.

◦ ◦ ◦

With Wellington Mara and his nephew Tim Mara unable to work together—they each owned 50 percent of the Giants—NFL commissioner Pete Rozelle intervened; at his suggestion, the team brought in George Young as general manager on February 14. On February 22, Ray Perkins was hired as head coach. Young began rebuilding the Giants by drafting quarterback Phil Simms.

◦ ◦ ◦

Behind goalie Shep Messing and Steve Zungul, the New York Arrows defeated the Philadelphia Fever, 9–5, on March 25 to sweep the best-of-three playoff series and capture the first MISL championship.

◦ ◦ ◦

On April 13, in the Eastern Division playoffs of the Women's Basketball League, the New York Stars fell to the Houston Angels, 93–84, losing the series in two straight.

◦ ◦ ◦

Under first-year coach Fred Shero, the Rangers reached the Stanley Cup playoffs. Behind goalie John Davidson, the Swedes Ulf Nilsson and Anders Hedberg, and Phil Esposito, Ron Duguay, and Pat Hickey, the Rangers dispatched the Flyers in five games. The Islanders, meanwhile, skating to the best record in the NHL on the stick of Mike Bossy, swept the Blackhawks. In the next round, the Rangers took the Islanders in six, ending with a 2–1 victory at Madison Square Garden on May 8. Mike Lupica wrote in the *Daily News*: "The Rangers and Islanders have spoiled us. New York will never forget these hockey games." In the finals, the Rangers lost to the Canadiens in five, losing the last game, 4–1, in Montreal on May 21. Bryan Trottier of the Islanders was the league's Most Valuable Player.

◦ ◦ ◦

Running for the Triple Crown in the Belmont Stakes on June 9, Spectacular Bid finished third, behind Coastal and Golden Act.

◦ ◦ ◦

With the Yankees struggling, George Steinbrenner dismissed Bob Lemon and brought back Billy Martin on June 17; the team finished in fourth place. On October 28, five days after Martin brawled with a businessman in a Bloomington, Minnesota, hotel, George Steinbrenner fired him. (By all accounts, the man had followed Martin out of the bar and started the altercation.) Dick Howser became manager.

▫ ▫ ▫

In his first at bat in the All-Star Game on July 17, Brooklyn-born Lee Mazzilli of the Mets hit a pinch-hit home run in the eighth inning. In the ninth, he drew a bases-loaded walk off Yankee ace Ron Guidry to force in the winning run for a 7–6 National League victory.

▫ ▫ ▫

On August 2, Yankee catcher Thurman Munson died in a crash at the Akron-Canton Airport in Ohio as he practiced takeoffs and landings in his private plane. He had been the American League's Most Valuable Player in 1976 and a seven-time all-star. The team retired his number, 15, in an emotional ceremony at the Stadium after his funeral.

▫ ▫ ▫

Walter O'Malley died at age seventy-five on August 9. There were no tears in Brooklyn.

▫ ▫ ▫

At the U.S. Open on August 30, umpire Frank Hammond lost control of a match between thirty-three-year-old Ilie Nastase and twenty-year-old John McEnroe midway through the fourth set when Nastase protested a point by refusing to serve. After begging into the microphone, "Let's go, Ilie, please," he awarded the match to McEnroe. The crowd howled and threw objects onto the court; tournament referee Mike Blanchard finally removed Hammond (a move that Hammond called "ludicrous"), and the match continued. McEnroe won the match and, in the final, beat Vitas Gerulaitis in straight sets for the first of his four singles titles.

▫ ▫ ▫

Early in the season, Ray Klivecka replaced Eddie Firmani as head coach of the Cosmos, and midfielder Rick Davis of California joined the roster. They finished with a 24–6 record. On September 1, the Cosmos faced the Vancouver Whitecaps in the conference final. They won the game (90 minutes,

plus a 15-minute overtime), 3–2, to tie the series at 1–1; the teams then played a scoreless 30-minute mini-game; finally, Vancouver won in a shoot-out.

▫ ▫ ▫

The Patriots shellacked the Jets, 56–3, on September 9, the worst loss in franchise history.

▫ ▫ ▫

The Mets finished 35 games back at 63–99, their third consecutive season with nearly 100 losses. Not surprisingly, they drew only 788,905 to Shea Stadium, the lowest season attendance in franchise history.

▫ ▫ ▫

Grete Waitz won the New York City Marathon in the world record women's time of 2 hours, 27 minutes, 33 seconds; Bill Rodgers won the men's race for the fourth consecutive year. For the first time, the event was televised.

▫ ▫ ▫

At the Felt Forum in Madison Square Garden on November 23, a near-capacity crowd of 2,590 saw middleweight Wilford Scypion knock out Willie Classen in the tenth round. Classen never regained consciousness and died after surgery for an acute subdural hematoma. After his death, the New York State Athletic Commission required an ambulance standing by at every prizefight.

▫ ▫ ▫

The Brooklyn Italian S.C. won the National Open Challenge Cup.

▫ ▫ ▫

Ashrita (originally Keith) Furman, a follower of Sri Chinmoy, performed 17,000 jumping jacks for the first of his record 78 entries in the *Guinness Book of Records*. He also traversed the 16 miles up and down Mount Fuji by pogo stick, race-walked the fastest mile while hula-hooping (15 minutes, 25 seconds), somersaulted the 12.2-mile route of Paul Revere's ride, and balanced 75 beer glasses on his chin. The keeper of the Guinness records called him "the most prolific record breaker."

1980—1989

New professional leagues brought new teams to the city in the 1980s, the New Jersey Saints of the Major Indoor Lacrosse League and the New Jersey Generals of the United States Football League joining the struggling New York Arrows of the Major Indoor Soccer League and the New York Stars of the Women's Basketball League. But those leagues did not survive, suggesting that the market was reaching the saturation point. The Meadowlands was the site of Grand Prix racing, but the event vanished when it could not move to the streets of Manhattan. The Cosmos began the decade as the preeminent team in the thriving North American Soccer League, but the team and the league collapsed. Under coach Al Arbour, the Islanders won the Stanley Cup in an unprecedented four straight years and generated enormous local interest in hockey. The Mets built a World Series winner, but could not sustain success. George Steinbrenner's managerial carrousel continued in the Bronx, always returning to Billy Martin, but this was the only decade since the 1910s when the Yankees did not win a World Series. On Staten Island, though, the South Shore Little League built a dynasty, and the Harlem Little League was founded, a modest step toward rectifying the neglect of team sports in the inner city. And, finally, radio station WFAN went on the air—all sports all the time—and immediately altered the way New Yorkers talked about sports.

1980

On January 24, the publisher Doubleday & Company, behind president Nelson Doubleday Jr., with Fred Wilpon of Sterling Equities, purchased a controlling interest in the Mets for $21 million, the highest price ever paid for a ballclub. The Payson family had owned the team since its inception in 1961.

■ ■ ■

With center Jeff Ruland, Iona College had its best basketball season, finishing in the top 20 with a 29–5 record. After a professional career cut short by injuries, Ruland returned to coach at his alma mater.

■ ■ ■

The Yankees signed with SportsChannel (the first all-sports cable-television channel, launched in 1976) to air 40 games, with WPIX broadcasting 100.

Before 8,469 at Nassau Coliseum on March 23, the New York Arrows defeated the Houston Summit, 7–4, to repeat as the champions of the Major Indoor Soccer League.

The New York Stars, with three players from Queens College—Debbie Mason, Gail Marquis, and Althea Gwynn—won the Women's Basketball League championship (their playoff games were held at Queens College). On April 9, the Stars defeated the Iowa Cornets, 125–114, to win the series, three games to one. Dean Meminger (an alumnus of Rice High School and a former Knick) was the WBL's Coach of the Year. During the season, the players received $5 a day. Unable to build a sufficient fan base, the Stars folded before the next season. The Dallas Diamonds made Nancy Lieberman the first pick in the WBL draft on June 16.

Knicks guard Micheal Ray Richardson became the first player to lead the National Basketball Association in both assists (10.1) and steals (3.23).

In the National Hockey League playoffs, the Rangers dispatched the Atlanta Flames, three games to one, but then were eliminated by the Philadelphia Flyers in five, losing the last game, 3–1, on April 22. The Islanders ousted the Los Angeles Kings in four, and then defeated the Boston Bruins in five. Bruins coach Harry Sinden said, "The reason we lost this series was because of the Islanders." In the semifinals, the Islanders took the Buffalo Sabres in six games. The Isles won their first Stanley Cup by beating the Flyers four games to two; Bob Nystrom's overtime goal won the final contest, 5–4, at Nassau Coliseum on May 24.

On May 19, former jockey Con Errico was convicted of having bribed jockeys in an organized-crime race-fixing scheme at Aqueduct Racetrack and Saratoga Race Course in 1974 and 1975. Jockey José Amy testified that he had accepted bribes from Errico to fix dozens of races. (His license had been suspended on May 13.) Errico was sentenced to 10 years in prison and fined $25,000.

New York United of the short-lived American Soccer League played their first game at Shea Stadium on May 28, drawing 1,109 (676 paid). They beat the Golden Gate Gales, 3–0. The team had played as New York Apollo at Hofstra Stadium for the four previous seasons.

At Baltusrol Golf Club, on June 15, Jack Nicklaus withstood a strong challenge from Isao Aoki of Japan to win the United States Open with a record score of 272 for 72 holes.

John McEnroe outlasted Bjorn Borg, 7–6, 6–1, 6–7, 5–7, 6–4, to win his second straight singles title at the United States Open. Chris Evert won her fifth singles championship.

Under new coach Hennes Weisweiler of Germany, the Cosmos finished with a record of 24–8. Giorgio Chinaglia again led the North American Soccer League in scoring, with 32 goals, and added a remarkable 18 goals in seven games in the playoffs to become the league's all-time scoring leader. In the Soccer Bowl on September 21, the Cosmos defeated the Fort Lauderdale Strikers, 3–0, for their fourth NASL championship.

Manager Dick Howser led the Yankees to a 103–59 record, but in the American League Championship Series they lost to the Kansas City Royals in three straight. Howser was dismissed on November 21. Gene Michael became manager, the seventh in eight years under George Steinbrenner.

John McEnroe during his five-set victory over Bjorn Borg for the U.S. Open Men's Singles Championship, his second straight, 1980. McEnroe went on to win the event two more times. (June Harrison)

After opening the season at 4–13–3, the Rangers fired coach Fred Shero and appointed Craig Patrick as interim coach on November 21. Patrick's father, Lynn, and his uncle Murray "Muzz" Patrick had played on the Rangers 1940 championship team, and his grandfather Lester had been the general manager.

The New York Pancyprian Freedoms won the National Open Challenge Cup.

On December 15, George Steinbrenner signed all-star outfielder Dave Winfield to a 10-year, $25 million contract, the highest for any player in team sports. Half of each year's cost-of-living increase would go to the David Winfield Foundation for Children.

With the Nets at 12–23 on December 22, coach Kevin Loughery resigned, and assistant coach Bob MacKinnon took over. Over seven and a half seasons, Loughery's record was 297–318, a winning percentage of .483, with four playoff appearances and American Basketball Association titles in 1974 and 1976.

1981

You never know. I'll keep it warm for you.

BOB LEMON TO GENE MICHAEL

The ship be sinking.

MICHEAL RAY RICHARDSON

On January 7, Bill Parcells joined the Giants as defensive coordinator, a key factor in turning a 4–12 team into a 9–7 contender.

While attending an indoor soccer game at Madison Square Garden on February 11, James F. Foster conceived of Arena Football, a 50-yard field set over the hockey rink.

On March 18, the Nets introduced Larry Brown as their new head coach, effective at the end of the season. Bob MacKinnon became general manager. Brown left UCLA to take the Nets job.

The Arrows won their third consecutive MISL title, defeating the St. Louis Steamers, 6–5.

In the best-of-three first round of the playoffs of the WBL, the New Jersey Gems fell to Most Valuable Player Nancy Lieberman and the Dallas Diamonds, 107–88, on April 6. The league folded after the season.

. . .

Behind center Bill Cartwright and guards Micheal Ray Richardson and Ray Williams, the Knicks finished with a 50–32 record, but lost to the Chicago Bulls in two straight games in the opening round of the playoffs.

. . .

In the playoffs, the Rangers, led by Ron Greschner and Barry Beck, beat the Los Angeles Kings and then ousted the St. Louis Blues. The Islanders swept the Toronto Maple Leafs in three straight games, and then eliminated the Edmonton Oilers in six. In the semifinals, the Islanders, with Billy Smith in goal, swept the Rangers, taking the fourth game, 5–2, at Madison Square Garden on May 5. In the finals, the Isles beat the Minnesota North Stars in five, winning the final game, 5–1, at Nassau Coliseum on May 21 for their second Stanley Cup.

. . .

On August 8, the Hambletonian, the most prestigious race for three-year-old trotters, was staged at the Meadowlands Racetrack for the first time. Shiaway St. Pat won the multiheat race. Named for the nineteenth-century horse from which almost all American thoroughbreds are descended, the race had begun in Syracuse, New York, in 1926.

. . .

On September 6, Bob Lemon became manager of the Yankees for the second time, replacing Gene Michael, who had expressed displeasure at interference from the front office. At the time, Lemon said to Michael, "You never know. I'll keep it warm for you." Former Yankees manager Dick Howser said, "I don't want to say he's better off, but when the guillotine is over your head, it's better to have it happen. His head's been on the block for a long time. Sometimes it's a relief. In my case it was."

. . .

Outside linebacker Lawrence Taylor, from the University of North Carolina, played his first game for the Giants. Dominant from the day he arrived, he was voted the NFL's Most Valuable Player in 1986; was named Defensive Player of the Year in 1981, 1982, and 1986; and played in the Pro Bowl 10 times. He retired in 1994 and was elected to the Pro Football Hall of Fame in 1999.

. . .

The New York Road Runners Club staged the inaugural Fifth Avenue Mile for elite runners on September 26. An estimated 100,000 spectators lined the avenue from Sixty-second to Eighty-second Street. Sydney Maree of South Africa won in 3 minutes, 47.52 seconds, the second fastest time ever; Leann Warren won the women's race in 4 minutes, 25.31 seconds. The race continued through 1998, and then resumed in 2005.

. . .

The Cosmos completed their fourth consecutive 20-win season, but in the Soccer Bowl on September 26, they lost to the Chicago Sting, 1–0, in a shoot-out, their first defeat in the NASL championship game.

. . .

On October 4, during the final game of the season, the Mets dismissed Joe Torre. Over four and a half

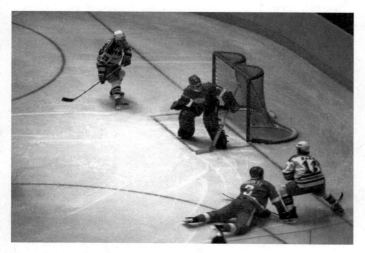

The Rangers in action against the Detroit Redwings at Madison Square Garden, 1981. (June Harrison)

seasons, the longest tenure of any Mets manager to date, his record was 286–420 (.404). On October 20, the Mets hired Staten Island native George Bamberger. The following season, the team finished last under Bamberger, too.

Because of the midseason players' strike, Major League Baseball scheduled the first divisional playoff series. The Yankees defeated the Milwaukee Brewers in five games, and then swept the Oakland Athletics in three straight in the ALCS, winning the final game, 4–0, on October 15 for their thirty-third pennant. In the World Series, the Yankees won the first two games, but then dropped four straight to the Los Angeles Dodgers. Pitcher George Frazier lost three games, a World Series record. On October 25, after the Yankees lost their third straight in Los Angeles, a pair of drunken Dodger fans approached George Steinbrenner in his hotel elevator. They called his team "chokers" and New Yorkers "animals." Steinbrenner responded with an obscenity and, in a brief brawl, landed two rights and a left, sending both men to the floor. At a press conference in his hotel room, the Boss said, "I clocked them. There are two guys in this town looking for their teeth, and two guys who will probably sue me." The men never surfaced. Or did he just slam his fist into a wall?

At the Rye Hilton in Port Chester on October 30, the United States won the world contract bridge championship, defeating Pakistan for the Bermuda Bowl. The previous night, Great Britain defeated the United States for the women's championship, the Venice Bowl.

The New Jersey Nets played their first season at the Brendan Byrne Arena in the Meadowlands. (It was renamed the Continental Airlines Arena in 1995, and in 2007 became the Izod Arena.)

The New Jersey Rockets joined the MISL, playing at the Meadowlands. After a 17–27 season, the team folded.

As the Knicks plummeted to 33–49, a reporter had this legendary exchange with Micheal Ray Richardson:

Reporter: What do you think is happening to the team?
Richardson: The ship be sinking.
Reporter: How far can it sink?
Richardson: Sky's the limit.

After an 11-year drought during which neither team reached the playoffs, both the Jets and the Giants made it. Behind running back Freeman McNeil and the aggressive defense of the "New York Sack Exchange"—Joe Klecko, Mark Gastineau, Marty Lyons, and Abdul Salaam—the Jets finished with a record of 10–5–1, their first winning season since the merger of the American Football League and the National Football League. In the wild-card games on December 27, the Giants defeated the Philadelphia Eagles, 27–21, behind backup quarterback Scott Brunner, while the Jets fell to the Buffalo Bills, 31–27, before 57,050 at Shea Stadium. The Bills intercepted quarterback Richard Todd's pass on the 1-yard line with 10 seconds remaining.

1982

In San Francisco on January 3, the Giants lost to the 49ers, 38–24, in the National Football Conference playoff game.

Red Smith died on January 15. A sportswriter since the 1920s, his regular column "Views of Sport" ran in the *New York Herald Tribune* from 1945 until that newspaper's demise; in 1971, he joined the *New York Times*; and in 1976, he was awarded the Pulitzer Prize for commentary, the first sportswriter so honored.

◦ ◦ ◦

The NBA All-Star Game was played at the Brendan Byrne Arena, with the Eastern Conference beating the Western, 120–118.

◦ ◦ ◦

The Arrows won their fourth consecutive MISL title, defeating the Steamers in a five-game championship series.

◦ ◦ ◦

John J. McMullen purchased the Colorado Rockies for about $30 million and moved the franchise to New Jersey. The team was renamed the Devils, after the former Eastern Hockey League team.

◦ ◦ ◦

The Yankees named third baseman Graig Nettles team captain on January 29.

◦ ◦ ◦

On April 18, Red Holzman coached his final game with the Knicks, a 119–99 loss to the Celtics at Boston Garden. Holzman's record was 613–484 (.559), taking his team to the playoffs in eight consecutive years and winning NBA championships in 1970 and 1973. His overall coaching record was 696–604 (.535). On May 20, Sonny Werblin, president of Madison Square Garden, appointed Dave DeBusschere executive vice president and director of basketball operations and named Hubie Brown head coach of the Knicks. General manager Eddie Donovan became vice president and director of player personnel. (He left the organization in 1986.) The team retired the number 613 for Holzman.

◦ ◦ ◦

In the playoffs, the Rangers beat the Flyers, three games to one, in the first round, while the Islanders survived a tough five-game series with the

Pittsburgh Penguins. Down 3–1 with 6 minutes to play in the deciding game on April 13, they won on a goal by John Tonelli in overtime. The Islanders then beat the Rangers, 5–3, at Madison Square Garden on April 23 to take the quarterfinals in six. On May 4, they completed a four-game sweep of the Nordiques with a 4–2 victory in Quebec City. The Isles then swept the Vancouver Canucks for their third straight Stanley Cup, taking the last game, 3–1, on May 16. Mike Bossy tied the record with seven goals in the finals (16 overall in the playoffs).

◦ ◦ ◦

The Washington Bullets defeated the Nets, 103–92, on April 23, taking the best-of-three first round of the playoffs in two straight. Nets forward Buck Williams was voted the NBA's Rookie of the Year.

◦ ◦ ◦

When the Yankees started at 6–8 under Bob Lemon, George Steinbrenner brought back Gene Michael on April 25. After the Yanks dropped a doubleheader to the Chicago White Sox in the Bronx on August 3 and fell to 50–50, Michael was out and Clyde King took over.

◦ ◦ ◦

Twelve swimmers challenged the 28.5-mile distance in the first competitive swim around Manhattan.

◦ ◦ ◦

Chris Evert won her record sixth U.S. Open singles championship, while Jimmy Connors won the fourth of his five singles titles.

◦ ◦ ◦

In the Soccer Bowl in San Diego, California, on September 18, the Cosmos defeated the Seattle Sounders, 1–0, on a goal by Girogio Chinaglia for their fifth and final NASL championship. The Cosmos averaged only 28,749 fans a game at Giants Stadium, down nearly 20,000 from 1978.

◦ ◦ ◦

Six-time women's singles champion Chris Evert at the U.S. Open, 1989. (June Harrison)

The New York Pancyprian Freedoms won their second National Open Challenge Cup.

▫ ▫ ▫

On December 16, the Cincinnati Reds traded Tom Seaver back to the Mets.

1983 ....

Giants coach Ray Perkins resigned on January 3 to become head coach at the University of Alabama. His record over four seasons was 23–34. The Giants named defensive coordinator Bill Parcells as the new head coach.

▫ ▫ ▫

On January 11, George Steinbrenner brought back Billy Martin for his third stint as manager of the Yankees.

▫ ▫ ▫

In the playoffs after a strike-shortened season, the Jets defeated the Cincinnati Bengals, 44–17; then beat the Los Angeles Raiders, 17–14; but lost to the Miami Dolphins, 14–0, in the American Football Conference title game in a rain-soaked Orange Bowl on January 23. On February 9, head coach Walt Michaels resigned (39–47–1; .454), and offensive coordinator Joe Walton took over.

▫ ▫ ▫

Hijos y Amigos de Altamira (Sons and Friends of Altamira), a dominoes club in the Bronx, was founded, named for the members' hometown in the Dominican Republic. The club gained national renown in June 2006 when ESPN2 broadcast dominoes there (following a successful debut on ESPN Deportes).

▫ ▫ ▫

After leading the Cosmos to the NASL title as interim coach the previous season, Julio Mazzei was named head coach on February 1.

▫ ▫ ▫

On February 23, the New Jersey Generals of the new United States Football League signed Heisman Trophy winner Herschel Walker, a junior at the University of Georgia, to the largest contract in professional football to date, an estimated $1.5 million a year. The USFL originally intended to follow the NFL and refuse to sign undergraduates, but facing likely legal action, commissioner Chet Simmons said, "We felt it was fruitless to maintain and defend that rule." Playing a spring season, the Generals took the field for the first time on March 6, losing to the Los Angeles Express, 20–15. They lost to the Tampa Bay Bandits, 32–9, before 53,370 in their first home game at Giants Stadium on March 20. (Their average attendance was 35,004 that first season.) The Generals finished with a record of 6–12 under coach Chuck Fairbanks. On September 22, Donald Trump bought the team for a rumored $8 million to $10 million (the exact sum was not disclosed).

For the first time in the five-year history of the MISL, the Arrows did not win the championship, losing in the first round to the Baltimore Blast.

With the Nets headed into the playoffs, coach Larry Brown resigned on April 7 to become basketball coach at the University of Kansas; team president and co-owner Joe Taub insisted that if Brown wanted the Kansas job, he leave immediately. Assistant coach Bill Blair took over. In the best-of-three first round, the Knicks swept the Nets, taking the second game, 105–99, on April 21. (The Nets had yet to win a game in three NBA playoff appearances.) On June 8, Stan Albeck became head coach. Nets player Foots Walker said, "He runs a team the way it should be run. Larry was the type of guy that you didn't know where he was coming from. I'm glad we've got a quality coach."

Tim McCarver joined Ralph Kiner and Steve Zabriskie in the Mets television booth; Bob Murphy would call the games only on radio.

The Rangers finished the season at .500, but in the opening round of the playoffs swept the Flyers, who had the second best record in the NHL. The defending champion Islanders (with only the sixth best record in the league) took the opening round from the Washington Capitals in four games. In the second round, the Isles beat the Rangers in six, winning the final contest, 5–2, at Madison Square Garden on April 22. After eliminating the Bruins in six games, the Islanders swept the Oilers for their fourth straight Stanley Cup,

taking the final game, 4–2, at Nassau Coliseum on May 17.

In the second round of the playoffs, the Philadelphia 76ers swept the Knicks, taking the fourth game, 105–102, on May 1. The Knicks had started the season at 15–26, but finished with a 44–38 record.

Using suction cups and metal clamps that hooked into the window-washing tracks, Daniel Goodwin climbed the 110-story North Tower of the World Trade Center on May 30. At first, he was charged with criminal trespass and reckless endangerment, but then was merely issued a summons for having staged an unlawful street performance.

Less than halfway through his second season as manager of the woeful Mets, George Bamberger resigned on June 3. "I probably suffered enough," he said. His record was 81–127 (.389). First-base coach Frank Howard took over for the season, finishing with a 52–64 record (.448). On October 13, the team hired Davey Johnson.

Running at 5–2 odds, August Belmont IV's Caveat won the Belmont Stakes on June 11. The 15-horse field was the largest in the event's history.

On June 20, the Yankees forced thirty-seven-year-old center fielder Bobby Murcer to retire to make room on the roster for Don Mattingly at first base. Murcer then became a broadcaster, joining Phil Rizzuto, Frank Messer, and Bill White in the WPIX television booth. At Yankee Stadium on July Fourth, George Steinbrenner's fifty-second birthday, Dave Righetti pitched a no-hitter to defeat the Boston Red Sox, 4–0. At the Stadium on July 24, an umpire ruled that a home run by George Brett of the Royals should be an out because, as Yankee manager Billy Martin pointed out, there was too much pine tar on his bat. Four days later, American League president Lee MacPhail overturned the umpire, ruling the home run legal and ordering the game resumed from that point; Kansas City won the continued game, 5–4, on August 18. Warming up in the out-field before the fifth inning in Toronto on August 4, Dave Winfield accidently killed a seagull with a baseball. The Ontario Provincial Police arrested him for cruelty to animals, but the charges were dropped the next day.

◦ ◦ ◦

Jimmy Connors defeated Ivan Lendl for his fifth and final singles title at the U.S. Open. Martina Navratilova won the first of her four singles championships.

◦ ◦ ◦

After finishing in first place for the sixth straight season, the Cosmos were bounced in the opening round of the NASL playoffs in two straight by the Montreal Manic, losing the second game in a shoot-out, 1–0, on September 12. Girogio China-glia retired after the game as the NASL's all-time scoring leader, with 165 goals. On November 7, Eddie Firmani returned as head coach, replacing Julio Mazzei. Firmani had led the team to the league title in 1977 and 1978.

◦ ◦ ◦

After holding the America's Cup for 132 years, the New York Yacht Club yielded to a challenger. *Australia II*, with its unusual and controversial winged keel, bested *Liberty* in the best-of-seven series off Newport, Rhode Island, taking the final race handily on September 26.

◦ ◦ ◦

In the Felt Forum at Madison Square Garden on September 30, lightweight Juan Roman Cruz knocked out twenty-four-year-old Isidro "Gino" Perez in the seventh round of a 10-round fight. According to Al Certo, Perez's manager,

> The first minute of the seventh round he done good. Then he got hit with the right hand, and he dropped right in our corner. He got right up right away, but his back was to me. I assumed he was all right, because the ref looked at him and let him continue. But when he moved away from the ropes, I seen him stagger. I started to move my hands to stop it, and Charley Norris, the ref, was seeing me, and he moved in too. But Cruz got there before any of us and landed another right hook while Gino was falling. By that time I was already reaching through the ropes. The doctor must have been flying, because he was in the ring, too, when I got there.

Perez wanted to get up, but the men held him down. Before passing out, Perez said, "Oh, jeez, my head." He never regained consciousness and died on October 6.

◦ ◦ ◦

Jimmy Connors at the U.S. Open, 1991. He won the Men's Singles Championship five times. (June Harrison)

Mets outfielder Darryl Strawberry, with 26 home runs and 74 RBIs, was voted the National League's Rookie of the Year.

- - -

The New York Pancyprian Freedoms won their third National Open Challenge Cup. New York soccer clubs had won the championship 14 times since the cup's inception in 1951.

- - -

Wagner College won the Eastern College Athletic Conference Metro NY/NJ football championship.

- - -

Twelve years after abandoning the sport, New York University again fielded a men's basketball team, but in Division III, not Division I.

- - -

The Jets played their final game at Shea Stadium on December 10, losing to the Pittsburgh Steelers, 34–7. They moved to Giants Stadium the next season.

- - -

On December 16, George Steinbrenner dismissed Billy Martin (while guaranteeing the four years left on his contract at $400,000 a year) and brought in Yogi Berra. The Yankees finished with a record of 87–75 the next season.

1984

Assuming that no team would want thirty-nine-year-old Tom Seaver, Mets general manager Frank Cashen left him off the team's protected list for the free-agent compensation draft, but the Chicago White Sox claimed him on January 20.

- - -

At the Millrose Games at Madison Square Garden, Carl Lewis set a new indoor long-jump record: 28 feet, 10¼ inches.

- - -

On February 9, Leon Hess bought out his last minority partner to become sole owner of the Jets.

- - -

For the second straight year, the Arrows lost to the Blast in the first round of the playoffs of the MISL. The team folded before the next season, with a record of 158–78 and four championships in six seasons.

- - -

In the Stanley Cup playoffs, the defending champion Islanders ousted the Rangers in the first round in a tough five-game series, taking the final game, 3–2, in overtime on April 10. They then ousted the Capitals in five games and the Montreal Canadiens in six. In the finals, the Islanders lost to the Oilers in five games.

- - -

In their first season under Stan Albeck, the Nets—with Buck Williams, Albert King, and Micheal Ray Richardson—upset the defending champion 76ers, led by Julius Erving and Moses Malone, in the first round of the playoffs, winning all three games on the road in Philadelphia. On April 26, they took the fifth game, 101–98, behind Richardson's 24 points and six steals. In the next round, they fell to the Milwaukee Bucks in six, losing the last game, 98–97, at the Brendan Byrne Arena on May 10.

- - -

In Detroit on April 27, the Knicks beat the Pistons, 127–123, in overtime to take the first-round series in five games. Bernard King had his fourth straight 40-point game and set an NBA record with 213 points in a five-game series. On May 13, the Knicks lost the seventh game of the Eastern Conference finals to the Celtics in Boston, 121–104.

- - -

The Department of Parks and Recreation closed McCarren Park Play Center in Greenpoint, Brooklyn, one of the pools built under Robert Moses in 1936. The bathhouse was later damaged by fire, and

McCarren Park Play Center in 1998, after years of abandonment by the Department of Parks and Recreation. (Queens Borough Public Library, Long Island Division, Anders Goldfarb Photographs)

the site remained abandoned for decades. In 2007, the pool was designated an official city landmark, and funds were promised for restoration.

■ ■ ■

Under Walt Michaels, the Generals finished with a 14–4 record, but in the playoffs on June 1, they lost to the Philadelphia Stars, 28–7. They averaged 37,716 fans a game at Giants Stadium.

■ ■ ■

At Winged Foot Golf Club on June 18, Frank "Fuzzy" Zoeller defeated Greg Norman by eight shots in an 18-hole playoff for the U.S. Open championship. On the second hole, Zoeller sank a 68-foot birdie putt to take a three-stroke lead and never looked back. The day before, Norman had sunk a 40-footer on the eighteenth green to force the playoff.

■ ■ ■

The Meadowlands Grand Prix for Indy cars was staged for the first time on July 1. Mario Andretti won the 168-mile event (100 laps around a 1.68-mile course). It had been planned as a 200-mile race, but was shortened to squeeze into the two-hour slot that NBC had allowed. After

the 1991 race, promoters proposed moving to the streets of Manhattan, but that did not happen and the race was not run again.

■ ■ ■

John McEnroe beat Ivan Lendl in straight sets for his fourth and final U.S. Open singles championship. (Lendl reached the finals every year from 1982 to 1989, winning in 1985, 1986, and 1987.) Martina Navratilova again won the women's singles title.

■ ■ ■

On September 6, the Jets played their first game at Giants Stadium in the Meadowlands, losing to the Steelers, 23–17. They previously played at the Polo Grounds (1960–1963) and Shea Stadium (1964–1983).

■ ■ ■

The Cosmos played their final game on September 15. The NASL collapsed after the season. What was left of the team joined the MISL, playing at Madison Square Garden. The Cosmos went 11–22 before folding in midseason.

■ ■ ■

For his second consecutive start, on September 17, Dwight Gooden struck out 16 batters—tying the major league record with 32 strikeouts in consecutive starts—but he still lost to the Phillies, 2–1. The Mets finished in second place, behind the Chicago Cubs, with a record of 90–72, nearly reversing their record from the year before, 68–94, and enjoying their first winning season since 1976. Going 17–9 with 276 strikeouts, Gooden was voted the National League's Rookie of the Year.

■ ■ ■

Columbia University's Lawrence A. Wien Stadium opened on September 22 with a football game against Harvard (the Lions lost). The new stadium had a capacity of 16,500; old Baker Field's wooden bleachers had held 32,000. The playing field was named for Robert Kraft in 2007 after he donated $5 million to his alma mater.

With barely 13,000 on hand at Shea Stadium on September 25, fan favorite Rusty Staub hit a pinch-hit home run in the ninth inning to beat the Phillies, 6–4, only the second player in major league history to homer in his teens and in his forties. (Ty Cobb was the other.)

On the last day of the season, Yankee first baseman Don Mattingly had four hits to finish at .343 and win the batting title; his teammate Dave Winfield had one hit to finish at .340.

On Christmas Day, Bernard King scored 60 points in a losing effort against the Nets, eclipsing Richie Guerin's Knicks record 57-point effort in 1959 and setting a new scoring mark in the fourth Madison Square Garden. (Wilt Chamberlain had scored 73 points against the Knicks in the third Garden in 1962.)

1985

On January 29, Joe Namath was elected to the Pro Football Hall of Fame, the first member of the Jets to be enshrined. On October 14, the team retired his number, 12, a franchise first.

Police officer Pat Russo and other officers from the Seventy-second Precinct founded the Sunset Park Boxing Club to give boys an alternative to street gangs; the club also recruited youth into the New York Police Department. It operated out of the Sunset Park Recreation Center until evicted in October 2006, the last such club in a facility run by the Parks Department, which claimed that the ring took up too much space.

Under coach Lou Carnesecca, the St. John's University men's basketball team reached the Final Four of the National Collegiate Athletic Association tournament. With Chris Mullin, Walter Berry, Willie Glass, Mark Jackson, and Bill Wennington, the team faced Patrick Ewing and Georgetown for the fourth time that season; they lost, 77–59. Carnesecca was named Coach of the Year.

Boxing match at the Cromwell Recreation Center on Staten Island, 1942. (New York City Parks Photo Archive)

On April 1, *Sports Illustrated* published George Plimpton's "The Curious Case of Sidd Finch," about a Mets pitcher who fired 168-mile per hour fastballs. Finch supposedly had studied with monks in Tibet, and threw with one bare foot and the other in a work boot. Joe Berton, an art teacher from Chicago, posed for the photos. The spoof took in several major league executives and at least one New York sports editor, who berated the Mets in print for having given the scoop to the magazine.

The surprising Nets—with Micheal Ray Richardson, Buck Williams, Albert King, Mike Gminski, and Darryl Dawkins—were bounced in the opening round of the playoffs by the Pistons in three straight, losing the final game, 116–115, on a last second shot by Isiah Thomas. Only 9,999 fans were on hand at the Brendan Byrne Arena.

Richardson was voted Comeback Player of the Year.

· · ·

With a 2–1 victory over the Capitals in Washington, D.C., on April 16, the Islanders became the first team in the history of the NHL to win a five-game series after being down by two games to none. In the second round, they fell to the Flyers, their earliest exit in seven years.

· · ·

With the Yankees starting the season at 6–10 under Yogi Berra, George Steinbrenner brought back Billy Martin on April 28. But rather than tell Berra directly, he dispatched Clyde King to deliver the news. Berra said, "He's the boss. He can do what he wants. I'm used to this. This is the third time I've been fired. That's what this game is." But he was deeply hurt and vowed never to return to Yankee Stadium as long as Steinbrenner owned the team. (They reconciled in 1999.) The Yanks finished second with a 97–54 record.

· · ·

Fifteen runners participated in the first Sri Chinmoy Self-Transcendence Marathon, run over five days, in Flushing Meadows–Corona Park. In 1988, the Sri Chinmoy Marathon Team staged a seven-day race; in 1996, a 10-day race.

· · ·

Gary Thorne joined Bob Murphy in the Mets radio booth, remaining with the team through 2002.

· · ·

Kathy Baker won the United States Women's Open Golf Championship at Baltusrol Golf Club.

· · ·

Behind rookie quarterback (and Heisman Trophy winner) Doug Flutie and running back Herschel Walker, the Generals finished with a record of 11–7. In the playoffs, they fell to the Baltimore Stars, 20–17, at the Meadowlands on July 1. The Generals averaged 41,268 fans a game in home attendance.

· · ·

Pitching for the White Sox, Tom Seaver hurled his 300th victory, beating the Yankees, 4–1, at Yankee Stadium on Phil Rizzuto Day, August 4. Seaver was later a broadcaster for the Yankees and the Mets.

· · ·

On August 13, nine weeks after Stan Albeck left for the Bulls, the Nets named thirty-five-year-old Dave Wohl as head coach.

· · ·

The South Shore Little League of Staten Island advanced to the Little League World Series.

· · ·

Dwight Gooden of the Mets struck out 16 batters in a 3–0 victory over the San Francisco Giants on August 20, becoming the first pitcher in the National League to strike out more than 200 in each of his first two seasons.

· · ·

At the Montclair Golf Club on September 1, Sam Randolph won the United States Men's Amateur Golf Championship.

· · ·

In the bar of the Cross Keys Inn in Baltimore on September 21, Yankee manager Billy Martin and pitcher Ed Whitson began to throw punches. The brawl continued in the lobby, the parking lot, and the hallway. Somehow Martin's arm was broken. He later told reporters that he had hurt himself while bowling. George Steinbrenner fired Martin on October 27 and hired Lou Piniella.

· · ·

After four unsuccessful outings, forty-six-year-old Phil Niekro of the Yankees finally notched his 300th win, beating the Toronto Blue Jays, 8–0, on the last day of the season. Known for his knuckleball, he threw everything but that pitch until he faced the final batter, when he struck out Jeff Burroughs on three knucklers. Niekro was the oldest pitcher to hurl a complete game shutout.

· · ·

Yankee first baseman Don Mattingly was voted the American League's Most Valuable Player. He hit .324, with 35 home runs and 145 RBIs, and won the first of nine consecutive Gold Glove awards.

▫ ▫ ▫

Aqueduct Racetrack hosted the Breeders' Cup on November 2, attracting 42,568 racing fans. (The event had been inaugurated the year before at Hollywood Park Racetrack in Inglewood, California.) The Big A received a $3 million spruce-up for the event.

▫ ▫ ▫

Wagner College won the ECAC South football championship.

▫ ▫ ▫

On December 28, in the AFC wild-card game, the Jets lost to the New England Patriots, 26–14.

1986 ....

At Madison Square Garden on January 10, the Rangers honored Bill Cook, team captain from 1926 until his retirement in 1937. "It makes you feel like you were somebody," he said.

▫ ▫ ▫

On February 25, NBA commissioner David Stern banned Micheal Ray Richardson of the Nets for two years for having tested positive for cocaine for the third time, as stipulated in the agreement between the league and the players' union. He was the first player to be banned for drug use. Larry Doby, the team's director of community affairs, said, "Micheal Ray is not a problem child; he's a child with a problem."

▫ ▫ ▫

On March 4, the Yankees named second baseman Willie Randolph and pitcher Ron Guidry as co-captains.

▫ ▫ ▫

At Nassau Coliseum on April 12, the Islanders lost to the Capitals, 3–1, and were eliminated in the open-

ing round of the playoffs in three straight, their earliest exit ever. Coach Al Arbour resigned on May 28 after 14 seasons and four NHL championships. Terry Simpson became head coach on June 18.

▫ ▫ ▫

Before only 7,784 fans at the Meadowlands on April 22, the Nets fell to the Bucks, 118–113, and were eliminated in the opening round of the playoffs in three straight.

▫ ▫ ▫

In the playoffs, the Rangers beat the Flyers, three games to two, and then took the Capitals in six. In the semifinals, they fell to the Canadiens in five, losing the final game, 3–1, on May 9.

▫ ▫ ▫

Knicks center Patrick Ewing, drafted number one out of Georgetown University, was named the NBA's Rookie of the Year.

▫ ▫ ▫

Running at 8–1 odds, Danzig Connection won the 118th Belmont Stakes on June 7, the fifth straight victory for trainer Woody C. Stevens.

▫ ▫ ▫

For the first time in 90 years, the U.S. Open was held at the Shinnecock Hills Golf Club in Southampton. Ray Floyd shot a final-round 66 for the championship, at forty-three, the oldest man to win the tournament.

▫ ▫ ▫

At twenty-one years, seven months, and thirty days, Dwight Gooden of the Mets became the youngest pitcher to start in the All-Star Game.

▫ ▫ ▫

On July 14, the Rangers named Phil Esposito as general manager, replacing Craig Patrick. On November 20, he fired coach Ted Sator (41–50–12) and went behind the bench himself, until hiring Tom Webster on November 26.

▫ ▫ ▫

On July 29, after a 10-week trial, a jury in the United States District Court in Manhattan ruled that the NFL had indeed violated the Sherman Antitrust Act, but awarded the USFL only $1 in damages (trebled to $3 in an antitrust case). The USFL had sought $1.69 billion. Lacking a network-television contract—the crux of the lawsuit—the USFL cancelled its upcoming fall season (after three spring seasons) on August 4. Founded with 12 teams in 1983, the USFL lost an estimated $150 million to $200 million.

The Ozone Howard Little League lost the championship game in the Eastern Regionals.

With a strong rotation of Dwight Gooden, Ron Darling, Sid Fernandez, Bob Ojeda, and Rick Aguilera; the relief pitching of Roger McDowell and Jesse Orosco; and the leadership of catcher Gary Carter and first baseman Keith Hernandez, the Mets won the National League East with a 108–54 record. In the sixth game of the tense National League Championship Series against the Houston Astros on October 15, the Mets scored three runs in the ninth inning to tie and won, 7–6, in the sixteenth for their third National League pennant. Down three games to two against the Red Sox in the World Series and down to their last out in the memorable sixth game at Shea Stadium on October 25, the Mets staged a three-run rally, highlighted by Mookie Wilson's easy grounder rolling through the legs of first baseman Bill Buckner. (This after Bob Stanley threw a wild pitch to allow the tying run to score.) The Mets won game seven, 8–5, on October 27 for their second world championship.

On November 14, Nelson Doubleday and Fred Wilpon purchased the Mets from Doubleday & Company.

Wagner College won the ECAC South football championship again.

The New York City Sports Commission was created to foster amateur and professional sports in the city.

Rodney Smith and Bruno Musso founded Shut Skateboards and sponsored a traveling skateboard team. The partners had connected as teenagers a few years before, skateboarding and writing graffiti in Riverside Park. The enterprise folded in 1991, but two years later Smith joined with Adam Schatz and Eli Morgan to launch Zoo York, designing and selling skateboards, surfboards, and clothing; they also sponsored a skateboard team.

Two years after the Arrows folded, and following a season without a MISL franchise in New York, the New York Express joined the league, playing at Nassau Coliseum. They went 3–23 before folding in midseason.

With the team sinking at 4–12, the Knicks fired Hubie Brown and promoted assistant Bob Hill to head coach on December 1. Over five seasons, Brown's record was 142–202 (.413), with two playoff appearances.

At Madison Square Garden on December 12, James "Bonecrusher" Smith won the World Boxing Association heavyweight title with a first-round knockout of Tim Witherspoon.

The Jets lost their last five games but still finished with a 10–6 record. In the AFC wild-card game, on December 28, they beat the Kansas City Chiefs, 35–15, at the Meadowlands.

1987

Stand up and boo.

DICK YOUNG

In the AFC divisional playoff on January 3, the Jets held a 20–10 lead over the Cleveland Browns with just 4 minutes to play, but lost, 23–20, in double overtime. A roughing-the-passer penalty called on Mark Gastineau kept the Browns' fourth-quarter drive alive.

▪ ▪ ▪

In the first game of the new Eagle Pro Box Lacrosse League (renamed the Major Indoor Lacrosse League in 1988), the New Jersey Saints defeated the Philadelphia Wings, 11–8, before 5,976 fans at the Meadowlands on January 10.

▪ ▪ ▪

On January 11, the Giants defeated the Washington Redskins, 17–0, in the NFC title game. In the Super Bowl, on January 25, they beat the Denver Broncos, 39–20, behind quarterback Phil Simms, who completed 22 of 25 passes for 268 yards and three touchdowns; he was named the game's Most Valuable Player. Linebacker Lawrence Taylor was voted the NFL's Most Valuable Player and, for the third time, was named Defensive Player of the Year. Running back Joe Morris set a team rushing record with 1,516 yards.

▪ ▪ ▪

On January 26, only two months after being hired as head coach of the Rangers, Tom Webster was fired, and general manager Phil Esposito again took over. On April 16, the Flyers beat the Rangers, 5–0, at Madison Square Garden, eliminating them in the first round of the playoffs in six games. The Rangers hired Michel Bergeron as coach on June 18.

▪ ▪ ▪

Irish runner Eamonn Coughlin, the "Chairman of the Boards," won the Wanamaker Mile at the Mill-rose Games on January 30 for a record seventh time (having won in 1977, 1979, 1980, 1981, 1983, and 1985), surpassing Glenn Cunningham's six victories in the 1930s.

▪ ▪ ▪

Mika'il Sankofa of New York University won the NCAA saber championship for an unprecedented fourth consecutive year.

▪ ▪ ▪

Down three games to one to the Capitals in the opening round of the playoffs, the Islanders forced a seventh game on April 18. At 8 minutes, 47 seconds of the fourth overtime of the deciding game, Pat LaFontaine scored to give the Islanders a 3–2 victory. In round two, the Islanders fell behind the Flyers, three games to one, and again forced a seventh game, but lost, 5–1, in Philadelphia on May 2.

▪ ▪ ▪

On July 1, all-sports radio WFAN went on the air, replacing WHN, a country-music station, at 1050 on the AM dial. The first voice heard belonged to Suzyn Waldman, who covered the Yankees for the station until 2001. The FAN moved to 660 on October 7, 1988, replacing WNBC-AM. Ten years later, it was the country's highest grossing station, the radio home of the Mets, Jets, Knicks, and Rangers.

▪ ▪ ▪

Al Bianchi became general manager of the Knicks on July 9. Four days later, he named Rick Pitino as the new head coach. Pitino had been an assistant with the Knicks from 1983 to 1985, and then head coach at Providence College.

▪ ▪ ▪

On July 18, Don Mattingly of the Yankees homered in his eighth straight game, tying the record set by Dale Long of the Pittsburgh Pirates in 1956. On September 29, he connected off Bruce Hurst of the Red Sox for a record sixth grand slam of the season.

▪ ▪ ▪

Sportswriter Dick Young died on August 31. He had started as a messenger at the *Daily News* in 1937 and rose to sports editor. He covered primarily baseball and boxing, and had a regular column,

"Young Ideas." In 1982, he moved to the *New York Post*. When Dwight Gooden returned from drug rehabilitation in 1987, he indignantly wrote, "Stand up and boo." Past president of the Baseball Writers Association of America, he was enshrined in the writers' wing at the Baseball Hall of Fame in 1978.

▫ ▫ ▫

Central State University defeated Grambling University, 37–21, in the seventeenth Whitney Young Jr. Memorial Urban League Classic before 29,411 at Yankee Stadium on September 12. It was the last football game played there.

▫ ▫ ▫

The Mets finished a disappointing three games out of first place, but topped 3 million in season attendance at Shea Stadium for the first time.

▫ ▫ ▫

Lou Piniella was out as Yankee manager on October 19, and Billy Martin returned for the fifth and final time.

▫ ▫ ▫

With the team at 2–13 on December 9, the Nets dismissed Dave Wohl. General manager Bob MacKinnon became interim coach. Over two-plus seasons, Wohl's record was 65–114, and 0–3 in the playoffs.

▫ ▫ ▫

On December 12, Wagner College defeated the University of Dayton, 19–3, in the Alonzo Stagg Bowl for the NCAA Division III football championship.

1988 ....

On February 29, Willis Reed took over as head coach of the Nets.

▫ ▫ ▫

The New Jersey Saints defeated the Washington Wave, 17–16, in the Eagle Pro Box Lacrosse League championship game on March 20.

▫ ▫ ▫

SportsChannel exercised its option to show 100 Yankee games, with only 40 to be broadcast over WPIX. At the time, the cable station had only 500,000 subscribers, mostly in Manhattan and the suburbs. Fewer than 10 percent of the homes in Brooklyn and Queens had access to cable; only 5 percent on Staten Island; and in the Bronx, only Riverdale was wired.

▫ ▫ ▫

In their first playoff appearance since moving to New Jersey from Colorado in 1982, the Devils beat the Islanders, 6–5, at the Meadowlands on April 14 to take the opening round in six games. In the Eastern Conference finals, the Devils fell to the Bruins in seven, losing the deciding game, 6–2, on May 14. Devils coach Jim Schoenfeld was suspended for the sixth game after insulting the officials. When the Devils obtained a restraining order, the referees refused to take the ice, so the game was played with amateurs officiating.

▫ ▫ ▫

Knicks guard Mark Jackson, a first-round pick out of St. John's University (and Bishop Loughlin Memorial High School in Brooklyn) was named the NBA's Rookie of the Year.

▫ ▫ ▫

Although the team was at 40–28, George Steinbrenner dismissed Billy Martin for the last time and brought back Lou Piniella on June 23. In five stints as Yankee manager, Martin's record was 556–385 (.591). On October 7, Piniella was dismissed and Dallas Green was hired, the sixteenth managerial change in 16 years. From 1986 through 1988, Piniella's record was 224–193 (.537).

▫ ▫ ▫

The South Shore Little League of Staten Island became New York State champion.

▫ ▫ ▫

Roosevelt Raceway canceled the racing season scheduled to begin on August 4 and never re-opened. The trotting venue had opened in 1940.

The action at Roosevelt Raceway. (Queens Borough Public Library, Long Island Division, Post Card Collection)

□ □ □

En route to winning the East, the Mets had their highest attendance to date at Shea Stadium: 3,055,445. In the NLCS, they lost to the Dodgers in seven games.

□ □ □

After setting an NCAA Division I record with 44 consecutive losses, Columbia University finally won a football game, defeating Princeton, 16–13,

on October 8. It was also the Lions' first win at Wien Stadium.

□ □ □

Finishing in 2 hours, 28 minutes, 7 seconds, Grete Waitz won the New York City Marathon for the ninth and final time on November 6. (She had won from 1978 to 1980 and 1982 to 1986.) The largest field to date, 22,912 runners, started on both levels of the Verrazano Narrows Bridge for the first time.

□ □ □

The New York Knights joined the Arena Football League. Playing their home games at Madison Square Garden, the team finished with a record of 2–10 and folded.

□ □ □

Wagner College lost to Ithaca College in overtime in the first round of the NCAA Division III football tournament.

□ □ □

On December 7, the Islanders dismissed head coach Terry Simpson and brought back Al Arbour.

1989

The Long Island University women's basketball team set an NCAA Division I record with 58 consecutive losses, dating back to 1986.

□ □ □

In its eighth appearance in the National Invitational Tournament finals, St. John's University defeated Saint Louis University, 73–65, for a record fifth NIT championship, and coach Lou Carnesecca's first. Jayson Williams was named the tournament's Most Valuable Player.

□ □ □

Iris and Dwight Raiford founded the Harlem Little League; 129 children played on eight teams at Colonel Charles Young Park (145th Street and Lenox Avenue).

□ □ □

Nine-time New York City Marathon winner Grete Waitz (left) running through Harlem, 1984. (June Harrison)

A member of the Harlem Little League. (Simon Benepe/New York City Parks Photo Archive)

Queens native Gary Cohen joined the Mets broadcasting team.

. . .

On April 1, with two games left in the season, general manager Phil Esposito fired Michel Bergeron (73–67–18) and went behind the bench himself. After leading the Patrick Division for three months, the Rangers had lost 12 of their last 15 games. Under Esposito, the Rangers lost their last two games, and then were swept by the Pittsburgh Penguins. On May 24, Esposito was fired. On August 15, Roger Neilson was named the twenty-fifth coach in the franchise's 53-year history.

. . .

The New Jersey Saints of the Major Indoor Lacrosse League relocated to Nassau Coliseum. They lost to the Philadelphia Wings, 11–10, in the championship game on April 7.

. . .

With the Yankees at an underachieving 56–65, Bucky Dent replaced Dallas Green as manager, the seventeenth managerial change in George Steinbrenner's 17 years as owner. Dent was gone a year later.

. . .

The Knicks reached the playoffs behind Patrick Ewing, Mark Jackson, and Charles Oakley. They swept the 76ers, but then fell to the Bulls in six games in the second round, losing the final game, 113–111, on a pair of free throws by Michael Jordan with 4 seconds left on May 19. On May 30, the Knicks released head coach Rick Pitino from the final three years of his contract so he could accept the coaching job at the University of Kentucky. Over two seasons, his record was 90–74 (.549). Stu Jackson, who had come from Providence College with Pitino as an assistant, became head coach on July 10, the team's fourth in five seasons and, at thirty-three, the league's youngest.

. . .

After finishing a close second to Sunday Silence in the Kentucky Derby and the Preakness, Easy Goer, with Pat Day up, won the Belmont Stakes on June

Easy Goer winning the Belmont Stakes, with Pat Day up, June 10, 1989. (Bob and Adam Coglianese Photographs)

High jumper competing at the New York Games, Wien Stadium, 1991. (June Harrison)

10, defeating his rival by eight lengths in the second fastest time after Secretariat: 2 minutes, 26.01 seconds. Easy Goer was the son of Alydar.

□ □ □

The New York Road Runners Club hosted the first New York Games on July 22, a track and field meet that attracted world-class international stars, including Carl Lewis, Jackie Joyner-Kersee, and many other Olympians. The games were held through 1995 at Columbia University's Wien Stadium, but never attracted large crowds.

□ □ □

The South Shore American Little League of Staten Island became New York State champion.

□ □ □

On August 11, Willis Reed resigned as coach of the Nets after one and a half seasons to become vice president for basketball and business development; his record was 33–77 (.300). Bill Fitch took over on August 21.

□ □ □

In August, after its real-estate taxes increased from $5.1 million to $38 million, the Richmond County Country Club, the city's last private golf club, agreed to sell to the city in exchange for a 99-year lease and $4 million, with $1 million going to the Staten Island Greenbelt.

□ □ □

Mike and the Mad Dog, with Mike Francesca and Christopher Russo, premiered in the afternoon slot on WFAN on September 5 and soon became one of the top-rated radio shows ever in the metropolitan area.

□ □ □

Herbert Warren Wind wrote his final piece in the *New Yorker*, a story about the U.S. Open tennis tournament. One of the preeminent golf writers in the country, Wind contributed 132 articles to "The Sporting Scene" feature in the magazine. He wrote for *Sports Illustrated* from 1954 to 1962.

□ □ □

Baseball writer Jack Lang retired from the *Daily News*. He had written for the *Long Island Press* from 1949 until the newspaper folded in 1977. Lang remained a member of Major League Baseball's Scoring Rules Committee and was an official scorer at the World Series for many years.

□ □ □

Former and likely future Yankee manager Billy Martin died in an automobile accident on Christmas Day. George Steinbrenner had fired Martin four times (a record, to be sure), and Martin resigned under pressure once.

□ □ □

After a dismal 4–12 season, the Jets dismissed head coach Joe Walton on December 26. Over seven seasons, his record was 53–57–1 (.482).

1990—1999

Professional sports proliferated in the last decade of the twentieth century. Major League Soccer was founded, with the Metrostars playing in Giants Stadium; the Liberty joined the new and instantly successful Women's National Basketball Association; minor league baseball arrived with the Staten Island Yankees; and an Arena Football League franchise came and went. The Giants won the Super Bowl under Bill Parcells, who ended the 1990s with the Jets, transforming a dismal team into a contender. Many teams—the Knicks, Nets, Islanders, Metrostars, Yankees, and Mets—endured a coaching-go-round and losing seasons. The Knicks had five coaches in five years before Pat Riley made them the toughest team in the National Basketball Association; still, they always fell short, usually at the hands of Michael Jordan and the Chicago Bulls. Bobby Valentine took the Mets to the National League Championship Series, and Joe Torre finally brought stability and championships back to the Bronx. After Al Arbour retired, however, the Islanders swiftly declined. The Rangers finally won the Stanley Cup, 54 years after their last triumph, and the Devils won their first the next year. Staten Island's Little League dynasty continued.

And New York again reached the top in chess, as players from the city's vibrant immigrant communities led high school and college teams to national championships.

1990 ....

Boys will be boys.
AL ARBOUR

Line drive. It's caught. It's over.... The Mets win the ballgame. They win the damn thing by a score of 10–9.
BOB MURPHY

At the Meadowlands on January 7, the Giants, winners of the Eastern Division of the National Football Conference with a 12–4 record, lost to the Los Angeles Rams, 19–13, in overtime in the playoffs.

▪ ▪ ▪

On February 9, Bruce Coslet became the eighth head coach of the Jets. The team went 6–10.

▪ ▪ ▪

The Nets finished with their worst record: 17–65, a winning percentage of .207.

▪ ▪ ▪

The New York Athletic Club, founded 1868, decided to admit women as members.

▪ ▪ ▪

In the first game of the Patrick Division semifinals, on April 6, the Rangers beat the Islanders, 2–1, at Madison Square Garden. With 1 minute, 17 seconds remaining, James Patrick of the Rangers delivered a hard check to Pat LaFontaine that left the Islanders' leading scorer out cold on the ice. Seconds before the game ended, the Isles started several brawls. Asked why he sent his enforcers onto the ice with 2 seconds remaining, Al Arbour replied, "Boys will be boys." The National Hockey League fined the team $25,000 and Arbour $5,000, and suspended Mick Vukota for 10 games and Ken Baumgartner for one. LaFontaine did not return until the last game. The Rangers took the ugly series, four games to one, but then fell to the Washington Capitals in five, losing the last game, 2–1, on April 25.

▪ ▪ ▪

On April 15, the Devils lost to the Capitals, 3–2, and were eliminated in the first round of the playoffs in six games.

▪ ▪ ▪

After dropping the first two games in the first round of the playoffs, including a record 157–128 drubbing in the second game, the Knicks roared back to take three straight from the Celtics, winning the final game, 121–114, at Boston Garden on May 6 (and breaking a 26-game losing streak there that dated back to 1984). The Knicks were only the third team in the history of the National Basketball Association to come back from a deficit of two games to none in a five-game series. They then fell to the Detroit Pistons in five, losing the last game, 95–84, on May 15.

▪ ▪ ▪

George Steinbrenner finally traded outfielder Dave Winfield to the California Angels for pitcher Mike Witt on May 16. On July 30, baseball com-missioner Fay Vincent banned the Yankee owner from day-to-day involvement with the club after determining that he had paid gambler Howard Spira $40,000 to dig up dirt on Winfield. (Spira had come up with nothing.) Steinbrenner's lifetime ban lasted until March 1, 1993.

▪ ▪ ▪

On May 29, the Mets dismissed Davey Johnson. Bud Harrelson, shortstop on the 1969 World Series championship team, became the team's twelfth manager. Over six seasons, the longest tenure of any Mets manager, Johnson went 595–417 (.588), the most wins in franchise history.

▪ ▪ ▪

Stump Merrill, manager of the Columbus Clippers, the Yankees' AAA club, replaced Bucky Dent on June 6. Dent's record over parts of two seasons was 36–53.

▪ ▪ ▪

In Philadelphia on July 25, the Mets started the ninth inning with a 10–3 lead over the Phillies, but allowed the tying run to reach third base. Radio announcer Bob Murphy made the call: "Line drive. It's caught. It's over. They win. The Mets win the ballgame. They win the damn thing by a score of 10–9." Certainly fitting, if out of character, it was the only such remark in Murphy's entire broadcasting career.

▪ ▪ ▪

South Shore American Little League of Staten Island repeated as New York State champion.

▪ ▪ ▪

Pete Sampras won the first of five Men's Singles Championships at the United States Open, defeating Andre Agassi in straight sets.

▪ ▪ ▪

The Breeders' Cup was held at Belmont Park on October 27. In the anticipated Distaff, the defending champion, Bayoka, and the three-year-old filly Go For Wand battled the entire way until Go For Wand, leading by a head in the final sixteenth,

Andre Agassi at the U.S. Open, 1988. He played in the men's finals six times between 1990 and 2005, winning in 1994 and 1999. (June Harrison)

shattered her right front leg. She was put down on the track. In the Sprint, Mr. Nickerson suffered a ruptured artery on the back stretch; Shaker Knit tumbled over him and was so badly injured that he, too, was put down.

□ □ □

After the team started at 7–8, the Knicks fired coach Stu Jackson on December 3 and hired John MacLeod, their fifth coach in five years. Jackson's record was a respectable 52–43.

1991 ....

With Phil Simms sidelined by injury, Jeff Hostetler quarterbacked the Giants through the playoffs, beating first the Chicago Bears, 31–3, on January 12, and then the San Francisco 49ers, 15–13, on Matt Bahr's record five field goals for the NFC title. In Super Bowl XXV, on January 27, the Giants

defeated the Buffalo Bills, 20–19. Bills kicker Scott Norwood missed a field goal with 4 seconds left. Running back Ottis Anderson was named the game's Most Valuable Player. Head coach Bill Parcells had Bill Belichick as defensive coordinator and Tom Coughlin as receivers coach. (They were the opposing coaches in Super Bowl XLII.)

□ □ □

On February 20, Preston Robert "Bob" Tisch, chairman of the Loew's Corporation, purchased the 50 percent share of the Giants controlled by Tim Mara for an estimated $75 million. "I think it's one of the great franchises in the sports world," he said.

□ □ □

Peter Westbrook, a member of the United States fencing team in saber at every Olympics from 1976 through 1996 and a bronze medal winner in the Los Angeles Games in 1984, founded the Peter Westbrook Foundation to bring the sport to minority youth. In 2004, four of the 14 members of the Olympic squad were from his academy, which is based at the New York Fencers Club (119 West Twenty-fifth Street).

□ □ □

First baseman Don Mattingly was named Yankee captain on February 28.

□ □ □

Knicks general manager Al Bianchi was fired on March 1. Dave Checketts was installed as team president, and Ernie Grunfeld became vice president of player personnel. With a 103–94 victory at Madison Square Garden on April 30, Michael Jordan and the Chicago Bulls swept the Knicks in the playoffs. Head coach John MacLeod, with a record of 32–35, resigned two days later. On May 31, Pat Riley became the team's sixth coach in seven years.

□ □ □

In the seventh game of the first round of the playoffs, on April 15, the Devils lost to the Pittsburgh

Penguins, 4–0. In the Patrick Division semifinals, the Rangers lost to the Capitals in six games, dropping the final contest, 4–2, in Washington.

◦ ◦ ◦

Forward Derrick Coleman of the Nets, drafted first overall out of Syracuse University, was named the NBA's Rookie of the Year.

◦ ◦ ◦

After leading the Giants to victory in Super Bowl XXV, coach Bill Parcells resigned on May 15, citing health concerns. Over eight seasons, his record was 85–52–1 (.620), with two Super Bowl titles. Offensive coordinator Ray Handley was promoted to head coach. General manager George Young later called Handley's hiring "my worst mistake."

◦ ◦ ◦

The South Shore American Little League of Staten Island finished third in the Little League World Series. One member of the team, Michael Cammarata, later joined the Fire Department and perished in the attack on the World Trade Center.

◦ ◦ ◦

On September 29, the Mets fired manager Bud Harrelson; third base coach Mike Cubbage took over for the final week of the season, going 3–4. In one and a half seasons, Harrelson's record was 145–139. On October 11, Jeff Torborg became manager.

◦ ◦ ◦

The Yankees finished fifth and fired Stump Merrill on October 7; his record was 120–155 (.436). On October 29, George Steinbrenner hired thirty-five-year-old Buck Showalter, who had been the third base coach for two years.

◦ ◦ ◦

With an 8–8 record, the Jets made the playoffs for the first time in five years, but in the American Football Conference wild-card game on December 29, they fell to the Houston Oilers, 17–10.

1992

On February 1, the Islanders retired Denis Potvin's number, 5; on March 3, they retired Mike Bossy's number, 22. Both had been key players on the Stanley Cup dynasty in the 1980s.

◦ ◦ ◦

The chess team at Edward R. Murrow High School in Brooklyn won its first national chess championship. The players successfully defended the title in 1993 and 1994, and won the state championship seven times between 1989 and 2001.

◦ ◦ ◦

Michael Kay began calling Yankee games over WABC Radio, joining John Sterling.

◦ ◦ ◦

At Nassau Coliseum on April 4, the New York Saints lost to the Philadelphia Wings, 8–6, in the divisional finals of the Major Indoor Lacrosse League playoffs.

◦ ◦ ◦

Lou Carnesecca retired as basketball coach at St. John's University on April 13. His record was 526–200, with a trip to the Final Four in 1985 and the National Invitational Tournament championship in 1989. His teams won the Lapchick Memorial Tournament 17 times and the Eastern College Athletic Conference Holiday Festival eight times.

◦ ◦ ◦

In the Patrick Division semifinals, the Rangers and the Devils battled for seven games, with the Rangers taking the deciding game, 8–4, at Madison Square Garden on May 1. They then lost to the Penguins in six, dropping the last game, 5–1, in Pittsburgh on May 16.

◦ ◦ ◦

After beating the Pistons in the opening round of the Eastern Conference playoffs, in five games, the Knicks fell to the Bulls. In the seventh game, on May 17, Michael Jordan scored 42 points to lead the Bulls to a 110–81 rout.

• • •

On May 28, Chuck Daly replaced Bill Fitch as coach of the Nets, the team's tenth in 11 years. Fitch's record over three seasons was 83–163 (.337), with one playoff appearance.

• • •

The South Shore National Little League of Staten Island became New York State champion.

• • •

On August 17, Long Island businessmen Robert Rosenthal, Stephen Walsh, Ralph Palleschi, and Paul Greenwood acquired a controlling interest in the Islanders. Don Maloney replaced Bill Torrey, architect of the Stanley Cup dynasty, as general manager.

• • •

The Wagner College football team won the ECAC Southeast championship.

• • •

In a game against the Kansas City Chiefs at the Meadowlands on November 29, Jets defensive end Dennis Byrd collided with teammate Scott Mersereau and was paralyzed. He underwent surgery at Lenox Hill Hospital three days later, and then endured months of rehabilitation at Mount Sinai Medical Center. On February 12, he walked with the aid of two canes into a press conference at the hospital. He eventually walked unaided.

• • •

At age seventy-four, play-by-play announcer Marty Glickman called his final game for the Jets in December. He had begun his broadcasting career at radio station WHN in 1939, becoming sports director there in 1943.

1993 . . . .

With Patrick Ewing, John Starks, Charles Oakley, Anthony Mason, Doc Rivers, and Charles Smith, the Knicks finished at 60–22, matching the record

of the championship team of 1969/1970. In the playoffs, they beat the Indiana Pacers in four games, and then eliminated the Charlotte Hornets in five. In the Eastern Conference finals, they took the first two games, but fell to Michael Jordan and the Bulls in six, losing the deciding game, 96–88, on June 4. Pat Riley was named Coach of the Year.

• • •

In the opening round of the playoffs, the Devils fell to the Penguins, losing the fifth game, 5–3, on April 26. The Islanders eliminated the Capitals in six games with a 5–3 win at Nassau Coliseum on April 28. After Pierre Turgeon scored the Isles' last goal, Dale Hunter of the Capitals slammed him into the boards; Turgeon suffered a concussion and a separated shoulder. (Hunter was suspended for the first 21 games of the next season.) In the second round, the Islanders eliminated the two-time defending champion Penguins, winning the seventh game, 4–3, on a goal by David Volek at 5 minutes, 16 seconds in overtime. The Islanders then lost to the Montreal Canadiens in the semifinals in five games.

• • •

With the team in last place at 13–25, the Mets fired manager Jeff Torborg and replaced him with Dallas Green on May 19. Torborg's record was 85–115 (.425).

• • •

Adelphi University defeated C. W. Post, 11–7, to win the National Collegiate Athletic Association Division II men's lacrosse championship.

• • •

The AquaCenter, designed by Richard Dattner, opened at the Asphalt Green Swim, Sports Training, and Rehabilitation Center in June. Asphalt Green, located on the site of a municipal asphalt plant at Ninetieth Street and the FDR Drive, had become a recreational facility in 1976.

▫ ▫ ▫

Riding Colonial Affair in the Belmont Stakes, Julie Krone became the first woman to win a Triple Crown race. Prairie Bayou, the favorite, fractured a foreleg and had to be put down.

▫ ▫ ▫

Lee Janzen won the United States Open at Baltusrol Golf Club.

▫ ▫ ▫

Carrying a 27-game losing streak, a major league record, as both a starter and a reliever, Mets pitcher Anthony Young finally won on July 28. Pitching in relief, he gave up a run and the lead in the ninth, but the Mets scored twice in the bottom of the inning to beat the Florida Marlins, 5–4. "It wasn't a monkey," he said, "it was a zoo."

▫ ▫ ▫

The Borough of Manhattan Community College chess team won the Pan American Intercollegiate Chess Tournament, soundly beating Harvard University in the finals. This was the first national title for any City University of New York school since 1950.

1994 ....

On January 7, the Jets dismissed Bruce Coslet and promoted defensive coordinator Pete Carroll to head coach. Coslet's record over four seasons was 26–38 (.406).

▫ ▫ ▫

Under new head coach Dan Reeves, the Giants returned to the playoffs, defeating the Minnesota Vikings in the NFC wild-card game, 17–10, but then losing to the 49ers, 44–3, in San Francisco on January 15. Linebacker Lawrence Taylor retired after the game; in June, the team released quarterback Phil Simms.

▫ ▫ ▫

The NHL All-Star Game was held at Madison Square Garden for the third time on January 22.

Ranger goalie Mike Richter was the Most Valuable Player as the Eastern Conference beat the Western, 9–8.

▫ ▫ ▫

Howie Rose joined the Mets broadcasting team.

▫ ▫ ▫

In the first round of the playoffs, the Knicks beat the Nets in four games, taking the last game, 102–92, at the Meadowlands on May 6. In the second round, they (finally!) defeated the Bulls (without Michael Jordan), winning the seventh game, 87–77, at Madison Square Garden on May 22. On June 5, they beat the Pacers, 94–90, at the Garden in game seven of the Eastern Conference finals. (They had lost the third game, 88–68, setting a record for the fewest points scored in a playoff game since the introduction of the 24-second clock in 1954.) In the finals, they led the Houston Rockets, three games to two, but dropped games six and seven, losing the deciding contest, 90–84, on June 22.

▫ ▫ ▫

Nets coach Chuck Daly resigned on May 26, with a record of 88–76 (.537). On June 28, Butch Beard took over.

▫ ▫ ▫

In the opening round of the playoffs, the Rangers swept the Islanders. In the thrilling sixth game of the semifinals against the Devils, Mark Messier scored three third-period goals to lead the Rangers to a comeback victory; they then beat New Jersey, 2–1, in double overtime in game seven on May 27. In the finals, the Rangers defeated the Vancouver Canucks for their first Stanley Cup since 1940, taking game seven, 3–2, at Madison Square Garden on June 14. Adam Graves set a team record with 52 goals in a season.

▫ ▫ ▫

Islanders coach Al Arbour retired on June 1 and became the team's vice president of hockey operations. He coached an NHL record 1,601 games and was second in victories (779), playoff games (209), and playoff wins (123). Lorne Henning became head coach on June 20.

▫ ▫ ▫

Devils goalie Martin Brodeur won the Calder Trophy as the NHL's top rookie, and Jacques Lemaire was voted Coach of the Year.

▫ ▫ ▫

On June 18 and 19, the Gay Games were held in New York. (The games originally were called the Gay Olympics, but the International Olympic Committee denied the organizers the right to use the name, unlike the Special Olympics.) Nearly 11,000 athletes from 40 countries competed in 31 sports. The opening ceremonies were held at Yankee Stadium; a diving exhibition by Greg Louganis at Asphalt Green was a highlight.

▫ ▫ ▫

Known as the Redmen since the 1920s (for the color of their uniforms, not a reference to American Indians), St. John's University became the Red Storm.

▫ ▫ ▫

In the midst of his contract dispute, Rangers coach Mike Keenan announced that he was a free agent and signed to coach the St. Louis Blues. Colin Campbell took over on August 9.

▫ ▫ ▫

With the Yankees in first place, the season ended when the players went on strike in mid-August. Still, Buck Showalter was Manager of the Year.

▫ ▫ ▫

On September 16, Tony Kubek resigned as the Yankee announcer for the MSG television network. He had played shortstop for the team from 1957 to 1965, and then called the games on *NBC Game of the Week* from 1966 to 1989 before joining MSG.

▫ ▫ ▫

Ruth Lovelace became coach of the boys' basketball team at Boys and Girls High School (origi-

nally, Boys High), the first woman to hold that position in the Public Schools Athletic League. Lovelace had graduated from the school in the 1980s and played at Seton Hall University.

▫ ▫ ▫

Fred Lebow, longtime president of the New York Road Runners Club, died of brain cancer at age sixty-two on October 9. Lebow originated the New York City Marathon (1970), the Empire State Building Run-Up (1978), the Fifth Avenue Mile (1981), and the Mini-Marathon for women in Central Park. Accompanied by nine-time winner Grete Waitz, Lebow ran his last marathon in 1992, finishing in 5 hours, 32 minutes, 35 seconds. A statue of Lebow in his standard running suit and hat stands in Central Park at Ninetieth Street and East Drive, and each year it is moved to the marathon's finish line near Tavern on the Green.

▫ ▫ ▫

Statue of Fred Lebow, president of the New York Road Runners Club, in Central Park. (Jeffrey A. Kroessler)

The Borough of Manhattan Community College chess team again defeated Harvard University to defend its title in the Pan American Intercollegiate Chess Tournament.

1995 ....

Rich Kotite replaced Pete Carroll as Jets coach on January 5. In Carroll's lone season, the Jets lost their last five games to finish with a record of 6–10.

■ ■ ■

The Professional and Amateur Pinball Association sponsored the World Pinball Championship at the Park Central Hotel.

■ ■ ■

The Tournament of Champions squash championship was staged in Vanderbilt Hall in Grand Central Terminal for the first time. The investment-banking firm Bear Sterns became the sponsor in 2004.

■ ■ ■

The golf course in Forest Park reopened, redesigned by Stephen Kay.

■ ■ ■

Howard Cosell died on April 23. From 1961 to 1974, he had been the sports anchor for WABC; had been one of the original announcers for *Monday Night Football*; and for many years had hosted *Speaking of Sports* on WABC Radio. He was one of the loudest supporters of Muhammad Ali when he was stripped of his heavyweight title for having refused induction into the military during the Vietnam War. During the second game of the 1977 World Series between the Yankees and the Dodgers, the camera focused on a tenement fire, and Cosell famously remarked, "There it is, ladies and gentlemen, the Bronx is burning."

■ ■ ■

In the Eastern Conference quarterfinals, the Rangers beat the Quebec Nordiques in six games, taking the last game, 4–2, at Madison Square Garden on May 16. In the semifinals, they were swept by the Philadelphia Flyers, losing the last game at the Garden, 4–1, on May 26.

■ ■ ■

In the playoffs, the Knicks defeated the Cleveland Cavaliers in the opening round, three games to one, and then fell to the Pacers in the Eastern Conference semifinals. In game one, at Madison Square Garden, Knicks nemesis Reggie Miller scored eight points in the final 18.7 seconds for a 107–105 Pacers win. At the Garden on May 21, the Pacers won game seven, 97–95, as Patrick Ewing's last-second lay-up bounced off the rim.

■ ■ ■

Adelphi University defeated Springfield College, 12–10, for the NCAA Division II men's lacrosse championship.

■ ■ ■

Only 37,171, the smallest crowd since World War II, saw Thunder Gulch win the Belmont Stakes.

■ ■ ■

With one year remaining on his five-year contract, Knicks coach Pat Riley resigned on June 15. His record was 223–105 (.680), and 35–28 in the playoffs, reaching the finals once. The Knicks introduced new coach Don Nelson on July 6.

■ ■ ■

After defeating the Boston Bruins in five games, the Penguins in five, and the Flyers in six—all without the home-ice advantage—the Devils swept the Detroit Red Wings to win their first Stanley Cup; they took the last game, 5–2 at, the Meadowlands on June 24.

■ ■ ■

The Shinnecock Hills Golf Club in Southampton hosted the U.S. Open for the third time. Corey

Pavin finished at even par, 280, two strokes ahead of Greg Norman, on June 18.

The Chelsea Piers opened. A 30-acre sports complex at Twenty-third Street and the Hudson River, it houses an ice-skating rink, a swimming pool, a gymnasium, bowling alleys, and a golf range.

Shelley Taylor-Smith swam 28.5 miles around Manhattan in the record time of 5 hours, 45 minutes, 25 seconds. In 1998, she won the race for the fifth time.

Mike Milbury replaced Lorne Henning as head coach of the Islanders on July 5. On December 12, Milbury also became general manager.

After 39 years in the Yankees broadcast booth, Phil Rizzuto retired. He was extremely upset that WPIX had strongly suggested that he broadcast a game against the Red Sox at Fenway Park instead of attending Mickey Mantle's funeral on August 18. On the air, he said, "I should have been there." He finally left the booth. "I took it hard and knew I made a big mistake," he said. "I got more upset as the game went on and left in the fifth. They tried to drag me back, but I wouldn't." The Scooter died on August 13, 2007.

The South Shore American Little League of Staten Island became New York State champion.

The Yankees made the playoffs as the wild card, returning to the postseason for the first time since 1981. In the American League Championship Series, they lost to the Seattle Mariners in five games. By the end of October, Buck Showalter was out as manager; his record over four seasons was 313–268 (.539). The team hired Joe Torre on November 2.

Jerry Bailey riding Cigar to victory in the Breeder's Cup Classic at Belmont Park, October 28, 1995. (Bob and Adam Coglianese Photographs)

In the Breeders' Cup Classic at Belmont Park on October 28, Jerry Bailey rode Cigar to a two-and-a-half-length victory on a muddy track to complete an undefeated year. Cigar was named Horse of the Year.

A night billed as "Extreme Fighting—Whatever It Takes to Win" was scheduled for November 18 at the Brooklyn Armory in Park Slope. The Division of Military and Naval Affairs, the agency with jurisdiction over the armories, canceled the event because it was "inappropriate for a state facility." Brooklyn district attorney Charles Hynes said that he considered the matches akin to assault, and Mayor Rudolph Giuliani said, "We have done everything we can to cancel this match." The promoter, Battlecade, a company part owned by *Penthouse* publisher Bob Guccione, abandoned its plans for the event.

On December 6, the New York Police Department busted a Gambino crime family sports-betting ring in Queens and Brooklyn that took in an estimated $13 million a year.

□ □ □

The Brooklyn College Chess Team won the Pan American Intercollegiate Chess Tournament on December 29. Team members were all immigrants: Gennady Sagalchick from Minsk, Yury Lapshun from Odessa, Alex Kalikshteyn from Tashkent, Oleg Shalumov from Baku, and Alex Beltre from Santo Domingo.

1996 ....

On March 8, the Knicks fired Don Nelson only 59 games into his first season and promoted Jeff Van Gundy, an assistant since 1989. The team finished the season with a 47–35 record. In the playoffs, the Knicks swept the Cavaliers, and then lost to the Bulls in five games.

□ □ □

Nancy Lieberman was elected to the Naismith Memorial Basketball Hall of Fame; in 1999, she was enshrined in the Women's Basketball Hall of Fame.

□ □ □

With the first overall draft pick for the first time in franchise history, the Jets selected wide receiver Keyshawn Johnson of the University of Southern California, a too-selfish star.

□ □ □

Ed Coleman joined the Mets broadcasting team.

□ □ □

In their first game in the inaugural season of Major League Soccer, on April 13, the Metrostars lost to the Los Angeles Galaxy, 2–1, at the Rose Bowl; in their home opener at Giants Stadium, on April 20, they lost to the New England Revolution, 1–0. Over 16 home games at the Meadowlands, the av-

erage attendance was 23,898 (the average dropped to 16,899 in 1997). Former Cosmos coach Eddie Firmani started the season, but Carlos Queiroz of Portugal replaced him after eight games. In the first round of the playoffs (eight of the 10 teams in the league made the playoffs), the Metrostars fell to D.C. United, dropping the third game of the best-of-three series, 2–1, on October 2. The first All-Star Game was held at Giants Stadium before a record crowd of 78,416 on July 14. The Eastern Conference defeated the Western, 3–2; in the second game, Brazil defeated the World All-Stars, 2–1.

□ □ □

The Rangers finished the season with a record of 41–27–14. In the playoffs, they defeated the Canadiens in six games, but in the Eastern Conference semifinals fell to the Penguins in five, losing the final game, 7–3, in Pittsburgh on May 11.

□ □ □

C. W. Post beat Adelphi University, 15–10, for the NCAA Division II men's lacrosse title.

□ □ □

The Nets dismissed Butch Beard, whose record was 60–104, after the season. On June 7, John Calipari, coach at the University of Massachusetts, took over.

□ □ □

The first Sri Chinmoy Self-Transcendence Ten-Day Race was staged in Flushing Meadows–Corona Park. Georgs Jermolajev covered 725 miles, and Dipali Cunningham of Australia set the women's mark with 723 miles.

□ □ □

Mel Allen, the voice of the Yankees, died on June 16. He had begun calling Yankee games in 1939 and broadcast 20 World Series and 24 All-Star Games. He was known for his home run call: "That ball is going, going, gone." A Yankee home run was a "Ballantine Blast," after the sponsor,

One of the Sri Chinmoy Self-Transcendence Races held in Flushing Meadows–Corona Park, 2007. (Jeffrey A. Kroessler)

and he regularly exclaimed, "How 'bout that!" An Alabama native, Melvin Allen Israel is buried in Temple Beth El Cemetery in Stamford, Connecticut.

◼ ◼ ◼

In the seventh round of a heavyweight bout at Madison Square Garden on July 11, referee Wayne Kelly disqualified Andrew Golota of Poland for a fourth low blow and awarded the victory to former champion Riddick Bowe of Brooklyn; Golota had been ahead on all cards. A near riot ensued, with whites and blacks brawling in the stands (a fan watching on television in Brooklyn actually alerted the police by calling 911); 11 were arrested.

◼ ◼ ◼

Again, the South Shore American Little League of Staten Island was New York State champion.

◼ ◼ ◼

On August 26, the Mets fired Dallas Green and named Bobby Valentine their fifth manager in seven years. Since taking over in midseason in 1993, Green had a record of 229–283 (.447).

◼ ◼ ◼

Behind Derek Jeter, Tino Martinez, Bernie Williams, Paul O'Neill, and Andy Pettitte, the Yankees reached the playoffs again, the first of 12 consecutive appearances in the postseason for Joe Torre's club. In the American League Division Series, the Yankees beat the Texas Rangers, three games to one. On October 9, in the first game of the ALCS against the Baltimore Orioles, Jeter hit a game-tying home run in the bottom of the eighth, aided by twelve-year-old Jeffrey Maier, who grabbed the ball before outfielder Tony Tarasco could catch it; Bernie Williams homered in the bottom of the eleventh inning for a 5–4 win. The Yankees took the series, four games to one. In the World Series, the Yankees dropped the first two games to the Atlanta Braves and were down, 6–0, in the third game before rallying to win in extra innings. They took the series in six games, winning the clincher, 3–2, at Yankee Stadium on October 26.

◼ ◼ ◼

In October, Governor George Pataki "reluctantly" signed a bill legalizing "combative sports," or

Joe Torre, manager of the Yankees. (Dan Goldfarb).

"extreme fighting," and granting regulatory authority to the New York State Athletic Commission. New York thus became the first state to sanction "human cockfighting." Four months later, on February 25, 1997, Pataki signed legislation banning ultimate fighting.

On December 15, the St. John's University men's soccer team won the NCAA Division I championship, defeating Florida International University, 4–1.

On December 20, two days before the final game of a dismal season, Rich Kotite resigned as head coach of the Jets. The team finished with records of 3–13 in 1995 and 1–15 in 1996 (.125).

1997

I think IBM owes me, and all mankind, a rematch.
GARRY KASPAROV

On January 6, Carlos Alberto Parreira, former coach of the Brazilian national soccer team, took over the Metrostars.

Mike Milbury, coach and general manager of the Islanders, stepped aside and named Rick Bowness as head coach on January 24.

On February 7, two weeks after taking the New England Patriots to the Super Bowl, Bill Parcells signed a six-year contract with the Jets as chief of football operations, including four years as head coach. Commissioner Paul Tagliabue brokered a deal whereby the Jets would surrender four draft picks to New England, including the first-round pick in 1999. The Jets had hired Bill Belichick as head coach, but he stepped aside for Parcells, becoming assistant head coach and defensive coordinator. The Jets finished the season with a 9–7 record.

On March 6, Charles F. Dolan's Cablevision gained control of Madison Square Garden Properties, including the arena, the MSG television network, the Knicks, and the Rangers; the total value was set at $1.53 billion. His son, James L. Dolan, became chairman of Madison Square Garden.

On March 22, the New York University women's basketball team won the NCAA Division III championship, defeating the University of Wisconsin at Eau Claire, 72–70. Marsha Harris of Jamaica, Queens, drove the length of the floor for a layup with 1.5 seconds left for the victory.

Jim Vogt founded the Metropolitan Oval Foundation to save the venerable soccer field in Mas-

Teams playing on Metropolitan Oval in Maspeth, Queens, the oldest soccer field in continuous use in the United States, 2007. (Jeffrey A. Kroessler)

peth, Queens, after the owners fell behind in their taxes. He convinced the owners of the 1,500 shares, descendants of the German and Hungarian immigrants who had built the field in the 1920s, to donate their shares to the foundation. It worked.

□ □ □

The New York City Hawks began play in the Arena Football League at Madison Square Garden. The New Jersey Red Dogs also joined the league, playing through 2000.

□ □ □

The Knicks finished the season at 57–25. In the Eastern Conference playoffs, they swept the Hornets in three straight games, but then lost to the Miami Heat in seven. The Knicks led the series three games to one, but with 1 minute, 53 seconds remaining in game five, P. J. Brown of the Heat tangled with Charlie Ward and tossed him off the court. In the ensuing mayhem, Buck Williams warned Patrick Ewing to stay on the bench, but he wandered onto the court, contrary to NBA rules; the Heat won, 96–81. Brown was suspended, but so were five Knicks: Ewing, Ward, and Allan Houston were out for game six at Madison Square Garden (won by Miami), and John Starks and Larry Johnson were lost for game seven, which Miami won at home, 101–90, on May 18.

□ □ □

After handily beating IBM's Deep Blue the year before, chess grand master Garry Kasparov took on the computer in a rematch at the Equitable Center. Blundering on his seventh move in the final game on May 11, Kasparov lost the series, 3½–2½. "I think IBM owes me, and all mankind, a rematch," he said.

□ □ □

The Rangers defeated the Devils, 2–1, on May 11 to win the Eastern Conference semifinals in five games, but lost to the Flyers in the conference finals in five, dropping the last game, 4–2, in Philadelphia.

. . .

Bryan Berard, a twenty-year-old defenseman, became the fourth Islander to win the Calder Trophy as the NHL's top rookie, and Brian Leetch of the Rangers won the Norris Trophy as the league's top defenseman.

. . .

New York Institute of Technology beat Adelphi University, 18–11, for its first NCAA Division II men's lacrosse title.

. . .

In the Belmont Stakes on June 7, Touch Gold came from behind and nosed out Silver Charm, winner of the Kentucky Derby and the Preakness.

. . .

On June 16, the Mets beat the Yankees, 6–0, at Yankee Stadium in their first interleague game. The Yanks took the next two games in this faux Subway Series.

. . .

With Rebecca Lobo, Teresa Weatherspoon, and Kym Hampton in the lineup, the New York Liberty of the new Women's National Basketball Association took the court for the first time on June 21, beating the Sparks in Los Angeles in the league's first game. They won their home opener against the Phoenix Mercury before 17,780 fans at Madison Square Garden on June 29. Coach Nancy Darsch took the Liberty to the first championship game, but they lost to the Houston Comets, 65–51, on August 30.

. . .

Major League Soccer's All-Star Game was played at Giants Stadium for the second year on July 9. The Eastern Conference beat the Western, 5–4, before a disappointing crowd of 24,816.

. . .

The South Shore American Little League of Staten Island three-peated as New York State champion.

. . .

At Winged Foot Golf Club on August 17, Davis Love III finished at 11 under par to win the Professional Golfers Association Championship by five strokes.

. . .

Giants owner Wellington Mara was inducted into the Pro Football Hall of Fame.

. . .

Arthur Ashe Stadium was dedicated at the National Tennis Center in Flushing Meadows–Corona Park on August 25. The largest tennis-only venue in the world, the 22,547-seat arena—plus 90 luxury boxes—cost $254 million.

. . .

In the longest nine-inning game in American League history—4 hours and 22 minutes—the Orioles beat the Yankees, 13–9, at Yankee Stadium on September 5 (eclipsing by 1 minute a 13–10 Yankee win over Baltimore at Camden Yards on April 30, 1996). The Yankees again won the American League East, but fell to the Cleveland Indians in the ALDS, three games to two.

. . .

On September 25, three days into his trial for forcible sodomy and assault and battery on his former girlfriend, longtime Knicks announcer and sportscaster Marv Albert pleaded guilty to a misdemeanor charge of assault and battery and received a 12-month suspended sentence. Hours later, NBC fired Albert, who then resigned from MSG. In September 1998, he returned to host *MSG Sports Desk*, and on February 7, 1999, he was back calling Knicks games on radio.

. . .

On November 26, playing on their home court, the former Paramount Theater in Brooklyn, Long Island University's Division I men's basketball team beat Medgar Evers, a Division III college of the City University of New York, 179–62, setting an NCAA record for the widest victory margin, field goals (79), and steals (39). Sportsmanship it wasn't.

▫ ▫ ▫

Under first-year head coach Jim Fassel, the Giants defeated the Washington Redskins, 30–10, on December 13 to win the NFC East with a 10–5–1 record. According to Fassel, general manager George Young "came into the coaches locker room, which was almost empty. He thanked me and broke down and cried and cried and cried. I think that championship validated everything he'd worked on." Young stepped down in January 1998. In the NFC wild-card game, on December 27, the Giants blew a 22–13 lead with 90 seconds to play and fell to the Vikings, 23–22. Fassel was named Coach of the Year.

▫ ▫ ▫

On December 29, the Borough of Manhattan Community College chess team won the fifty-second Pan-American Intercollegiate Chess Tournament, its third national title.

1998 . . . .

Former Yankee catcher Rick Cerone founded the Newark Bears as a charter team in the independent Atlantic League.

▫ ▫ ▫

Madison Square Garden hosted the NBA All-Star Game on February 8; the Eastern Conference won, 135–114.

▫ ▫ ▫

The Rangers, with the highest payroll in the NHL and a losing record, fired head coach Colin Campbell on February 18. Over three and a half seasons, Campbell's record was 118–108–43. John Muckler took over the next day.

▫ ▫ ▫

Steven Gluckstern and Howard Milstein, co-chairmen of New York Sports Ventures, purchased the Islanders.

▫ ▫ ▫

Thirty-year-old Brian Cashman succeeded Bob Watson as general manager of the Yankees.

▫ ▫ ▫

On March 11, Mike Milbury, general manager of the Islanders, fired head coach Rick Bowness and went behind the bench himself.

▫ ▫ ▫

Twenty-seven men, including Brooklyn police officer Richard "Pasta" Sacco, were arrested on March 18 on charges of running a $50 million sports-betting ring for the Genovese crime family in Brooklyn, Queens, and Staten Island.

▫ ▫ ▫

The Nets finished second in the Atlantic Division with a 43–39 record, but were swept by the Bulls in the first round of the playoffs.

▫ ▫ ▫

For the second year, the playoff series between the Knicks and the Heat was marred by a brawl and suspensions. With 1.4 seconds remaining in the fourth game of the intense best-of-five series at Madison Square Garden on April 30, Knicks coach Jeff Van Gundy raced onto the court to break up a fight between Larry Johnson of the Knicks and Alonzo Mourning of the Heat. The 5-foot, 9-inch Van Gundy ended up being dragged across the floor while holding the leg of the 6-foot, 10-inch Mourning. The Knicks won, 90–85. Mourning, Johnson, and Chris Mills were suspended for the last game in Miami; the Knicks won, 98–81. In the second round, Patrick Ewing returned to the lineup for the first time since breaking his wrist in December, but it was not enough; the Knicks fell to the Pacers, four games to one, losing the last game, 99–88, in Indianapolis on May 13.

▫ ▫ ▫

On May 2, the Devils fell to the Ottawa Senators, 3–1, and were eliminated in the first round of the playoffs in six games.

▫ ▫ ▫

Earl "The Goat" Manigault died at age fifty-three on May 14. A playground legend, he got involved with drugs, was expelled from Benjamin Franklin High School in Harlem, and served time in prison. He later founded the "Walk Away from Drugs" basketball tournament, which was interrupted when he was again imprisoned for drug possession. The playground at Ninety-ninth Street and Amsterdam Avenue was known as Goat Park and was officially renamed Goat Courts after Manigault's death. Kareem Abdul-Jabbar once named Manigault as the toughest opponent he ever played against.

▪ ▪ ▪

The men's tennis team of Kingsborough Community College won the National Junior College Athletic Association championship on May 21, defeating DuPage College of Illinois.

▪ ▪ ▪

The New Jersey Jackals began play in the independent Northern League; their home field was Yogi Berra Stadium on the campus of Montclair State University. In 2005, they joined the reborn Canadian American League.

▪ ▪ ▪

Adelphi University again won the NCAA Division II men's lacrosse title, defeating Long Island rival C. W. Post, 18–6.

▪ ▪ ▪

The Goodwill Games took place from July 17 to August 2, 15 sports staged at venues from Nassau Coliseum to Madison Square Garden to Central Park to Staten Island. The aquatic center at the Mitchell Field Athletic Complex, in Uniondale, was built for the games.

▪ ▪ ▪

The South Shore American Little League of Staten Island was New York State champion for the fourth straight year.

▪ ▪ ▪

The Yankees beat the Red Sox, 7–5, to clinch the American League East on September 9, the earli-

Jackie Joyner-Kersee ending her career with a victory in the heptathlon at the Goodwill Games at the Mitchell Field Athletic Complex in Uniondale, on Long Island. (June Harrison)

est in the league's history. They won a record 112th game on September 25. (The 1927 Yankees had won 110 games.) In the ALDS, they swept the Texas Rangers in three straight, and in the ALCS took the Indians in six. The Yankees captured their twenty-fourth world championship on October 21, beating the San Diego Padres in four straight games, the seventh World Series sweep by the Yankees. Mariano Rivera saved three games, and third baseman Scott Brosius was the Most Valuable Player of the series, batting .417 with two home runs and six RBIs.

▪ ▪ ▪

On September 21, after the team had lost six straight games heading into the playoffs, the Metrostars replaced coach Alfonso Mondelo with Serbian-born Bora Milutinović. They fell to the

Columbus Crew in the first round, two games to one.

■ ■ ■

A referendum would have determined whether to spend public money for a new Yankee Stadium on the West Side of Manhattan, but Mayor Rudolph Giuliani kept it off the ballot because he did not think the voters would approve.

1999 ....

On January 6, George Steinbrenner made a pilgrimage to the Yogi Berra Museum on the campus of Montclair State University and apologized to Berra for having sent Clyde King to fire him 16 games into the 1985 season. Berra had vowed never to set foot in Yankee Stadium as long as Steinbrenner owned the team. "I know I made a mistake by not letting you go personally," said the Boss. "It's the worst mistake I ever made in baseball."

■ ■ ■

After finishing atop the AFC East at 12–4, the Jets, behind thirty-five-year-old quarterback Vinnie Testaverde and running back Curtis Martin, gained their first playoff victory since 1986, defeating the Jacksonville Jaguars, 34–24, at the Meadowlands on January 10. In the AFC championship game a week later, they built a 10–0 lead over the defending champion Broncos, but Denver prevailed, 23–10.

■ ■ ■

Islander coach and general manager Mike Milbury stepped aside and named Bill Stewart head coach on January 21; on April 30, Butch Goring replaced Stewart.

■ ■ ■

After two seasons in Madison Square Garden, the New York City Hawks of the Arena Football League relocated to Hartford, Connecticut, and became the New England Sea Wolves.

■ ■ ■

The Mets, apparently unhappy with his second-guessing the team's on-field moves, fired broadcaster Tim McCarver on February 3; he had called Mets games on television for 16 years. Tom Seaver replaced him. Thirteen days later, McCarver signed to announce Yankee games. At the press conference at Mickey Mantle's restaurant, McCarver remarked, "When I came to New York 16 years ago, it was not nearly as big a story as it seems this time."

■ ■ ■

Joe DiMaggio, the "Yankee Clipper," died at age eighty-four on March 8. The three-time Most Valuable Player had a lifetime batting average of .325 and a historic 56-game hitting streak in 1941. His plaque in Monument Park at Yankee Stadium was unveiled on April 25, with many Yankee greats in attendance; Paul Simon sang "Mrs. Robinson," with its famous lyric, "Where have you gone, Joe DiMaggio? / Our nation turns its lonely eyes to you."

■ ■ ■

A much-anticipated 12-round heavyweight unification bout on March 13 between Evander Holyfield, World Boxing Association and International Boxing Federation champion, and Lennox Lewis, World Boxing Council titleholder, ended in a draw. The crowd of 21,284 at Madison Square Garden lustily booed the result, as Lewis clearly had dominated. (Lewis won the rematch in November—in Las Vegas.)

■ ■ ■

After the team began its season at 3–17, the Nets fired John Calipari on March 15. His record over two-plus seasons was 72–112. Assistant Don Casey took over. The Nets finished their season with a 16–34 record.

■ ■ ■

The Knicks fired team president and general manager Ernie Grunfeld on April 21.

. . .

The Adelphi University men's lacrosse team won its fourth NCAA Division II championship in seven years, defeating rival C. W. Post, 11–8.

. . .

Behind Allan Houston, Latrell Sprewell, and Larry Johnson, the Knicks made a dramatic run to make the playoffs as the eighth and final seed. In the deciding fifth game against the Heat on May 16, Houston hit a shot at the buzzer for a 78–77 win. The Knicks next swept the Atlanta Hawks and, in the Eastern Conference finals, eliminated the Pacers, four games to two. In the finals, they fell to the San Antonio Spurs in five, losing the last game, 78–77, at Madison Square Garden on June 25.

. . .

Running for the Triple Crown in the Belmont Stakes on June 5, Charismatic (grandson of Secretariat) broke his left foreleg at the finish line. Jockey Chris Antley saved the horse by quickly jumping off and cradling the leg. Lemon Drop Kid, a 29–1 long shot, won before a record crowd of 85,818.

. . .

The Staten Island Yankees, a Class A affiliate of the Bronx Bombers, played their first game on June 20 before a capacity crowd of 4,500 at the College of Staten Island. They beat the Hudson Valley Renegades, 5–1. The City Council allocated funds for a new ballpark in St. George.

. . .

Madison Square Garden hosted the first WNBA All-Star Game on July 14; the capacity crowd of 18,649 saw the Western Conference beat the Eastern, 79–61. In the championship series, the Liberty fell to the Houston Comets in three games.

. . .

Bears and Eagles Riverfront Stadium opened in Newark, New Jersey, on July 16. The Bears defeated the Lehigh Valley Black Diamonds, 9–8.

. . .

The Rolando Paulino Little League of the Bronx won the New York State championship.

. . .

At the U.S. Open, Andre Agassi won his second singles title with a five-set victory over Todd Martin, and Serena Williams beat Martina Hingis for her first singles title.

. . .

Behind Mike Piazza, Edgardo Alfonzo, Rickey Henderson, and John Franco, the Mets entered the playoffs as the wild-card team, their first postseason appearance since 1988. In the National League Division Series, they eliminated the Arizona Diamondbacks, three games to one, but in the National League Championship Series fell to the Braves in six, losing the final game, 10–9, when Kenny Rogers threw a walk in the eleventh inning with the bases loaded.

. . .

The Yankees set a new home attendance mark, drawing 3,293,659 to the Bronx. After sweeping the Texas Rangers in three straight in the ALDS, the Yankees faced the Red Sox. Yogi Berra told center fielder Bernie Williams, "We've been playing these guys for 80 years. They cannot beat us." The Yankees indeed beat the Red Sox for the pennant, taking the fifth game, 6–1, on October 18. In the World Series, the Bombers swept the Braves, taking the final game on October 27 for their twelfth straight World Series victory, third title in four years, and twenty-fifth world championship.

. . .

The Metrostars fired Bora Milutinović on October 29. In his one season, the team finished with a record of 7–25, the worst in franchise history, and managed only 32 goals. Octavio Zambrano became the sixth coach in five seasons.

■ ■ ■

At the Mitchell Field Athletic Complex on December 11, the Long Island Sharks, a women's flag-football team, defeated the Minnesota Vixens, one of the two teams in the new Women's Professional Football League, 12–6, in a full-contact tackle game. The Sharks joined the league the next year.

2000—2009

The new millennium saw few significant changes in sports. Teams made the playoffs, changed coaches, or signed new superstars. New professional sports arrived, including women's leagues, but none really grabbed public attention. With so great an investment, a win-or-else mentality defined the attitude of team owners more than ever. Few players in any sport embody the character of the city, and fewer seem willing to even try. Fans know that most athletes are merely mercenaries. A bit of hometown confidence returned to the Mets when they hired Willie Randolph, and a native of Brooklyn and the team's first black manager. (Is it still necessary to mention that?) Professional teams also sucked up enormous public subsidies, from the Staten Island Yankees, playing in the most expensive minor league park in the country, to the replacements for Shea Stadium and Yankee Stadium. Surprisingly, there was surprisingly little public outcry when the Yankees abandoned "The House That Ruth Built." There was just too much big money, too much political muscle, and too little respect for history to argue. The Nets announced a move from New Jersey to Brooklyn, but their arena is a Trojan horse for a massive real-estate development, again de-

manding huge public subsidies. Ironically, it was to rise where Walter O'Malley wanted to move the Dodgers in 1957, but the city refused to allocate any public money for that private purpose. The city tried to get the 2012 Olympic Games and used that effort to try to build a stadium for the Jets on the Far West Side of Manhattan, an idea repeatedly rejected by the citizenry. Between the heightened security, massive long-term construction, and stratospheric costs, many New Yorkers were relieved when the bid failed. Still, despite the scandals and the big money and the contempt for loyal fans, sport remains as popular as ever, and New York is still the place to be.

2000

On January 3, Jets coach Bill Parcells announced his retirement: "I'm not going to coach any more football games. This is definitely the end of my career." (He later coached the Dallas Cowboys.) His record with the Jets was 29–19, a winning percentage of .604. Parcells remained in charge of football operations. Bill Belichick was named head coach, but abruptly resigned the next day. On January 11, Robert Wood "Woody" Johnson IV bought the

Jets from the estate of Leon Hess for $635 million, outbidding Charles F. Dolan, chairman of Cablevision and owner of Madison Square Garden, the MSG television network, the Knicks, and the Rangers. Within two weeks, Al Groh was appointed head coach.

• • •

With four games remaining on March 28, John Tortorella replaced John Muckler (70–91–24) as coach of the Rangers; the team finished the season with a 0–3–1 record. Glen Sather became team president and general manager on June 1. On July 12, Ron Low was named coach.

• • •

On March 29, in the first major league baseball game ever played outside North America, the Mets opened the season against the Chicago Cubs in Tokyo, losing 5–3, but winning the next day, 5–1.

• • •

The Nets opened the season at 1–10 and lost their final 11 games, to finish with a record of 31–51. Don Casey (44–68) was fired on April 26. On June 27, the Nets hired former Los Angeles Laker Byron Scott; in his first season the team went 26–56.

• • •

Charles Wang and Sanjay Kumar of Computer Associates purchased the Islanders on April 26. On November 1, they bought the Iowa Barnstormers of the Arena Football League to play in Nassau Coliseum; the team was renamed the New York Dragons.

• • •

The Long Island Ducks joined the independent Atlantic League, playing in the new 6,002-seat Citibank Park in Central Islip. Former Met Bud Harrelson was the first manager and a part owner of the team.

• • •

In Dallas on June 10, the Devils beat the Stars, 2–1, on Jason Arnott's goal at 8 minutes, 20 seconds of the second overtime to take the Stanley Cup in six games. (Dallas had won the fifth game, 1–0, in triple overtime.) Martin Brodeur was brilliant in goal, and Scott Stevens was the series's Most Valuable Player.

• • •

On June 15, Devils center Scott Gomez, the first Latino to play in the National Hockey League, received the Calder Trophy as Rookie of the Year. He signed with the Rangers in 2007.

• • •

The Rangers drafted Swedish goalie Henrik Lundqvist in the seventh round, 205th overall. During the decade, he emerged as a key member of the team.

• • •

The Queens Kings, a minor league affiliate of the Toronto Blue Jays, played at St. John's University for one season.

Henrik Lundqvist, goalie with the Rangers. (Dan Goldfarb)

On July 10, Richard A. Kahan, president of the Urban Assembly; Bob Tisch, part owner of the Giants and co-chairman of the Loew's Corporation; and Anthony Kiser, president of the William and Mary Greve Foundation, founded Take the Field, pledging $1 for every $3 the city budgeted to refurbish high school playing fields. They raised about $130 million and renovated more than 40 fields.

John J. McMullen sold the Devils to the short-lived Yankees-Nets Corporation for $176 million. He had bought the team in 1982 for about $30 million.

The Rolando Paulino All-Stars of the South Bronx were the New York State Little League champions.

In the finals of the Women's National Basketball Association, the Liberty lost to the Houston Comets in two straight, dropping the second game, 79–73, in overtime on August 26.

On August 26, the National Tennis Center in Flushing Meadows hosted the World Team Tennis championship for the first time; the Sacramento Capitals won for the fourth straight year. The finals also were held there in 2001 and 2002.

Jeff Quinney won the United States Men's Amateur Golf Championship at Baltusrol Golf Club.

On September 20, the Knicks traded 11-time all-star Patrick Ewing to the Seattle Supersonics in a four-team, 12-player deal. Dave Checketts, president of Madison Square Garden, later remarked, "When we traded him, I would say that was probably a lose–lose." Ewing held team records for most games played (1,039), minutes played (37,586), field goals made (9,260) and attempted (18,224), free throws made (5,126) and attempted (6,904), rebounds (10,759), steals (1,061), blocks (2,758), personal fouls (3,676), and games of 40 or more points (30). He retired before the 2002 season.

Under Octavio Zambrano, the Metrostars, with German star Lothar Matthaus, won the Eastern Conference of Major League Soccer with their best record: 17–12–3. In the first round, they swept the Dallas Burn, but fell to the Chicago Fire in the semifinals in three games, dropping the deciding game, 3–2, on October 6.

For the first time since 1956, there was a Subway Series. The Yankees again swept the Texas Rangers in three straight, and then beat the Seattle Mariners in six. The Mets defeated the San Francisco Giants in four, and then took the St. Louis Cardinals in five for their fourth pennant. In the World Series, the Yankees won the first two games for a record 14 straight series victories. Facing Roger Clemens in game two for the first time since Clemens had beaned him in July, Mets catcher Mike Piazza shattered his bat. Clemens picked up the barrel and tossed it in front of Piazza as he ran to first base. (Clemens subsequently was fined $50,000.) On October 26 at Shea Stadium, the Bronx Bombers won game five, 4–2, for their third straight championship.

In late November, after the Giants lost their second straight game, coach Jim Fassel told the press, "This is a poker game. I'm shoving my chips to the middle of the table. I'm raising the ante. This team is going to the playoffs." The Giants reeled off five straight wins and made it to the Super Bowl.

The New York (formerly Long Island) Sharks joined the 11-team Women's Professional Football League. Finishing with a 4–2 record, the Sharks lost to the New England Storm, 10–7, in the playoffs.

After a 9–7 season, Jets coach Al Groh resigned on December 29 to coach at the University of Virginia, his alma mater.

2001 ....

Sportscaster Marty Glickman died on January 3. He had been the voice of the Giants from 1948 to 1971, the Jets from 1972 to 1979 and 1987 to 1989, and the Knicks from their first season in 1946 through 1970. He popularized "swish" for baskets and often said, "Good! Like Nedicks!" (the sponsor). For 22 years, he hosted pre- and postgame shows for the Dodgers and the Yankees, and for 12 years called races at Yonkers Raceway, in addition to broadcasting collegiate sports. In 1936, he was bumped from the 4 × 100-meter relay team at the Berlin Games at the last minute, denying him the chance for Olympic gold. He received the Curt Gowdy Media Award from the Naismith Memorial Basketball Hall of Fame in 1991 and was inducted into the Sportscasters Hall of Fame in 1993.

□ □ □

Bill Parcells resigned as director of football operations for the Jets on January 9; Terry Bradway became general manager. Herman Edwards was named head coach on January 18. (As a Philadelphia Eagle, Edwards had grabbed and run with "The Fumble" in a game against the Giants on November 19, 1978.)

□ □ □

At the Meadowlands on January 14, the Giants, behind quarterback Kerry Collins and running back Tiki Barber, won the National Football Conference championship with a 41–0 trouncing of the Minnesota Vikings, the largest victory margin ever in that game. In Super Bowl XXXV, on January 28, they lost to the Baltimore Ravens, 34–7.

□ □ □

The New Jersey Storm joined the National Lacrosse League, playing at the Continental Airlines Arena in the Meadowlands. After the 2003 season, they moved to California.

□ □ □

James Ferraro bought the New Jersey Red Dogs of the Arena Football League and renamed them the Gladiators. In 2003, he moved the team to Las Vegas.

□ □ □

In March, St. John's University won the National Collegiate Athletic Association fencing championship.

□ □ □

Lorne Henning replaced Butch Goring (41–88–14) as coach of the Islanders on March 4; on May 23, Pete Laviolette became head coach.

□ □ □

In the first and only season of the XFL, a made-for-television league created by NBC and the World Wrestling Federation that embraced a thuggish playing style, the New York–New Jersey Hitmen finished with a 4–6 record. They drew surprisingly well at Giants Stadium, but the league mercifully collapsed after one season.

□ □ □

At the Theater at Madison Square Garden on April 14, International Boxing Federation middleweight champion Bernard Hopkins won a 12-round decision over Keith Holmes for the World Boxing Council title. In the main arena on September 29, thirty-six-year-old Hopkins stopped World Boxing Association champion Felix Trinidad in the twelfth round, unifying the middleweight crown for the first time since 1987.

□ □ □

In the opening round of the playoffs, the Knicks fell to the Toronto Raptors, losing game five, 93–89, on May 4.

□ □ □

On May 27, Adelphi University defeated Limestone College, 14–10, for the NCAA Division II men's lacrosse championship. C. W. Post defeated

West Chester University, 13–9, for the Division II women's lacrosse title.

∎ ∎ ∎

In the first Major League Lacrosse game, on June 7, the Long Island Lizards lost to the Baltimore Barrage, 16–13. On September 3, the Lizards beat the Barrage, 15–11, in the first title game.

∎ ∎ ∎

Led by goalie Martin Brodeur, Jason Arnott, Petr Sykora, and Patrik Elias, the defending champion Devils beat the Carolina Hurricanes, four games to two, in the first round of the playoffs; then won a seven-game series against the Toronto Maple Leafs; and finally eliminated the Pittsburgh Penguins in five games to reach the Stanley Cup finals for the second consecutive year. They led the Colorado Avalanche, three games to two, but lost games six and seven, dropping the deciding contest, 3–1, in Denver on June 9.

∎ ∎ ∎

On June 24, the Staten Island Yankees beat the Hudson Valley Renegades, 3–1, in the first game played at Richmond County Bank Ballpark at St. George. The city-funded $71 million field was the most expensive minor league ballpark in the country. The Brooklyn Cyclones, the Class A affiliate of the Mets, won their first game at Keyspan Park in Coney Island on June 25, beating the Mahoning Valley Scrappers, 3–2.

∎ ∎ ∎

On June 26, in the first night of boxing on the deck of the Intrepid Air and Space Museum, light-heavyweight George Jones knocked out Beethavaen Scottland. Scottland fell into a coma and died a few days later.

∎ ∎ ∎

In a home game at Nassau Coliseum against the Carolina Cobras on July 7, Dragons quarterback Aaron Garcia threw an Arena Football League record 11 touchdowns. During the season, he tossed a record 104 touchdowns. But in the opening round of the playoffs, the Dragons fell to the Toronto Phantoms, 64–57.

∎ ∎ ∎

The New York Power began play at the Mitchell Field Athletic Complex in Uniondale in the new professional Women's United Soccer Association. In the semifinals on August 18, they fell to the Bay Area CyberRays in San Jose, 3–2. The league folded after three seasons.

∎ ∎ ∎

In August, the first Bronx International Championship Rodeo was staged in Crotona Park. As Cord McCoy of Oklahoma, put it, "I came to ride broncs in the Bronx."

∎ ∎ ∎

On August 5, with Gary Stevens up, Point Given, winner of the Preakness and the Belmont Stakes, won the thirty-fourth Haskell Invitational at Monmouth Park in Oceanport, New Jersey, before a record crowd of 47,127.

∎ ∎ ∎

More than 1,000 athletes participated in the first New York City Triathlon on August 12, with a 1,500-meter swim in the Hudson River, a 40-kilometer bicycle ride into the Bronx, and a 10-kilometer run that finished in Central Park. Hunter Kemper was the men's winner, finishing in 1 hour, 41 minutes, 20 seconds; Karen Smyers was the women's champion, completing the race in 1 hour, 57 minutes, 55 seconds. Both winners received $6,250. In 2006, the triathlon drew 3,200 competitors from 42 states and 20 countries.

∎ ∎ ∎

On August 25, the Rolando Paulino All-Stars of the South Bronx lost the United States final in the Little League World Series to a team from Apopka, Florida. It was soon revealed that their star pitcher, Dominican-born Danny Almonte, was fourteen years old, two years older than the legal age for Little League and thus ineligible. The team's record was erased.

• • •

The Liberty lost the best-of-three WNBA Eastern Conference final to the Charlotte Sting, losing the deciding game, 48–44, at Madison Square Garden before more than 14,000 fans on August 27.

• • •

On September 8, defending champion Venus Williams defeated her sister Serena, the 1999 winner, in straight sets in the women's singles final of the United States Open. Not since 1884 had sisters met in a Grand Slam final.

• • •

The Metrostars finished their season with a 13–10–3 record, but fell to the Los Angeles Galaxy in

Venus Williams playing at the U.S. Open, 2002. (June Harrison)

the MLS playoffs on September 29. Forward Rodrigo Faria was named Rookie of the Year, and Tim Howard was Goalkeeper of the Year.

• • •

The baseball season was briefly suspended after the attack on the World Trade Center on September 11. The Yankees won the American League East, and in the American League Division Series defeated the Oakland Athletics in five games (after losing the first two at Yankee Stadium). They went on to beat the Mariners in five games, but lost to the Arizona Diamondbacks in an emotional World Series. In game seven, on November 4, seemingly invincible closer Mariano Rivera gave up two runs in the bottom of the ninth for a 3–2 loss. Roger Clemens won his sixth Cy Young Award, his first with the Yankees.

• • •

Knicks coach Jeff Van Gundy, the third winningest in franchise history with a record of 248–172 (.590), abruptly resigned on December 8, citing his "diminished focus." Assistant Don Chaney took over.

• • •

On December 13, the Yankees signed Athletics first baseman Jason Giambi to a seven-year, $120 million deal. At Giambi's insistence, any mention of steroids was omitted from the contract. Two years later, before a federal grand jury in San Francisco, he admitted to having used steroids.

• • •

Sportswriter Dick Schaap died on December 21. The former city editor of the *New York Herald Tribune*, Schaap was also editor of *Sport* magazine and the local sports reporter for WNBC-TV. In 1974, he had referred to Secretariat and Riva Ridge as "the most famous stable mates since Mary and Joseph," for which he issued an on-air apology. Schaap pioneered the "as told to" sports autobiography, including his own: *Dick Schaap, as Told to Dick Schaap*.

2002

On January 3, after broadcasting Yankees games for three seasons, Tim McCarver resigned. Michael Kay moved from radio to television, joining Ken Singleton, Jim Kaat, Bobby Murcer, and Suzyn Waldman.

Defensive end Michael Strahan of the Giants set a National Football League record with 22$\frac{1}{2}$ sacks, eclipsing the record set by Mark Gastineau of the Jets in 1984. He recorded his last sack in the final game of the season, on January 6, a loss to the Green Bay Packers. (Quarterback Brett Favre seemed to intentionally allow the sack.) Strahan was named Defensive Player of the Year. He retired before the 2008 season.

Stars and Stripes, Dennis Conner's new 79-foot entry for the America's Cup, was moored on West Forty-fourth Street in front of the New York Yacht Club for its formal christening on January 10. Was this the club's final challenge for the cup?

The Jets defeated the Raiders on the last day of the season to reach the playoffs, but then fell to Oakland, 38–24, in the American Football Conference wild-card game on January 12.

Before a capacity crowd at the Theater in Madison Square Garden on January 26, Vernon Forrest (33–0) won a unanimous 12-round decision over Shane Mosley (38–0) for the welterweight title.

On January 28, the Devils fired Larry Robinson, who had led the team to the Stanley Cup finals the previous season; Kevin Constantine took over. Pat Burns became head coach on June 13.

The New York University School of Law won the World Universities Debating Championship, held in Toronto.

Failing to make the playoffs for the fifth straight season, the Rangers dismissed Ron Low, whose record was 69–86–9. On June 6, former Islander Bryan Trottier became head coach.

A year after finishing with the worst record in the NHL, the Islanders made the playoffs for the first time in eight seasons. They fell to the Maple Leafs in seven in the quarterfinals, losing the deciding game, 4–2, in Toronto on April 30. The Devils, too, reached the postseason, but fell to the surprising Hurricanes in six, losing the last game, 1–0, on April 27.

Under coach Byron Scott, the Nets finished with their best record since joining the National Basketball Association, 52–30 (.634), and won the Atlantic Division for the first time. Point guard Jason Kidd led them over the Indiana Pacers in five, winning the deciding game, 120–109, in double overtime at the Meadowlands on May 2. They beat the Charlotte Hornets in five games and, in the Eastern Conference finals, eliminated the Celtics in six, taking the last game, 96–88, in Boston on May 31. The defending champion Los Angeles Lakers then swept the Nets, taking the final game, 113–107, on June 12 at the Continental Airlines Arena.

On June 8, a record 103,222 spectators saw Sarava, a 70–1 long shot, win the Belmont Stakes and foil War Emblem's bid for the Triple Crown.

Tiger Woods won the United States Open by three strokes on the Black Course at Bethpage State Park on Long Island on June 16, the first time the event was played on a public course.

Joel Sherman of the Bronx, winner of the World Scrabble Championship in 1997, won the National Scrabble Championship.

Twenty-two-year-old Johnson Wagner of Garrison, New York, won the Metropolitan Golf Association Ike Tournament on June 25, making him the first player to hold the MGA's three major titles simultaneously. In 2001, he had captured the MGA Amateur and the MGA Open. On August 22, a week after turning pro, Wagner won the eighty-seventh MGA Open.

Ivan Dominguez, a Cuban who had defected to the United States, won the inaugural New York City Cycling Championship, a 50-lap race over a 1.2-mile circuit through the financial district.

Finishing with a season record of 7–0, the Sharks defeated the Austin Outlaws, 24–4, in the WPFL championship game in Ashland, Oregon, on July 6.

The Harlem Little League reached the Little League World Series, but lost to the team from Worcester, Massachusetts, in the United States semifinal game on August 22.

On August 23, Fred Wilpon and partners bought out Nelson Doubleday to gain full ownership of the Mets.

For the fourth time in six years, the Liberty lost the WNBA championship series, falling to the Los Angeles Sparks, 68–66, on August 31 to lose in two straight.

The Mets did not win at Shea Stadium in August, and on September 3 dropped their fifteenth straight home game—a National League record—losing to the Florida Marlins, 3–2, in the first game of a doubleheader. But they took the nightcap, 11–5.

Pete Sampras playing at the U.S. Open. (June Harrison)

At the U.S. Open on September 7, the Williams sisters again met in the women's singles final; Serena defeated Venus, 6–4, 6–3. The next night, thirty-one-year-old Pete Sampras bested thirty-two-year-old rival Andre Agassi, 6–3, 6–4, 5–7, 6–4, for his fifth men's singles title, tying Jimmy Connors for the most in the Open era. Sampras also had beaten Agassi in the finals in 1990 and 1995.

Becky Lucidi won the United States Women's Amateur Golf Championship at Sleepy Hollow Country Club in Westchester.

The Brooklyn Cyclones sold a record 317,124 tickets, the first Class A short-season team to surpass the 300,000 attendance mark.

Before 2,852 fans at Richmond County Bank Ballpark on September 12, the Staten Island Yankees defeated the Oneonta Tigers, 2–0, to take the New York–Penn League championship in two straight.

The Newark Bears won their first Atlantic League championship, sweeping the Bridgeport Bluefish in three straight.

A capacity crowd of 2,266 attended the first soccer game at St. John's University's Belson Stadium on September 21. The Red Storm played Wake Forest to a 1–1 tie.

On October 1, the Mets fired manager Bobby Valentine, who suffered his only losing season with the team. His final record was 536–467 (.543), 13–11 (.542) in postseason play. On October 28, the Mets introduced Art Howe as manager.

Despite finishing with 103 wins, the best record in baseball, the Yankees fell to the Anaheim Angels in the ALDS in three games, ending a four-year run of World Series appearances.

The Metrostars missed the MLS playoffs, and on October 8 Octavio Zambrano was fired. Over three seasons, his record was 41–37–8 (.526).

On November 26, the Baruch College men's basketball team played on its new home court in the Academic Building on East Twenty-fourth Street for the first time, beating New Paltz, 86–66. Previously, the team played at the Sixty-ninth Regiment Armory and Xavier High School, on West Sixteenth Street. The team also had a new nickname: the Statesmen were now the Bearcats.

In a preseason game against the Buffalo Bandits on December 6, goaltender Ginny Capicchoni of the New Jersey Storm became the first woman to play in the National Lacrosse League.

On December 8, the Queens College men's water polo team finished third in the NCAA tournament.

2003

With victories on the last weekend of the season, both the Giants and the Jets reached the playoffs for the first time since 1986. In the NFC wild-card game, on January 5, the Giants lost to the San Francisco 49ers, 39–38, after leading by a score of 38–14. After thrashing the Indianapolis Colts in the AFC wild card, the Jets fell to the Oakland Raiders, 30–10, on January 12.

From January 26 to February 7, the New York Athletic Club hosted a six-game chess match between the thirty-nine-year-old Russian champion and grand master Garry Kasparov and Deep Junior. After 27 moves and close to 4 hours, man vanquished machine in the first game; the computer won the third, and the others ended in draws.

With the team at 21–26–6, the Rangers fired first-year coach Bryan Trottier on January 29. President and general manager Glen Sather took over. In five and a half seasons, the Rangers went through six coaches.

The girls' basketball team of Murry Bergtraum High School won the New York State Federation Basketball Tournament (pitting the top public school against the top private school) and was ranked first in the nation.

On March 8, Brooklyn-born Keeth Smart became the first American to be ranked number one in the world in men's saber. A graduate of Brooklyn Tech and St. John's University, he won the NCAA title as a freshman.

Just before the first pitch on opening day on March 31, Attorney General Elliot Spitzer brokered a deal between the Yankees Entertainment and Sports Network (YES) and Cablevision to broadcast Yankee games. Because of the dispute,

Yankees captain Jerek Jeter. (Dan Goldfarb)

Cablevision had not carried Yankee games the previous season.

■ ■ ■

At Madison Square Garden on April 3, St. John's University defeated Big East rival Georgetown University, 70–67, for its record sixth National Invitational Tournament championship.

■ ■ ■

The Knicks home-game sellout streak ended at 433 games, no doubt the result of their uninspired play.

■ ■ ■

The Ottawa Senators eliminated the Islanders in the first round of the playoffs in five games on April 17. Steve Stirling replaced Pete Laviolette (77–68–19) as Islanders coach on June 3, the team's seventh in seven seasons.

■ ■ ■

In May, for the first time since hosting the Tournament of Champions in 1989, the West Side Tennis Club hosted a professional tournament, the Forest Hills Tennis Classic for men ranked below fiftieth in the world.

■ ■ ■

In the NCAA Division II men's lacrosse championship game on May 25, New York Institute of Technology defeated Limestone College, 9–4.

■ ■ ■

On May 27—72 days, 21 hours, 11 minutes, 38 seconds after leaving Hong Kong—Rich Wilson and Rich du Moulin arrived off Sandy Hook, New Jersey, in their 53-foot trimaran *Great American II*. They set a new record for the 15,000-mile voyage. The *Sea Witch*, a 192-foot clipper built for the China trade, had set the old mark of 74 days, 14 hours in 1849.

■ ■ ■

Derek Jeter was named the Yankees eleventh captain, the first since Don Mattingly in 1995. George Steinbrenner said, "I cannot think of a single player that I have ever had who is more deserving of this honor than Derek Jeter. He is a young man of great character and has shown great leadership qualities. He believes, as I do, what General MacArthur said, that 'there is no substitute for victory.' To him, and to me, it's second only to breathing."

■ ■ ■

Funny Cide finished third in the Belmont Stakes on June 7, failing to become the first New York–bred horse to win the Triple Crown.

■ ■ ■

At the Meadowlands on June 9, the Devils won their third Stanley Cup, beating the Anaheim Mighty Ducks, 3–0, in game seven. Goalie Martin Brodeur had recorded seven shutouts in the playoffs.

■ ■ ■

The Mets fired general manager Steve Phillips on June 12 and brought in Jim Duquette. Phillips had held the job since 1997.

■ ■ ■

In the playoffs, the Nets eliminated the Milwaukee Bucks in six games, and then swept the Celtics and the Detroit Pistons. In the NBA finals, Jason Kidd, Richard Jefferson, Kenyon Martin, and company fell to the San Antonio Spurs in six, losing the final game, 88–77, on June 15.

∙ ∙ ∙

Before a capacity crowd at Madison Square Garden on July 12, the Western Conference beat the Eastern, 84–75, in the WNBA All-Star Game.

∙ ∙ ∙

The Sharks, now of the Independent Women's Football League, finished with a record of 8–0, with seven shutouts, yielding only six points all season. In the Eastern Conference championship game, they beat the Bay State Warriors, 20–6, but in the championship game at St. John's University's Da Silva Stadium on July 12, they fell to the Sacramento Sirens, 41–30.

∙ ∙ ∙

In the Arena Football League playoffs, the Dragons beat the Chicago Rush, but then fell to the Orlando Predators. Todd Shell of the Dragons was Coach of the Year.

∙ ∙ ∙

The New York Saints, an original franchise in the National Lacrosse League, suspended operations on August 22.

∙ ∙ ∙

At Keyspan Park in Coney Island on September 10, the Brooklyn Cyclones fell to the Williamsport Crosscutters, 4–3, in 11 innings to lose the New York–Penn League championship series in two straight.

∙ ∙ ∙

The voice of the Mets since 1962, radio play-by-play man Bob Murphy called his final game on September 25. (The Mets lost to the Pirates, 3–1.) When the Mets won, he always ended with "the happy recap." Inducted into the broadcasters' wing of the Baseball Hall of Fame in 1994, Murphy died on August 3, 2004.

Logo of the New York Sharks. (Andra Douglas)

∙ ∙ ∙

The Duke Kahanamoku Surfing Tournament was held off Beach Ninetieth Street in the Rockaways on October 4. The city's first surfing contest attracted competitors from South Africa and Brazil, as well as locals.

∙ ∙ ∙

Again winning the American League East, the Yankees beat the Minnesota Twins, three games to one, in the ALDS. In game seven of the American League Championship Series, against the Boston Red Sox on October 16, the Yankees trailed, 5–2, in the eighth but rallied to tie; third baseman Aaron Boone hit a lead-off home run in the bottom of the eleventh for a dramatic 6–5 victory. Mariano Rivera worked the last three innings. The *New York Post* went to press before the game ended and opined: "Looks like the Curse of the Bambino boomeranged this year. . . . [T]he Yankees couldn't get the job done at home; their season ended last night in the seventh game of the American League Championship Series. Or, maybe the Yanks have acquired a curse of their own: After all, the Bombers haven't won the seventh game of a championship series since 1962." In the World Series, the Yankees were up two games to one over the Marlins, but lost three straight, dropping the final contest, 2–0, at Yankee Stadium on October 25. The next day, bench coach

Don Zimmer resigned, saying that he had had enough of George Steinbrenner. In January 2004, the Yankees voided Boone's contract after he tore knee ligaments in a pickup basketball game.

■ ■ ■

After the last game of the year at Yankee Stadium, Eddie Layton retired. An organist for CBS soap operas, he began to play for the Yankees in 1967 and also played at Madison Square Garden for the Knicks and Rangers and at Nassau Coliseum for the Islanders. Layton claimed to have originated the "Charge" cheer and once said, "I think I'm the only organist in the world with five world championship rings."

■ ■ ■

The Harlem Hellfighters of Frederick Douglass Academy, Harlem's first high school football team, played their first game on November 1, losing to Garden City High School, 34–6. Former NFL player Duke Fergerson organized the team when he learned that there was no team for boys after Pop Warner.

■ ■ ■

On November 2, Margaret Okayo of Kenya won the New York City Marathon in 2 hours, 22 minutes, 31 seconds, cutting 2 seconds off the mark that she had set in 2002. Martin Lel, also of Kenya, won the men's race.

■ ■ ■

Under Bob Bradley and with sixteen-year-old Eddie Gaven on the team, the Metrostars finished with a record of 11–10–9, but lost to the New England Revolution in the playoffs.

■ ■ ■

At the New York Athletic Club in November, grand master Garry Kasparov took on the supercomputer X3D Fritz. The first and fourth games ended in draws, Fritz won the second, and Kasparov took the third.

■ ■ ■

Despite finishing below .500, St. Francis Prep defeated Holy Cross, 2–0, for its first city soccer title in 20 years, and then defeated Canisius of Buffalo, 1–0, to win the state's Catholic schools championship. On November 16, Martin Luther King Jr. High School defeated Midwood High School for its fourth consecutive Public Schools Athletic League boys' soccer championship.

■ ■ ■

St. John's University lost to Indiana University, 2–1, in the NCAA men's soccer championship game on December 14.

■ ■ ■

Certain that he would be fired after the 4–12 season, Giants coach Jim Fassel announced on December 16 that he was resigning, effective after the last game. In seven seasons, he took the team to the playoffs three times and reached the Super Bowl in 2000; his record was 58–51–1 (.532), the third winningest in franchise history behind those of Bill Parcells (.611) and Steve Owen (.605).

■ ■ ■

Everlast, the sporting goods company founded in 1910, abandoned the Bronx in December. In 2004, John Golomb, grandson of Everlast founder Jacob Golomb, founded Legacy, a Bronx-based company producing hand-sewn boxing gear.

■ ■ ■

The Knicks fired general manager Scott Layden on December 22 and hired Isiah Thomas. Under Layden, the payroll had ballooned to $88 million, $40 million over the salary cap, with decidedly disappointing results on the hardwood.

2004

Let's go to the videotape.

WARNER WOLF

The Giants hired Tom Coughlin, a one-time assistant under Bill Parcells, as head coach on January 6.

■ ■ ■

Knicks coach Don Chaney arrived for a game at Madison Square Garden on January 14, only to learn that he had been fired by Isiah Thomas. Assistant Herb Williams took over until Lenny Wilkins arrived. Chaney's record was 72–112 (.391).

◦ ◦ ◦

On January 21, real-estate developer Bruce C. Ratner agreed to purchase the New Jersey Nets for $300 million, intending to move the franchise to a new arena, designed by Frank Gehry, in Brooklyn.

◦ ◦ ◦

The National Track and Field Hall of Fame (founded in Charleston, West Virginia, in 1974 and moved to Indianapolis in 1985) was dedicated at the New Balance Track and Field Center at the Armory (168th Street and Fort Washington Avenue) on January 24. Built in 1912, the Armory had hosted its first track meet in 1914.

◦ ◦ ◦

Atop the Atlantic Division with a 22–20 record on January 26, the Nets fired Byron Scott; assistant Lawrence Frank became interim coach. In three-plus seasons, Scott went 149–139 (.517), 25–15 in the playoffs, reaching the finals twice. Frank began his tenure with 13 straight wins, an NBA record.

◦ ◦ ◦

On February 5, St. John's University expelled or suspended six basketball players after a woman they had picked up at a strip club in Pittsburgh at 2:30 A.M. falsely accused them of rape. (They lost to Pitt that night.) The players were disciplined "for violation of team rules and behavior inconsistent with St. John's mission and values."

◦ ◦ ◦

The Yankees acquired all-star shortstop Alex Rodriguez from the Texas Rangers on February 14 for Alfonso Soriano and a player to be named later. Derek Jeter was at short, so A-Rod, with the biggest contract in baseball at the time, moved to third.

◦ ◦ ◦

The New York/New Jersey Juggernaut joined the eight-team women's National Pro Fastpitch Softball League; their home field was at Montclair State University. On August 29, they defeated the New England Riptide for the championship. In 2006, the team was inactive.

◦ ◦ ◦

On February 25, citing the distraction of the frequent "Fire Sather" chants in what he always called "the Gardens," Glen Sather resigned as Rangers coach, but remained as general manager. (The team had the highest payroll in the NHL.) Tom Renney became interim coach.

◦ ◦ ◦

Courtney Prince, captain of the City Skaters, the Rangers' ice-skating cheerleaders, was fired after informing the other members of the squad that a Madison Square Garden executive had solicited her for sex. She then filed a sexual harassment suit, charging that the cheerleaders were expected to be sexually alluring, particularly toward management. The Garden finally settled out of court in December 2007.

◦ ◦ ◦

The Yankees lost their season opener to the Tampa Bay Devil Rays, 8–3, in Tokyo on March 30, but won the next day, 12–1.

◦ ◦ ◦

In his final game, forty-three-year-old Rangers captain Mark Messier scored in a 4–3 loss to the Buffalo Sabres on March 31. The team retired his number, 11, on January 12, 2006. In 1994, "The Captain" had led the team to the Stanley Cup.

◦ ◦ ◦

In the first round of the playoffs, the Philadelphia Flyers eliminated the defending Stanley Cup champion Devils, four games to one.

◦ ◦ ◦

The Kissena Park Velodrome reopened on April 21 after a year-long renovation.

◦ ◦ ◦

With the fourth pick in the draft on April 24, the Giants selected quarterback Philip Rivers of North Carolina State University and immediately traded him to the San Diego Chargers for the first overall pick, Eli Manning of the University of Mississippi. Four days later, they released Kerry Collins, their quarterback in Super Bowl XXXV; he was second in franchise history in completions (1,447), behind Phil Simms, and third in passing yardage (16,875), behind Simms and Charlie Conerly.

• • •

The Nets won the Atlantic Division for the third straight year. In the opening round of the playoffs, Jason Kidd and company swept the Knicks, taking the fourth game, 100–94, at Madison Square Garden on April 25. They then lost to the Pistons in seven.

• • •

On May 11, the Chelsea Recreation Center, the Department of Parks and Recreation's first in nearly 30 years, opened on Twenty-fifth Street between Ninth and Tenth Avenues. Construction had begun in 1973, but stopped in 1976 during the fiscal crisis. The six-story building has a 25-yard pool; aerobic, weight, and cardiovascular rooms; pool tables; and a basketball court.

• • •

Adelphi University defeated West Chester University, 12–11, for the NCAA Division II women's lacrosse championship on May 15.

• • •

On May 28, CBS fired veteran sportscaster Warner Wolf, who had immortalized the phrase "Let's go to the videotape." Wolf had been a sportscaster on local television since 1976 and later was featured on *Imus in the Morning*.

• • •

A record 120,139 spectators saw Birdstone win the Belmont Stakes and thwart Smarty Jones's bid for the Triple Crown on June 5.

• • •

Scott Niedermeyer of the Devils won the Norris Trophy as the NHL's top defenseman.

• • •

Unhappy with Marv Albert's on-air criticism of the Knicks, MSG fired him on June 15. The voice of the Knicks on radio and television since 1967, Albert said, "They confuse negativity with objectivity. If the team didn't play well the previous game, just don't deal with it. Don't talk about Knick turnovers, don't talk about the opposition. It was constant things that cut into your integrity or your credibility. It wasn't like I was killing them, either." He then began calling NBA games for TNT.

• • •

Sebastian Telfair of Coney Island, the highest scorer in New York State boys' basketball history and leader of the three-time PSAL champion Abraham Lincoln High School, was selected thirteenth in the draft by the Portland Trailblazers. He is the cousin of fellow Lincoln alumnus and point guard Stephon Marbury—Starbury.

• • •

The New York Storm played in American Pro Cricket, the nation's first professional league. Its field was Richmond County Bank Ballpark at St. George. The league expired after one season.

• • •

With the Liberty at 7–9 on July 3, two days after they fell to the Sacramento Monarchs, 73–47, the worst loss in franchise history, general manager Carol Blazejowski dismissed coach Richie Adubato; over five and a half seasons, Adubato's record was 100–79, with three Eastern Conference titles. Assistant coach Pat Coyle took over. In October, the Liberty lost the conference final to the Connecticut Sun in two straight.

• • •

The Sharks again went undefeated. In the IWFL playoffs, they beat the Chicago Force, 40–0, and then the Tampa Bay Terminators, 29–7. In the title game on July 12, they lost to the Sacramento Sirens, 29–27.

At Winged Foot Golf Club, Ryan Moore won the United States Men's Amateur Golf Championship.

. . .

The Long Island Ducks won the Atlantic League championship, sweeping the Camden Riversharks in three straight games.

. . .

Dominican-born, Corona-raised Omar Minaya became general manager of the Mets on September 30. He dismissed Art Howe, whose record was 137–186 (.424), after the season. Brooklyn-born Willie Randolph became manager on November 4. Randolph had played second base for the Yankees for 13 years, and then was a coach for 11 years.

. . .

Again winning the American League East, the Yankees beat the Twins in four games. But after taking the first three games of the ALCS, they dropped four straight to the Red Sox, losing the seventh game, 10–3, at Yankee Stadium on October 20. (They were the first team to lose a series after being up by three games.) The "Curse of the Bambino" had been exorcised (and there's skating on the River Styx).

. . . .

Metropolitan Opera baritone Robert Merrill (born Moishe Miller in Brooklyn) died on October 23. Merrill's rendition of "The Star-Spangled Banner" was a regular feature at Yankee Stadium, and he sang in person on opening day and on other important occasions.

. . .

On October 30, the Metrostars fell to D.C. United, 2–0, and were eliminated in the first round of the playoffs. Midfielder Armando Guevara shared the scoring title and was MLS's Most Valuable Player.

. . .

Representatives of the New York attorney general's office and other agencies raided Aqueduct Racetrack on December 15. Braulio Baeza, a Hall of Fame jockey, and Mario Sclafani, clerk of scales, were suspended on January 12, 2005, for allegedly having falsified the recorded weights of certain jockeys racing at Belmont Park, Aqueduct, and Saratoga Race Course. They were fired on September 21, 2005, but ultimately were exonerated at great personal cost.

. . .

On December 31, longtime sportswriter Joe Durso of the *New York Times* died. He had covered the Yankees and the Mets and had written biographies of Casey Stengel and Joe DiMaggio.

2005

Take it easy. This is sport.

PAUL TERGAT

In a 32–29 overtime loss to the St. Louis Rams on January 2, Curtis Martin of the Jets ran for 153 yards to claim the rushing title with 1,697 yards, 1 yard ahead of Shaun Alexander of the Seattle Seahawks. Martin also set the Jets single-season rushing mark and rose to fourth on the all-time list, with 13,366 yards. The same day, Tiki Barber set a Giants single-season rushing record with 1,518 yards. His 3-yard touchdown run with 16 seconds remaining in the fourth quarter lifted the Giants over the Cowboys, 28–24. Barber passed Rodney Hampton to become the team's all-time rushing leader.

. . .

On January 15, a week after beating the Chargers, 20–17, in overtime in the AFC wild-card game, the Jets lost to the Pittsburgh Steelers, 20–17, in overtime in the next round. Doug Brien missed two field goals late in the fourth quarter.

. . .

Naismith Memorial Basketball Hall of Fame player and coach Lenny Wilkins resigned as coach of the Knicks on January 22 after the team had lost nine of 10 games; his record was 40–41. Assistant coach and former Knick player Herb Williams took over for the remainder of the season.

· · ·

In February, for the 900th consecutive game, retired accountant Burt Beagle, class of 1956, was the official scorer for the Baruch College men's basketball team. He had begun with Baruch's first game, in December 1968; he missed the seventh game that season, but not one since. He worked every City University of New York tournament since its inception in 1970, as well as more than 6,000 basketball games at every level.

· · ·

At Aqueduct on February 16, officials of the New York Racing Association tested horses for doping before a race for the first time. This examination followed the bust of a Gambino family gambling ring that had doped a horse in at least one race.

· · ·

In March, after years of being harassed by police officers and the Parks Department for "swimming" without lifeguards present, surfers finally got a dedicated surfing beach at Beach Ninetieth Street in the Rockaways.

· · ·

The women's basketball team of Monroe College fell to Anoka-Ramsey Community College, 64–60, in the National Junior College Athletic Association Division III championship game.

· · ·

David Elwell and other members of the New York Yacht Club created the NYYC 42 (sold as the Club Swan 42 outside the club), a new one-design offshore racing boat, the ninth one-design created by the club since 1900.

· · ·

Suzyn Waldman, who had covered the Yankees for WFAN from 1987 to 2001, joined John Sterling in the radio booth as a color commentator.

· · ·

The Nets won seven of their last eight games to reach the playoffs, but were swept by the Miami Heat in the first round, their earliest exit in Jason Kidd's four years with the team.

· · ·

In May, 36 men were arrested for running a sports-betting ring that had taken in $360 million over two years. On August 15, Dominic Valila, the former head groundskeeper at Shea Stadium, pleaded guilty to the charge.

· · ·

On May 22, 20 yachts in three classes—Grand Prix, Classics, and Performance Cruising—sailed from New York Harbor in the Rolex Transatlantic Challenge, aiming to break the record of 12 days, 4 hours, 1 minute, 19 seconds set by the three-masted schooner *Atlantic* in a 1905 race for the Kaiser's Cup. With Mike Sanderson at the helm, *Mari-Cha IV*, a 140-foot carbon-fiber schooner owned by Robert Miller, broke the record, reaching Lizard Point off Cornwall in 9 days, 15 hours, 55 minutes, 23 seconds—even after repairing the mast for 12 hours in 40-knot winds.

· · ·

New York Institute of Technology defeated Limestone College, 14–13, in overtime for its second NCAA Division II men's lacrosse title.

· · ·

After clinching their third straight division title, the Dragons lost to the Orlando Predators, 47–42, at Nassau Coliseum on May 29 in the Arena Football League playoffs.

· · ·

At a meeting of the Public Authorities Control Board on June 6, Assembly Speaker Sheldon Silver and Senate Majority Leader Joseph Bruno refused to support the construction of a stadium for the Jets on the Far West Side of Manhattan, a project requiring a $300 million allocation from the state (Mayor Michael Bloomberg had pledged $300 million from the city), effectively derailing New

York's bid for the 2012 Olympics. Six days later, Bloomberg and Mets owner Fred Wilpon announced plans to build a new ballpark adjacent to Shea Stadium that would accommodate the Olympics. While pushing the Manhattan site, Bloomberg had dismissed the Queens option. "You should . . . see the places where the Olympics have taken place," he said. "You will realize that Shea Stadium is not of the same order of magnitude or grandeur that the I.O.C. wants for the Olympics." For the revised bid, he said, "You can't have a better place." To the relief of many, many New Yorkers, the International Olympic Committee rejected the city's bid for the games on July 6.

▪ ▪ ▪

Takeru Kobayashi consumed 49 hot dogs and buns in 12 minutes to win the ninetieth annual Nathan's Famous Fourth of July International Hot Dog Eating Contest in Coney Island. His fifth straight triumph fell four and a half franks shy of his own record. American Sonya Thomas finished second with 37, breaking her own American record.

▪ ▪ ▪

At the new Icahn Stadium on Randall's Island (the old Downing Stadium, redesigned by Ricardo Zurita), the LeMans Track Club of New York City captured the women's title at the USA Track and Field National Club Championships on July 16. The Shore Athletic Club of New Jersey won the men's title.

▪ ▪ ▪

Ending the season with a 10–0 record and winning the Eastern Conference for the fourth straight year, the Sharks lost to the Atlanta Xplosion, 3–0, in the IWFL playoffs at Monsignor Farrell High School on Staten Island on July 23.

▪ ▪ ▪

On July 28, the Knicks signed Brooklyn native Larry Brown to a five-year, $50 million contract as their new coach.

Icahn Stadium on Randall's Island, built on the site of Downing Stadium. (Zurita Architects)

▪ ▪ ▪

In a rain-delayed finish, Phil Mickelson won the Professional Golfers Association Championship by one stroke at Baltusrol Golf Club on August 15.

▪ ▪ ▪

The NCAA and the NIT reached an out-of-court agreement on August 16, settling the NIT's suit accusing the NCAA of "deliberately set[ting] out to get a monopoly." The NCAA agreed to buy the NIT's pre- and postseason tournaments from the Metropolitan Intercollegiate Basketball Association—made up of Fordham University, New York University, Wagner College, Manhattan College, and St. John's University—for $56.6 million.

▪ ▪ ▪

On August 28, at the National Tennis Center, Patrick McEnroe's New York Sportimes defeated the Newport Beach Breakers, 21–18, to win the World Team Tennis championship and take home the Billie Jean King Trophy for the first time. The team's home court was the Sportime Tennis Club at Harbor Island in Mamaroneck.

▪ ▪ ▪

On their home field on September 15, the Staten Island Yankees defeated the Auburn Doubledays, 3–2, to take the New York–Penn League championship series in two straight.

. . .

On October 4, with three games to play and the team three points out of the playoffs, the Metrostars fired Bob Bradley and made Mo Johnston coach. Bradley's record was 32–31–26, but his team never made it out of the first round in two playoff appearances; his 114 victories overall made him the winningest coach in MLS history. The Metrostars reached the playoffs, but fell to the New England Revolution.

. . .

En route to another Eastern Division title, the Yankees set a new attendance mark, drawing 4,090,696 fans, an average of 50,502 a game. In Anaheim on October 10, the Yankees fell to the Angels, 5–3, in the fifth game of the ALDS. Pitching coach and former Yankees pitcher Mel Stottlemyre resigned two days later, having served beside manager Joe Torre for 10 years. Third baseman Alex Rodriguez was the American League's Most Valuable Player.

. . .

The Breeders' Cup was held at Belmont Park on October 29. Silver Train won the $1 million Sprint; Pleasant Home, a 30–1 long shot, won the Distaff; and Saint Liam, with Jerry Bailey up, won the $4.7 million Breeders' Cup Classic.

. . .

The New York State Athletic Commission ruled that so-called white-collar boxing was illegal, even if all the requirements for amateur bouts were fulfilled (a doctor at ringside, an ambulance outside, headgear and other protective equipment on the fighters). At these bouts, amateur boxers—typically white-collar professionals—matched by weight and ability met for three 2-minute rounds; the gyms would charge admission and sell refreshments.

. . .

On November 1, a statue of Pee Wee Reese and Jackie Robinson was unveiled outside Keyspan Park in Coney Island, commemorating a moment in the 1947 season when Reese put his arm around Robinson to silence abusive fans.

. . .

On November 6, in the closest finish in the history of the New York City Marathon, Paul Tergat of Kenya crossed the finish line .32 second ahead of Hendrick Ramaala of South Africa. Afterward, Tergat approached Ramaala and said, "Take it easy. This is sport." Jeļena Prokopčuka of Latvia was the women's winner.

. . .

The St. Francis College men's water polo team reached the Final Four in the NCAA tournament, but lost to the University of Southern California, 14–8, and then to Loyola Marymount, 10–6, in the consolation game. With players from Serbia, Moldova, Canada, Israel, Hungary, Croatia, Azerbaijan, Venezuela, and Texas (but not Brooklyn!), the team had won the Eastern College Athletic Conference championship, the Collegiate Water Polo Northern Championship, and the Collegiate Water Polo Eastern Championships.

. . .

Devils coach Larry Robinson resigned on December 18; over one full season and parts of three others, his record was 87–56–24. General manager Lou Lamoriello went behind the bench.

. . .

By defeating the Raiders on December 31, the Giants clinched the NFC East with an 11–5 record. Tiki Barber led the league with 2,390 total yards, the second highest total in NFL history.

. . .

Bob Sheppard retired as the Giants public-address announcer. His tenure began when the team moved from the Polo Grounds to Yankee Stadium in 1956.

2006

Once you fall here, you're done.

JAROMIR JAGR

With two years remaining on his contract, the Jets released coach Herman Edwards on January 6; he went to the Kansas City Chiefs, the Jets receiving a fourth-round draft pick in compensation. Edwards was 39–41 overall and had led the team to the playoffs in three of his five seasons, going 2–3 in the postseason. On January 17, the Jets named thirty-four-year-old Eric Magnani head coach; he had been the defensive coordinator of the New England Patriots under Bill Belichick.

At the Meadowlands on January 8, the Giants fell to the Carolina Panthers, 23–0, in the NFC wild-card game. The Giants had not been shut out since 1996 and had not been held scoreless in a home playoff game since 1943.

On January 12, with the team at 18–22–2, Islander owner Charles Wang fired coach Steve Stirling; assistant Brad Shaw became interim coach.

In January, the Knicks fired Anucha Browne Sanders, head of business and marketing operations. A former Big-Ten basketball star, she filed a sexual harassment suit against general manager Isiah Thomas and Madison Square Garden. On October 2, 2007, a Manhattan jury found Thomas and Garden chairman James L. Dolan guilty of sexual harassment and awarded Sanders $11.6 million.

On February 1, Epiphanny Prince of the perennial powerhouse Murry Bergtraum High School girls' basketball team played the entire 32-minute game and scored 113 points in a 137–32 win over Brandeis (breaking Cheryl Miller's single-game scoring record of 105, set in 1982). The Lady Blazers defeated

Francis Lewis High School, 81–66, on March 19 for their eighth straight PSAL championship under coach Ed Grezinsky. In the New York State Class AA girls' basketball championship on March 25, Christ the King of Queens, ranked first in the United States, defeated second-ranked Murry Bergtraum, 79–66.

The Devils retired Scott Stevens's number, 4, the first ever retired by the franchise, on February 3. He played 956 games with the Devils and was the captain of three Stanley Cup champion teams.

On February 7, Mike Tannenbaum replaced Terry Bradway as general manager of the Jets.

The co-ed rifle team of John Jay College of Criminal Justice won its fourth consecutive Mid-Atlantic Rifle Conference championship on March 4.

Major League Soccer approved the sale of the Metrostars to Austrian beverage company Red Bull for more than $100 million on March 8. The team was renamed Red Bull New York, and the colors were changed to the energy drink's red, blue, and silver.

On March 16, SportsNet New York (SNY), the Mets' television network, went on the air.

On March 18, the Monroe College's women's basketball team defeated Mohawk Valley Community College, 100–70, in the NJCAA Division III championship game, completing an undefeated season. Fantasia Goodwin of the Lady Mustangs finished as the NJCAA Division III career scoring leader (1,681 points) and set records for single season scoring (867), single season scoring average (28), and career scoring average (27.1).

The Skate Key, a roller rink in Mott Haven, closed in March. Home to a new roller derby team—the Gotham Girls—since 2003, the venue had been plagued by crime.

* * *

On March 26, Brooklyn district attorney Charles Hynes announced the arrest of 10 men associated with the Gambino crime family and with Chinese gangs for having operated a sports-betting ring in Brooklyn, Queens, and Manhattan. Hynes used the occasion to call for legalizing sports betting: "People are going to bet. That's a reality, and we've got to do something about recovering this revenue."

* * *

In a 5–1 victory over the Islanders on March 29, Jaromir Jagr of the Rangers had four assists to reach 113 points for the season, surpassing Jean Ratelle's mark of 109 points set over 63 games in 1971/1972. (A broken ankle had prematurely ended Ratelle's season.) Jagr established franchise records with 54 goals and 123 points. On playing in New York, he remarked, "You have to be a winner to be successful. And that's what's probably pushing everybody. You cannot fall. Once you fall here, you're done. And that's what pushes you."

* * *

Gail Richards and Sharon Joseph opened Harlem Lanes at 126th Street and Adam Clayton Powell Boulevard on April 1, the first bowling alley in Harlem since the Lenox Lanes closed in the 1980s.

* * *

Under Larry Brown, the Knicks finished at 23–59, the second worst record in franchise history. In April, he said, "I never in my life thought I'd have to be in a position where you're begging guys to play. Somehow, you've got to find five guys that care enough to compete." He was fired on June 22, and Isiah Thomas appointed himself coach.

* * *

The Nets again won the Atlantic Division. They ousted Reggie Miller and the Pacers in six games, but fell to the Heat in five games in the semifinals.

* * *

After beating the Rangers in four straight in the first round of the playoffs, the Devils fell to the Hurricanes in five games, losing the final contest, 4–1, on May 14. Lou Lamoriello stepped aside on June 13 and named Claude Julien the new head coach, the twelfth coaching change since Lamoriello became general manager in 1987.

* * *

Adelphi University defeated West Chester University, 16–8, for the NCAA Division II women's lacrosse championship on May 14.

* * *

On June 8, the Islanders named Ted Nolan head coach and Neil Smith general manager. Barely six weeks later, Islanders owner Charles Wang named back-up goalie Garth Snow general manager; thirty-six-year-old Snow immediately retired as a player.

* * *

At Winged Foot Golf Club on June 18, Geoff Ogily won the U.S. Open by one stroke when Phil Mickelson double-bogeyed the eighteenth hole.

* * *

On June 27, the Red Bulls dismissed Mo Johnston, whose record was 2–3–7; assistant Richie Williams took over. On July 18, Bruce Arena was hired, the ninth coach in the team's 11-year history. Williams, who had played for Arena at the University of Virginia, became an assistant.

* * *

The WNBA All-Star Game was again held at Madison Square Garden, on July 12. For the first time in

The New York Sharks, 2007. (Andra Douglas)

seven contests, the Eastern Conference beat the Western, 98–82.

▪ ▪ ▪

In the IWFL playoffs, on July 15, the Sharks lost to the Xplosion, 35–14, at Monsignor Farrell High School.

▪ ▪ ▪

In the first round of the Arena Football League playoffs at Nassau Coliseum, the Dragons lost to the Georgia Force, 72–69.

▪ ▪ ▪

The Mid-Island Little League of Staten Island advanced to the Little League World Series, but was eliminated in two straight games.

▪ ▪ ▪

On August 16, ground was broken for the new Yankee Stadium in Macombs Dam Park. For years, George Steinbrenner had complained about the crime and decay in the Bronx and threatened to move the team to New Jersey if the city did not build him a new stadium on the West Side of Manhattan. The city and state would contribute $400 million, including the cost of demolition, and the

Yankees pledged $800 million; the city ceded the land to the team, eliminating the annual $5 million the Yankees paid in rent. Only the *Staten Island Advance* lamented the loss: "Have you grown accustomed to seeing one precious bit of New York history after another fall to the wrecker's ball?"

▪ ▪ ▪

At Coney Island on August 20, a crowd of 4,000 saw Misty May Treanor and Kerri Walsh defeat Jennifer Boss and Rachel Wacholder in the Association of Volleyball Professionals' first Brooklyn Open.

▪ ▪ ▪

On August 21, the Yankees completed a five-game sweep of the Red Sox at Fenway Park with a 2–1 victory to open a lead of six and a half games in the American League East. The Yanks won by 12–4 on Friday afternoon; 14–11 on Friday night (a record for the longest nine-inning game, at 4 hours, 45 minutes); 13–5 on Saturday; and 8–5 on Sunday night. They finished with a season record of 97–65 and won their ninth straight Eastern Division title, but fell to the Detroit Tigers in the ALDS, winning game one and then dropping three straight.

▪ ▪ ▪

At the opening ceremonies for the U.S. Open on August 28, the National Tennis Center was renamed in honor of Billie Jean King. The women's sports hall of fame planned for the Sports Museum of America in the former Standard Oil Building, at 26 Broadway, was named the Billie Jean King International Women's Sports Center on October 17.

▪ ▪ ▪

On their home field on September 15, the Staten Island Yankees defeated the Tri-City Valley Cats, 2–0, to repeat as New York–Penn League champions.

▪ ▪ ▪

Closed for 16 months, Yonkers Raceway reopened on October 11, not with trotters, but with 1,870 slot machines, ostensibly to support harness racing. One patron remarked, "I used to come here to play the horses, but not for a long time. I started going to Atlantic City instead. The slots are just a lot more fun to me. There's nothing wrong with horse racing, but I never seemed to win."

▪ ▪ ▪

On October 11, Yankee pitcher Corey Lidle and pilot Tyler Stanger died when their airplane crashed into a 42-story apartment building on Manhattan's East Side.

▪ ▪ ▪

Behind veterans Tom Glavine, Orlando Hernandez, and Carlos Delgado and rising stars David Wright, José Reyes, and John Maine, the Mets won the National League East with a 97–65 record. The franchise set a new home attendance mark of 3,379,551, topping 3 million for the first time. In the National League Division Series, the Mets swept the Los Angeles Dodgers, but fell to the Cardinals in the National League Championship Series in seven, dropping the deciding game at Shea Sta-

dium, 3–1, on October 19. The score was tied 1–1 going into the ninth, but Carlos Beltran looked at a third strike with two out and the bases loaded to end the game.

▪ ▪ ▪

In November, eight years after the Giuliani administration awarded a contract to Ferry Point Partners to build an 18-hole golf course designed by Jack Nicklaus on a former dump in Ferry Point Park in the Bronx, the project was abandoned. The city had spent more than $8 million on the toxic cleanup, and costs had ballooned from $22.4 million to $84 million.

▪ ▪ ▪

Aviator Sports and Recreation—a $38 million complex with ice-skating rinks, indoor and outdoor playing fields, basketball courts, and a climbing wall—opened at Floyd Bennett Field in Brooklyn in November.

▪ ▪ ▪

Australian Kurt Fearnley set a new record for wheelchair competitors in the New York City Marathon on November 5, finishing in 1 hour, 29 minutes, 22 seconds.

▪ ▪ ▪

On November 13, the Mets broke ground for Citi Field, a 42,500-seat, $800 million ballpark. Citigroup agreed to pay $20 million annually for 20 years for the naming rights.

▪ ▪ ▪

At the thirtieth annual Double Dutch Holiday Classic at the Apollo Theater in Harlem on December 3, a Japanese team won for the fourth time in five years.

▪ ▪ ▪

On December 4, in the face of strong local opposition, the International Speedway Corporation abandoned plans to build an 82,000-seat Nascar track on Staten Island.

▪ ▪ ▪

In the inaugural Texas Bowl in Houston on December 28, Rutgers University defeated Kansas State, 37–10, the university's first victory in a bowl game.

2007

Nappy-headed ho's.

DON IMUS

The first time you're coming through that tunnel, knowing you're here in this arena with its history, you can't describe it.

BUDDY MCGIRT

Madison Square Garden hosted the Versus Invitational on January 6, the first time the Professional Bull Riders tour visited New York.

In wild-card games on January 7, the Jets fell to the Patriots, 37–16, and the Giants lost to the Eagles, 23–20.

Ernie Accorsi retired after nine seasons as general manager of the Giants. The team introduced Jerry Reese, who had begun with the Giants as a scout in 1994, as its new general manager on January 16.

On January 20, the New York Titans of the National Lacrosse League played their first home game at Madison Square Garden, defeating the Chicago Shamrox, 11–9. It was the first lacrosse game played at the Garden.

On April 2, with the Devils in first place and the playoff games beginning in a week, Lou Lamoriello fired first-year coach Claude Julien and again took over. The Rangers and the Islanders also reached the playoffs. The Isles were swept by the Sabres in the opening round. The Devils beat the Tampa Bay Lightning in six games, but then fell to the Ottawa Senators in five. The Rangers swept the Atlanta Thrashers in four straight, but then lost to the Sabres in six; in game five, they were 7.7 seconds away from winning their third straight to take a lead of three games to two when Buffalo scored to tie, and the Rangers lost in overtime.

In the NCAA women's basketball championship game on April 3, Rutgers University lost to the University of Tennessee, 59–46. Tennessee had Nicky Anosike of Staten Island and Harlem's Shannon Bobbitt of Murry Bergtraum High School; Rutgers freshman Epiphanny Price, also of Murry Bergtraum, was held to two points. The day after the game, WFAN morning host Don Imus called the Rutgers players "nappy-headed ho's." The next day, after receiving a few complaints, he wondered on the air about the big deal being made over "some idiot comment meant to be amusing." Broadcast live over MSNBC and carried by 70 stations nationwide over CBS Radio, the hugely profitable *Imus in the Morning* was dropped amid a growing controversy on April 12. But Imus was back on the air in December.

The chess team of Edward R. Murrow High School in Brooklyn won its fourth straight national championship on April 15, with Alex Lenderman named the national scholastic chess champion.

The Empire Roller Skating Center in Crown Heights closed on April 22. Located at Empire Boulevard east of Bedford Avenue, the venue had opened in 1941 in a former garage for Ebbets Field. The Empire invented roller disco in the 1970s. With a capacity of 2,500, it was sometimes so crowded that, according to competitive skater

Chester Fried, "if you fell, you couldn't fall." It sold for $4.5 million and became a storage facility.

◦ ◦ ◦

On April 23, over Mayor Michael Bloomberg's veto, the City Council passed Staten Island Republican James Oddo's bill banning the use of aluminum bats in high school games. The ball flies off metal bats quicker than off wooden bats, although some coaches and Little League Baseball dispute that. Oddo said: "Gone are the days of kids learning to hit a line drive or a homer off the sweet part of a wooden bat—the same tool that the 'Splendid Splinter' and 'Teddy Baseball' utilized to become legends in the game that was made for wood, and in the game that has unfortunately become perverted by metal. For the sake of the sanctity of baseball, yes, but much more importantly for the safety of our young people."

◦ ◦ ◦

The Claremont Riding Academy, at 175 West Eighty-ninth Street, closed on April 29. It had opened as a livery stable in 1892 and became a riding academy in the 1920s.

◦ ◦ ◦

On May 13, C. W. Post defeated West Chester University, 15–7, for the NCAA Division II women's lacrosse championship.

◦ ◦ ◦

Running at 4–1 odds on June 9, Rags to Riches became the first filly to win the Belmont Stakes since 1905.

◦ ◦ ◦

At Brooklyn's Spring Creek Park in June, the Parks Department staged its first cricket tournament, attracting 20 teams.

◦ ◦ ◦

At the ninety-second annual Nathan's Famous Fourth of July International Hot Dog Eating Contest at Coney Island on July 4, Joey Chestnut con-

Roger Federer winning his second U.S. Open Men's Singles Championship, 2005. (June Harrison)

sumed 66 franks in 12 minutes to break his own world's record and dethrone six-time champion Takeru Kobayashi, who ate 63.

◦ ◦ ◦

On July 13, the Devils introduced Brent Sutter as their seventh coach in nine years. Sutter had played for 17 seasons in the NHL, 10 with the Islanders.

◦ ◦ ◦

At Yankee Stadium on August 4, third baseman Alex Rodriguez hit his 500th home run, at thirty-two years and eight days old the youngest player to reach that milestone, joining Babe Ruth and Mickey Mantle as the third to do so in pinstripes. The Yankees clubbed the Kansas City Royals, 16–8. The next day, Tom Glavine of the Mets defeated the Cubs, 8–3, at Wrigley Field for his 300th career win, the twenty-third pitcher to reach that milestone and only the fifth left-hander.

. . .

On September 9, Roger Federer won his fourth straight U.S. Open Men's Singles Championship at Arthur Ashe Stadium with a 7–6, 7–6, 6–4 victory over Novak Djokovic.

. . .

After eliminating the Staten Island Yankees, the Brooklyn Cyclones lost the New York–Penn League championship to the Auburn Doubledays in two straight, dropping the final game, 4–1, at Keyspan Park on September 14.

. . .

On September 15, former NBA referee Tim Donaghy pleaded guilty to two felonies in the United States District Court for the Eastern District in Brooklyn for having bet on games, including those he was officiating, and having provided information to gamblers (conspiracy to commit wire fraud and conspiracy to transmit wagering information over state lines). A referee for 13 years, Donaghy had resigned in July.

. . .

Madison Square Garden's historic boxing ring, first used in 1925 for a light-heavyweight title fight between Paul Berlenbach and Jack Delaney (Berlenbach won on points), was retired on September 19 and donated to the international Boxing Hall of Fame in Canastota, New York. The ring was also used at Yankee Stadium and the Polo Grounds. Buddy McGirt, who had fought 25 times at the Garden, recalled, "The first time you're coming through that tunnel, knowing you're here in this arena with its history, you can't describe it. And I had to love it because I never got knocked out in it."

. . .

The ring at Madison Square Garden, 1948. (Museum of the City of New York, *Look* Collection)

The Newark Bears defeated the Somerset Patriots, four games to one, to win the Atlantic League championship.

. . .

Atop the National League East since May 19 and enjoying a seven-game lead over the Phillies with 17 games to play, the Mets suffered a historic collapse, losing six of seven on their final home stand, including a season-ending 8–1 loss to the last-place Marlins on September 30. Tom Glavine yielded seven runs in one-third of an inning, the worst moment for the worst start of his 20-year career.

. . .

The Yankees entered the postseason as the wild card, but for the third straight year they fell in the ALDS, losing to the Cleveland Indians in four games. During the year, George Steinbrenner had

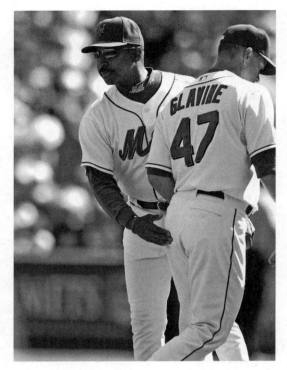

Mets manager Willie Randolph removing Tom Glavine in the first inning of the last game of the season at Shea Stadium, September 30, 2007. (Dan Goldfarb)

yielded control of the team to his sons Hank and Hal, and after the season they forced out Joe Torre, who went to the Dodgers. On October 29, Joe Girardi was named manager. Alex Rodriguez was again the American League's Most Valuable Player.

■ ■ ■

Curlin won the Breeders' Cup Classic at Monmouth Park.

■ ■ ■

On October 25, the $375 million Prudential Center in downtown Newark, New Jersey, opened, the new home of the Devils, Seton Hall University basketball, and the Ironmen of the Major Indoor Soccer League.

■ ■ ■

Ryan Hall won the men's Olympic marathon trial in Central Park on November 3. Tragically, his friend and training partner Ryan Shay, twenty-eight years old, dropped dead 5 miles into the race.

■ ■ ■

The Red Bulls fired Bruce Arena after the team lost to the New England Revolution in the playoffs. Managing director Marc de Grandpre said, "I understand there's been numerous coaches throughout this franchise history. I've only been responsible for one. I do understand that stability is important, but with the amount of resources that we committed to this franchise, we expect results quickly." Arena's record was 16–16–10. Juan Carlos Osorio became coach in December.

■ ■ ■

On December 13, former senator George Mitchell issued his report on steroid use, naming dozens of current and former major leaguers, including Roger Clemens, Andy Pettitte, and other Yankees and Mets. He used information provided by Clemens's personal trainer, Brian McNamee, and former Mets batboy and clubhouse assistant Kirk Radomski, who had pleaded guilty in April to distributing steroids and laundering money.

2008

[W]e have the greatest fans in the world.

DEREK JETER

In January, Major League Baseball announced that it would be the anchor tenant in Harlem Park, a new 21-story building at 125th Street and Park Avenue, in partnership with Vornado Realty Trust. In July, the building was lowered to 14 stories; in December, the project died, a victim of the economic collapse.

■ ■ ■

The Rangers retired Brian Leetch's number, 2, on January 24. A member of the team for 16 seasons,

Giants quarterback Eli Manning. (Dan Goldfarb)

he retired as the highest-scoring defenseman in franchise history and the second leading scorer.

▪ ▪ ▪

In the NFC wild-card game, the Giants beat the Tampa Bay Buccaneers, 24–16, and then went on to defeat the Cowboys, 21–17, in Dallas. Enduring a temperature of –4 degrees in Green Bay for the NFC title game, Big Blue beat the Packers, 23–20, in overtime, their tenth straight win on the road— an NFL record. Against the 18–0 Patriots in Super Bowl LXII on February 3, Eli Manning directed an 83-yard drive late in the fourth quarter, high- lighted by a miraculous catch by receiver David Tyree; with 39 seconds left, Manning found Plax- ico Burress in the corner of the end zone for a stunning 17–14 upset. It was the greatest Super Bowl ever!

▪ ▪ ▪

On February 12, Uno (K-Run's Park Me in First), a 15-inch beagle, was named Best in Show at the 132nd Westminster Dog Show, the first of his breed so honored.

▪ ▪ ▪

With an Olympic-size pool and an NHL regula- tion hockey rink, the Aquatic Center at Flushing Meadows–Corona Park opened on February 29 after almost a decade of construction and at a fi- nal cost of $66.3 million.

▪ ▪ ▪

The Yankees signed sixty-year-old comedian Billy Crystal to a two-day contract on March 13; in an exhibition game against the Pirates at Legends Field, the Yankees' spring-training facility in Tampa, Florida, he led off and struck out.

The last opening day at Shea Stadium, with Citi Field under construction, April 8, 2008. (Dan Goldfarb)

▪ ▪ ▪

On March 15, The Monroe College women's basketball team defeated Mohawk Valley Community College for its second NJCAA Division III championship.

▪ ▪ ▪

Legends Field, which opened in 1996, was renamed George L. Steinbrenner Field on March 27.

▪ ▪ ▪

On April 2, the Department of Education launched a 14-team interscholastic cricket league, the only one in the United States. It was financed through a marketing contract with Snapple.

▪ ▪ ▪

The popular Woodhaven Lanes, a Queens fixture since 1959, was demolished.

▪ ▪ ▪

In their final home opener at Shea Stadium, on April 8, in front of the largest opening-day and largest weekday crowd (56,350), the Mets fell to the Phillies, 5–2, their ninth straight loss to the team that had denied them the pennant in 2007. Also, SNY, the Mets' network, hired Darryl Strawberry as a part-time analyst, joining other members of the 1986 championship team: Lee Mazzilli, Ron Darling, and Keith Hernandez.

▪ ▪ ▪

On April 13, construction workers used jackhammers to exhume a Red Sox jersey embedded in concrete at the new Yankee Stadium, planted by a Boston fan working on the site. A curse averted?

▪ ▪ ▪

On April 18, two weeks after stepping in as president of the Knicks, Donnie Walsh dismissed Isiah Thomas as head coach. Over two seasons, his record was 56–108, and during his five years as team president, the Knicks never had a winning season, although their payroll had ballooned. On May 13, Mike D'Antoni, noted for his up-tempo style of play, was introduced as the new coach.

◦ ◦ ◦

The Rangers beat the Devils, 5–3, on April 18 to take the opening round of the playoffs, four games to one; in the next round, they fell to the Penguins in five, dropping the final game, 3–2, in overtime on May 4.

◦ ◦ ◦

The Sports Museum of America, located in the former Standard Oil Building at 26 Broadway, opened to the public on May 7. Philip Schwalb was the founder and chief executive of this private venture, which was home to the Heisman Trophy (homeless since the Downtown Athletic Club closed after September 11). The museum closed within a year.

◦ ◦ ◦

In the NCAA Division II men's lacrosse championship game, on May 25, New York Institute of Technology defeated Le Moyne College, 16–11, for its fourth title.

◦ ◦ ◦

On May 31, just over 8,000 attended a night of mixed martial arts at the Prudential Center in Newark. CBS Entertainment—not CBS Sports—broadcast the event live in prime time, a breakthrough for the brutal sport, but the ratings disappointed.

◦ ◦ ◦

A crowd of more than 94,000 jammed Belmont Park on June 7 to witness Big Brown's attempt to win the Triple Crown, but the 1–4 favorite failed in the mile-and-a-half Belmont Stakes, "The Test of the Champion." Jockey Kent Desormeaux pulled up when the horse did not respond around the final turn. The winner was Da' Tara, a 38–1 long shot trained by Nick Zito. For months, trainer Rick Dutrow had given Big Brown regular injections of the steroid Winstrol (legal in New York), but not for this race. On August 3, Big Brown came back to win the $1 million Haskell Invitational at Monmouth Park.

◦ ◦ ◦

On June 15, hours away from Mayor Michael Bloomberg's deadline for shutting down Off-Track Betting, the state agreed to take over the money-losing operation, with the city retaining a portion of the revenues.

◦ ◦ ◦

At 3:00 A.M. New York time on June 17, hours after the Mets beat the Angels in Anaheim, general manager Omar Minaya fired manager Willie Randolph, along with pitching coach Rick Peterson and first base coach Tom Nieto. Bench coach Jerry Manuel took over. In the *Daily News*, Bill Madden wrote: "Never in the history of New York baseball has there been a more shameful, indecent, undignified or ill-conceived firing of a manager." Over three-plus seasons, Randolph's record was 302–253 (.544), the second highest winning percentage in franchise history, with one divisional championship and a monumental collapse at the end of 2007.

◦ ◦ ◦

On July 12, former Yankee outfielder Bobby Murcer died from brain cancer at age sixty-two. He had broken in with the team as a teenager in September 1965. After stints with the Cubs and the Giants, he returned to the Yanks. In 1983, he retired and moved to the broadcasting booth.

◦ ◦ ◦

Two years into a three-year contract, the Islanders dismissed coach Ted Nolan on July 14. He had taken the team to the playoffs in 2007 with a 75–68–21 record, but general manager Garth Snow said, "It just wasn't good enough." A month later, Scott Gordon became head coach.

■ ■ ■

On July 15, with 49 Hall of Famers on hand, Yankee Stadium hosted the All-Star Game for the fourth time, a fitting moment for the final season of "The House That Ruth Built." The American League beat the Nationals, 4–3, in 15 innings, extending its unbeaten streak to 12 years.

■ ■ ■

On July 16 and 18, Billy Joel performed at Shea Stadium, the final concerts in the venue that had hosted the Beatles, Grand Funk Railroad, Simon and Garfunkel, Jethro Tull, the Who, the Police, Eric Clapton, the Rolling Stones, Bruce Springsteen, and the Newport Jazz Festival. "Last Play at Shea" featured guest appearances by Tony Bennett and Paul McCartney.

■ ■ ■

At the Meadowlands on August 2, Deweycheatumnhowe became the first undefeated horse (15–0) to win the Hambletonian, the richest purse in trotting.

■ ■ ■

Chris Russo left WFAN and Mike Francesa, his on-air partner of 19 years, on August 14 for his own show on satellite radio. *Mike and the Mad Dog* was among the top-grossing shows in the nation.

■ ■ ■

On August 24, during the Battle of the Bay powerboat race in the Great South Bay off Long Island, Philip Dejana and Kevin Graff were killed when Dejana's 37-foot twin-engine catamaran flipped while racing at 90 miles an hour.

■ ■ ■

The Jets opened their new training facility in Florham Park, New Jersey, on September 2. They had been based at Hofstra University since 1974, but relocated as part of their contract for the new stadium they would share with the Giants in the Meadowlands.

■ ■ ■

On September 7, Serena Williams defeated Jelena Janković, 6–4, 7–5, for her third U.S. Open singles title (and a return to the number-one ranking); she did not drop a set during the tournament. The next day, Roger Federer won his fifth straight Open title, defeating Andy Murray, 6–2, 7–5, 6–2.

■ ■ ■

In the final game at Yankee Stadium, on September 21, with many Yankee greats on hand, the Bronx Bombers beat the Baltimore Orioles, 7–3; catcher Jose Molina hit the last home run, Andy Pettite was the winning pitcher, and Mariano Rivera pitched the final inning. During that last home stand, Derek Jeter passed Lou Gehrig (1,269) for the most hits at the Stadium. Speaking to the crowd after the last game, Jeter said,

> Although things are going to change next year and we're going to move across the street, there are a few things with the New York Yankees that never change. That's pride, tradition, and most of all, we have the greatest fans in the world. We're relying on you to take the memories from this stadium and add them to the new memories we make at the new Yankee Stadium and continue to pass them on from generation to generation. We just want to take this moment to salute you, the greatest fans in the world.

■ ■ ■

At a soggy Belmont Park on September 27, Robby Albarado rode Curlin to victory in the $750,000 Jockey Club Gold Cup by a neck, surpassing Cigar to become the highest-earning horse in North America, with more than $10 million in total purses.

■ ■ ■

On September 28, the final day of the season, thirty-nine-year-old Mike Mussina defeated the

Red Sox, 6–2, for his twentieth victory, becoming the oldest player to reach that milestone for the first time. Still, the Yankees missed the playoffs for the first time in 13 years.

□ □ □

For the second year, the Mets suffered a late-season swoon and missed the postseason. Needing a win to force a one-game playoff with the Milwaukee Brewers on the last day of the season, September 28, they lost to the Marlins, 4–2, a sad ending to the final game at Shea Stadium. Still, in their final season at Shea, the Mets topped 4 million in attendance for the first time (4,047,404).

□ □ □

After dispatching the Connecticut Sun, two games to one, the Liberty fell to the Detroit Shock in the WNBA Eastern Conference finals, losing the deciding third game, 75–73, on September 29. (They were down by 17 points at the half.)

□ □ □

In their first game beyond North America, the Rangers opened their season with a 2–1 victory over the Tampa Bay Lightning in Prague on October 4; they won again the next day by the same score.

□ □ □

On October 23, Governor David Paterson announced that the Buffalo-based company Delaware North had received the contract to build a casino at Aqueduct Racetrack. The facility would have 4,500 video terminals, restaurants, a 300-room hotel, and a conference center. In March 2009, the plan was put on hold because the company could not obtain $370 million in financing.

□ □ □

In Portland, Oregon, the Gotham Girls won the Women's Flat Track Derby Association (roller derby) championship.

□ □ □

The Brooklyn Aces began play in the new four-team Eastern Professional Hockey League on November 1; their home ice was the Aviator Arena at Floyd Bennett Field. On March 28, 2009, the Aces fell to the Jersey Rockhoppers, 4–1, to lose the championship series, two games to one

□ □ □

In the first round of the MLS playoffs, the Red Bulls ousted the defending champion Houston Dynamo, 3–0, on November 9, and then beat Real Salt Lake, 1–0, on November 15 to reach the championship game for the first time in franchise history. They fell to the Columbus Crew, 3–1, before only 27,000 fans in Carson, California, on November 27.

□ □ □

On November 10, former Mets catcher and Hall of Famer Gary Carter became manager of the Long Island Ducks.

□ □ □

At about 1:30 A.M. at the Latin Quarter Nightclub (Forty-eighth Street and Lexington Avenue) on November 29, Giants wide receiver and Super Bowl hero Plaxico Burress shot himself in the leg with his unlicensed .40-caliber Glock pistol. His teammate, linebacker Antonio Pierce, hid the gun in the glove compartment of his car and took Burress to New York Presbyterian Hospital (which failed to immediately inform the police, as required by law). Burress was arrested on December 1 and charged with two counts of criminal possession of a handgun. The Giants suspended him without pay for the rest of the season.

□ □ □

On December 1, the Knicks ordered Stephon Marbury, their $21.9 million a year point guard, to stay away from the team after he twice refused to play for coach Mike D'Antoni. Since arriving in January 2004, Starbury had brought the organization nothing but problems, and on February 24, 2009, the Knicks bought out his contract of $20.8 million.

. . .

Forest City Ratner abruptly stopped work on the $4.2 billion Atlantic Yards complex, including the arena for the Nets, on December 3.

. . .

On December 6, Stevens Institute of Technology fell to Messiah College, 2–1, on penalty kicks in the NCAA Division III men's soccer finals.

. . .

The Yankees signed twenty-eight-year-old left-hander C. C. Sabathia to a seven-year, $161 million contract on December 10. It works out to about $727,848 a game; $107,366 an inning; $6,934 a pitch—the largest contract ever negotiated for a pitcher. Two weeks later, they agreed to an eight-year, $180 million deal with first baseman Mark Teixeira.

. . .

On December 11, Newark hosted a night of title fights for the first time since the welterweight bout between Tony Zale and Rocky Graziano in 1948. At the Prudential Center, International Boxing Federation bantamweight champion Joseph Agbeko won a split decision over challenger William Gonzalez, and former light-heavyweight champion Tomasz Adamek (a Polish-born resident of Jersey City) took the IBF cruiserweight title from Steve Cunningham with a 12-round split decision.

. . .

In the semifinals of the NCAA men's Division I soccer tournament on December 12, St. John's University fell to the University of Maryland, 1–0, the fourth time the Terrapins eliminated the Red Storm.

. . .

After 22 seasons, the Arena Football League suspended its upcoming season, scheduled to begin in March.

. . .

Seemingly bound for the playoffs with an 8–3 mark behind thirty-nine-year-old Brett Favre, the Jets sputtered to a 9–7 finish, ending on December 28 with a 24–17 defeat at home at the hands of former Jet quarterback Chad Pennington and his AFC East champion Miami Dolphins (rebuilt from 1–15 the previous season by Bill Parcells). The next day, the team dismissed head coach Eric Mangini, whose record over three seasons was 23–26, with one playoff appearance. On January 21, Rex Ryan was hired as head coach (the son of Buddy Ryan, an assistant coach on the 1969 Super Bowl champions), and Favre retired in February 2009.

. . .

At the request of Rutgers University president Richard L. McCormick, athletic director Robert E. Mulcahy III stepped down effective December 31. Mulcahy had guided Rutgers athletics into the big time, hiring football coach Greg Schiano and launching a $102 million expansion of the football stadium. He also gave Schiano a contract worth $1.6 million a year, and women's basketball coach C. Vivian Stringer almost $1 million. He doubled the budget to nearly $48 million while cutting men's swimming and diving, men's tennis, and men's crew, as well as men's and women's fencing. On December 29, Rutgers had defeated North Carolina State, 29–23, in the Papajohns.com Bowl in Birmingham, Alabama.

2009

On January 1, a ban on the use of steroids on racehorses in New York State took effect.

. . .

After starting the season at 11–1, the Giants lost three of their last four games (following the Plaxico Burress incident). In a playoff game at Giants Stadium on January 11, they lost to the Eagles, 23–11 (the first such score in NFL history).

. . .

THE INNOCENTS

BY BILL GALLO BGALLO @NYDAILYNEWS.COM

(Courtesy of Bill Gallo, *Daily News*)

After 51 consecutive losses, the men's basketball team of New Jersey Institute of Technology finally won, defeating Bryant College, 61–51, on January 21. It would have been a Division I record, but NJIT was in the final reclassification year, moving up from Division II.

- - -

Ultimate Fighting Championship—mixed martial arts—lobbied the legislature to legalize the sport in New York State, as it was in 37 other states. Lawrence Epstein, the organization's general counsel, said, "Let me say how important New York is to our company. New York is the world media center. When you do events in New York, you get more attention."

- - -

The Knickerbocker Yacht Club in Port Washington, founded by Jewish yachtsmen in 1874 on the Harlem River, dissolved.

- - -

On February 5, thousands flocked to East River Park to witness the Red Bull Snowscrapers, the first world-class snowboarding event held in the city. A nine-story, 150-yard-long ramp had been erected for the competition.

- - -

On February 7, *Sports Illustrated* reported that Alex Rodriguez had tested positive for steroids in 2003, a year before he signed with the Yankees as the highest paid player in baseball. The tests were supposed to be anonymous, and Major League Baseball did not test for banned substances at the time.

- - -

The new four-team United Football League was announced on February 9, to begin play in October, with franchises in New York–Hartford, Orlando, Los Angeles–Las Vegas, and San Francisco–Sacramento.

- - -

On February 22, the Rangers retired Harry Howell's number, 3, and Andy Bathgate's number, 9 (joining Adam Graves's 9 in the Garden's rafters). The next day, the team fired coach Tom Renney (whose record was 164–121–42 and three playoff

The new Yankee Stadium seen from Macombs Dam Park, with the old ballpark to the right. (Jeffrey A. Kroessler)

appearances since 2004) and brought in John Tortorella, who took the team to the playoffs.

◦ ◦ ◦

Devils goaltender Martin Brodeur stopped 30 shots in a 3–2 win over the Chicago Blackhawks at the Prudential Center on March 17 for his 552nd victory, surpassing Patrick Roy for the most in NHL history.

◦ ◦ ◦

Double Dutch became a varsity sport in public schools; competition began on March 21.

◦ ◦ ◦

At Madison Square Garden on March 21, the Abraham Lincoln High School Railsplitters from Coney Island trounced John F. Kennedy High School of the Bronx, 78–56, for their fourth consecutive PSAL Class AA boys' basketball championship. Also, the Lady Blazers of Murry Bergtraum High School defeated South Shore High School of Brooklyn, 51–36, for their eleventh straight Class AA girls' basketball championship.

◦ ◦ ◦

On April 1, Len Berman, the sports anchor at WNBC since 1985, was let go in a cost-cutting move. Berman had created the popular sports blooper segment "Spanning the World" and had been honored as Sportscaster of the Year five times.

◦ ◦ ◦

In their first game in the inaugural season of Women's Professional Soccer, Sky Blue F.C., the New Jersey–New York franchise, fell to Los Angeles Sol, 2–0, at TD Bank Ballpark in Bridgewater, New Jersey, on April 5.

◦ ◦ ◦

Citi Field, the new home of the Mets, opened on April 13. Tom Seaver threw the ceremonial first pitch to Mike Piazza. Unhappily, the Mets lost to the Padres, 6–5. San Diego's lead-off hitter, Jody Gerut, hit the first home run; David Wright hit the first homer for the Mets. During the third inning, a stray cat ran on to the field, an omen of . . . what?

◦ ◦ ◦

Yogi Berra threw the ceremonial first pitch to open the new Yankee Stadium on April 17 before 48,271 fans (about 4,000 below capacity). But the Yankees lost to the Indians, 10–2; catcher Jorge Posada hit the first home run. After the disappointing game, manager Joe Girardi said, "It's not how you want to start out a new Stadium, but one game is not going to make the history of this Yankee Stadium or this year."

□ □ □

The women's tennis team of Kingsborough Community College won the NJCAA Division III championship.

□ □ □

With one year remaining on his contract, Brent Sutter resigned as coach of the Devils on June 9. Over two seasons, his record was 97–56–11, but the team lost in the first round of the playoffs in both years. On July 13, the Devils brought back Jacques Lemaire, coach of their 1995 Stanley Cup champions.

□ □ □

The New York Sportimes of World Team Tennis, led by John McEnroe, played seven home matches at the new 2,000-seat Tennis Center on Randall's Island.

□ □ □

On Monday, June 22, Lucas Glover won a rain-soaked U.S. Open on the Black Course at Bethpage State Park by two strokes over Phil Mickelson, who finished second for a frustrating fifth time; David Duval; and a surprising Ricky Barnes, who held a six-stroke lead in the third round and set an Open record for 36 holes at 132. Persistent rain extended play into a fifth day.

□ □ □

Mariano Rivera earned his 500th save as the Yankees beat the Mets, 4–2, at Citi Field on June 28. He also collected the first RBI of his career with a bases-loaded walk in the top of the ninth. Rivera's first save had come against the Angels on May 17, 1996.

□ □ □

On July 26, Australian Greg Bennett won the New York City Triathlon for the fourth consecutive year, taking the $30,000 first prize. Rebeccah Wassner won the women's race. More than 3,400 athletes participated.

□ □ □

At the Meadowlands on August 8, Muscle Hill, the 1–5 favorite, won the $1.5 million Hambletonian by six lengths, trotting the mile in the record time of 1 minute, 50.2 seconds.

□ □ □

With his 2,675th hit, on August 16, Derek Jeter passed Luis Aparicio to become the all-time hit leader among major league shortstops. At Yankee Stadium on September 11, Jeter collected his 2,722nd base hit to pass Lou Gehrig and become the Yankees' all-time leader in base hits. "I just try to be consistent year in and year out," he said. "If you are consistent, good things happen."

□ □ □

Sky Blue F.C. defeated Los Angeles Sol, 1–0, in California on August 22 to capture the first Women's Professional Soccer championship.

□ □ □

In the bottom of the ninth at Citi Field on August 23, Phillies second baseman Eric Bruntlett completed an unassisted triple play and secured a 9–7 win over the Mets. It was only the second game-ending unassisted triple play in major league history. Leading off in the first, Angel Pagan of the Mets hit the first inside-the-park home run in the new ballpark.

Index